BRITAIN

AND THE

UNITED NATIONS

by

GEOFFREY L. GOODWIN

Prepared for the
ROYAL INSTITUTE OF INTERNATIONAL AFFAIRS
and the
CARNEGIE ENDOWMENT FOR INTERNATIONAL PEACE

Manhattan Publishing Company
New York
1957

BRITAIN AND THE UNITED NATIONS

Published simultaneously in the United Kingdom by Oxford
University Press for the Royal Institute of International Affairs.

VOLUMES PREVIOUSLY PUBLISHED IN THIS SERIES

CANADA AND THE UNITED NATIONS, prepared for the Canadian
Institute of International Affairs by F. H. Soward and Edgar
McInnis with the assistance of Walter O'Hearn.

DENMARK AND THE UNITED NATIONS, by Max Sørensen and
Niels J. Haagerup.

LA GRECE ET LES NATIONS UNIES, prepared for the Société d'Etudes
Internationales d'Athènes by S. Calogéropoulos-Stratis in collaboration with P. A. Argyropoulo, S. Castanos and D. Sidjanski.

INDIA AND THE UNITED NATIONS, Report of a Study Group set
up by the Indian Council of World Affairs.

ISRAEL AND THE UNITED NATIONS, Report of a Study Group set
up by the Hebrew University of Jerusalem.

LA SUISSE ET LES NATIONS UNIES, by Jacqueline Belin, under the
direction of Paul Guggenheim.

SWEDEN AND THE UNITED NATIONS, Report by a Special Study
Group of the Swedish Institute of International Affairs.

PRINTED BY BRÜDER ROSENBAUM, VIENNA (AUSTRIA)

Preface

This volume is one of a series of national studies on international organization initiated by the Carnegie Endowment for International Peace and carried out by private institutions and individuals in more than twenty countries. This particular study has been written by Mr Geoffrey L. Goodwin, with the assistance of a Study Group of the Royal Institute of International Affairs under the chairmanship of the Rt Hon. Kenneth Younger, M.P., P.C.

The decision, taken in 1952, to initiate this programme reflected both the Endowment's long-standing conviction that international organizations, such as the United Nations, are central to the quest for peace and the assumption that their significance and functioning depend first and foremost upon the attitudes and policies of their members. The fact that the question of Charter review would be on the agenda of the General Assembly in 1955 also seemed to afford a unique opportunity for assessing the strengths and weaknesses of the United Nations in terms of national expectations and their fulfilment during the brief but rich testing period of the first ten years. Thus, in sponsoring this series of studies the Endowment has sought to encourage an exchange of unofficial national views on international organization, with the object of stimulating a closer examination of the past record and future potentialities of the United Nations and of increasing understanding of differences and similarities in national attitudes towards the organization.

In the pursuit of these objectives, the participants in each country have been asked to appraise their national experience in international organization, especially in the United Nations. In doing so they have considered such questions as: What impact has the

United Nations had on both the content and the conduct of national policy? To what extent have the purposes and principles set out in the Charter served as adequate guides to the organs of the United Nations in their operations? Have developments in the practices and the procedures of the United Nations made the organization more or less effective as an agency to achieve the purposes for which it was established? What is, and should be, the relationship of the United Nations to other forms of international organization, including regional systems? Does experience suggest the need for formal revision of the Charter?

These studies have been undertaken on the initiative of the Carnegie Endowment for International Peace. However, they have been carried out independently of that organization and the responsibility for the contents of the individual volumes, therefore, lies with the authors.

In exercising its responsibility for the decision to publish the volumes in this series, the Endowment has been assisted by an advisory review committee, comprising Dr Alberto Lleras Camargo, former President of Colombia and former Secretary General of the Organization of American States; Sir Ramaswami Mudaliar, Vice-Chancellor of Travancore University, India; and Dr Bernard H. M. Vlekke, Secretary-General of the Netherlands Institute of International Affairs. Their faithful and wise counsel is most gratefully acknowledged.

The conclusions of the individual studies will be summarized and their significance analyzed in two final volumes which are being prepared independently by Robert MacIver, Lieber Professor Emeritus of Political Philosophy and Sociology at Columbia University; and Maurice Bourquin, Professor of International Public Law at the University of Geneva.

No prefatory note can possibly acknowledge all the debts which the Endowment owes to scholars and officials in many parts of the world for the help which they have given in making this series possible. To the officers of the Royal Institute of International

Affairs, to the members of its Study Group, and especially to its Chairman, the Rt Hon. Kenneth Younger, M.P., and to its Rapporteur, Mr Geoffrey L. Goodwin, particular thanks are due for their co-operation in making the present volume possible. The Endowment wishes to record its deep appreciation not only for the scholarship and thought which are reflected in the following pages but also for the patience and unfailing courtesy they have shown in this venture in co-operation over several years.

The Endowment wishes to express its gratitude to the Ford Foundation for providing a grant which, by supplementing funds supplied by the Endowment and the co-operating institutions themselves, made it possible to carry out the project on a broad and comprehensive basis.

January 1957   JOSEPH E. JOHNSON
President
Carnegie Endowment for International Peace

Foreword

At the invitation of the Carnegie Endowment for International Peace, the Council of the Royal Institute of International Affairs agreed to arrange for the preparation of the United Kingdom volume in the Endowment's series of national studies on international organization. A Study Group under the chairmanship of the Rt Hon. Kenneth G. Younger, M.P., Vice-Chairman of the Institute, was set up by the Council in November 1952 with responsibility for carrying out the task. The membership of the Study Group included, in addition to Mr Younger, Peter Calvocoressi, Dame Kathleen Courtney, Major-General L. O. Lyne, the Rt Hon. John S. Maclay, M.P., the late the Rt Hon. Hector McNeil, M.P., A. D. Marris, S. R. Pawley, T. E. Utley, with Geoffrey L. Goodwin as Rapporteur.

The report has been written by Mr Goodwin, Lecturer in International Relations at the London School of Economics and Political Science, who wishes to acknowledge the assistance he has received from members of the Group at all stages and also from Miss Coral Bell, Sir Alexander Cadogan, A. C. L. Day, D. H. N. Johnson, Dr F. C. Jones, Brigadier Stephen Longrigg, Professor C. A. W. Manning, Professor J. E. Meade, Dr F. S. Northedge, Kenneth Robinson, and Sir Charles Webster, and from others whose official position precludes their mention by name.

Although the members of the Study Group accept general responsibility for the study as a whole, this should not be taken to mean that each member of the Group necessarily subscribes to every opinion expressed in it. Readers are also reminded that the Royal Institute of International Affairs is precluded by its

Charter from expressing an opinion on any aspect of international affairs. Any views expressed in the study are not, therefore, attributable to the Institute. It should also be noted that, except for Chapter 5 on disarmament, it has only been found possible to cover events up till the end of 1955 in this study.

The Council records its thanks to the Group and to Mr Goodwin for so ably fulfilling its undertaking to the Carnegie Endowment by the production of this study.

London, December 1956   C. M. WOODHOUSE
Director General and *Director of Studies*
Royal Institute of International Affairs

Abbreviations*

BYIL	*The British Year Book of International Law* (London, Oxford University Press for RIIA).
Churchill, i-vi	Winston S. Churchill, *The Second World War*, vols. i-vi (London, Cassell, 1948-54; Boston, Houghton Mifflin, 1948-53).
CLP	*Current Legal Problems*.
Goodrich and Hambro	L. M. Goodrich and E. Hambro, *Charter of the United Nations: Commentary and Documents*, 2nd ed. (London, Stevens for London Institute of World Affairs, 1949; Boston, World Peace Foundation, 1949).
H. C. Deb. and H. L. Deb.	House of Commons and House of Lords Debates (Hansard). All references to Debates are to the fifth series.
Hull, *Memoirs*, i-ii	*The Memoirs of Cordell Hull*, vols. i-ii (London, Hodder & Stoughton, 1948; New York, Macmillan, 1948).
ICJ Pleadings	International Court of Justice, *Pleadings, Oral Arguments, Documents*.
ICJ Reports	International Court of Justice, *Reports of Judgments, Advisory Opinions and Orders*.
ICLQ	*International and Comparative Law Quarterly*.
ILQ	*International Law Quarterly*.
Kirk, *Middle East in the War*	George Kirk, *The Middle East in the War* (London, Oxford University Press for RIIA, 1952; *Survey of International Affairs, 1939-1946*).
Kirk, *Middle East, 1945-50*	George Kirk, *The Middle East, 1945-1950* (London, Oxford University Press for RIIA, 1954; *Survey of International Affairs, 1939-1946*).

* This list does not include such familiar abbreviations as EPU, FAO, GATT, NATO, &c.

McNeill, *America, Britain and Russia*	W. H. McNeill, *America, Britain and Russia: Their Co-operation and Conflict, 1941-1946* (London, Oxford University Press for RIIA, 1953; *Survey of International Affairs, 1939-1946*).
OUP	Oxford University Press.
Preparatory Commission Report	*Report of the Preparatory Commission of the United Nations*, PC/20, 23 December 1945.
Repertoire of the Practice of the Security Council	United Nations, Dept. of Political and Security Council Affairs, *Repertoire of the Practice of the Security Council* (New York, 1954).
Repertory of United Nations Practice, i-v	United Nations, *Repertory of Practice of United Nations Organs*, vols. i-v (New York, 1955).
RIIA, *Survey* and *Documents*	Royal Institute of International Affairs, *Survey of International Affairs* and *Documents on International Affairs* (London, Oxford University Press for RIIA, published annually).
UNCIO, i-xxii	United Nations Conference on International Organization, San Francisco, 1945, *Documents of the United Nations Conference on International Organization*, vols. i-xxii (London and New York, U.N. Information Organizations and The Library of Congress, 1945).
Vandenberg Papers	*The Private Papers of Senator Vandenberg*, ed. by A. H. Vandenberg, Jr., with the collaboration of J. A. Morris (Boston, Houghton Mifflin, 1952).
White House Papers, i-ii	Robert E. Sherwood, *The White House Papers of Harry L. Hopkins: an Intimate History*, vols. i-ii (London, Eyre & Spottiswoode, 1948-9); English ed. of *Roosevelt and Hopkins: an Intimate History* (New York, Harper, 1948).
YBUN	United Nations, *Yearbook of the United Nations*.
YBWA	*The Year Book of World Affairs* (London, Stevens for London Institute of World Affairs).

NOTE: Symbols of United Nations documents are composed of capital letters combined with figures, e.g. A/1938. Mention of such a symbol indicates a reference to a United Nations document. Official records of the United Nations General Assembly, Security Council, Economic and Social Council, and Atomic Energy Commission are indicated by *GAOR, SCOR, ESCOR,* and *AECOR,* respectively.

British parliamentary Command papers are referred to by their Command number, e.g. Cmd. 6666.

Contents

BACKGROUND TO BRITISH POLICY

PART ONE

chapter one

The Genesis of the United Nations[1]

The United Nations has obvious similarities with the League
of Nations. Broadly speaking, the Charter and the Covenant express
the same aims; in each case the basis of association is the sovereign
equality of member states; and the institutional framework follows
much the same pattern. Yet the United Nations is not just a refashion-
ed League; nor could it have been. Those in Britain who believed
that it was not so much the League that failed as the nations that
had failed the League were not blind to the alleged weaknesses
in the Covenant, while they were firmly convinced that the organization would be valueless without the whole-hearted co-operation
of the United States, and even, indeed, of the Soviet Union. And
it was clear almost from the start that the United States, which
had consistently viewed the League with suspicion, and the Soviet

---

[1] Only the main threads in the tangled skein of negotiations leading up to the
San Francisco Conference can be unravelled here.

Union, which had joined it only to be expelled five years later, were determined to start afresh and were wholly unwilling to revive the League.

Even if this had not been decisive, for some time both Mr Churchill and President Roosevelt showed a marked preference for the organization of the world on the basis of regional groupings held together by a Great Power triumvirate, rather than for the universalism of the League. Despite their subsequent change of front, not only are many traces of their early views to be found in the Charter, but they have by no means been without their relevance to developments since 1945, both in the world at large and within the United Nations itself.

REGIONALISM IN FAVOUR

It is, of course, the fashion to trace the genesis of the United Nations back to the Atlantic Charter, or, to give it its full title, the 'Joint Declaration by the President and the Prime Minister', of 14 August 1941. This can be misleading. The resounding phrases of the Declaration did indeed give hope and assurance of final victory and open up encouraging new vistas of the future world order; yet during the preliminary negotiations President Roosevelt was reluctant to commit himself on the subject of international organization.[2] Thus he rejected a proposal by Mr Churchill that the Declaration should affirm the joint intention of Great Britain and the United States to set up an 'effective international organization' after the war. Only with some difficulty was he persuaded to accept Mr Churchill's alternative suggestion for the insertion of a clause which looked vaguely to the disarmament of potential aggressors 'pending the establishment of a wider and more permanent system of general security'.[3] The impact of Pearl Harbor led the

---

[2] For an explanation of President Roosevelt's attitude, see Sumner Welles, *Seven Major Decisions* (London, Hamish Hamilton, 1951), pp. 171-75, and Sir Charles Webster, *Sanctions* (David Davies Memorial Lecture, 1950), p. 9.
[3] Churchill, iii. 388-92.

President to shed much of his initial caution, but during the ensuing critical period of the war the Allies' main energies were naturally concentrated on paving the way to final victory. It was not, therefore, until early in 1943 that ideas on both sides of the Atlantic about the post-war international organization began to take firmer shape.

The picture of the post-war world that was then developing was not altogether a reassuring one for Britain. Whatever might be the fruits of victory, the growing preponderance of the American and Soviet war effort pointed to the probability that Britain's power would soon be dwarfed by that of her major allies; that her freedom of choice would consequently be limited to a degree unprecedented in modern times; and that many long cherished beliefs of British policy, whether in the virtues of the 'free hand' or in the beneficence of 'free trade', would have to be discarded. But the supreme anxiety for the future appears to have been that after victory the Grand Alliance might disintegrate and the United States return, as in 1919, to isolationism, leaving a weary and impoverished Britain virtually alone to face a re-emergent and militant Germany and, possibly, an expansionist Soviet Union. This had two major consequences. In the first place, it was clearly incumbent upon Britain to do everything possible to preserve for the peace the close and intimate war-time co-operation between the United States and herself, as well as to encourage the Soviet Union to remain in friendly association with both. Accordingly, all plans for the future looked to the war-time alliance of the Great Powers to form the hard core of the post-war system for the maintenance of peace. In the second place, the crucial importance of the American attitude made Britain strongly disposed both to defer to American views on the post-war system and to avoid taking any initiative which might embarrass the Administration in its task of securing popular support for American participation in it.

It should also be remembered that Britain's most immediate and special concern was with the future of Europe. Thus, in his broadcast of 23 March 1943, Mr Churchill expressed the hope

that the three Great Powers would immediately begin to confer
about the future world organization, but he stressed that it was
'upon the creation of the Council of Europe and the settlement
of Europe that the first practical task will be centred'.[4] The grounds
for this concern were obvious enough. Plans for tackling the gigantic
problems of the relief and rehabilitation of the devastated territories
of Europe were already well advanced, but much remained to be
done. Furthermore, the ease with which the small nations of Europe
had succumbed to successive German incursions seemed to show
the need for them to come together into more compact and powerful
units. A great deal of thought was, therefore, given by the 'exile'
governments in London to the possibilities of political and economic
integration; of special interest to Britain were proposals for a
Danubian Confederation, which could be both economically viable
and capable of standing up to either German or Soviet pressure.[5]

Nor was this preoccupation with the development of regional
arrangements confined to Western and Central Europe. In the Middle
East, negotiations bearing the blessing of Great Britain were in
train for the formation of the Arab League, while in the Western
Hemisphere the Latin American states were multiplying their
machinery for consultation and defence. The tide in early 1943 was,
in fact, running strongly in favour of regionalism, with both President
Roosevelt and Mr Churchill looking to the formation after the war
of regional councils held together by an armed triumvirate of the
victorious Great Powers. Mr Churchill's views along these lines
were first sketched out in a paper entitled *Morning Thoughts* (sent
to President Roosevelt on 2 February 1943)[6] and later amplified
during his visit to Washington at an informal luncheon party on
22 May 1943.

---

4 Churchill, *Onwards to Victory* (London, Cassell, 1944), p. 36.

5 On one occasion it was suggested by Mr Churchill that this Confederation
should include the southern states of a dismembered Germany (*White House
Papers*, ii. 789).

6 Churchill, iv. 636-37.

The first preoccupation, Mr Churchill said, must be to prevent further aggression by Germany and Japan by the continued association of the United States, Great Britain, and Russia.

> On these Powers would rest the real responsibility for peace. They together, with certain other Powers,[7] should form a Supreme World Council. Subordinate to this World Council there should be three Regional Councils, one for Europe, one for the American Hemisphere, and one for the Pacific . . . The members of the World Council should sit on the Regional Councils in which they were directly interested,[8] . . . [but] the last word would remain with the Supreme World Council, since any issues that the Regional Councils were unable to settle would automatically be of interest to the World Council.

To the Great Powers of the World Council should be added others, he suggested, 'by election in rotation from the Regional Councils. The central idea of the structure was that of a three-legged stool—the World Council resting on three Regional Councils'. But he attached great importance to the regional principle.

> It was only the countries whose interests were directly affected by a dispute who could be expected to apply themselves with sufficient vigour to secure a settlement. If countries remote from a dispute were among those called upon in the first instance to achieve a settlement the result was likely to be merely vapid and academic discussion.[9]

In outlining his conception of the Regional European Council as consisting of some twelve states or confederations, including Danubian and Balkan groupings, Mr Churchill emphasized the importance of re-creating a strong France, 'for the prospect of having no strong country on the map between England and Russia

---

[7] Mr Churchill consistently pressed for the inclusion of France; he doubted the wisdom of including China but did not oppose the American desire to do so.

[8] Mr Churchill hoped that the United States would be represented on the European Regional Council as well as on those for the American Hemisphere and for the Pacific.

[9] Churchill, iv. 717, 718.

was not attractive'. Moreover, his anxiety about the future course
of Soviet policy and his conviction of the need for continuing close
Anglo-American co-operation led him to add that his proposals
were not intended to exclude 'special friendships devoid of sinister
purpose against others'. He could see small hope for the world
'unless the United States and the British Commonwealth worked
together in fraternal association.' He looked forward, therefore,
'to an extension of bases for the common defence of common
interests.'[10]

THE MOSCOW DECLARATION (OCTOBER 1943)

The views Mr Churchill set forth at Washington offered an
attractive and practical alternative to the universal approach to
world organization. But they did not represent settled British
policy; nor is it certain that they were shared in every respect by
all the Prime Minister's colleagues. In London, as in Washington,
it was still a period for exploring and testing out ideas. And there
is a strong hint in Mr Harry Hopkins's diary that Mr Eden was closer
than Mr Churchill to the view that all the United Nations should
be members of one body for the purposes of recommending policy.
Mr Eden is reported to have explicitly agreed that the United
Nations should be organized on a global basis.[11] Nevertheless,
the change from the conception of May 1943 of an all-powerful
Great Power alliance underpinned by regional councils to the Moscow
Declaration of 30 October 1943 is striking. The fourth clause of

---

10 ibid. pp. 717-21. Mr Churchill reports that the following day he and President Roosevelt agreed upon the need to continue the Anglo-American Combined Staff 'for a good long time after the war — at any rate until we could all
be sure that the world was safe' (ibid. p. 722).

11 *White House Papers*, ii. 716. Mr Churchill also seems to have modified his
own views within a few months, since on 11 October 1943 he wrote to Mr Eden
(just before the Moscow Conference): 'We hold strongly to a system of a League
of Nations which will include a Council of Europe, with an International Court
and an armed Power capable of enforcing its decisions' (Churchill, v. 251).

that Declaration was based upon a United States draft,[12] subscribed
to by the four Foreign Ministers;[13] it recognized

> the necessity of establishing at the earliest practicable date
> a general international organization, based on the principle
> of the sovereign equality of all peace-loving states, and open
> to membership by all such states, large and small, for the
> maintenance of international peace and security.[14]

The Declaration did, of course, leave a great deal open. Indeed,
from reports of subsequent conversations between President
Roosevelt and Premier Stalin at Teheran (November 1943), the
former still seems to have favoured government of the post-war
world by the 'Four Policemen',[15] while the latter is said to have
preferred the setting up of regional councils, with the United
States a member of that for Europe.[16] Yet to all outward appearances
it clearly pointed in the direction of a universal organization not
unlike the League of Nations, within which both the Great Power
caucus and regional groupings would be contained.

The considerations which led Britain to accept this shift in
emphasis can only be surmised.[17] It is known that Mr Cordell
Hull, who had not been present at the Washington luncheon party,
was strongly in favour of 'a universal international organization,
as opposed to regional organizations, although regional associations
of the Pan American type should of course continue and be brought
into a proper relationship with the world organization.'[18] And he
was evidently concerned lest regionalism might prove a 'haven for
the isolationists, who could advocate all-out United States co-

---

[12] Britain had accepted the draft at the Quebec Conference (August 1943)
as a basis of negotiation with the Soviet Union.

[13] The Chinese Foreign Minister was the fourth.

[14] For full text of the Declaration see Goodrich and Hambro, pp. 571-72.

[15] Namely, the United States, the United Kingdom, the Soviet Union, and
China.

[16] Churchill, v. 321; also *White House Papers*, ii. 780-81.

[17] Access to official documents has not been requested for this report.

[18] Hull, *Memoirs*, ii. 1643.

operation in a Western Hemisphere council on condition that we did not participate in a European or Pacific council.'[19] After much argument he and his advisers[20] were able to dissuade President Roosevelt from continuing to press for the more thorough-going regionalism advocated a few months earlier by Mr Churchill. This change of front on the part of President Roosevelt was all-important.

> From Churchill's point of view, there was much that seemed unrealistic in American attitudes, but acceptance of American leadership in post-war planning had the great advantage of committing the United States to an active part in post-war international affairs.[21]

Moreover, if regionalism might encourage the United States to withdraw from European affairs, that was a most powerful argument in favour of universalism. Although it was still hoped that the proposed Danubian and Balkan Confederations (together with a restored France) might eventually fill the power vacuum that would follow the defeat of Germany, it was by no means certain whether on their return the 'exile' governments, who had formally subscribed to the proposals, would remain in power or be willing and able to carry their plans through. In any event, the new political groupings would take several years to fructify; in the interval active American support would be needed in Europe both to reduce the danger of German resurgence and to set a check on possible Soviet ambitions.

Nor should it be forgotten that Soviet co-operation was still eagerly sought. And the Soviet Union did not conceal her hostility to the British-sponsored plans for Central and South-Eastern Europe, recognizing, not without foundation, that one of their main aims was to check or counterbalance the greatly increased influence which the Soviet Union hoped to exercise in this area when victory

---

[19] ibid. p. 1645.

[20] Mr Sumner Welles who, as Under Secretary of State in the State Department, had been a strong advocate of regionalism, had resigned in September 1943 after a series of differences with Mr Hull.

[21] McNeill, *America, Britain and Russia*, p. 323.

was won. 'Thus the sacrifice of a scheme which, while far more attractive to Great Britain, was in all probability unworkable, seemed a small price to pay for active American collaboration in the post-war world.'[22]

The regional approach was also not without its critics in Britain. It was argued that the regionalism of Locarno and after had weakened the League of Nations by casting doubt on the efficacy of the Covenant and by encouraging states to put their commitments under these regional arrangements before their obligations under the Covenant. Also, if regionalism were carried too far, was there not a serious risk that regional groupings might crystallize into powerful 'blocs', each dominated by a Great Power, with the supreme World Council consequently incapable of dealing with disputes between them? And might not these disputes constitute the most serious threat to world peace? The misgiving may also have been present that despite the world-wide character of Great Britain's interests and possessions, she might not be able to secure a seat on every regional body. Since the Soviet Union was avowedly anti-imperialist and the United States seemed intent on ensuring the early liquidation of the British Colonial Empire in Asia, this was not a risk that could be faced with equanimity.

In the economic field also Mr Hull's anxiety lest regional groupings might develop into closed trade areas or discriminatory systems was coming to be shared by most of those in Britain responsible for post-war economic planning. Indeed, plans for setting up functional organizations on a universal basis to deal with economic questions were already well advanced.[23] The International Labour Organisation (ILO) had remained in existence during the war, having migrated from Geneva to Montreal; the United Nations Conference on Food and Agriculture had already been held (Hot Springs, Virginia, May-June 1943); a draft agreement looking to the establishment of the United Nations Relief and

---

[22] ibid.
[23] See Chapter 10.

Rehabilitation Administration had been circulated in June 1943, prior to a meeting in Washington in the following November; the International Monetary Fund (IMF) was starting to take shape and some kind of International Civil Aviation Organization had already been mooted.

> The United States Administration took the lead in the creation of these institutions, and, though for some time it was uncertain whether Congress would accept them, it was clear that the idea of the economic interdependence of all states had made great progress in the one country which had the power to make it a reality. It was not easy to reconcile this conception with a world planned on the basis of regions.[24]

The arguments against a superior and rather exclusive Great Power triumvirate were no less weighty. Unlike either the United States or the Soviet Union, Britain was both a major Power and the centre of a Commonwealth otherwise made up of 'middle' and 'small' Powers. It was only to be expected that the latter would be reluctant to yield up to a Great Power caucus exclusive responsibility for decisions on matters which might be of supreme importance to them. The majority were now influential Powers in their own right and all had important strategic facilities; their willingness to contribute these to the future security system might well depend upon their having a real voice in its functioning. In addition, the League of Nations had helped to give them a status in international affairs which they were anxious to retain; indeed, they could fairly claim that the distinguished representatives which they (and several European Powers of the same stature) had sent to Geneva had not only helped to 'put them on the international map' but had also exercised a very healthy influence there.

This firm rejection of a *condominium mundi* of the Great Powers was to become more articulate as final victory drew nearer, but even at this stage it was clear that

---

[24] Sir Charles Webster, *The Making of the Charter of the United Nations* (Creighton Lecture, University of London, Nov. 1946), p. 20.

the peoples of the United States and British Commonwealth instinctively rejected the idea of forming a naked Great Power Alliance. They wished it to be embedded in a larger organization and subjected to the restraints of an ordered constitution expressing a moral purpose. This object could only be achieved in a universal system. Thus, while the special position of the Great Powers and the usefulness for certain purposes of regional organization still remained important, it was clear that they could only be put into practical effect inside the framework of a world organization embracing all states, great and small.[25]

The Moscow Declaration in favour of a general international organization was, therefore, welcomed in Britain. There was little disposition to believe that the deep-seated problems of the peace could be solved merely by setting up an international organization, but the Declaration (and the cordial atmosphere in which the negotiations in Moscow had taken place) seemed to indicate not only the unlikelihood of America's return to isolationism but also the Soviet Union's willingness to co-operate in the post-war world. There were, of course, reservations. Mr Hull's reiteration of his views on the future of dependent peoples showed how great a gulf still existed between British and American thinking on this subject, while Mr Molotov's sharp rejection of all schemes for Danubian and Balkan Confederations caused some dismay. Britain also continued to be mainly concerned about the fate of Europe. In this respect, some progress was made with the setting up of a European Advisory Commission, but its competence fell considerably short of British hopes.[26] On the whole, however, the Declaration strengthened confidence in the possibilities of creating

---

[25] ibid. p. 21.

[26] In July 1943 Britain is reported to have proposed the creation of a European Commission not only to 'coordinate the execution of surrender or armistice terms imposed on the enemy', but also to 'assume far-reaching functions with regard to long-range European arrangements in the fields of security and economic integration' (Hull, *Memoirs*, ii. 1642). The Commission now set up was to have the former function only.

an effective world-wide organization; the next step was to give greater substance to its wraith-like features.

DUMBARTON OAKS: THE BRITISH CONTRIBUTION

A suggestion that all the signatories of the United Nations Declaration of 1 January 1942 should be invited to adhere at once to the clause of the Moscow Declaration envisaging a universal organization was rejected in favour of a British proposal that the four signatories should first seek agreement upon a more detailed scheme. In Britain planning on the official level up to this time had been the responsibility of the Foreign Office and a special committee working under the Chiefs of Staff. Their conclusions had been submitted to a special Cabinet Committee but this had not yet gone very far into the question. To this machinery was now added an interdepartmental committee which was responsible for producing the papers to be exchanged with the other three Governments.[27] Public debate was also growing amongst such bodies as the League of Nations Union; the London Assembly of April 1944 held under its auspices was attended by representatives from the exile governments as well as by many notable public figures in Great Britain. Such extra-official discussions, however, played a smaller part in influencing official policy than parallel activities in the United States. Of greater importance were the discussions which took place at the Conference of Commonwealth Prime Ministers held in London early in May 1944.[28]

In their communiqué of 18 May 1944 the Prime Ministers limited themselves to declaring, *inter alia*, 'We affirm that after the war a world organization to maintain peace and security should be set up endowed with the necessary power and authority to prevent aggression and violence.'[29] The proposals which Britain communicated

---

[27] Webster, *Making of the Charter*, p. 23.

[28] There were also discussions with American officials who visited London in April 1944.

[29] *The Times*, 18 May 1944.

on 22 July 1944 to the other signatories of the Moscow Declaration took into account, however, the observations which the Prime Ministers had made in private, while at Dumbarton Oaks the British delegation met daily with representatives of the diplomatic missions in Washington of other Commonwealth members (including India). And it may be conjectured that the latter reaffirmed their opposition to an unadulterated Great Power dictatorship and their hope that the special responsibilities of the Great Powers for the maintenance of peace would be shared with all like-minded states both great and small and exercised in accordance with principles of international justice.

Perhaps it should be explained in parenthesis, however, that this close and continuous consultation was not intended by any of the participants to lead to the creation of a 'British Empire' bloc. At one time such a hope may have been entertained in some quarters in Britain, but any real possibility of a concerted Commonwealth policy or that Britain might be entitled to speak at Dumbarton Oaks for the other members of the Commonwealth had been effectively ruled out several months earlier by the adverse reaction, especially in Canada, to Lord Halifax's Toronto speech of 24 January 1944.[30] The myth of the Commonwealth 'bloc' was cited at Dumbarton Oaks by Soviet spokesmen to justify their demand for the admission to the new organization of all sixteen const uent republics of the Soviet Union. That it was a myth completely without substance was amply demonstrated by the vigorous part played by individual members of the Commonwealth at San Francisco.

---

[30] Lord Halifax was then British Ambassador in Washington. In the course of his speech, and following a line of thought voiced by Field-Marshal Smuts the previous November, Lord Halifax expressed the view that in the post-war world Britain, apart from the rest of the Commonwealth and Empire, could hardly claim equal partnership with the three 'Titans': the United States, the Soviet Union, and China. He appealed, therefore, for greater Commonwealth unity as 'a condition necessary to that working partnership with the United States, Russia, and China to which we look.' For the full text, see Nicholas Mansergh, ed., *Documents and Speeches on British Commonwealth Affairs, 1931-1952* (London, OUP for RIIA, 1953), i. 575-79; also Mansergh's *The Commonwealth and the Nations* (London, RIIA, 1948), pp. 67-70.

The Dumbarton Oaks Proposals for the Establishment of a General International Organization,[31] which were made public simultaneously by the four Governments on 9 October 1944, need not be examined in detail since the Charter itself will be analysed later in this chapter. The evidence on Britain's contribution that has so far been made public is rather meagre. But the dominant conception seems still to have been that of a continuing 'Armed Concert' of the Great Powers, invested with supreme responsibility for the maintenance of peace and backed by regional arrangements. From the official commentary and other official statements it also appears that the experience of the League was very much in the minds of the British delegates. Thus the new Organization was to be in accordance with the spirit and principles of the League, and much stress was laid on its role as 'an international centre where members may confer', the establishment of which was said to have been 'one of the constructive acts of the League of Nations'.[32] But the main weaknesses in the League were to be remedied so as to clothe the Organization with the necessary authority. These were said to be: the unanimity rule; the absence of any obligation on its members to intervene with force to repress violence until war had actually broken out; the decentralized character of sanctions which allowed each member to decide for itself whether to put them into force; and the muted emphasis on economic and social co-operation.

As to the structure of the Organization, Sir Charles Webster has disclosed that all three Powers

> envisaged an Assembly and a Council composed of the Great Powers and some smaller states chosen in the same manner as in the Covenant. All agreed that the responsibility for the

---

[31] Cmd. 6560. For the official commentary see Cmd. 6511. The negotiations at Dumbarton Oaks were conducted at the official level in two stages: between the United States, Great Britain, and the Soviet Union from 21 August to 28 September 1944, and then between the United States, Great Britain, and China from 29 September to 7 October.

[32] Cmd. 6571, para. 14.

> maintenance of international peace and security should be placed on the Council, and that the members of the Organization should confer on it adequate powers for this purpose; that these should not be shared with the Assembly, and that a unanimous vote in the Council should not be required for their exercise.[33]

On the other hand, an American proposal to set up a separate organ for economic and social questions was viewed with misgiving by both Britain and the Soviet Union. Unlike the Soviet Union, Britain did not wish to exclude these questions from the purview of the Organization altogether; despite some qualifications, the arguments of the Bruce Report of 1939 for a Co-ordinating Committee on Economic Questions were accepted.[34] But she would have preferred a closer relation between the Security Council and the Economic and Social Council than is allowed for under the present Article 65, on the grounds that many security questions and economic questions were intrinsically inseparable, as in the case of economic sanctions. Indeed, some members of the delegation questioned the wisdom of limiting the competence of the Council exclusively to security questions, of constituting a body which would be 'professionally concerned with trouble', instead of making it, like the League Council, competent to discuss any matter within the sphere of action of the whole organization. In their view, in order to develop that feeling of corporate responsibility which had proved of such value in the League Council, the new Council should have under its aegis the kind of problems which were most propitious for constructive work and collective action. And such problems, it was held, were more commonly found in the 'technical' or 'non-political' field where the technological interdependence of nations tended to make co-operation a virtual necessity, whereas in security matters dissension and suspicion were the norm.

---

33 Webster, *Making of the Charter*, pp. 26-27.
34 *The Development of International Co-operation in Economic and Social Affairs* (Bruce Report), special suppl. to *Monthly Summary of the League of Nations*, Aug. 1939.

Furthermore, the recently negotiated Bretton Woods institutions, the well-tried ILO, which had recently agreed upon an ambitious programme at the Philadelphia Conference of July 1944, and the projected Food and Agriculture Organization (FAO) seemed to offer a more solid basis for co-operation in economic and social matters. There was perhaps room for a co-ordinating committee within the United Nations to pull together the work of these institutions, especially in preventing the spread of economic depressions and in tackling the economic and social injustices which were thought to be one of the root causes of war. But anything more grandiose would in all probability encroach upon the activities of the functional (later known as the 'specialized') agencies and become little more than an irritating international 'busybody'.

This viewpoint did not prevail, however, against the strong pressure by the United States in favour of an Economic and Social Council and against the Soviet Union's insistence that the scope of the Security Council be limited to security matters. Moreover, the issue was not of crucial importance and Britain may well have hoped, by acceding to the American point of view on the Economic and Social Council, to make the United States more amenable on the trusteeship question, on which agreement had not yet been reached.[35]

Rather surprisingly, the principle of majority voting as the normal voting procedure for all the organs of the United Nations seems to have struck nearly all concerned as a welcome improvement upon the unanimity rule of the League and to have been accepted with little difficulty. No doubt its acceptance was made easier not only by the fact that the Assembly's powers were limited to recommendation only but also by the fact that the issue of the voting rights of the permanent members of the Security Council, which alone would have the power to act, was left unresolved at Dumbarton Oaks.

---

[35] Nor was it discussed at Dumbarton Oaks; see Chapter 14.

The postponement of this crucial issue was not allowed, however, to hold up negotiations on the Council's enforcement machinery. The growing realization that each of the permanent members would probably be vested with the right to veto the use of this machinery may well have lent a certain air of unreality to the negotiations, but it must be remembered that Britain's proposals[36] were at this stage based on the supposition that a voting formula could be agreed upon which would not allow a Great Power party to a dispute to veto the use of sanctions, and, perhaps more notably, on the belief that even after victory Germany might remain the most potent threat to world peace. Consequently, whatever the outcome of the veto issue, there was clearly a lot to be said for a scheme which might help both to perpetuate Anglo-American military co-operation and to broaden it to include the Soviet Union. Moreover, if all went well, this machinery could meet what was thought to be a major defect in the League system, namely, the absence of armed forces upon which the League Council could call for enforcement action. Thus, with the model of the Anglo-American Combined Chiefs of Staff Committee in mind, Britain

> made in some detail suggestions for the creation of a Military Staff Committee, composed of representatives of the supreme military authorities of the Great Powers, to organize, under the authority of the Security Council, the machinery of sanctions and the regulation of armaments. It was hoped that, by this means, direct and continuous contact would be maintained between those responsible for the armed forces of the Great Powers.[37]

These suggestions, together with United States proposals for 'special agreements', by which each state would undertake to make available to the Security Council armed forces, facilities, and

---

[36] And, no doubt, those of the United States also.
[37] Webster, *Making of the Charter*, p. 28; see also Webster, *Sanctions*, pp. 11-13.

c

assistance, were to form Articles 43-47 of the Charter.[38] These ambitious proposals represented, perhaps, the most striking change from the League system. Since, however, the Security Council would have no forces at its disposal until the 'special agreements' had been concluded, the four states parties to the Moscow Declaration reserved to themselves the right in the interim period to take 'such joint action on behalf of the Organization as may be necessary for the purpose of maintaining international peace and security.'[39]

A United States proposal that the Security Council should be 'so organized as to be able to function continuously' met with a mixed reception from the British delegation. The Security Council should be able to act at a moment's notice if necessary, but should not its main purpose be to serve as a centre for personal contact between the leading statesmen? A Security Council in permanent session might, it was feared, tend to discourage such periodic meetings of principals. And was there not a hint in the American proposal that the Security Council was intended to supersede rather than to 'supplement and humanize' ordinary diplomacy? Certainly, it might encourage the submission to the Council of innumerable issues, perhaps often of a trifling nature, which could be better dealt with through normal diplomatic channels.

In the event, the American proposals were accepted, and only a half-hearted provision was tagged on for periodic meetings of the kind advocated by Britain. But the role of orthodox diplomacy (and of judicial procedure) was safeguarded by the obligation on parties to disputes 'first of all, to seek a solution by negotiation, mediation, conciliation, arbitration or judicial settlement.' And it was a relief to those members of the delegation who feared that Britain might occasionally be faced by an anti-colonial majority,

---

[38] The provision for national air force contingents originated in a Soviet proposal for an international air force.
[39] Cmd. 6560.

that the provisions for the pacific settlement of disputes 'should not apply to situations or disputes arising out of matters which by international law are solely within the domestic jurisdiction of the State concerned',[40] and that the right of the Security Council to impose the terms of settlement of a dispute, as was at first suggested by the United States, was left in doubt.

In two respects Commonwealth wishes were catered for. Although Britain failed to secure some kind of semi-permanent representation on the Security Council for 'middle' Powers, the non-permanent membership of the Council was set at six partly to allow of a seat for a Commonwealth country (other, of course, than Britain). The Council was also enjoined to 'act in accordance with the Purposes and Principles of the Organization'; the main task of the new Leviathan would be to maintain order and to keep the peace,[41] but this precept might dissuade it from altogether disregarding considerations of justice and fair dealing.

Despite the impasse over the voting procedure on the Security Council, the Dumbarton Oaks proposals had a sympathetic reception in Great Britain. Their cumbrous phraseology met with some criticism, while nearly all recognized that the success of the Organization would depend not so much on the perfection and elegance of its structure as on the policies of the Great Powers. Whatever reservations there might have been in official circles, however, the general public welcomed the proposals as encouraging evidence that the war-time alliance was firmly welded together and that victory would usher in a long period of peace in which there would be an effective safeguard against the re-emergence of a militant Germany or, for that matter, Japan.

---

[40] ibid.

[41] 'The mere existence of a quarrel, or of the grievance of some small State against a mighty neighbour, will concern the Council only in the unlikely event of peace appearing in peril. The organization will exist rather for security as such than for justice as such, and will, it seems, leave less doubt on this point than did its Geneva precursor' (*The Times*, 12 Oct. 1944).

THE YALTA FORMULA[42]

The powers conferred upon the Security Council in order to ensure 'prompt and effective action' were recognized, however, to be so far-reaching as to make the method by which its decisions were reached of crucial importance. That it had proved to be the chief source of dissension between the Great Powers at Dumbarton Oaks came, therefore, as no great surprise; until it had been settled, judgement was to some extent reserved.

The negotiations on this issue were long and involved; but the most salient features merit brief mention if only because they have a direct bearing on recent proposals for amending the veto. At Dumbarton Oaks all four Powers were agreed that decisions (and, of course, recommendations) of the Security Council should, as in the other organs, be arrived at by a majority vote only, and that the votes of some of the small states should be required to make up the necessary majority; Britain favoured a two-thirds majority, the Soviet Union a simple majority, and the United States was willing to accept either. But as a safeguard against being outvoted, possibly by a group of small Powers, and against being bound by decisions which, despite their dissent, might commit them to put their armed forces at the disposal of the Security Council, all were agreed that for decisions on matters of substance this majority vote should, in principle, include the concurring votes of the permanent members (i.e. the Great Powers). The bone of contention was whether an important exception should be made to this principle, namely, whether a permanent member should be precluded from voting on a dispute to which it was a party. Britain, while admitting that unanimity of the permanent members should normally be required for decisions on matters of substance, consistently took the view that 'in any event the votes of parties to a dispute should

---

42 The formula agreed upon at the Yalta Conference by the three war leaders was tentatively worked out by the United Kingdom and United States delegates during the Dumbarton Oaks negotiations and communicated by President Roosevelt to Mr Churchill and Premier Stalin on 5 December 1944.

not be taken into account.'[43] In other words Britain wished to follow the precedent of the Covenant and to exclude a Great Power from voting on a dispute to which it was a party, not only on recommendations for the pacific settlement of disputes but also on decisions involving enforcement measures. After considerable hesitation, and with some dissenting voices within her delegation, the United States supported this view.[44] The Soviet Union, in contrast, emphatically refused to agree to any abrogation whatsoever of her veto powers and insisted upon the unqualified unanimity of the permanent members, not only for enforcement action but also for the pacific settlement of disputes.

In retrospect, this clash can be seen to have reflected fundamental differences about the role of the Organization.

> Was the organization to be a device whereby the Great Powers would act in concert to impose their will upon any refractory small nation, while settling their own differences through other channels of negotiation? Or was the organization to pretend to authority over the Great Powers themselves?[45]

Yet at the time the issue probably did not seem so clear-cut. Not only did the continued unity of the Great Powers appear to Great Britain to be of supreme importance for the successful prosecution of the war,[46] but the concept of a continuing 'Armed Concert' of

---

[43] Sir Alexander Cadogan: *SCOR*, 2nd yr., 125th mtg., 3 Apr. 1947, p. 683.

[44] Mr Cordell Hull records that even during the Dumbarton Oaks Conference: 'There was still some difference of opinion among us, however, as to whether this abstention from voting should apply only to the pacific settlement of disputes in which one or more of the major nations were involved or should apply also to enforcement action' (*Memoirs*, ii. 1678; see also E. R. Stettinius, *Roosevelt and the Russians* (London, Cape, 1950), pp. 26-28). From both sources it appears that the retention by the United States of the right to prevent the use of American armed forces was generally thought to be a pre-condition of Congressional approval of United States participation in the Organization.

[45] McNeill, *America, Britain and Russia*, p. 507.

[46] Germany was on the verge of defeat but she still seemed to have plenty of fight left in her, while there was every prospect of a long and bitter struggle with Japan.

the victorious Great Powers after the war had by no means been discarded.[47] Certainly, their continued co-operation seemed vital to the effective functioning of the new Organization; whatever the voting formula, there could be little doubt that if a majority of the Great Powers should feel called upon to inflict sanctions upon one of their own number, the Organization would in fact have broken down. Furthermore, the immediate risk was that the Soviet Union might refuse to participate in the Organization if her viewpoint were not accepted. And as Field-Marshal Smuts pointed out to Mr Churchill in commending to him the principle of unanimity: 'Should a World Organization be formed which does not include Russia she will become the power centre of another group. We shall then be heading towards a third World War.'[48] Nor was it overlooked that the strong distaste shown by President Roosevelt and many of his colleagues for all forms of 'colonialism', a distaste which the Soviet Union might be expected to exploit, might possibly put Britain in a position in which she herself might wish to be able to resort to the veto to prevent any encroachment on her colonial responsibilities. Against these considerations, however, had to be set the fact that if the Security Council's exercise of its powers was made wholly dependent upon the unqualified unanimity of the Great Powers, not only would a security system of great potential value to Britain be completely stultified, but the Council would also be prevented even from pronouncing upon the rights and wrongs of any dispute to which a Great Power was a party. And an all-powerful Great Power oligarchy, which was both a law unto itself and immune from criticism by the smaller Powers, would almost certainly not be acceptable either to domestic opinion or to the countries of the Commonwealth.

---

[47] Many still thought that the re-emergence of Germany and Japan after defeat as militant, dissatisfied Powers would constitute the major threat to the future peace of the world.

[48] Churchill, vi. 183.

As is well known, the compromise formula first tentatively worked out at Dumbarton Oaks and later accepted with little difficulty at Yalta,[49] was to become Article 27 of the Charter. Its essential feature was the distinction drawn between recommendations for the peaceful adjustment of disputes and decisions relating to the use of enforcement measures, whether diplomatic, economic, or military. The main effect was that a Great Power could under no circumstances be subjected to any form of sanctions; but when it was a party to a dispute it could not prevent the Council—if the necessary majority of seven affirmative votes including the concurring votes of all permanent members not parties to the dispute could be mustered—from discussing the dispute, from deciding whether its continuance was likely to endanger peace, from calling upon the parties to settle the dispute by peaceful means, and from making recommendations as to methods and procedures of settlement.

Although falling short of the original British proposal, the Yalta formula marked a significant advance on the position previously firmly adhered to by the Soviet Union. Since the United States also now claimed it as her own, the formula evidently represented the maximum derogation from the unanimity rule which it was possible to secure. Above all, despite its painful implications for the new security system, the formula went far to ensure both American and Soviet participation in the organization and to allow the conduct of a Great Power to be discussed and commented upon by the Council.

It was also encouraging that at Yalta the Soviet demand that all sixteen constituent republics of the Soviet Union should be individually represented in the Organization was reduced to cover the Ukraine and White Russia only.[50] For the United Kingdom to have opposed this claim might well have prejudiced India's membership

---

[49] For an account of the Yalta discussions see Churchill, vi. 309-12, and Stettinius, *Roosevelt and the Russians*, pp. 132-42.

[50] Thus giving the Soviet Union three votes.

since, although a full member of the League, she was not in 1945
a fully sovereign state; thus, in contrast to the furore in the United
States when acceptance of the Soviet claim was made public, very
little exception to it was taken in Britain.

With the settlement of these two issues the way was open for the
inaugural conference. It must be admitted, however, that Britain
did not altogether share the United States view that the conference
should be convened as rapidly as possible. Indeed, President Roosevelt's disclosure at Yalta that he did not expect American troops
to remain in Europe for more than two years after Hitler's overthrow[51] served but to deepen Britain's conviction both that European
problems were of greater urgency and that their settlement was a
necessary condition of the successful functioning of the organization.
But the American insistence that the Senate's approval would be
easier to obtain while wartime fervour prevailed could not be
gainsaid. The Yalta Conference finished on 11 February 1945;
on 5 March the United States, on behalf of the four sponsoring
Powers, issued invitations for the United Nations Conference on
International Organization to the forty-six Governments which
had declared war on the Axis Powers by 1 March 1945 and had
signed the Declaration by the United Nations of 1 January 1942.
All accepted and the Conference opened at San Francisco on 25 April
1945.

THE SAN FRANCISCO 'POLISH'[52]

At the San Francisco Conference the five Great Powers[53] were,
as might be expected, more concerned to defend the privileged
position they had reserved for themselves in the Dumbarton Oaks

---

[51] Churchill, vi. 308.

[52] On the organization of the conference see McNeill, *America, Britain and
Russia*, pp. 591-606, and Goodrich and Hambro, pp. 10-20.

[53] France refused to become a Sponsoring Power, but from 4 May she joined
the private discussions of the four Sponsoring Powers.

proposals than to defer to the pressure of the smaller Powers to reduce their hegemony.[54] And since, apart from an initial brush over the admission to the Conference of Argentina and a more serious dispute over the veto, they usually presented a united front —at any rate in public—their views almost invariably prevailed. The submission of the proposals to such a representative international gathering was, nevertheless, unprecedented; neither at Vienna nor at Versailles had the smaller states been treated with such consideration. Moreover, throughout the Conference both the United Kingdom and the United States paid careful heed to the comments of the not-so-great Powers, especially those of the Commonwealth and Latin America.

Consequently, although the Dumbarton Oaks proposals, together with the Yalta voting formula, came through the Conference without radical revision, many drafting improvements and several important additions were made. Thus the powers of the General Assembly and of the Economic and Social Council were strengthened, the provisions concerning dependent territories[55] and an International Court of Justice[56] were agreed upon, those parts of the Dumbarton Oaks proposals dealing with regional arrangements were amended, and the strong pressure from the smaller Powers to restrict the veto rights of the Great Powers led to a purported 'clarification' of these rights—though not until after a disagreement between the Soviet Union and the other Great Powers which threatened to wreck the Conference.

The procedures of the Security Council for pacific settlement were also clarified and strengthened. Thus, the right of the Security Council to recommend terms of settlement in the case of a dispute

---

[54] Although a number of amendments were submitted jointly by the four Sponsoring Powers during the Conference, most of which were intended to meet the criticism of the smaller Powers.

[55] See Chapter 14.

[56] The Conference had before it a draft statute prepared by a Committee of Jurists, which had met in Washington from 9 to 20 April 1945. See also Chapter 15.

the continuance of which it considers is in fact likely to endanger the maintenance of international peace and security was made quite explicit (Art. 37(2)), mainly at the instance of Britain, while the Council was also given the right, strangely omitted in the Dumbarton Oaks proposals, to make recommendations for the pacific settlement of any dispute, if requested to do so by all the parties to that dispute (Art. 38). The final version of Chapter VI (Pacific Settlement) was not devoid of ambiguities, but at least the right of the Security Council to pronounce on the merits of a dispute was left in no doubt. To Britain this seemed a real achievement.

At one stage, however, this achievement was in jeopardy. This was when Mr Gromyko[57] unexpectedly argued that, under the Yalta formula, a dispute could not even be considered or discussed by the Security Council unless all five permanent members were agreed that it should be admitted to the Council's agenda. This interpretation cut right across the firm understanding of both Britain and the United States that the admission of an item to the agenda was a procedural matter to be decided by the affirmative vote of *any* seven members. To allow a single Great Power to veto even discussion would be to deprive the Security Council of almost its sole remaining *raison d'être*. Fortunately, strong representations in Moscow[58] led to Soviet acceptance of the American and British interpretation, which was embodied in the 'Statement by the Delegations of the Four Sponsoring Governments on Voting Procedure in the Security Council'.[59]

The Joint Statement on Voting Procedure attempted, not altogether successfully, to clear up the many ambiguities in the Yalta voting formula. Some difficulties of interpretation remain, but, broadly speaking, and taking both Article 27 (Voting) and the

---

[57] On 9 May Mr Gromyko had succeeded Mr Molotov as the senior Soviet delegate.

[58] *White House Papers*, ii. 900-1.

[59] Hereafter referred to as the 'Joint Statement on Voting Procedure' (UNCIO, xi. 711).

Joint Statement together, a permanent member's voting rights may be summarized as follows:

1. A permanent member cannot prevent the Security Council from, *inter alia*, considering and discussing a dispute or situation in which it is claimed that the maintenance of international peace and security is threatened; nor can it prevent the Council from inviting a member not represented thereon to participate in its discussion when that member's interests are 'specially affected', or from inviting 'any state when it is a party to a dispute being considered by the Council to participate in the discussion relating to that dispute'; all these are procedural matters[60] to be decided by the affirmative vote of *any* seven members.

2. So long as it is not a party to the dispute (not situation)[61] under consideration (in which case it must abstain from voting), a permanent member *can* prevent the Council from, *inter alia*, making an investigation into a dispute or situation, calling upon states to settle their differences by peaceful means, referring a local dispute to a regional agency, making recommendations to the parties to a dispute (even when all the parties request it to do so).[62]

3. A permanent member has an unqualified right, i.e. even when it is a party to a dispute, to prevent both the determination by the Council of the 'existence of any threat to the peace, breach of the peace, or act of aggression' (Art. 39) and any kind of enforcement measures by the United Nations or a regional agency or arrangement.[63]

There was never, of course, any question of the permanent members relinquishing their right of veto over enforcement measures, yet in other respects the intensity and bitterness of the attack on

---

[60] See para. 2 of the Joint Statement on Voting Procedure.

[61] For the distinction between a 'dispute' and a 'situation', see below, p. 235.

[62] On the grounds that such acts 'may well have major political consequences and may even initiate a chain of events which might, in the end, require the Council . . . to invoke measures of enforcement'; see Joint Statement on Voting Procedure, para. 4.

[63] Other than measures taken against an ex-enemy state; see below, p. 31.

the veto by the smaller states may well have served but to make more hard and definite everything which they most disliked in Chapter VI of the Charter (Pacific Settlement). For instance, after indicating in Part I, paragraph 2, the kind of questions to be regarded as procedural, the Joint Statement took the very rigid line in Part II that a decision whether any other matter was procedural 'must be taken by a vote of seven members of the Security Council, including the concurring votes of the permanent members'. According to the Joint Statement, therefore, any one permanent member is able to prevent:

    i. the admission of a new Member (Art. 4(2));[64]

    ii. the suspension of a Member from the exercise of the rights and privileges of membership (Art. 5), and the expulsion of a Member from the Organization (Art. 6);

    iii. the election of a Secretary-General (Art. 97).

The inflexible attitude of the Great Powers on the issue of the veto led many delegates to base their hopes upon the early revision of the Charter. As an apparent concession to this point of view, provision was made for a General Conference to review the Charter, if so requested by two-thirds of the members of the General Assembly and by any seven members of the Security Council (Art. 109(1)); if such a conference were not held by the Assembly's tenth session, only a simple, instead of a two-thirds, majority of the Assembly would be required to convene it (Art. 109(3)). As Charter reformers have discovered, however, this circumventing of the veto was robbed of almost all its content by the requirement that no amendment to the Charter can come into force until it has been ratified by *all* the permanent members; in other words, any one permanent member can prevent amendment of the Charter (Arts. 108 and 109(2)).

The firm reassertion by the Great Powers of their veto rights made the relationship between regional arrangements and the

----

64 For the consequent difficulties, see below, pp. 220 ff.

Security Council of crucial importance. Since the security system of the Charter could be rendered impotent by the dissent of a single permanent member, many states saw in these regional arrangements their main source of protection. They discovered to their dismay, however, that although the Dumbarton Oaks proposals had stressed their role as instruments for enforcement action, under the existing draft of Article 53 they could not properly be used either for this purpose or for the purpose of collective self-defence without the prior authorization of the Security Council. And such authorization could be vetoed by a single permanent member. The net effect seemed to be that no security system was entitled to function without the approval of all five permanent members. This was to stake a great deal on the perpetuation of the 'Grand Alliance'. Could not some loophole be devised to guard against the possibility of future dissension amongst its members?

The Soviet Union's main concern (and one which was shared by France) was to remove from the control of the Security Council any action under the bilateral pacts which she had concluded with Great Britain (26 May 1942), Czechoslovakia (12 December 1943), France (10 December 1944), Yugoslavia (11 April 1945), and Poland (21 April 1945). Since these pacts purported to be directed against a renewed threat from Germany, the draft of Article 53 was amended so as to except 'measures against any enemy state'[65] from the need for prior authorization by the Security Council, 'until such time as the Organization may, *on request of the Governments concerned*,[66] be charged with the responsibility for preventing further aggression by such a state.'

The Soviet Union and France having secured their own freedom of action through this 'escape clause', the Latin American states pressed for a similar exemption for collective action under the

---

[65] As defined in the second paragraph of Art. 53. See also Art. 107.
[66] Author's italics.

recently concluded Act of Chapultepec,[67] arguing that to give European and Asian Powers a veto over action within the Western Hemisphere would be a violation of the sacrosanct Monroe Doctrine. In this they were supported by the United States[68] and by other countries which contemplated similar regional arrangements.

Britain appears, however, to have had some reservations about such an exemption. The loophole for measures against ex-enemy states was, in her view, a temporary expedient to meet the special circumstances of the moment. To release regional arrangements from the Security Council's supervision might be held to imply their equal or even superior status; certainly, to give regional groups virtually a free hand could hardly fail to undermine the Council's authority. And it was in upholding that authority rather than in the merits of regionalism that the British delegation now seemed most interested.[69] In the compromise eventually worked out, regional arrangements remained formally subordinate to the Security Council (Arts. 52 and 53), but a new article (Art. 51) was inserted, which made explicit the right of Member States to take measures of individual or collective self-defence against an armed attack until the Security Council was able to take over. Article 51 was also generally interpreted as covering collective self-defence through regional agencies, such as that envisaged in the Act of Chapultepec.

At Dumbarton Oaks the right of individual and collective self-defence against armed attack was thought to be inherent in the

---

67 March 1945. For a summary of its main provisions see Goodrich and Hambro, pp. 298-99, which also contains an instructive account of the regional issue at San Francisco.

68 The United States delegation was rather divided, however; see *Vandenberg Papers*, pp. 188-89.

69 The British attitude towards regionalism appears to have become notably cooler; for instance, McNeill points out that in contrast to earlier British proposals for a Balkan Federation, by the end of 1944 Britain opposed any South Slav federation, fearing that a powerful Communist state might emerge as a potential core for a still wider Balkan federation (McNeill, *America, Britain and Russia*, p. 530).

proposals; nevertheless, its explicit recognition in Article 51 was of the utmost significance. The regional issue was not, of course, the only reason for this recognition. Article 51 was also designed to cover the not inconsiderable interval that might elapse between the onset of an armed attack and subsequent action by the Security Council, in which states would be bound to defend themselves, quite possibly in concert with other states. But the article was primarily an insurance against the breakdown of the Charter security system. Indeed, although outwardly no more than a legal loophole to allow states to fall back upon regional defence arrangements in such an eventuality, for some at least it was essentially an expression of no confidence in that system and a reaffirmation of their preference for the more limited forms of protection.

The great importance of Article 51 was recognized in informed circles in Britain. Though it did no more than give a veneer of legitimacy to political realities, it might at least help to stifle charges that measures of individual or collective self-defence were incompatible with the Charter and so remove a possible obstacle to continued Anglo-American co-operation. Otherwise, the article seems to have been regarded mainly as a necessary insurance against an eventuality which most people devoutly hoped might never arise. Few could have foreseen that in less than four years it was to become one of the most frequently quoted articles of the Charter.

A foretaste of things to come was also provided by the success of the smaller Powers, with the active assistance of the United States, in obtaining an increase in the powers and authority of the General Assembly. In contrast to the League theory of the parallel competences of the Council and the Assembly, the Dumbarton Oaks proposals left no doubt that the General Assembly was expected to be subordinate to the Security Council in all questions relating to the maintenance of international peace and security. At San Francisco the primary responsibility of the Security Council in these questions was reaffirmed, but the General Assembly was given the right not only to discuss but also to make recommendations

upon them (Art. 11(2)), so long as they were not being dealt with
by the Security Council (Art. 12). Subject to the same proviso, the
General Assembly was also given the right to discuss and to make
recommendations upon 'any questions or any matters within the
scope of the present Charter' (Art. 10) and 'to recommend measures
for the peaceful adjustment of any situation, regardless of origin,
which it deems likely to impair the general welfare or friendly
relations among nations' (Art. 14). The former would, its supporters
hoped, turn the Assembly into 'the town meeting of tomorrow's
world';[70] the latter represented 'a modest approach to the problem
of "peaceful change" in a dynamic world'.[71]

Britain was not opposed to this extension of the Assembly's
competence, for the latter's potentialities as a 'great instrument for
the formulation of world opinion'[72] were admitted. Nor did Britain
wish to see the *status quo* maintained for all time. On the contrary,
she had opposed proposals at Dumbarton Oaks[73] for writing in
a guarantee of the territorial integrity or political independence
of all Member States for much the same reasons as had caused her
to view Article 10 of the Covenant with misgiving, namely, that
such a guarantee would vastly extend Britain's commitments, that
it would invite intransigence on the part of the 'have' states, and
that it would imply that political frontiers were unalterable under
all circumstances. Moreover, the seeming indifference of the principal
members of the League (and especially France) to German claims
for an adjustment of the political frontiers drawn up at Versailles
and to Italian and Japanese claims for a more 'equitable' sharing
of the world's material wealth, was considered by many in Britain

---

70 *Vandenberg Papers*, p. 190.

71 Goodrich and Hambro, p. 178.

72 Cmd. 6666 (1945), para. 89.

73 Cmd. 6571 (1944), para. 16, which begins: 'Now that the undertaking to
prevent war is absolute and much more definite responsibilities to secure that
end are laid on all States, such a guarantee, if literally interpreted, would prevent any change in frontiers being carried out, even if all the other members
of the Organisation thought such a change was just and desirable'.

to have been one of the main reasons for the failure of the League and to have contributed to the installation or confirmation in office of the exponents of militaristic expansion in the 'have-not' countries. But the problem of 'peaceful change' was thought to be one for the Security Council not for the Assembly. Thus, at the Conference, it was made quite clear that the Council could not only consider any dispute in which the maintenance of the *status quo* was alleged to constitute a threat to the peace, but that it could also recommend the terms of settlement (Art. 37(2)) if the allegation were upheld.[74] The strong support both at home and throughout the Commonwealth for bringing the problem of 'peaceful change' within the purview of the more representative and so, it was supposed, more democratic, Assembly, did not altogether still the doubts as to whether the Assembly would use its powers wisely or the fear that Britain might occasionally be outvoted by an anti-colonial majority; the Assembly could, of course, only recommend, but it was not impossible to foresee circumstances in which an adverse recommendation might become a serious source of embarrassment. Above all, Britain was determined not to prejudice the prospects of collaboration between the Great Powers by undermining the authority of the Security Council. It was a matter for satisfaction, therefore, that the Assembly's new powers were explicitly made subject to the Security Council's primary responsibility for the maintenance of peace (Art. 12).

Britain also had some reservations about the general desire to strengthen the provisions on 'human rights', mainly on the grounds that the Charter should not include matters which did not lend themselves to international action, while there appear to have been some misgivings within the United Kingdom delegation about

---

[74] Sir Charles Webster comments: 'The question as to how far this right extends is a controversial one, but, in my view, the Security Council has the power to impose a settlement on the parties to a dispute, even if this means the alteration of their legal rights, provided that it determines that such a settlement is necessary for the maintenance of international peace and security'. *Sanctions*, p. 14.

d

the numerous amendments[75] designed to give a more prominent place, especially in the settlement of disputes, to 'principles of justice and international law'. The importance of such principles, both in themselves and as a check on possible arbitrary action by the Great Powers, was not denied, but should not the Security Council's prime purpose be the adjustment of conflicting interests so as to avoid armed conflict, in other words, with the preservation of peace and order rather than with the remedying of an unending succession of injustices, very few of which might ever pose a really serious threat to the peace? Although Britain supported the amendments, these mental reservations on the part of some members of the delegation persisted.

No less notable than the growth in the Assembly's powers was the elaboration of the economic and social objectives of the Organization and the inflation of the status of the Economic and Social Council into one of the 'principal organs' of the United Nations. Many delegates argued[76] that the economic and social work of the Organization could not only add to the sum of human welfare but that it also constituted the most hopeful approach to the problem of 'peaceful change'. The 'positive' or 'constructive' approach to peace was, indeed, a favourite talking-point for most delegates. This, broadly speaking, took two forms: the first, the so-called 'functional' approach,[77] was based upon the argument that by extending the opportunities for common action in those non-political matters in which the interdependence of states was most marked, the United Nations and the specialized agencies could foster a habit of co-operation between states, which might eventually help to lessen the strain of political divisions. The second held that the human

---

[75] Often at the instance of Commonwealth delegates, especially of Dr Evatt, the leader of the Australian delegation.

[76] This argument no doubt reflected the disappointment of some delegates with what they held to be the inadequate provision made elsewhere in the Charter for 'peaceful change'.

[77] Of which Professor David Mitrany was perhaps the best-known proponent; see his 'A Working Peace System', in RIIA, *Post-War Problems* (London, 1943).

misery and degradation caused by mass unemployment was not only abhorrent in itself but that it might also provide fertile soil for the growth of militarism; similarly, the sense of injustice engendered by glaring inequalities between living standards in different parts of the world could give rise to serious political friction and unrest. Both needed to be tackled at their source if world peace was to be assured.

On grounds both of human welfare[78] and as a contribution to world peace, Britain was anxious to accord to the new international system a more extensive role in economic and social affairs than had been permitted to the League of Nations. But there was little disposition to take the extreme view of some delegates that the causes of war were primarily economic, or to suppose that increased prosperity necessarily made for greater security. Indeed, some feared that the enthusiasm for the 'positive' approach might obscure the paramount importance of the problem of security.

Nor did the co-ordinating or residuary functions which would be the Council's main responsibility seem to most of the British delegation to justify its designation as a 'principal organ' of the United Nations.[79] Moreover, the hastily compiled jumble of goals set out in Article 55 no doubt reflected noble aspirations, but were they sufficiently premeditated or specific enough to be of practical value? In contrast, the specialized agencies[80] had carefully worked out and precisely defined tasks to perform, which were closely

---

[78] In a political broadcast of 5 June 1945 Mr Attlee said: 'I hold that it should be a principal object of the United Nations to wage war on hunger, poverty, disease, and ignorance, and to promote the greatest measure of economic co-operation between all nations in order to raise the standard of life of the masses of the people' (*The Times*, 6 June 1945).

[79] Although itself a 'principal organ', the Council was nevertheless made subordinate to the General Assembly.

[80] More especially the ILO, FAO, IMF, and the International Bank. These and other specialized agencies are autonomous bodies, with membership different from that of the United Nations, but the Charter seeks to establish an organic link between them and the United Nations by bringing them 'into relationship' with the United Nations (Art. 57). See Goodrich and Hambro, pp. 324-50.

geared in with Britain's own needs. In addition, the ILO[81] had
both a long and successful career behind it and ambitious plans
for the future. The Fund and the Bank possessed considerable
resources to dispense and the advantage of weighted voting,[82]
while their autonomous status would, it was hoped, keep these
and other specialized agencies unsullied by the political *arrières-
pensées* which would almost certainly be the daily concern of the
Economic and Social Council.

A further cause of misgiving was that in the one field of 'full
employment' in which the Council might have been able to perform
a useful service in pulling together the work of the specialized
agencies and in mobilizing political support for full employment
policies, much of its authority had been whittled down by the
transfer of the 'domestic jurisdiction' clause from the chapter in
the Dumbarton Oaks proposals dealing with the pacific settlement
of disputes to Chapter I (Principles) of the Charter.[83] Thus the
limitation was to apply to every aspect of the Organization's
activities, including all the provisions of Chapter IX. To emphasize
this, the relevant Committee at San Francisco placed on record
its agreement that 'nothing contained in Chapter IX [Economic
and Social Co-operation] can be construed as giving authority
to the Organization to intervene in the domestic affairs of member
states'.[84] But the successful attainment of the goals set out in
Chapter IX would be directly dependent on the domestic policies
pursued by member states. Not a great deal could be expected
from a Council (or an Assembly) whose powers were so closely
circumscribed.

---

[81] Britain at first pressed for the ILO to be recognized formally in the Charter
as one of the principal agencies for pursuing the objectives of the Charter.
[82] See below, p. 276.
[83] Mainly at the behest of the United States and Australia, both of which,
paradoxically, were amongst the foremost proponents of the 'positive approach';
see Goodrich and Hambro, pp. 110-12 and 320-21.
[84] UNCIO, x. 271-72.

On the other hand, it was admitted that the growing constellation of specialized agencies had made overlapping more likely and the need for co-ordination more obvious. This could best be achieved, many thought, by locating them in the same place, by close co-operation between their secretariats, and by member governments co-ordinating their own policies; but the Economic and Social Council might also come in handy for the purpose, as well as for initiating action in those matters not covered by the specialized agencies.

There were also strong political arguments in favour of elevating the Council's status. The fact that the Great Powers had no special privileges on the Economic and Social Council (e.g. permanent membership[85] or a veto) was not only one of the reasons for the Council's popularity but it had already gone some way towards reconciling the smaller states to the privileged position of the Great Powers on the Security Council; the wider powers and improved status now proposed for the Economic and Social Council might further mitigate their discontent at the refusal of the Great Powers to relinquish their veto rights. The thought also no doubt occurred that Britain's support would be a small price to pay for ensuring a better hearing for her own case on dependent and trust territories, a matter of the utmost importance to her but one on which many of the states[86] most anxious to advance the Economic and Social Council's position might be expected to be rather unsympathetic. These political considerations and Britain's genuine sympathy with the general aims of Chapters IX and X were sufficient to ensure her support for the majority proposals. Yet there are some grounds for believing that those most intimately concerned with the economic and social problems under discussion remained rather dubious about the elaboration of objectives and of the Council's machinery which was the most obvious achievement of the Conference; some,

---

[85] Much the same result was ensured, however, by the provision that 'A retiring member shall be eligible for immediate re-election' (Art. 61(2)).

[86] Especially Australia and the United States.

indeed, appear to have been seriously perturbed lest the Council might turn out to be little more than a distraction from more urgent and important tasks.

The provisions of Chapter XI (Declaration regarding Non-Self-Governing Territories) and Chapter XII (International Trusteeship System) will be examined later in this study.[87] It suffices to mention here that the Declaration was in close accord with the general objectives of British colonial policy and that the trusteeship system was essentially a strengthened mandates system. Finally, the International Court of Justice (Chapter XIV), whose Statute forms an integral part of the Charter, was in effect a renovated Permanent Court of International Justice, while the provisions of the Charter dealing with the Secretariat (Chapter XV) were closely based on League experience. The International Court and the Secretariat are the subject of later chapters in this study.[88]

COLLECTIVE SECURITY IN THE COVENANT AND IN THE CHARTER

As its tangled wording indicates, the Charter, like the Covenant, is the end-product of a long and complicated series of negotiations; it is, therefore, a compromise, in places an uneasy and ambiguous one, between competing conceptions.[89] Yet the main aim at San Francisco, as *mutatis mutandis* at Versailles, was the maintenance of international peace through, in the first place, the acceptance of undertakings not to commit any act of aggression, and, in the second place, the institution of a system of collective security under

[87] See Chapter 14.

[88] See Chapters 15 and 16, respectively.

[89] Professor Alfred Zimmern's description of the Covenant is apposite; he wrote: 'Unlike most other great declarations and constitutions, it [the Covenant] is not the expression of a single political doctrine. It does not emanate from a body of men animated by a common thought or purpose. On the contrary it represents a dovetailing of doctrines and the adjustment of widely differing and, in some cases, contending wills' (*The League of Nations and the Rule of Law, 1918-1935* (London, Macmillan, 1939), p. 271).

which the readiness of all (or nearly all) states to take collective action against aggression, wherever it occurred,[90] would ensure that any state that might be tempted to make illicit use of its strength would be faced by such an array of strength that it would regard the attempt as hopeless and desist; by reducing the feeling of insecurity inherent in a society of sovereign states such a system would also, it was hoped, pave the way for a reduction of armaments and for 'peaceful change'.

The premises on which the collective security formulae of the Covenant and the Charter were based differed considerably, however. A major assumption underlying the Covenant was that the First World War might never have occurred had not the Concert system broken down. Hence the need to set up machinery which would automatically bring the Great Powers together whenever there was a threat to peace and to provide for a breathing space—a 'cooling-off' period—during which the parties to a dispute that might lead to a rupture would forbear to go to war. War was not to be outlawed altogether, but the hope was that 'war delayed would be war averted', since the machinery for pacific settlement would then have time to come into play. In addition, since secret diplomacy and the armaments race were believed to have contributed substantially to the outbreak of war, much stress was laid on 'open diplomacy' and the limitation of armaments, while the success of the economic blockade of Germany highlighted the importance of economic sanctions.

By contrast, the conflict which was still being waged when the Dumbarton Oaks negotiations were in progress seemed not so much the product of a lack of machinery as the inevitable consequence of the overweening cupidity of the Axis Powers; and against the calculated aggressions of a Hitler, the Covenant process of 'inquiry

---

[90] Integral to the concept of collective security is the notion of the 'indivisibility of peace' and the belief that since aggression by its very nature is a threat to the whole world order it must be stamped out wherever it occurs, irrespective of the political complexion of the aggressor.

and delay' seemed a puny defence. The overriding need, it was argued, was for the comprehensive renunciation of war as an instrument of policy and for a security system of irresistible power which could nip aggression in the bud; in brief, the aim was to 'put teeth into the Kellogg Pact'. Little emphasis was placed on the regulation of armaments (Art. 26); far from the Second World War having resulted from an armaments race, the failure of the United States and Great Britain to rearm rapidly enough in the late 1930's was of too recent memory, while the compulsory disarmament of 'aggressor' nations by an 'Armed Concert' of the victorious Great Powers seems to have been uppermost in the minds of the three war leaders.

Nor was the sanctions system of the Covenant as revolutionary as that of the Charter. Its guiding principle was that in a society of sovereign states any system of restraints must necessarily be founded in the loyalty of Member States to their obligations, in other words, in mutual consent rather than compulsion from above, as in the Charter. Throughout the Covenant the League figured as little more than a permanent association, or 'club', of sovereign states—a 'they' rather than an 'it'[91]—and the emphasis was on the obligations of Members rather than on the authority of its organs.[92] Similarly, the effectiveness of its sanctions system did not depend upon the ability of the League Council to reach a decision, but rather upon the observance by individual Members of a precisely defined and automatic obligation, namely, to 'excommunicate' any Member State that resorted to war in disregard of its covenants (Art. 16(1)).[93] Thus the system of voting was not of crucial

---

[91] J. L. Brierly, 'The Covenant and the Charter', in *BYIL, 1946*.

[92] Only in Art. 11 was the 'League' specifically mentioned as such, and this may have been a drafting error.

[93] The lack of definition of aggression was, therefore, unimportant. Incidentally, despite the concern in the 1920's over the gap in the Covenant (i. e. the right of a state to go to war, after the stipulated interval, either if the Council was unable to reach a unanimous recommendation or if the other party was unwilling to comply with the recommendation), no state ever made use of it.

importance since it did not confer upon a dissenting state the right to veto the action of the others. The Council could *advise* on whether an occasion for economic and financial sanctions had in fact arisen and it could also recommend further military measures to 'protect the covenants of the League' (Art. 16(2)), while arrangements could be made to co-ordinate the action of those members participating in collective sanctions. But the Council could not *decide* or *call upon* Members; in each and every case the immediate responsibility for fulfilment of the Covenant's requirements lay with Member States.

This decentralized system depended, of course, upon the continuing good faith of its members. But at least it was thoroughly realistic in recognizing that no one had the power to compel them to live up to their obligations. Furthermore, at least in theory the system had the great merit of allowing those states that conceived it to be their duty to act to do so without having first to secure the agreement of all their fellows, including the delinquent state itself. Consequently, under the Covenant system sanctions could properly have been taken against Japan in 1931 and they were taken against Italy in 1935, both countries being generally regarded as Great Powers at the time.

The drafters of the Charter sought to confer upon the Security Council powers far exceeding those exercised by the League Council. In the Charter the Security Council purports to exercise powers of a supranational kind—it is an 'it' rather than a 'they'—with the right to take decisions for the maintenance of international peace and security on behalf of all the Members of the United Nations (Arts. 24 and 25) and the capacity to secure compliance with those decisions (through the forces made available to the Council under the special agreements of Art. 43).[94] Even apart from the uncertainty whether those forces would in fact be made

---

[94] This organic conception of the Security Council reflects the Hobbesian precepts which permeate the Charter in contrast to the principles of Lockeian liberalism mirrored in the Covenant (see below, pp. 425-26).

available when a crisis threatened, the formula itself is wholly dependent, however, both on the Council's being able to reach a decision and on the conclusion of the special agreements.[95] The veto made it certain that the Council would be unable to decide whenever a threat to the peace had the connivance of a permanent member, while even at San Francisco the atmosphere did not seem very propitious to the conclusion of the 'special agreements'.

In so far as the veto was no more than a reassertion by the permanent members of their right—and of their capacity—as sovereign states to refuse to be bound by decisions in which they did not concur, it was, in the existing state of international society, both realistic and inevitable. What was more contentious was the right accorded to every permanent member—on a strict reading of the Charter—to prevent all the other permanent members from taking enforcement measures not merely against itself (which, as the official commentary advised,[96] would probably lead to the major war which it was the prime purpose of the United Nations to prevent), but also against any state whatsoever. The elaborate provisions of Chapter VII of the Charter made some sense if they were drafted on the assumption that a permanent member would be unable to prevent their operation when, as a party to a dispute, it was required to abstain from voting, or if the Dumbarton Oaks delegates had the possibility of renewed aggression by Germany or Japan in the forefront of their minds. But the former assumption was outmoded by the Yalta formula and the latter contingency could hardly have seemed a very pressing one by the time of the San Francisco Conference. The Yalta formula was, in fact, the price that had to be paid to secure the participation of both the Soviet Union and the United States in the new Organization. That it was not generally considered to be a prohibitive price could not conceal the fact, however, that, *on paper*, 'we have discarded the

---

[95] Or, at least, on the conclusion of enough of them to give the Council a reasonable margin of power over any potential aggressor.
[96] Cmd. 6666, para. 87.

system of the Covenant which, though not certainly, might possibly have worked, and we have substituted for it one which hardly even professes to be workable'.[97]

HOPES AND MISGIVINGS

The realization, after Yalta, that the proposed collective security system had virtually no chance of working whenever there was a real threat to world peace came as a shock. Hopes of a continuing 'Armed Concert' of the Great Powers still lingered on, while it was generally anticipated that the veto would be used only as a last recourse, not as a routine obstruction. But claims by government spokesmen in the House of Commons debate of 17 April 1945 that the blue-print for the projected world organization represented an advance upon the Covenant were greeted with some reserve. Sir Arthur Salter was not alone in his criticism that the 'new instrument would in fact be actually weaker than the League', or in his fear that 'the very elaboration of these provisions may merely cause misconception as to what this new organization can do'.[98] Consequently, when on 26 June 1945 the delegates assembled at San Francisco signed the Charter, the response in Great Britain was on the whole rather lukewarm. The wide measure of agreement achieved at San Francisco excited favourable comment, but the prevalent mood was one of cautious commendation rather than of marked enthusiasm. And it was on the prospects for Great Power collaboration that attention continued to be concentrated. Thus *The Times* leader of 27 June 1945, while generally sympathetic and politely sanguine about the prospects for the United Nations, pointed out that there was little disposition to consider the Charter as more than a first step:

It is far more widely recognized than it was in 1919 that no

---

[97] J. L. Brierly, *The Law of Nations*, 5th ed. (London, OUP, 1955), p. 307.
[98] H. C. Deb., vol. 410, col. 136.

> international instrument, no constitutional specific, will suffice
> to maintain peace . . . The Charter by itself is nothing, if it
> fails to rally the loyalty of the major Powers who alone can
> give it body and life.

This is not the whole picture, however. As compared with a
generation earlier, the League 'way' now had powerful adherents
in ministerial and official circles. Not only did the initial success
of Hitler's 'one-by-one' technique seem to testify to the indivisibility
of peace and to the truth of the old adage 'hang together or hang
separately', but it was perceived that in the post-war world the
relative diminution of British power (both political and economic)
would make her more a 'consumer' than a 'producer' of security.
It was more than ever in her interest, therefore, to do everything
possible to build a more peaceful and orderly world. Moreover,
in addition to the habit of international co-operation which the
League had instilled in many walks of official and unofficial life,
the technological contraction of the world and the interlocking
character of contemporary inter-state relations appeared once and
for all to have outmoded the slow-moving processes of traditional
diplomacy and to have made 'diplomacy by conference' a daily
necessity, not only for idealistic reasons but on grounds of practical
self-interest and convenience. The League 'idea' had also become
firmly embedded in the public mind. The alleged cold-shouldering
of the League by Britain (and France) was by now widely regarded
as having contributed to the terrible conflagration which was just
drawing to its end. In men and women sickened by the brutality
and waste of war, by the violation of human rights in totalitarian
states, and by the misery of the economic depression of the 1930's,
the picture of a new and nobler world mirrored in the Preamble to
the Charter struck a responsive chord. There might be misgivings
about particular provisions of the Charter but few were opposed
to making this second attempt.

The supreme merit of the Charter for most people, however,
was that it was acceptable to both the United States and the Soviet

Union, as the Covenant had not been.[99] The new world organization might not be everything that Britain desired, but it might at least help to keep the Great Powers together and to prevent them from splitting into two rival blocs. The flaw in the collective security formula was regretted, but, as Mr Attlee pointed out,

> the British delegation took a foremost part in seeking to make the Security Council something more than a policeman who is called in when there is already a danger of a breach of the peace. We sought, and sought successfully, to make it a place where the policies of the States, and especially the greater States, could be discussed and reconsidered for the time, especially when they showed signs of such divergencies as to threaten the harmony of international relations. Collective security is not merely a promise to act when an emergency occurs, but it is active co-operation to prevent emergencies occurring . . . What, I think, is required is a continuous discussion of international affairs, not spasmodic action at times of crisis.[100]

More especially, although American suspicion of British policies and aims militated against that more intimate association which Britain sought, the United Nations could help to harness American power to the cause of world security and to counter any tendency to revert to isolationism; it might even help to postpone the threatened early withdrawal of American troops from Europe.[101] It was also the 'definite and reasoned conviction on the part of the British and United States Governments—the change of party control in Great Britain made no difference in this respect—that there would be no hope for the future of Europe and indeed of the world

[99] The fact that the new organization was not tied to a peace settlement, as the League had been, also excited favourable comment, as did the expanded provisions for economic and social co-operation.

[100] 22 Aug. 1945, H. C. Deb., vol. 413, col. 665.

[101] In Mr Eden's view, it was 'impossible to exaggerate . . . the significance for this organisation of the fact that the United States is not only in it from the start, as one of the authors of the organisation, but . . . is a whole-hearted supporter of this new world organisation' (ibid. col. 676).

without the collaboration of Russia.'[102] Hence, despite the growing resentment at Soviet policy in Poland, Roumania, and Germany, real encouragement was drawn from the concessions made by the Soviet Union at San Francisco, especially their agreement that no one Great Power should be able to prevent the discussion of any dispute.

The ratification of the Charter was approved by the House of Commons without a division, and Britain deposited her instrument of ratification on 20 October 1945. On 24 October 1945 the United States Secretary of State formally declared that the Charter had come into effect. Meanwhile, the Preparatory Commission and its Executive Committee busied themselves with setting the scene for the first session of the General Assembly which was to open in London on 10 January 1946. The advent of the atomic bomb lent new urgency to their deliberations. Indeed, the need to secure effective international control of atomic energy suggested that the United Nations might have to be transformed to meet this grave new challenge to the future of civilized man. Mr Bevin, then Foreign Secretary, himself wondered, when opening the Executive Committee of the Preparatory Commission on 16 August 1945, what might be 'the effects of the atomic bomb on the organization of security', and whether 'a great many of their previous conceptions and a great many of the assumptions on which they worked at San Francisco would have to be radically revised.'[103] Certainly this development gave new force to declarations that the United Nations would be the 'cornerstone' of British policy.

---

[102] Sir Llewellyn Woodward, 'Some Reflections on British Policy, 1939-45', *International Affairs*, July 1955, p. 283.
[103] *The Times*, 17 Aug. 1945.

chapter two

British Foreign Policy since 1945

Before turning to a more detailed examination of the impact of the United Nations on the content and conduct of British foreign policy from 1946 until December 1955[1], it may be helpful to give a very brief résumé of that policy, and to indicate some of the main issues that will be discussed in later chapters. A word of warning is necessary, however. Recent events are too close to be seen in their true perspective; brevity may conceal the baffling complexity of the post-war scene, while hindsight may read a logic and coherence into policies which were in reality little more than tentative and confused gropings.

Nevertheless, despite the immense rise in the power and influence of the United States and the Soviet Union, and the consequent narrowing of Britain's own range of choice and freedom of manoeuvre,

---

[1] The period covered by this study, with the single exception that the story of the disarmament discussions is taken up to July 1956 (Chapter 5).

the problems that have preoccupied British Ministers since 1945 are not unfamiliar ones and the main lines of British policy stand out fairly clearly. Of first importance has been the old anxiety lest Western Europe should fall under the dominance of a hostile Power, in this instance the Soviet Union. To meet this threat the first priority for British policy has been to anchor American power firmly in Western Europe and to preserve the close ties which knit the United States and Britain together during the Second World War. Hardly less important, especially since 1950, has been the need to heal the breach between France and Western Germany and to obtain French acquiescence in the latter's rearmament. Mainly for this reason Britain has been led, albeit rather hesitantly, to enter into the closest possible association, short of surrendering her ultimate sovereignty, with the nations of Western Europe. Of special significance also have been Britain's relationships within the Commonwealth. Indeed, the evolution of the 'multi-racial Commonwealth' is regarded by the British people as perhaps the most challenging political experiment of modern times, which requires Britain to listen attentively to Asian views even at the cost of an occasional strain on her relations with the United States and her European allies. The bearing of the United Nations on these three enduring, but sometimes conflicting, sets of relationships will frequently be touched upon in this study.

As in the past, the other areas of principal concern to Britain have been, on the one hand, the Eastern Mediterranean and Middle East, and on the other, Asia and the Far East. The former area is still of vital strategic importance to Britain as a focal point of air and sea communications, as a source of oil, and as the gateway to the newly emerging continent of Africa. In the Far East the American stake is considerably greater than the British, but Britain's Commonwealth ties and responsibilities, her commercial interests, and her dependencies in South East Asia still make this area one of real concern to her. The problems of both these areas have figured prominently on the agenda of United Nations organs;

they are examined in some detail, therefore, in the following two chapters.

Three other elements in British policy since 1945 are rather less familiar. In the first place, the fear of economic collapse haunted British Ministers in the early post-war years. Indeed, the early pruning of British overseas military commitments was partly dictated by the need to reduce overseas expenditure, while the initial dependence on American economic aid helped to orientate policy towards the United States. Ever since, the struggle to become and to remain economically solvent has coloured every aspect of policy and has directly affected Britain's standing in the counsels of the nations. In this struggle the economic agencies of the United Nations have played a secondary but not an unimportant role.[2] Secondly, the ideological conflict has introduced a new, though not entirely novel, element, the precise importance of which it is difficult to assess. Certainly in so far as it has deepened mutual mistrust and suspicion, it has contributed to the impasse over disarmament,[3] while in many parts of the world the relative appeal of Western and Soviet conceptions of the 'democratic' way of life may play a considerable part in shaping future alignments. Thirdly, familiar problems have taken on a new dimension with the perfection of a wide range of weapons of mass destruction; in their formidable power may lie either the best hope of future peace or the instrument of civilization's eclipse.

It is evident that in all these matters Anglo-American relations have been of first importance. Consequently, the bearing of the United Nations on these relations will form one of the main themes of this study. For Britain the basic fact about the United Nations is that almost from the outset the system of collective security envisaged in the Charter was found to be a wholly ineffective instrument for ensuring the safety of the British Isles and the

---

[2] See Part IV.
[3] See Chapter 5.

e

protection of British possessions and interests overseas. This was
not entirely unexpected. Indeed, Article 51 had been inserted in
the Charter at San Francisco partly as a safeguard against such
a contingency. But few had foreseen that a deep and intractable
rift between the West and an expansionist Soviet Union, seemingly
intent on promoting 'all mischief short of war', would develop so
rapidly as to compel the United Kingdom and her European
neighbours, within hardly more than eighteen months, to look to
arrangements outside the United Nations for their security.

These facts were not immediately apparent, however. The disintegration of the 'Grand Alliance' was not instantaneous, and a
modicum of co-operation between the Great Powers persisted into
1947. At first, therefore, both politicians and the general public
were more aware of the destruction wrought by the atomic explosions
over Hiroshima and Nagasaki than of Soviet ambitions. Mainly
for this reason in late 1945 and January 1946 there was some talk
of the United Nations as a step towards world government.[4] During
this period Britain was determined to do everything possible to
make the collective security system of the Charter work. High-
ranking delegates were sent to the Military Staff Committee and
much thought and energy were devoted to its deliberations. This
was possibly more a matter of faith than of conviction. Even the
more optimistic found it difficult to believe in a Committee whose
members were instructed to plan against the possibility of aggression
by one of their own number; but the attempt had to be made.
Similarly, from the start Britain stressed the importance of the
work of the Atomic Energy Commission and sought to bridge
the gap between the Western and Soviet proposals. In the Security
Council, despite his vigorous rebuttal of Soviet charges against
British policy in Greece and elsewhere, Mr Bevin strove to build
up the authority of the Council, especially as an instrument for

---

[4] See the Foreign Secretary (Mr Bevin), 23 Nov. 1945, H. C. Deb., vol. 416,
coll. 785-86, and the Minister of State (Mr P. J. Noel-Baker), 28 Jan. 1946,
ibid. vol. 418, coll. 630-31.

the pacific settlement of disputes. At the same time he was anxious not to burden an infant United Nations, so dependent upon Great Power co-operation, with issues which divided, or threatened to divide them; in his view these[5] could be better discussed within the smaller and more private circle of the Council of Foreign Ministers. But the wrangling within the Council of Foreign Ministers quickly spilled over into the United Nations. The very first meetings of the Security Council were marked by long verbal duels between Mr Bevin and Mr Molotov, which received considerable publicity and did much to dispel all but the most cautious hopes entertained in Britain at the time of San Francisco.

In addition, the Soviet Union's actions in Eastern Europe and Iran, her verbal assaults at the United Nations on British policy in Greece, and the failure to make any progress over the future of Germany soon led to the abandonment of earlier assumptions and hopes with regard to the Soviet Union. Thinking in official circles was already turning to the possible development of more limited and closely-knit collective defence arrangements under Article 51. By early 1947 Mr Bevin himself seems to have been converted to Mr Churchill's belief that regional arrangements were the essential pillars of an effective collective security system. Until these supporting pillars were built, would not the Charter system be like a roof suspended in mid-air?

The refusal of the Soviet Union to take part in the European Recovery Programme eased the way to a closer association of Western Europe. Mr Bevin's hint on 22 January 1948 that 'the time is ripe for the consolidation of Europe'[6] was swiftly followed by the signature of the Brussels Pact on 17 March 1948, the second treaty to invoke Article 51.[7] The Organization for European Economic

---

[5] Apart from the control of atomic energy and the regulation of armaments.

[6] H. C. Deb., vol. 446, col. 383.

[7] The first was the Inter-American Treaty of Reciprocal Assistance of 2 September 1947. The Treaty of Dunkirk (4 March 1947) was directed against a revival of German aggression, and so came principally under Art. 107, although Art. 51 was also cited.

Co-operation bore witness to the United Kingdom's stake in the prosperity of Western Europe; the Brussels Pact committed her to the defence of Western Europe more firmly than ever before. But those intent on drawing Britain further into Europe found, to their dismay, that she set greater store either by her transatlantic or by her Commonwealth and imperial connexions. Close association was one thing, but full membership of a federated Europe—or of schemes which pointed in that direction—was another. Would it not threaten the 'welfare state' and the disintegration of the Common-wealth? Almost as important was the fear that many of the early proposals for European Union were motivated by a 'neutralist' or 'third-force' philosophy. For it has been a central tenet of British policy, certainly since early in 1947, that the resolve of the countries of Western Europe to resist aggression can be effective only with American help. Consequently, although Western European Union could serve as a useful military planning prototype, it needed to be underpinned by American power if an effective deterrent to Soviet expansion was to be built up. Thus, even before the signature of the Brussels Pact, Mr Bevin's prime aim was to draw America, Canada, and Western Europe together.[8] With the Brussels Pact the seed of NATO sprouted into life.

The development of closer ties with the United States was viewed with some hesitation, however, by a section of the rank and file of the Labour Party, which had long cherished hopes of friendly relations with the Soviet Union and was apt to be distrustful of American ways. Misgivings about Soviet intentions were growing, but Germany was seen as the chief threat for the future by many in the Labour Party, while others were extremely reluctant to pursue any policy which might be construed as by-passing the United Nations. But pro-Soviet feeling was alienated by the per-secution of the Social Democrats in Eastern Europe, by the coup d'état in Czechoslovakia (February 1948), and by the defection of

[8] See *NATO, the First Five Years, 1949-1954*, by Lord Ismay (Paris, NATO, 1954), pp. 7-9.

Yugoslavia from the Soviet camp. Anti-American feeling also gradually abated as the generosity of Marshall Aid came to be appreciated. In addition, Mr Bevin was a man of character, independent spirit, and robust determination, and his high standing in his party enabled him to make changes in policy which others might have hesitated to advocate. Consequently, when Mr Bevin found himself forced to abandon the idea of preserving world peace through a harmonious concert of Great Powers, and he turned to work for a closer Atlantic grouping as an effective counterpoise to Soviet power, he was able to count upon the support of the vast majority of the Labour Party.

The whole course of political and economic events since 1945 thus emphasized the supreme importance of Anglo-American co-operation; but the omens on the other side of the Atlantic were not at first very encouraging for the continuance of the close and intimate co-operation which had grown up during the war. Many not uninfluential Americans seemed to see little to choose between Soviet ambitions and what they still termed 'British imperialism'. Indeed, those who argue that the setting up of the United Nations distracted attention from the prime need for an Anglo-American alliance overlook the volume of American opinion which favoured instead a United States-Soviet rapprochement.

When Mr Winston Churchill advocated, in his Fulton speech of 5 March 1946, a 'fraternal association' between the United States and the British Commonwealth because of his doubts about Soviet intentions, the American response was cool in the extreme. Through the United Nations American power had been harnessed to the cause of world security, thereby mitigating the fears of renewed American isolationism which haunted British statesmen.[9] But the fears were by no means removed. The Charter obligations were 'general', not 'particular', and American policy in the late summer

---

[9] It can be argued that this fear was an unrealistic one, but it certainly existed; it also led to British pressure to locate the United Nations headquarters on the eastern seaboard of the United States.

of 1945 was to negotiate the peace treaties as promptly as possible
in order to permit an American withdrawal from active participation
in European affairs.[10] Not until the open rupture, in May 1946,
between the United States and the Soviet Union over German
reparation deliveries, followed shortly by Congressional approval
of the loan to Britain, did a common Anglo-American front start
to develop. Only with the enunciation of the Truman Doctrine in
March 1947 did the United States set her face firmly against further
Soviet expansion. And it may well be that the willingness of the
American people to undertake such revolutionary new commitments
was induced to no small extent by their dedication to the purposes
and principles of the Charter and by the impact on their thinking
of the open display of Soviet intransigence at the United Nations.[11]

It is also notable that the United States responded rather
differently from Britain to the stultification of the Security Council.
Mr Bevin was anxious to limit the abuse of the veto rights of the
Great Powers in regard to the pacific settlement of disputes,[12] but
he viewed with serious misgivings a tentative suggestion from
General Marshall in September 1947 to circumvent the veto by
developing the Assembly's role in the field of collective security.
In the British view the veto was a symptom, not a cause, of a
basic weakness in the whole collective security idea, which would
only work if the Great Powers were more or less of one mind
on basic principles, or if the 'peace-loving'—or *'status-quo'*—states
had a clear preponderance of power. And the real test was not
the number of votes they could muster but the military power
that they could mobilize. Clearly neither of these conditions was
present. If, then, the dissident minority were as powerful as the
majority—or more powerful—or if the majority were hesitant to
use the one weapon in which they had an overwhelming superiority,
what point was there in trying to patch up the United Nations

10 McNeill, *America, Britain and Russia*, pp. 611-12.
11 See below, p. 83.
12 See below, p. 232.

collective security system? In such a situation those Powers who felt themselves threatened by the Soviet Union should draw together into a closely-knit system of collective self-defence which, by redressing the balance of power, might put them in a better position to negotiate or, if need be, to defend themselves successfully. Article 51 provided a convenient 'umbrella' for such an effort. Meanwhile the United Nations could usefully remain as a readily available instrument of negotiation and point of contact between East and West.

On the whole the British view prevailed, and with the coup d'état in Czechoslovakia and the Berlin blockade (June 1948-May 1949), most Americans came to accept the need for a closer association of the Atlantic countries. The North Atlantic Treaty of April 1949, which also owed a great deal to Canadian initiative, may be said to be the crown of post-war British foreign policy. In the first place NATO was the means by which Britain could harmonize her interests and obligations in Europe with her ties with America and Canada. Secondly, it was, from Britain's point of view, in nearly every respect the ideal type of international organization. It was inter-governmental, with adequate opportunities for Great Power leadership, and it was of the size and consistency which made for effective collaboration. More important still, NATO was not simply an assurance of American help in the event of war, but the framework for building up an effective counterpoise to Soviet power.

The Atlantic Treaty had obvious and momentous consequences. No amount of delicate phrasing could gloss over the fact that the Atlantic alliance was a response to the demonstrated incapacity of the United Nations to deal with the fundamental cleavage of the post-war period, and that NATO rather than the United Nations had become the hub of British foreign policy. In some quarters in Britain there was a tendency to assume a slightly apologetic air towards the United Nations because of its apparent supersession as the principal vehicle of British foreign policy. Some asked whether the Treaty was consonant with the letter and spirit of the Charter. But the rather legalistic debate that ensued aroused little interest. The legal case made out by apologists for the Treaty, though perhaps a trifle disingenuous, seemed plausible, while few doubted that the Charter system of security had been stillborn, that the Soviet threat was a real one, and that the Treaty represented the best means of creating that 'position of strength' for the West which might bring nearer the possibilities of peaceful coexistence.

However, though the United Nations was, and is, a tribute to the ideal and NATO a response to reality, the ideal lived on. Despite its relegation to the wings as regards the cold war, the United Nations' record for 1949 was, in other respects, not unimpressive. Armistice agreements had been concluded under United Nations auspices in Palestine in January, while in November the General Assembly was able to agree on a feasible plan for the future of Libya.[13] Moreover, the Berlin blockade had been lifted in May after negotiations initiated at Lake Success.[14] Thus, in the British view, though collective defence in the free world could best be organized outside the United Nations through smaller, more tightly-knit groups of like-minded states, the experience of 1949 seemed to show that the United Nations should be kept alive and oecumenical as the essential framework for an international order, as an instrument of conciliation and mediation between the smaller Powers, and as a valuable point of contact between the Great Powers.

The Korean War, which is discussed in Chapter 4, modified this rather austere view of the United Nations; for a time the resolute American response revived languishing faith in the collective security principle. Britain was active in support of United Nations action in Korea and appreciated the major part played by the United States. But in making the Far East the focus of international

---

[13] See below, p. 87.
[14] See below, p. 238.

interest, the Korean War also posed delicate problems for Anglo-American relations, particularly as regards their respective attitudes towards Communist China, the emergence of which has been the dominant feature of the Far Eastern scene. Previously the United Nations had been esteemed for its part in awakening the American people to the Soviet threat; now the Organization came to assume more importance in most British minds as a means of restraining the United States from taking what was, rightly or wrongly, considered to be over-precipitate action. Further, Britain viewed with grave misgivings a disposition in the United States to treat the United Nations as merely an alliance of belligerents; in the British view the United Nations had still a valuable role to perform as a restraining influence and as a diplomatic meeting place where the possibilities of a settlement could be explored.

The Korean War also faced London with the often difficult task of preventing too acute a divergence between Washington and Delhi. For, although Britain is determined to play her full share in Western defence, the preservation of the multi-racial Commonwealth is an integral part of British policy. Indeed, the post-war evolution of a formerly predominantly British and imperial grouping into a multi-racial society of sovereign states is an experiment that the British people have followed with such pride that Britain's Commonwealth connexions are almost as highly prized as Anglo-American friendship, while the United Nations itself is apt to be compared unfavourably with the Commonwealth, which is held up as a happier model of international co-operation that has worked and is working—even though how and why it works is something of a puzzle.[15] And although India is the only member of the Commonwealth which has consistently pursued a policy of non-alignment, the fact that relations with India are by way of being a symbol

---

15 Many people in Britain take almost a perverse pride in not being able to explain the nature of the Commonwealth to others, as though the invention of something which is at once both effective and inexplicable were the *ne plus ultra* of political genius.

of the new Commonwealth, the growing importance of New Delhi as a diplomatic centre, and her appreciation of India's standing as an 'honest broker' between Communist China and the West, have all made Britain inclined to take a more sympathetic view of India's policy of non-alignment than has the United States. By giving India a *locus standi* in the Korean armistice negotiations which she might not otherwise have had, the United Nations may well have helped to ease what threatened at one time to become a source of serious tension in Anglo-American relations.

The United Nations has also had a direct bearing on intra-Commonwealth relations as a result of its intervention in the dispute between India and Pakistan over Kashmir.[16] It is true that at present the dispute does not appear much closer to a settlement that when it first came before the Security Council on 1 January 1948.[17] Yet the achievement of a cease-fire on 1 January 1949 was of the utmost significance. The United Nations cannot claim all the credit for bringing it about. An important contributory factor was that the military 'commanders on both sides were always conscious of their grave responsibilities and the need to limit operations'.[18] The military situation was indeed a most unusual one. Both armies were commanded by British generals,[19] while many of the senior officers on both sides had served together in the Indian army and had trained together at Sandhurst or Dehra

---

[16] For an account see Lord Birdwood, *A Continent Decides* (London, Hale, 1953), pp. 211-56, and Michael Brecher, *The Struggle for Kashmir* (Toronto, Ryerson Press for Canadian Institute of International Affairs and Institute of Pacific Relations, 1953).

[17] On that date India complained under Art. 35 of the Charter that Pakistan's complicity in the invasion of Kashmir by tribesmen from the north (including what came to be known as the Azad forces) had given rise to a situation likely to endanger international peace and security. Two weeks later, i. e. on 15 January, Pakistan counter-charged that the tribal invasion was a by-product of Indian actions since partition which, she alleged, were aimed at the destruction of Pakistan.

[18] Birdwood, *A Continent Decides*, p. 237.

[19] General Sir Douglas Gracey (Pakistan) and General Sir F. R. R. Bucher (India).

Dun. It is also the case that towards the end of 1948 it had become clear to both sides that the chances of a quick decision had passed and that there was a real danger of a full-scale war, which neither country desired. Nevertheless, United Nations mediation was probably decisive in tipping the scales in favour of a cease-fire, while subsequently its Military Observer Group has helped to check incidents which might have led to another outbreak. Thus United Nations intervention has almost certainly been instrumental in keeping alive the chances of a more permanent settlement and in preventing a full-scale war, which would have engulfed a sub-continent of 400 million people and would almost certainly have disrupted the Commonwealth. In addition, by its very existence the United Nations has made possible the transfer of the dispute to an arena where Britain and other members of the Commonwealth have been able to avoid identifying themselves with one side or the other, a choice that might have rendered extremely difficult the continued membership of both.

By contrast, the strong anti-colonial pressure at the United Nations of the Arab-Asian bloc, in which India and Pakistan play a prominent part, has caused some resentment in Britain. Although the cold war has split the United Nations most deeply, the rift between the colonial and highly industrialized Powers of the West (with the United States often a reluctant partner) and the underdeveloped and newly independent countries of Asia and the Middle East has become of increasing significance. As will be seen in Chapters 9 and 14, the United Nations merely mirrors, it is not the cause of, this antagonism. And even though the members of the Commonwealth often figure as the chief protagonists in the opposing camps, their disagreements usually centre on timing and method rather than on ends, on which Britain and the Asian members of the Commonwealth usually seem to be in broad agreement. Yet the open display of differences at the United Nations may have tended occasionally to weaken the intangible ties that hold the Commonwealth together, especially since by consistently aligning herself with other colonial Powers Britain may run the risk of becoming stigmatized as an unrepentant imperialist Power. Moreover, the Arab-Asian attack is also directed at all forms of race discrimination, at least when practised by Europeans against non-Europeans. The consequences may be serious for a Britain grappling with the formidable problems of multi-racial dependent territories in East and Central Africa and for a multi-racial Commonwealth in which one member pursues an avowed policy of discrimination. These tensions would exist even if there were no United Nations, but may the United Nations not aggravate rather than ease them?

SOME CASE STUDIES

PART TWO

PART TWO

chapter three

The Middle East and Eastern Mediterranean

In the very first months of its existence Middle East problems thrust themselves upon the United Nations. The first dispute to be discussed at the Security Council was an Iranian complaint against the Soviet Union in January 1946, which was followed shortly by a complaint by Syria and Lebanon against France and Britain. From early 1946 until 1948 the situation in Greece figured prominently on the Council's agenda, and in 1947-48 events in Palestine and the creation of the State of Israel burdened the United Nations with a most onerous task, which had defied Anglo-American attempts to find a solution; ever since the United Nations has been concerned to prevent a 'second round' between the Arab States and Israel and to bring succour to nearly a million Arab refugees. The disposal of the Italian colonies, which was entrusted to the General Assembly in September 1948, faced the latter with a problem which had defeated the Council of Foreign Ministers and gave to it quasi-legislative powers of a novel kind. In addition, Britain and France have been under fire at the United Nations from the Arab States, either on the grounds of their alleged refusal to treat them in a manner appropriate to their status as sovereign states, or, more recently, because of the so-called denial of the national rights of Arab peoples in North Africa.

Events in this area do not fit easily into a coherent pattern, but in the period shortly after the Second World War three main forces can be detected at work. In the first place, the Soviet probing towards the Persian Gulf and through the Dardanelles and Macedonia to the Eastern Mediterranean looked suspiciously like a Soviet version of former Tsarist pressure in this area.[1] In the second place, there was the coming to fruition of Zionist aspirations for the creation of a Jewish state in Palestine, followed by persistent Arab-Israel tension. In the third place, the growth of Arab nationalism was accompanied by an upsurge of resentment against any status that could be construed as 'clientship' or 'tutelage'. These were forces that Great Britain was no longer in a position to contain or regulate single-handed.[2] Unhappily, closer Anglo-American co-operation was made peculiarly difficult, first of all by a certain amount of rivalry over oil rights and by the strong feeling of certain Americans that Britain was still playing her old 'imperialist' game in the traditional cockpit of Anglo-Russian rivalry, and then by differences between the two countries over the creation of the State of Israel.[3] The impact

---

[1] Although Soviet pressure may have been partly explicable by her fear that Turkey and Persia might be used as bases for Anglo-American blows at her 'soft under-belly', the suspicion was reinforced by Soviet claims on Tripolitania and it seemed to be confirmed by the exposure of the Soviet Government's stipulation in the negotiations of November 1940 with Germany that the 'area south of Batum and Baku in the general direction of the Persian Gulf [should be] recognized as the center of the aspirations of the Soviet Union' (U.S. Dept. of State, *Nazi-Soviet Relations, 1939-41*, ed. R. I. Sontag and J. S. Beddie (Washington, 1948), p. 259).

[2] The diminution of British power in this region was accelerated by the recognition of the independence of the countries of the Indian subcontinent.

[3] There were also those in Britain who feared that increased American interest in the area might adversely affect British influence there.

of the United Nations on these differences forms a recurrent theme in the brief case studies that follow.

IRAN

Stated very simply, the events leading to the Iranian Government's complaint of 19 January 1946 (under Art. 35(1) of the Charter)[4] against 'the interference of the Soviet Union . . . in the internal affairs of Iran' were as follows. In November 1945, when the Iranian Government attempted to send a detachment of troops to put down armed uprisings in the northern province of Azerbaijan,[5] the Red Army barred the way. At this time it looked as if the Soviet Union was attempting to install a Communist puppet régime in the northern province of Azerbaijan, and as if she intended to use the Communist-dominated Tudeh Party to secure control of the whole country and to gain access to the Persian Gulf, with all that this would portend for British security and oil interests in the area. British and American protestations at the Moscow Conference of Foreign Ministers (December 1945) that the Soviet Union's actions contravened the three-Power Teheran Declaration of December 1943 to respect the 'independence, sovereignty, and territorial integrity of Iran' were of no avail. Nor would Stalin undertake to evacuate the Red Army from Iranian soil by 2 March 1946 (i.e. six months after the end of the war with Japan, as prescribed by the Anglo-Soviet Treaty of 1942 which regulated the joint occupation of Iran).[6] Mr Bevin proposed a three-Power commission to investigate and make recommendations on the situation in Iran as an alternative to a public airing of the dispute before the Security Council. After some hesitation Mr Molotov rejected

---

[4] *SCOR*, 1st yr., 1st ser., suppl. no. 1, Annex 2A, p. 16.

[5] Soviet efforts during the wartime occupation to stir up separatist feeling had led to the establishment of an Azerbaijan National Committee of Liberation.

[6] The United States had unilaterally announced on 28 August 1945 that U.S. troops would be withdrawn by 1 November 1945. See Kirk, *Middle East, 1945-50*, for a detailed account of these and subsequent events.

f

the proposal and the matter was left to be pursued through diplomatic channels.

Mr Bevin later tried to dissuade the Iranian Government from bringing the matter before the Security Council,[7] but when it did so on 19 January 1946 both Britain and the United States defended its right to be heard. Both were anxious, however, to avoid an open rupture with the Soviet Union[8] and to find a formula which would solve the problem without loss of face by the United Nations. This was not difficult since both parties claimed at the Security Council hearing that they were willing to negotiate a direct settlement. Moreover, on 21 January 1946 the Iranian Cabinet fell, and the new Prime Minister, Qavam as-Saltana, was thought to favour a compromise with the Soviet Union. Consequently, the Council's resolution of 30 January, which was adopted unanimously, merely requested that it be kept informed of the progress of the negotiations. However, these proceeded very unsatisfactorily, the Iranian Premier refusing to accede to Soviet demands for the right to station troops in certain parts of Iran for an indefinite period, for the recognition of the autonomy of Azerbaijan, and for the formation of a joint Soviet-Iranian company to exploit oil resources in the north.

The failure of the Soviet Union to withdraw her troops by 2 March precipitated a new crisis and produced a strong reaction in both Britain and the United States.[9] On 18 March the Iranian representative complained to the Security Council that the Soviet Union had failed to evacuate her troops and that interference in the internal affairs of Iran continued. When the Security Council considered the question on 26 March, the Soviet Union pressed for a postponement of discussion until 10 April on the grounds that negotiations were still in progress and in the obvious hope that an agree-

---

[7] 21 Feb. 1946, H. C. Deb., vol. 419, coll. 1357-58.

[8] Though this did not inhibit Mr Bevin from using some rather brusque language.

[9] See statement by Mr Bevin, 14 March 1946, H. C. Deb., vol. 419, coll. 1290-92, and Harry S. Truman, *The Truman Memoirs* (London, Hodder & Stoughton, 1956), ii. 99-101.

ment satisfactory to her would soon be reached. Despite some apparent discrepancies between the attitude of the Iranian representative at the Council and that of his Premier in Teheran, members of the Council refused to agree to postponement, Mr Byrnes arguing strongly against it. Thereupon Mr Gromyko staged the first Soviet walk-out, not returning till 15 April. On 29 March it was agreed that the two Governments should be asked to report on the progress of their negotiations by 3 April. In the meanwhile in Teheran the Iranian Prime Minister skilfully used the Security Council's discussions as a lever to extract better terms from the Soviet Union.

In a reply to a message from Mr Gromyko, reiterating that agreement had been reached between the two Governments on the withdrawal of troops, the Iranian delegate said that the Soviet Ambassador had confirmed the promise to evacuate Iran, 'but on the condition that no unforeseen circumstances should occur'. He further stated that if the Soviet representative withdrew this condition and would assure the Council that withdrawal would be completed by 6 May, Iran would not at that time press the matter, provided that it remained on the Council's agenda. The Council agreed to defer further proceedings until 6 May, and on 5 April the Iranian Cabinet approved an agreement with the Soviet Union whereby Iranian territory was to be evacuated within six weeks of 24 March, a proposal for a joint stock oil company[10] was to be submitted to the Majlis within seven months of 24 March, and Azerbaijan was to be recognized as an integral part of Iran. The members of the Security Council received this news with relief when they met on 15 April, but refused, mainly on United States insistence, to take the matter off the agenda. This they did despite the Iranian Government's withdrawal of its complaint on the same day, and a consequent opinion from the Secretary-General to the effect that since the Council had not invoked Articles 34 or 36, it might well be that there was no way in which it could remain

---

[10] In which the Soviet Union would hold 51 and Iran 49 per cent. of the shares.

seized of the matter.[11] On 22 May, on receipt of a report from
Teheran that evacuation had been completed, discussion was adjourned.

It is frequently claimed that the Security Council, by providing
a forum in which a small nation could state its case against a Great
Power and by continuing, despite Soviet pressure, to be seized of
the case while doubt still existed about the Great Power's compliance
with its undertakings, had vindicated the hopes of the vast majority
of delegates at San Francisco, and had dramatically shown that
a small nation could look to the United Nations for effective support
against even such a gigantic neighbour as the Soviet Union. Moreover,
had not the discussions led to the removal of a dangerous threat
to an area of vital concern to Great Britain, both strategically and as
an important source of oil? These claims are not without foundation.
The general sympathy shown for Iran in the United Nations debates
may well have influenced the Soviet Union to evacuate her troops
earlier than she had planned, if only because she was anxious not
to draw attention to the presence of Russian occupation troops in
other countries. But there were more important forces at work
than the intervention of the United Nations. The most important
was almost certainly the Soviet belief, by May 1946, that the Iranian
Prime Minister had been won over and that the Soviet Union's main
objectives had been attained. In addition, the Soviet Government
was probably surprised by the firm stand taken by the United States,
especially from March 1946, and alarmed at the common Anglo-
American front which its actions were helping to bring into being.
In the event, the leading members of the Tudeh Party were dismissed
from the Cabinet in November 1946 and the Iranian Government
sent its troops into Azerbaijan in the following month, whereupon
the autonomous Azerbaijan Government collapsed. Neither these

---

11 See letter from the Secretary-General to the President of the Security Council
concerning the question of the retention of the Iranian case on the agenda of
the Security Council (S/39) 16 Apr. 1946; also Report of the Chairman of the
Committee of Experts on the same question (S/42), 18 Apr. 1946.

developments nor the action of the Majlis (which did not meet until August 1947) in refusing to sanction the proposed joint stock oil company provoked Soviet retaliation.

There can be little doubt that American policies became more closely attuned with those of Britain as a result of the Security Council's discussions on Iran. Not only did Soviet tactics contribute to the hardening of the Administration's attitude towards the Soviet Union,[12] but the wrangles at the United Nations forcibly demonstrated to the American public the marked deterioration in Great Power relations and accustomed them to the necessary reorientation of American policy. If the American people knew and cared little about Iran, they did care about the United Nations, especially now that its meetings were held so near to New York. Thus, when Mr Byrnes spoke of America's duty to uphold the principles of the Charter, he had far more hope of enlisting strong support from domestic opinion than if he had spoken of the need for containment.

Against their healthy influence on Anglo-American co-operation must be set, however, the possibility that the Council's debates directly contributed to the broadening of the gulf between the Big Three. This was one of Mr Bevin's fears. The Iranian complaint was eminently justified, but it gave rise to some bitter exchanges which can hardly have failed to influence the attitudes of the chief protagonists. The Soviet retort of lodging formal charges against British action in Greece and Indonesia also marked the beginning of the technique of using the United Nations as a propaganda platform to embarrass less friendly Powers. This technique has done much to discredit the United Nations. Yet in the conditions of the cold war was it not inevitable sooner or later? A rather different misgiving (which strengthened Mr Bevin's desire to secure a settlement in the more private circles of the Council of Foreign Ministers) was that Iran's ventilation of her grievances against

---

12 Although this was chiefly the result of the impasse over Germany, the Soviet war of nerves against Turkey, and the disputes in the Council of Foreign Ministers.

the Soviet Union might encourage nationalist forces ultimately inimical to Britain's own oil interests in the area.[13] Later events were to show the prescience of this misgiving.

SYRIA AND LEBANON

A not dissimilar dispute was brought to the United Nations on 4 February 1946 with the request to the Security Council by Syria and Lebanon that it should recommend the total and simultaneous evacuation of foreign troops from their territories.[14] The complaint was directed far more against the presence of French troops than British, but it raised some delicate issues for Franco-British relations.[15] British intervention in the previous summer to put an end to French military authority in Syria had mollified the Arab world, but it had naturally excited strong French resentment.[16] However, both Governments were agreed in principle to the withdrawal of their troops, though partly in deference to French views they had declared, on 13 December 1945, that evacuation should be effected in such a way that it would ensure the maintenance of sufficient forces to keep order until such a time as the United Nations had decided on the organization of collective security in the Levant.[17]

When the matter came before the Security Council both M. Bidault, the French Foreign Minister, and Sir Alexander Cadogan announced

[13] In the first week of September 1947 the British Ambassador in Teheran handed a note to Qavam in which it was recommended that a blank refusal should not be returned to the Soviet Union (Kirk, *Middle East, 1945-50*, p. 87). However, the American Ambassador took a different view; on 11 September he made a statement in which he declared: 'Iran's resources belong to Iran. Iran can give them away free of charge, or refuse to dispose of them at any price, if it so desires' (ibid.).

[14] *SCOR*, 1st yr., 1st ser., 19th-23rd mtgs., 14-16 Feb. 1946.

[15] Ever since 1918 many Frenchmen have suspected Britain of trying to replace French influence in the Levant States.

[16] For background and details of the Security Council's discussions, see Kirk, *Middle East, 1945-50*, pp. 106-13.

[17] *The Times*, 22 Dec. 1945. On their request, the British Government gave an assurance to Syria and Lebanon that British troops would not be withdrawn from the Levant as long as other foreign troops remained.

their Governments' willingness to withdraw their troops and their approval of an American draft resolution to the effect that the Council 'expresses its confidence that the foreign troops in Syria and Lebanon will be withdrawn as soon as practicable, and that negotiations to that end will be undertaken by the parties without delay'.[18] They did, however, oppose the contention of Egypt and the Soviet Union that as parties to a 'dispute threatening international peace and security' they were not entitled to vote, since they held that the Council was discussing a *situation*, not a *dispute*, and that Article 27(3) did not stipulate that states involved in a situation must abstain from voting. This issue and the related point whether the determination of the existence of a dispute was to be treated as a procedural or substantive question were eventually left undecided;[19] on this occasion both Britain and France voluntarily refrained from voting, though they expressly declared that they did so without prejudice to the question whether a dispute existed or not. Later, the Soviet Union exercised the first veto in voting against the American resolution on the grounds that Soviet amendments to it had been rejected. Nevertheless, on Mr Bevin's initiative, both he and M. Bidault declared that their countries would 'carry out the majority decision of the Council as expressed in the vote'.[20]

This magnanimous gesture was well calculated to uphold the authority of the Security Council and to allay rather widespread suspicions about French, and to a lesser extent, British intentions in the Middle East. It earned Britain and France considerable political goodwill in the United States and made Senator Vandenberg declare that he was 'proud of Western democracy that night'.[21] The airing of the complaint at the Security Council was not, of course, responsible for the initial decision to withdraw. On the

---

[18] *SCOR*, 1st yr., 1st ser., 22nd mtg., 16 Feb. 1946, p. 333.

[19] See p. 235 below.

[20] *SCOR*, 1st yr., 1st ser., 23rd mtg., 16 Feb. 1946, p. 368. The bulk of British and French troops were withdrawn by the late summer of 1946.

[21] *Vandenberg Papers*, p. 242.

British side this resulted primarily from the desire not to alienate
the moderate wing of Arab nationalism, from the economic need
to limit overseas commitments, and from the lack of any strong
strategic argument against withdrawal.[22] On the other hand, it
almost certainly speeded up the carrying out of this decision. In the
circumstances this was all to the good, but the incident did again
suggest that far from being an instrument of a Great Power hegemony, the United Nations might come to serve the smaller nations
as a not ineffective lever for securing concessions from their greater
brethren.

GREECE

The situation in Greece first came before the Security Council
on 25 January 1946, when the Soviet Union claimed that the presence
of British troops there constituted interference in the internal
affairs of Greece and endangered peace and security. This charge,
like that of the Ukraine concerning British troops in Indonesia,
was apparently intended as a reply to the Iranian charges against
the Soviet Union.[23] But the real issue was whether Greece was to
pass under Soviet hegemony, as had the Balkan States; if it did
so, either through internal subversion or external pressure, or
through a combination of both, Great Britain's position in the
whole Middle East would be most seriously jeopardized. Moreover,
the Soviet move was a shrewd one since British policy was still
under fire from a section of American opinion[24] as well as from

[22] The Labour Cabinet was also concerned not to incur the charge of 'imperialism'.

[23] Mr Molotov had pursued similar tactics at the Council of Foreign Ministers;
whenever conditions in Roumania and Bulgaria were criticized by Britain and
America he riposted with criticisms of British action in Greece.

[24] British intervention in December 1944 to prevent the overthrow of the Greek
Government by the Communist-led EAM (National Liberation Front) and
ELAS (National People's Liberation Army) had evoked far stronger criticism
in the United States than in Great Britain. For background material see W. H.
McNeill, *The Greek Dilemma* (London, Gollancz, 1947) and C. M. Wood-
house, *Apple of Discord* (London, Hutchinson, 1949).

members of Mr Bevin's own party. If British support of the régime could be weakened or the latter's strength sapped and the United States could be persuaded to stand aside, power would be bound sooner or later to pass to the Communists. Mr Stettinius said little during the long and often bitter exchanges between Mr Bevin and Mr Vyshinsky, but he finally proposed that the Council should drop the matter altogether, thus supporting the British view that since their troops were in Greece at the request of the Greek Government, they could not constitute interference or a threat to peace and security. The Council's final decision merely to 'take note' of the views expressed by the various governments could perhaps be construed as the 'clean bill' for which Mr Bevin had pleaded; but this 'unhappy incident' in Anglo-Soviet relationships had certainly not been closed.

A marked hardening in the official United States attitude towards Greek affairs came with the Greek elections of 31 March 1946. American initiative had resulted in the organization of an international mission consisting of American, French, British, and South African observers,[25] to supervise the elections, which it described as 'on the whole free and fair'. After the elections the American Administration evidently felt under an obligation to defend the Greek Government against verbal attacks by the Soviet Union and its satellites.[26] Communist-led guerrilla activity was once again on the increase, however, and in an attempt to blacken the international reputation of the Greek Government[27] the Ukrainian Government on 24 August 1946 complained to the Security Council that the Greek Government's policy constituted a threat to the peace;[28] they also claimed that frontier incidents on the Albanian border had been caused by the

---

25 McNeill, *America, Britain and Russia*, pp. 735-36. The Soviet Union did not participate though invited, probably for fear of setting a precedent for Eastern Europe.

26 American economic aid through UNRRA was also supplemented by a display of American naval power off the Greek coast in April and early September.

27 McNeill, *America, Britain and Russia*, p. 736.

28 *SCOR*, 1st yr., 2nd ser., suppl. no. 5, S/137.

Greek authorities with the 'obvious object of provoking armed conflict with Albania'—one of the first instances of the Communist technique of making unsubstantiated allegations against a potential victim in order to provide a smoke screen for their own activities. The charges were couched in such immoderate language that the United Kingdom delegate (Sir Alexander Cadogan) opposed their admission (in their existing form) to the agenda. The United States voted with the Soviet Union in favour of admission, on the grounds that all complaints should be discussed, but in the subsequent heated debate the United States delegate, Mr Herschel Johnson, strongly supported Britain in holding that Mr Manuilsky, the able but fiery Ukrainian delegate, had failed to produce any evidence to substantiate his charges.[29] An American suggestion for an investigation on both sides of Greece's northern frontier was vetoed by Mr Gromyko, the Soviet delegate. On 20 September the item was dropped from the agenda over Soviet and Polish objections, thus clearing Greece of the Ukrainian charges.

Nevertheless, the position inside Greece continued to deteriorate, with the Communist guerrillas receiving considerable help from across the northern frontiers and virtual civil war raging in the northern provinces. Despite British and American economic aid, the Greek economy was in a parlous condition. A decision by Britain, said to have been communicated privately to the United States in November 1946, that for economic reasons it might be necessary to withdraw troops from Greece in the near future, was particularly alarming. The problem posed for American policy was very serious. The Administration might be convinced of the need for the United States to move in to fill the vacuum that would result from the British withdrawal; but were the American people?[30]

---

[29] ibid. 69th mtg., 18 Sept. 1946, pp. 366 ff.

[30] American public opinion was still not actively alive to Soviet pressure. Even at the end of 1946 Great Power relations exhibited some signs of co-operation; agreement had been reached at the Council of Foreign Ministers on the peace treaties with the Balkan States, Finland, and Italy, while a vaguely worded disarmament resolution had been agreed unanimously at the General Assembly.

On 3 December 1946 the Greek Government complained to the Security Council that Albania, Yugoslavia, and Bulgaria were 'lending their support to the violent guerrilla warfare now being waged in northern Greece against public order and the territorial integrity' of Greece.[31] On this occasion discussion was brief. An American proposal[32] was unanimously accepted (on 19 December) to 'establish a Commission of Investigation to ascertain the facts relating to the alleged border violations along the frontier between Greece on the one hand and Albania, Bulgaria and Yugoslavia on the other'. The Commission was also given authority to conduct its investigations in these countries so as to ascertain the 'causes and nature of the above-mentioned border violations and disturbances'.[33] All members of the Council were to be represented on the Commission. Further consideration of the Greek complaint was postponed until the Commission could report its findings. Soviet acceptance of the investigating Commission (as compared with its previous rejection) may have reflected a hope that its report would publicize any shortcomings in the Greek Government and so help make the guerrilla movement appear a popular rising against an intolerable tyranny. The British and American Governments no doubt hoped that the Commission, by sifting evidence on the spot, would show that the Greek Government's charges were well founded and so silence public criticism of their support for that Government. They also probably hoped that the Commission would be able to exercise some check on the aid being given to the guerrillas.

Not surprisingly, the Commission was unable to agree on the facts. The Soviet and Polish members sought to advance the belief that the cause of the trouble lay with the allegedly oppressive nature of the Greek Government. The majority (Australia, Belgium,

---

[31] *SCOR*, 1st yr., 2nd. ser, suppl. no 10, S/203, p. 170.

[32] ibid. 87th mtg., 19 Dec. 1946, p. 700.

[33] This clause was inserted on Polish initiative with Soviet support, probably to allow investigation of the behaviour of the Greek Government.

Brazil, China, Colombia, France[34], Syria, the United Kingdom, and
the United States) saw sufficient evidence to convince them of the
reality and importance of the aid reaching the guerrillas from
across the border. Consequently, although the report[35] (considered
by the Security Council on 27 June 1947 and at following meetings)
did not exempt the Greek Government from some responsibility
for the disturbed condition of the country, it supported the charges
that Yugoslavia and, to a lesser extent, Albania and Bulgaria,
were assisting the guerrillas by supplying arms and military supplies
and by permitting them to cross the frontier to and from Greece,
and it considered that the continuance of such action should be
considered 'as a threat to the peace within the meaning of the Charter
of the United Nations' (i.e. Art. 39). It also found that the Yugoslav
and Bulgarian Governments were encouraging a separatist movement
in Macedonia. The minority conclusions were that the civil war was
the result of internal causes and that the allegations of interference
on the part of Albania, Bulgaria, and Yugoslavia were unfounded.

In the meanwhile, developments of far greater importance were
taking place outside the United Nations.[36] On 18 January 1947 an
American economic mission under Mr Paul A. Porter arrived in
Athens to look into the economic conditions of Greece and to report
what measures were necessary for its recovery.[37] But the crisis in
Greece was made more urgent by the public announcement by
Great Britain on 24 February 1947 that she could not continue
economic support of Greece and Turkey after the end of March 1947,
and that the remaining 16,000 British troops in Greece would be
withdrawn shortly thereafter. Events now moved rapidly in Washington; on 12 March 1947 President Truman propounded to Congress

---

[34] France did not subscribe to the whole of the majority report.

[35] S/360 and S/360 (Corr. 1).

[36] For a detailed account see RIIA, *Survey, 1947-8*, pp. 180-83, and *Survey, 1949-50*, pp. 120-26.

[37] As a first step towards securing a tighter grip over the distribution of American relief the Administration had, in December 1946, persuaded the General
Assembly to wind up UNRRA.

the policy which has become known as the Truman Doctrine.[38] He asserted 'that it must be the policy of the United States to support free peoples who are resisting attempted subjugation by armed minorities or by outside pressures'. He therefore asked Congress to appropriate $400 million[39] for aid to Greece and Turkey and to authorize the dispatch to them of American military and economic missions. The Truman Doctrine was a logical step in the development of American policy over the past months, but for many Americans it appeared to hasten the demise of the United Nations and to stretch America's strategic frontier on to the hills of Macedonia and into the Bosphorus, a giant's stride for which they were ill prepared. But though the American people might hesitate, Senator Vandenberg's own reaction—that the United Nations was unfortunately incapable at present of dealing with the situation—was shared by most of his colleagues, for had they not witnessed at first-hand its impotence in face of Great Power differences? And the criticism that it was being by-passed was robbed of much of its sting when Senator Vandenberg succeeded in inserting a provision permitting the abandonment of the programme if the Security Council or the General Assembly found that 'action taken or assistance furnished by the United Nations makes the continuance of such assistance unnecessary or undesirable'.[40]

The rest of the story can be told quite shortly. During 1947 the Greek Government was bolstered up by American aid, guerrilla activity increased, and the general situation did not perceptibly improve. Meanwhile the Security Council had considered the report of its Commission of Investigation but had been unable to find a solution acceptable to all the permanent members. On American initiative the item was then removed from the Council's agenda and

---

[38] *U. S. Congressional Record*, 80th Congress, 1st sess., vol. 93, pt. 2, pp. 1980-81.
[39] Half of this was expected to be used for military expenditure.
[40] *Vandenberg Papers*, p. 146. Two other contingencies for the termination of aid were also envisaged, viz. a request by the Greek or Turkish Government or a decision by the President.

brought before the General Assembly in September 1947. After an acrimonious debate the Assembly 'called upon' Albania, Bulgaria,[41] and Yugoslavia to desist from giving aid to the Greek guerrillas and resolved, by 41 votes to 6, to establish a United Nations Special Committee on the Balkans (UNSCOB).[42] Poland and the Soviet Union were invited to serve on this Committee; both refused. The Committee continued to keep the situation in Greece under observation, but Greece's northern neighbours refused to co-operate with it and it had no success in promoting a peaceful settlement. Its findings[43] confirmed and very largely reproduced the majority report of the Security Council's Commission. The third session of the General Assembly on 27 November 1948 decided by 47 votes to 6 to keep UNSCOB in being.[44] A special Conciliation Commission, under the Chairmanship of the Assembly's President (Dr Evatt), was also set up, though to no purpose.

An unexpected turn was given to the situation by the secession of Yugoslavia from the Cominform in June 1948. Apart from its wider repercussions, this development broke up the anti-Greek front.[45] The report of UNSCOB to the fourth session of the General Assembly, covering the period from October 1948 to July 1949,[46] noted that Yugoslav aid to the guerrillas had declined or possibly ceased, and that Albania was then the principal source of assistance. But Albania, being isolated from the remaining Cominform countries and somewhat fearful of her own safety, had to restrict supplies to the Greek guerrillas. Bulgaria was less suitably placed geo-

---

[41] During the debate in the First Committee, Bulgaria and Albania (neither of which was a member of the United Nations) were invited to make statements. They would not give an unqualified undertaking to accept all the obligations of the Charter with respect to the pacific settlement of disputes (Art. 35), but, after some debate, they were heard nevertheless.

[42] *GAOR*, 2nd sess., Resolution 109(II).

[43] A/574, A/644, A/692.

[44] *GAOR*, 3rd sess., pt. 1, Resolution 193(III).

[45] RIIA, *Survey, 1949-50*, pp. 120-26.

[46] A/935 and A/981.

graphically to give aid, while Titoist dissension among the guerrillas, culminating in the removal of General Markos, their former leader, considerably weakened them. Even so, efforts at mediation by the President of the General Assembly and by the Secretary-General yielded no result and heavy fighting continued until the autumn of 1949 when, in a report issued on 16 September 1949,[47] UNSCOB announced that rebel resistance had been broken. The life of UNSCOB was renewed by the General Assembly on 8 November, however, which also rather belatedly and ineffectually recommended to all Members of the United Nations and all other states that they 'refrain from the direct or indirect provision of arms or other materials of war to Albania and Bulgaria until . . . the unlawful assistance of these States to the Greek guerrillas has ceased'.[48] Happily, by December 1951 the internal situation in Greece had improved[49] to such an extent that at the request of the Greek Government the General Assembly decided to dissolve UNSCOB, subject to the establishment by the Peace Observation Commission of a Balkan Sub-Commission.[50]

How much credit for the restoration of peaceful conditions in Greece should go the vigilance of the members of UNSCOB—often at considerable personal risk—and to the efforts at conciliation made through the United Nations? Probably not a great deal. A number of delegates were no doubt persuaded by UNSCOB's reports and by the debates in the General Assembly that the Greek Government's charges were better founded than they had at first been willing to allow, while the Soviet Union's attitude excited much adverse criticism. But peace was restored primarily by force of Greek arms (backed by substantial British and American aid),

---

[47] *GAOR*, 4th sess., suppl. no. 8.

[48] ibid. Resolution 288(IV).

[49] Persistent attempts by the international Red Cross organizations and by the Secretary-General to secure the repatriation of Greek children deported to her northern neighbours were mostly unsuccessful, however.

[50] *GAOR*, 6th sess., suppl. no. 20, Resolution 508 A & B (VI).

through the defection of Yugoslavia from the Cominform, and as a result of the Soviet Union's unwillingness to extend unlimited support to the rebels.[51] The limitations of the United Nations had indeed been strikingly demonstrated. Although the Security Council's incapacity to coerce one of its permanent members was evident enough, could it not exercise effective pressure on these smaller Balkan States? But small states have powerful protectors, especially when, as in this case, wider strategic issues are at stake. The quarrel was in făct nearly as much between the United States and Britain on the one hand, and the Soviet Union on the other, as between Greece and her northern neighbours; and such quarrels are not resolved by the passing of resolutions, however impressive a majority they receive. In the Security Council the resolutions proposed by the Soviet Union criticizing the Greek Government uniformly met defeat at the hands of the majority, which did not need to use the veto, while most of the resolutions presented by the Western Powers in support of that Government were vetoed by the Soviet Union, who found herself, with Poland, constantly in a minority of two. Nor were the Soviet Union and her satellites impressed by the massive majorities mobilized by the West in the General Assembly in support of resolutions 'calling upon'[52] Albania, Bulgaria, and Yugoslavia to cease rendering assistance to the Greek guerrillas. In addition, despite the protracted attempts at mediation, there was a strong tendency from the start for the Security Council and the General Assembly both to be treated mainly as sounding-

---

51 RIIA, *Survey, 1947-8*, p. 182. The Soviet Union never accorded recognition to the rebel Greek Government and seemed anxious throughout to avoid doing anything which might result in the fighting spreading. It may also be recalled that in 1944 Stalin had conceded pre-eminent influence in Greece to Britain (Churchill, vi. 198).

52 According to the Charter, only the Security Council is entitled to 'call upon' (i.e. to require) members to comply with its decisions (viz. Arts. 33(2), 40, 41); the General Assembly's competence under Arts. 10 and 11 is limited to making recommendations. The terminology of these resolutions was indicative both of the habitual loose drafting of Assembly resolutions and of the desire of many delegates to devolve some of the Security Council's powers on to the General Assembly (see below, pp. 228-29).

boards for propaganda either for or against the Greek Government, and for the lobbies to be used more for marshalling the greatest number of votes than for private and informal negotiation—for voting-power politics[53] rather than for diplomacy.

The record of UNSCOB is rather more impressive. Although there was little room for compromise on the central issue, namely, the cessation of aid to the guerrillas, the Commission put some check on the volume of that aid, if only because any very marked increase might have produced an unmanageable conflagration out of a local bonfire—the very contingency which the Soviet Union, as well as the Western Powers, was intent on avoiding. Without its reports the General Assembly would also have been even more in the dark about the actual situation in the northern provinces of Greece, while if events had taken a more ominous turn and guerrilla war had turned into open war, UNSCOB might have been able to fulfil the same verifying role as did the Korean Commission in June 1950. It is a wise man who insures against such contingencies.

The United Nations debates on Greece and the comments on them in the press were also instrumental in awakening the American people to the true nature of the threat to Greek independence and in acclimatizing them to their new responsibilities in the Eastern Mediterranean. The Charter seems to have acted as a kind of 'overall' commitment through which the Administration could secure the American people's acceptance of obligations which, however burdensome, could be made to appear inescapable for a good United Nations member. In addition, the contempt with which the General Assembly's exhortations were treated by Greece's northern neighbours demonstrated in the most effective way possible that the United Nations lacked the capacity to do what the United States undertook to do under the Truman Doctrine. Even in Great Britain, where Mr Bevin's shoulders would in any case probably have been strong enough to shrug off domestic criticism of British

---

[53] See pp. 212 ff. below.

G

policy in Greece, the resentment aroused by the extravagance of the Soviet bloc's charges almost certainly eased his task and helped to soften attacks on the much harassed Greek Government. The protracted and acrimonious debates at the United Nations may possibly have tended to aggravate Great Power discords; but this is by no means certain, and there can be little doubt that, by helping to rid many people's minds of facile, but dangerous, illusions about the Organization, they gave a much-needed impetus to the growth of the Western security system. The Soviet Union's behaviour at the United Nations on the Greek issue may well have played a not insignificant part in bringing that system into being.

THE ITALIAN COLONIES

The Italian colonies, the disposal of which was eventually entrusted to the United Nations, were Eritrea and Italian Somaliland in East Africa, and Libya (Tripolitania, Cyrenaica, and the Fezzan) in North Africa. Though they had been conquered by troops under British command, Great Britain had not only renounced all territorial ambitions in the Atlantic Charter, but it was evident at an early date that she could not afford prolonged military occupation. Some form of trusteeship seemed the obvious answer, since, in British eyes, the people did not appear ready for the full independence which the politically conscious Libyans, who had rallied round Sayid Idris el-Senussi[54] at an early stage in the Second World War, were pressing for. Stalin's announcement at Potsdam on 20 July 1945 that the Soviet Union wanted to be given trusteeship over one of the Italian colonies came as a distinct shock, however, especially as Mr Molotov reiterated the Soviet claim at the Council of Foreign Ministers in September 1945, instancing Tripolitania as the territory his Government had in mind. This claim may have been only a bargaining counter, but it posed a disturbing picture of a Soviet

---

[54] In October 1946 he was formally recognized by Britain as Amir of Cyrenaica.

foothold in Africa, of strengthened Soviet claims for freer passage through the Dardanelles, and of a new and potent threat to vital British air and sea communications. The Soviet claim was later modified to a proposal for joint Russo-Italian administration, but without noticeably reducing Mr Bevin's fear of seeing Russian power clamped across the 'life-line' of the British Empire[55]. Nor did Britain feel very happy about American proposals for United Nations trusteeship as a prelude to full independence;[56] the scheme seemed quite impractical and divided counsels and policies only too likely to result—an opportunity which the Soviet Union could be expected to exploit. For her own part Britain would probably have preferred at this stage to advance the date of full independence for a Libya temporarily under British trusteeship, to create a new political unit under British trusteeship of the Somalilands (Italian, French, and British) and the Ogaden, and to allot various portions of Eritrea to Ethiopia and the Sudan.

At the Council of Foreign Ministers on 27 June 1946 Mr Molotov accepted an American proposal, supported by Britain, that, failing agreement between the United States, the Soviet Union, Britain, and France within one year after the ratification of the peace treaty with Italy, the matter should be referred to the General Assembly for decision. It was also agreed that a four-Power commission should visit the territories between October 1947 and May 1948 to ascertain the wishes and welfare of their inhabitants. Meanwhile they remained under British and French administration. The four Powers being unable to agree on a solution within the time-limit, the problem devolved in September 1948 upon the General Assembly, which discussed it during the second part of

---

[55] There was the further complication of Mr Eden's declaration on 8 January 1942 (H. C. Deb., vol. 377, col. 78) that 'His Majesty's Government are determined that at the end of the war the Senussis in Cyrenaica will in no circumstances again fall under Italian domination'. This undertaking had in fact been considerably 'strengthened' in the Arabic translation.

[56] Except for Somaliland, where trusteeship would be of an indefinite duration.

its third session (April-May 1949). By this time the Soviet Union[57] had come to favour the original American proposal for United Nations trusteeship, but the Americans had now abandoned it on much the same grounds as those originally advanced by the British. However, hopes of a solution rose with the news of an agreement reached between Mr Bevin and Count Sforza in May 1949 envisaging the independence of Libya at the end of ten years. During these ten years Cyrenaica and the Fezzan would be under British and French trusteeship respectively, while Tripolitania would be administered for two years by the British, assisted by an Advisory Council, and by the Italians for the remaining eight years. The Bevin-Sforza proposals[58] were approved by the First (Political) Committee of the General Assembly on 13 May but, despite energetic lobbying, the clause of the resolution regarding Tripolitania failed by one vote to secure the necessary two-thirds majority, thus alienating Latin American support for the draft resolution as a whole, which was rejected. The General Assembly thereupon decided to postpone the whole question of the colonies to its fourth session.[59] The rejection of the Bevin-Sforza plan was not without compensations. From Britain's point of view its implementation would have raised grave problems. In Tripolitania the Arabs demonstrated fiercely against the return of the Italians, whose safety could probably only have been ensured by the use of British troops. Such action would have had the most unfortunate repercussions on Britain's relations with the Arab world.

By 30 September 1949, when the First Committee of the General Assembly resumed discussion on the matter, opinion had shifted considerably. In the summer the Italian Government had come out

---

[57] The Soviet resolution (A/881) envisaged the appointment by the Trusteeship Council of an administrator for each territory and an Advisory Council which would include the Great Powers.

[58] For text see *GAOR*, 3rd sess., pt. 2, 1st Committee, Annexes, A/C1/466, p. 19.

[59] RIIA, *Survey, 1949-50*, pp. 540 ff.

in favour of immediate independence for Libya and Eritrea. Britain, having already decided that constitutional developments in Cyrenaica should no longer be delayed, now proposed: early independence for Libya (leaving the question of Libyan unity to be decided by the Libyans themselves); that Italian Somaliland should be placed under Italian trusteeship; and that Eritrea should be incorporated into Ethiopia.[60] The United States likewise favoured an independent and united Libya. So did the Soviet Union—as long as all foreign troops were withdrawn and military bases liquidated.

Consequently, on 21 November 1949, the General Assembly was able to agree[61] that Libya (comprising Cyrenaica, Tripolitania, and the Fezzan) should become an independent and sovereign state not later than 1 January 1952, with a Constitution drafted by a National Assembly of the representatives of the three territories; a United Nations Commissioner,[62] aided by a Council of ten,[63] would help to draft the Constitution and to establish the Government.[64] Somaliland was to be placed under Italian trusteeship[65] for a period of ten years, at the end of which she would become independent. No agreement was reached on the disposition of Eritrea, but a Commission was established to ascertain the wishes and interests of the inhabitants and to prepare proposals for the General Assembly. A year later, on 2 December 1950, the General Assembly recommended that Eritrea should constitute an autonomous unit federated

---

60 Except for the Western provinces, which should be annexed by the Sudan.

61 *GAOR*, 4th sess., Resolution 289(IV).

62 On 10 December 1949 Mr Adrian Pelt of the Netherlands, at that time Assistant Secretary-General in charge of Conferences and General Services, was elected by the General Assembly to the office of United Nations Commissioner.

63 Egypt, France, Italy, Pakistan, the United Kingdom, the United States, one representative from each of the three regions of Libya, and one representative of the minorities.

64 As the Administering Authority, Great Britain undertook to transfer power and to help in the establishment of the new Government.

65 Italy was to be assisted by an advisory commission of three: Colombia, Egypt, and the Philippines.

with Ethiopia.[66] Señor Eduardo Anze Matienzo of Bolivia was elected as United Nations Commissioner to supervise the transfer of power from the British Administering Authority to the new federation not later than 15 September 1952.

Later developments can be recounted very briefly.[67] On 2 December 1950 the Libyan National Assembly adopted a unanimous resolution in favour of an independent, federal, constitutional, and democratic kingdom under the Amir of Cyrenaica. On 24 December 1951 Libya was declared independent. In Somaliland Italy undertook provisional administration after power was handed over by Great Britain on 1 April 1950, and pending final approval by the General Assembly of the trusteeship agreement. This was given on 3 December 1950.[68]

The General Assembly's decisions were not unsatisfactory for Britain. Doubts might be entertained about the readiness of the Libyan people for independence, especially in view of the poverty of the country. But the dangers inherent in the original American and Soviet proposals had been avoided, and Britain had been relieved of the cost of military occupation and administration while retaining her close wartime ties with the peoples of the new state. Thus a treaty of friendship and alliance was signed on 30 July 1953[69] in Benghazi, together with military and financial agreements under which Britain was granted military facilities in Libya, including the right to station British forces for twenty years,[70] while, on her part, she undertook to continue to furnish financial aid to

---

[66] *GAOR*, 5th sess., suppl. no. 20, Resolution 390(V). The United Kingdom delegation played a leading part in securing acceptance of this solution by both Italy and Ethiopia.

[67] For details see RIIA, *Survey, 1949-50*, pp. 545-51.

[68] *GAOR*, 5th sess., suppl. no. 20, Resolution 442(V).

[69] See statement by the Minister of State (Mr Selwyn Lloyd), H. C. Deb., vol. 518, coll. 1540-42.

[70] The Libyan army was also to be trained by a British military mission.

Libya for the same period.[71] British strategic interests and air communications were, therefore, well secured at a time when similar rights and facilities in Egypt and Iraq were threatened by the rising tide of Arab nationalism. These developments were not altogether to the liking of the Indian and Soviet delegates at the sixteenth session of the Economic and Social Council (August 1953) on the grounds that the military facilities were incompatible with Libyan independence, while other delegates (e.g. Egypt) feared that the United Nations was in danger of being squeezed out of any share in the shaping of Libya's future. But without British protection during the first years of independent life, Libya might possibly have fallen under less sympathetic influences, while the risk that too marked a United Nations influence might encourage an over-elaborate administrative structure, far beyond the resources of the country, could not be neglected.

It must be conceded that the United Nations decisions which resulted in Libyan independence were the result both of hard, and often rather disreputable, bargaining, and of the infinite capacity for lobbying of certain of the interested parties. Nevertheless, it is to the credit of the United Nations that where the Council of Foreign Ministers had failed, a solution was arrived at which has on the whole proved workable. It can be argued that Britain, France, and the United States might have been able to come to a better solution outside the United Nations; but 'better' from whose point of view? The Bevin-Sforza proposals, which had the tacit approval of France and the United States, hardly showed a very lively sensitivity to the wishes or interests of the peoples of the territories. The General Assembly was, of course, only able to exercise these rather novel quasi-legislative powers because it had been empowered to do so by the four Great Powers and—even more important—because

---

[71] During the first five years Britain agreed to subsidize the budget to the amount of £2,750,000 and to pay £1 million for economic development, contributions to which would also be made by the United States (under Point Four), France, and Italy.

Great Britain co-operated fully in the transfer of power and in helping to equip the new state to tackle its new responsibilities. But had not the United Nations been able to arrive at a majority decision, and had not the negotiations taken place in a setting where at least some deference was paid to the Principles and Purposes of the Charter, it might well have proved even more difficult to reach a solution generally acceptable to the peoples of the territories concerned.

PALESTINE

The issues which constituted the vexed and emotionally charged 'Palestine problem' are well known, and no attempt will be made here to analyse them or to recount the events which preceded Britain's reference of the problem to the United Nations. Nor will it be possible to give more than a brief thumbnail sketch of the tortuous negotiations at the United Nations.[72]

As will be recalled, although the report of the Anglo-American Committee of Inquiry into conditions in Palestine, submitted on 30 April 1946, was unanimous, it did not succeed in bridging the deep gulf between the Arabs and Jews or, indeed, in resolving the growing differences between London and Washington. With the failure of the London Conference also, the British Government announced on 14 February 1947 its decision to refer the whole problem to the United Nations without recommending any particular solution. Britain's decision was formally communicated to the Secretary-General on 2 April 1947, with the request that a special

---

[72] There is, of course, a vast literature on the subject; see especially RIIA, *Great Britain and Palestine, 1919-1945*; Kirk, *Middle East in the War*, pp. 10-14, 228-50, and 306-33; and *Middle East, 1945-50*, pp. 187-319. To balance the picture see also J. C. Hurewitz, *The Struggle for Palestine* (New York, Norton, 1950). A graphic account of the atmosphere in which United Nations debates were conducted is given in Susan Strange, 'Palestine and the United Nations', in *YBWA, 1949*.

session of the General Assembly[73] be called to appoint a committee to study the problem and to report back to the Assembly at its regular autumn session. The session met at Flushing Meadows on 28 April 1947. The sharp conflict between the claims of the Arab Higher Committee and the Jewish Agency was highlighted by their testimony before the First Committee, while Sir Alexander Cadogan made the first of many statements to be made by United Kingdom spokesmen pointing out that the United Kingdom 'should not have the sole responsibility for enforcing a solution which is not accepted by both parties and which we cannot reconcile with our conscience.'[74] The Assembly agreed, however, to set up a Special Committee on Palestine (UNSCOP), with the widest powers, consisting of representatives of eleven states.[75] The Committee was instructed to report back not later than 1 September; this it managed to do with a few hours to spare. All members of the Committee were agreed on the early termination of the Mandate and that Palestine should become independent at the earliest practicable date.[76] The majority plan[77]—political partition with economic union—recommended that Palestine be divided into independent Arab and Jewish States with an international régime for Jerusalem. The minority[78] considered partition impracticable and proposed that after a three-year transitional United Nations administration, an independent federal state, comprising Arab and Jewish States, be created, with Jerusalem as

---

[73] In view of the Soviet Union's ready use of the veto, the Security Council was thought to be an 'imperfect instrument', while any trusteeship agreement would have to be approved by the Assembly, of which also all Arab States were Members.

[74] *GAOR*, 1st special sess., 1st Committee, 52nd mtg., 9 May 1947, *SR*, p. 184.

[75] Australia, Canada, Czechoslovakia, Guatemala, India, Iran, the Netherlands, Peru, Sweden, Uruguay, and Yugoslavia. The Great Powers and the Arab States were excluded on the grounds that they were interested parties.

[76] U.N., Special Committee on Palestine, *Report to the General Assembly* (*GAOR*, 2nd sess., suppl. 11), i. 42.

[77] Canada, Czechoslovakia, Guatemala, the Netherlands, Peru, Sweden, and Uruguay.

[78] India, Iran, and Yugoslavia. The Australian delegate declined to be committed to either plan.

its capital. However, no mention was made of how either of these plans was to be implemented.

The second regular session of the General Assembly on 23 September referred the Palestine question to an *Ad Hoc* Committee on the Palestinian Question, composed of all Members. Mr Creech Jones expressed to this Committee Britain's substantial agreement with the majority recommendations (particularly the termination of the Mandate and early independence for Palestine),[79] but he drew a sharp distinction, as had Sir Alexander Cadogan earlier, between accepting an Assembly recommendation in the sense of not impeding its execution by others, and accepting responsibility for carrying it out. Britain would place her knowledge and experience at the disposal of the Assembly and would give effect to any plan on which agreement was reached between the Jews and Arabs, but she was not prepared to undertake the task of imposing a policy in Palestine by force of arms.[80] Furthermore, in the absence of a settlement she had to 'plan for an early withdrawal of British forces and of the British administration from Palestine'.[81]

Meanwhile, the *Ad Hoc* Committee set up two Sub-Committees, the first[82] of which (consisting almost wholly of delegates favouring partition) slightly modified the boundaries recommended in the majority plan, strengthened the provisions for economic union, and asked the Trusteeship Council to work out a statute for the City of Jerusalem. But the crucial question of how partition was to be

---

[79] A decision to transfer the main British Middle East military stores depot from the Canal Zone to Kenya (*The Times*, 13 and 16 Sept. 1947) had probably reduced Palestine's strategic importance (Kirk, *Middle East, 1945-50*, p. 8).

[80] Though the possibility of Britain's participating in the execution of a settlement was not absolutely excluded.

[81] GAOR, *Ad Hoc* Committee on the Palestinian Question, 2nd mtg., 26 Sept. 1947, pp. 3-4.

[82] The second Sub-Committee, consisting exclusively of anti-partition delegates, considered Arab proposals for an independent unitary state. There was also an ineffective and inactive three-man conciliation group. See Susan Strange, 'Palestine and the United Nations', in *YBWA, 1949*, pp. 155-58.

brought about was sedulously avoided,[83] despite repeated warnings from United Kingdom delegates. Indeed, on 20 November 1947 Sir Alexander Cadogan not only intimated to the *Ad Hoc* Committee that British troops would not be available as an instrument for the enforcement of a settlement against either the Arabs or Jews, but he reserved Britain's right to lay down the Mandate and to end her civil administration at any time after it had become evident that the Assembly was unable to reach a settlement acceptable to both sides.[84]

Despite the misgivings of several 'neutral' delegates at the lack of 'teeth' in the partition plan, the fear that the rejection of the plan would lead to deadlock, together with the pressure that is said to have been brought to bear on waverers by the United States (the necessary two-thirds majority being uncertain), led the Assembly, on 29 November 1947, to recommend (by 33 votes to 13, with 10 abstentions) 'to the United Kingdom, as the mandatory Power for Palestine, and to all other Members of the United Nations the adoption and implementation . . . of the plan of Partition with Economic Union'.[85] In view of Arab threats to resist partition and the United Kingdom's refusal to enforce it herself, the resolution also, on Soviet initiative, rather forlornly requested the Security Council to take the necessary measures for the implementation of the plan.

The prospects for the Commission of five members[86] appointed by the Assembly to supervise the transition to independence were not improved by the Colonial Secretary's announcement in the House of Commons on 11 December that Great Britain would

---

[83] A proposal for a volunteer force by the United States delegate (Mr Herschel Johnson) was short-lived.

[84] He had previously announced that Britain was preparing to evacuate Palestine by 1 August 1948.

[85] *GAOR*, 2nd sess., Resolution 181(II).

[86] Bolivia, Czechoslovakia, Denmark, Panama, and the Philippines. The work of the Commission was also handicapped by the time taken by these Governments to designate their representatives.

terminate the Mandate by 15 May 1948 and that she proposed to retain undivided control until that date; in other words, she would not hand over her responsibilities piecemeal to the Commission. Nor, with conditions rapidly deteriorating in Palestine, would she allow the Commission into Palestine until just before 1 May.[87] Thereafter British troops in Palestine would only maintain order so far as necessary for their own security and speedy withdrawal.

Faced with this situation, the five members of the Commission —or the 'five lonely pilgrims' as they had by now been nicknamed— reported to the Security Council on 16 February 1948 that they would be unable to discharge their responsibilities at the end of the Mandate unless they received armed assistance. This appeal fell on deaf ears; armed assistance from the Soviet Union would not have been welcomed (even if she had been prepared to give it), Britain was intent on evacuating her troops as rapidly as possible, and Senator Austin now declared that his Government was prepared to consider the use of armed force to restore peace, but not to enforce partition—in the circumstances rather a subtle distinction. On 19 March Senator Austin electrified delegates by proposing that action on partition be suspended and that the General Assembly be convened in special session to consider the establishment of a temporary trusteeship over Palestine.[88]

Meanwhile fierce fighting was taking place in Palestine, with Jewish forces gradually gaining the upper hand despite the volunteers who were joining the Palestinian Arabs from neighbouring Arab countries. A Security Council order for a general truce on 17 April

---

[87] Although a small party of the Commission's staff were allowed to enter in February.

[88] On the probable reasons for this change of front see Council on Foreign Relations, *The United States in World Affairs, 1947-1948*, p. 339. This marked shift in American policy seems to have been induced mainly by the mounting tension in Soviet-American relations which caused the strategic considerations (including fears about American oil concessions), which had always been prominent in the thinking of Secretary of Defence Forrestal and of the Middle East experts of the State Department, to outweigh the domestic political considerations of the White House.

was ignored and discussions at the special session of the General Assembly which opened on 16 April seemed to hold out no hope of a solution. On 14 May, however, the establishment of the State of Israel was proclaimed in Tel Aviv. Much to the surprise of delegates, including the American ones, President Truman immediately announced his Government's recognition of the Provisional Jewish Government in Tel Aviv as the *de facto* Government of the new state. This radically transformed the situation and the General Assembly at once appointed a Mediator—Count Folke Bernadotte, the President of the Swedish Red Cross—with terms of reference[89] that did not bind him to the letter of the Assembly's partition resolution.

By now units of the regular armed forces of the neighbouring Arab States[90] were actively engaged in the fighting, but this time a Security Council call (on 29 May) for a cease-fire was heeded; the month's truce which started on 11 June was generally observed. The British Government was now bringing pressure to bear on the Arab States to abide by the Security Council's truce calls, and when fighting began again on 9 July Britain supported an American resolution, adopted by the Security Council on 15 July, ordering the cessation of fighting on pain of sanctions under Chapter VII of the Charter—though of what kind and by whom was not disclosed.[91] This call was effective and, despite not infrequent violations, the subsequent truce was fairly well observed. Consequently Count Bernadotte, in his report to the third session of the General Assembly which met in Paris on 21 September 1948, proposed the replacement

---

[89] *GAOR*, 2nd special sess., suppl. no. 2, Resolution 186 (S-2), pp. 5-6.

[90] Including Iraq and Saudi Arabia.

[91] Previously the United Kingdom had strongly deprecated all talk of sanctions. In deference to sharp criticism both at home and abroad, the British Government also agreed in June 1948 to stop the supply of arms to the Arab States, to ensure that British officers seconded to the Arab Legion should not serve in Palestine, and to reconsider the payment of the subsidy to Transjordan. The United States had imposed an arms embargo in December 1947, but arms continued to reach Israeli forces from various sources, including Czechoslovakia.

of the truce by a formal peace or armistice; the revision of the frontiers of the original partition plan and the merger of Arab Palestine with Jordan; an international régime for Jerusalem (with the right of unimpeded access to it); assistance to Arab refugees with recognition of their right to return home and compensation for their loss of property; and the creation of a United Nations Conciliation Commission.[92] These proposals, which were followed by the announcement of Count Bernadotte's assassination, were fully endorsed by Britain and, somewhat less certainly, by the United States, so raising hopes of a settlement. But American policy was still very divided and unpredictable (a Presidential election was due in November) and discussion was shelved until 15 November, that is, until after the election. Not surprisingly both sides sought to take advantage of the United Nations' temporary incapacity, and in the fighting which continued, despite a Security Council call (on 16 November) for an immediate general armistice, the Israeli armies achieved further successes; they were determined to cling to the gains thus achieved regardless of further Security Council injunctions to give them up.

Conditions for a more permanent cease-fire were becoming more propitious, however. On the Arab side discontent at home and internal dissension gravely weakened their hand; Transjordan, having in December taken over that part of Arab Palestine occupied by its forces, showed rather less reluctance to come to terms with Israel; Lebanon's participation in the war had been half-hearted from the start; Israeli successes on the Egyptian frontier had effectively convinced the Egyptians of the wisdom of negotiation; and both Iraq and Saudi Arabia were disposed to follow suit. For their part the Israelis had established control over an area considerably more extensive than that recommended in the Assembly's original (1947) partition plan, while they were deterred from exploiting their successes further by the firm resistance of the Arab

---

[92] *GAOR*, 3rd sess., pt. 1, suppl. no. 11, A/648.

Legion; by a British threat to invoke the 1936 Treaty with Egypt if the Israeli forces were not promptly withdrawn from Egyptian frontiers; and by an American warning that further Israeli expansion might cause her to review her attitude towards the new state. Accordingly, the new Acting Mediator, Mr Ralph Bunche, was able to inform the Security Council on 6 January 1949 that both Israel and Egypt had unconditionally accepted a cease-fire proposal and were willing to enter into direct negotiations for an armistice under his mediation.On 29 January 1949 the British Government announced its *de facto* recognition of the State of Israel. On 24 February a military armistice agreement was signed between Egypt and Israel, which was followed shortly by similar agreements with Lebanon and Jordan,[93] and a few months later by one with Syria.[94] On their conclusion, the three-man[95] Conciliation Commission, which had been set up by the General Assembly on 11 December 1948, embarked on exploratory talks in the hope of negotiating a formal peace settlement. On 11 May 1949 Israel was admitted to the United Nations, Britain having abstained on the substantive votes in both the Security Council and the Assembly. On 11 August 1949 the Security Council took formal cognizance of the end of the war in Palestine by terminating the office of Acting Mediator.

Since the armistice agreements the United Nations has continued to be seized of three aspects of the Palestine problem: (1) plans for an international régime for Jerusalem, (2) the relief, repatriation or resettlement of the Arab refugees, and (3) the prevention of violations of the armistice agreements and the promotion of a permanent settlement. Only the briefest comment on each of these is possible.

After the armistice Israel's hold on New Jerusalem and Jordan's on Old Jerusalem quickly came to assume an air of permanence.

---

[93] In the summer of 1949 King Abdullah took over that part of central Palestine which remained under Arab control to form 'the Hashimite Kingdom of Jordan'.

[94] The armistice with Syria was delayed by a coup d'état in Damascus.

[95] France, Turkey, and the United States.

But this did not deter an oddly assorted majority[96] at the fourth session of the General Assembly (1949) from proposing to place Jerusalem under an international régime administered by the Trusteeship Council.[97] However, at the Assembly's seventh session (1952) a Philippine proposal which would have reaffirmed the principle of internationalization was rejected.[98] Since then the United Nations has taken little interest in the subject.

The United Nations Relief and Works Agency for Palestine Refugees in the Near East has done a great deal to mitigate the plight of nearly a million Arab refugees;[99] but no progress has been made in repatriating them, while projects designed to assist in their resettlement or rehabilitation have made little headway. Consequently, expenditure on relief has taken a far higher proportion of the Agency's funds than was originally anticipated. Israel firmly rejects the Arab insistence on repatriation, while the Arab States declare that resettlement is still unacceptable to the vast majority of the refugees and that it is economically quite impossible for the host countries. Yet, as the United Kingdom delegation stated at the fifth session of the Assembly (1950), 'whilst the refugees undoubtedly had the right to return, their own interests and those of the Middle East as a whole would best be served by the payment of compensation to them and their resettlement in the Arab countries'.[100] This also now seems to be the Agency's main aim.

---

96 Consisting of the Arab States (except Jordan, not then a member of the United Nations), Catholic countries (mainly those of Latin America and including France), and the Soviet bloc. On their motives see Hurewitz, *Struggle for Palestine*, pp. 326-29.

97 In doing so, they rejected a proposal by the Conciliation Commission (A/973), supported by the United Kingdom and the United States, for a United Nations régime over a demilitarized Jerusalem, divided into semi-autonomous Arab and Jewish zones, with a United Nations Commissioner responsible for the protection of the Holy Places and for free access to them.

98 *GAOR*, 7th sess., Plen., 406th mtg., 18 Dec. 1952, p. 413.

99 As of June 1954 the Agency had on its rolls 887,058 refugees. See its annual report, *GAOR*, 9th sess., suppl. 17; also A/2727/Add. 1 on the future of the Agency.

100 Cmd. 8264, p. 40.

That no early solution is in sight was recognized by the General Assembly at its ninth session, when it extended the Agency's mandate until 30 June 1960. Britain has throughout strongly supported the work of the Agency and has contributed very substantially to its funds.

Although six years have elapsed since the conclusion of the armistice agreements, the prospects of a permanent territorial settlement seem as remote as ever. The ever-present possibility of renewed large-scale fighting is a constant source of instability throughout the Middle East, a serious impediment to the economic development of the region,[101] and an embarrassment to Western plans for regional defence. In this situation the task of the United Nations Truce Supervision Organization has been a difficult one indeed. As is well known, the whole period of the armistice agreements has been marked by repeated violations, each of which frequently leads to a chain of retaliatory measures. In the Gaza area, in the El Auja demilitarized zone, and along the Syrian and Jordanian borders serious fighting has more than once broken out. Moreover, the Security Council's exhortations have not carried great weight,[102] the United Nations force of unarmed observers has been far too small to be deployed effectively, its freedom of movement has been severely restricted, and its authority has come to depend very largely on the personal prestige of its Chief-of-Staff (General E. L. M. Burns) and his subordinates. In these difficult circumstances the record of General Burns and his predecessors has been most creditable; by making known to the world where responsibility for an incident lies and by mediating between local commanders to secure a cessation of fighting, they have helped to

---

[101] The Arab States still impose an economic blockade upon Israel.

[102] For example, the Council's resolution of 1 September 1951, calling upon Egypt to terminate the embargo on shipping passing through the Suez Canal bound for Israel, has been completely ignored, while the Council's condemnation of 29 March 1955 of an Israeli attack in the Gaza area has not deterred the Israelis from instigating further incidents of this kind.

h

reduce bloodshed. But the chief external restraint on really large-scale fighting has been not the United Nations but the Anglo-French-American Tripartite Declaration of 25 May 1950[103] that they would take action, both within and outside the United Nations, to prevent a violation of frontiers or armistice lines.

In briefly commenting upon the part played by the United Nations in regard to Palestine, it is instructive to consider first the contention that from the British point of view the United Nations served as a convenient depository for a problem which had defeated all British efforts to arrive at a settlement. Though crudely put, this contention is not without foundation. No doubt there were those who in early 1947 still thought of the United Nations as a 'higher authority' to which such a problem could be referred with every hope of a successful solution. But this belief is so much at variance with the orthodox British 'official' view of the United Nations as essentially a new form of 'diplomacy by conference' that the British decision to refer the problem to the United Nations was almost certainly primarily a case of *faute de mieux*. Caught between the fires of Arab and Jewish intransigence and faced by rising American indignation, especially at the methods used to prevent illegal immigration, it probably seemed to the United Kingdom that the least unpromising line of action was to return her embarrassing responsibility to the authority under whose supervision it had been exercised. Originally this had been the League of Nations, but the United Nations was the League's legal successor and the Charter provided that mandated territories might be placed under the trusteeship system (Art. 77). Nor should it be forgotten that at this stage the Government was not going to the United Nations to surrender the Mandate; indeed, there were thought to be strong strategic reasons for retaining a foothold in Palestine. As Mr Creech

---

103 *The Times*, 26 May 1950. It was in this declaration that they also declared their opposition to the development of an arms race between the Arab states and Israel. The Declaration was reaffirmed by Mr Eden on 4 April 1955 (H. C. Deb., vol. 539, coll. 899-902).

Jones stated in the House of Commons,[104] the Government's aim in early 1947 was to seek the advice of the United Nations as to how the Mandate could be administered and, if that were impossible in its present form, how it could be amended. In other words, the bilateral attempt of the Anglo-American Committee to draw the United States into sharing the British responsibility had failed; should not the collective approach now be tried? At the very least it might ensure that Arab and Zionist hostility to whatever course of action was recommended by the Assembly would not have to be borne by Great Britain alone.

By the time the Assembly met in September 1947 Britain had come to favour an early withdrawal,[105] but she still seems to have been willing to play her part in whatever method of handing over the Mandate was evolved by the United Nations. Only in November when the Assembly seemed intent on adopting a thoroughly impracticable plan, did Britain's attitude harden. Sir Alexander Cadogan's disclosure that British troops would not take part in enforcing a settlement was dictated partly by growing domestic pressure for their early withdrawal and by Britain's anxiety not to alienate the Arab States, but it was also designed to shock delegates into facing up to the crucial question of how partition could be enforced. The Assembly's adoption of the partition plan only reinforced Britain's determination to evacuate her troops as rapidly as possible. Thus Britain's widely resented refusal to co-operate with the Palestine Commission was dictated, rightly or wrongly, primarily by the belief that the completion of this difficult military operation without grave loss of British lives required her to retain undivided control until the very last moment.

Whether reference to the United Nations made for a more constructive and consistent American policy is doubtful. Nor is it certain that Britain incurred any less odium in the Arab world by handing over the problem to the United Nations and by refusing

---

[104] 25 Feb. 1947, H. C. Deb., vol. 433, col. 2007.
[105] Partly because the strategic picture had changed; see above, p. 92n.

to take any part in enforcing partition. There may be a *prima facie* case for believing so. On the other hand, if it had not been for the United Nations' existence, might not both Britain and the United States have faced up to the problem of Palestine more realistically? The final territorial solution might not have been very different, but the refugee problem might not have become so grievous; and it is this problem which is perhaps the greatest single obstacle to a permanent settlement. Thus the United Nations may have provided Britain with a convenient depository, but it may also have tended to serve as an incitement to escapism on Britain's part and as a camouflage for the absence of any coherent policy on America's part.

To turn to the partition proposals themselves. These did not, of course, secure a 'just' solution for all the parties concerned—an impossible task in the circumstances, while the suspicion that their adoption was very largely the result of shrewd lobbying disillusioned many previous supporters of the United Nations in Great Britain. That the United Nations had correctly expressed the general consensus of world opinion in proposing the creation of a Jewish State was fairly widely conceded, however. The main point of criticism was the Organization's failure to face up to the problem of giving effect to its proposals. Yet this criticism was misdirected, for it made the United Nations a scapegoat for the unwillingness of the United States and Britain, whether jointly or separately, to enforce either partition or any alternative plan. It was the marked divergence between American and British policies rather than any shortcomings in the United Nations machinery which resulted in partition being effected by Jewish arms rather than through the United Nations. Nor can the latter's impotence be ascribed to the obstructionist tactics of the Soviet Union; in fact, the adoption of the Assembly's partition proposals was marked by fairly close American and Soviet agreement. In short, the United Nations could do no more than its principal members were prepared to do, which was virtually nothing.

In spite of the very creditable record of the United Nations in bringing about the 'cease-fire', in limiting the number of 'incidents', and in relieving the misery of nearly a million refugees, the Security Council's edicts have frequently been flouted with comparative impunity. The fact is that neither Israel nor the Arab States can be deterred from the use of force by mere exhortations. Nor has it been easy to preserve a stable balance between them by restrictions on the supply of arms. In addition to a strengthened Truce Supervision Organization and possibly a small force of armed police to check minor incidents, what the United Nations has needed is a military arm which can make the price of aggression appear prohibitive. It has been forced to look primarily for this to the armed forces of the signatories to the Tripartite Declaration. But in return the Security Council could provide a forum where these Powers (and, it is to be hoped, the Soviet Union) could publicly demonstrate their identity of purpose, and it could cloak with its authority whatever action they might jointly decide upon.

THE ANGLO-IRANIAN OIL DISPUTE

The use of the United Nations as a means of bringing pressure to bear on those Western Powers who have acquired special rights in Africa and the Middle East or of restraining them from protecting their rights in the traditional manner, will be discussed more fully in Chapter 9. Two instances only of this pressure will be recalled here. The first was the Egyptian complaint to the Security Council on 8 July 1947 against the presence of British troops on Egyptian territory which, it was alleged,[106] was 'contrary to the letter and spirit of the United Nations Charter, and to the resolution adopted

---

[106] See letter from the Egyptian delegate to the President of the Security Council: *SCOR*, 2nd yr., 159th mtg., 17 July 1947, pp. 1343-45; also speech to the Council by the Egyptian Prime Minister: ibid. 175th mtg., 5 Aug. 1947, pp. 1753-65.

unanimously by the General Assembly on 14 December 1946'.[107]
The United Kingdom delegate sought to rebut these charges by
citing the 1936 Treaty and by pointing out that the Egyptian
Government's refusal to admit the Sudan's full right of self-
determination had been chiefly responsible for the failure of earlier
negotiations to revise the treaty.[108] There never appeared any
great danger of a finding prejudicial to Britain, and the Council
adjourned the discussion on 10 September without having been
able to agree on any resolution. But the general tone of the debate
was rather disturbingly indicative of a climate of opinion not
sympathetic to the maintenance of legal rights, which many delegates
seemed to regard as merely the expression of a vanishing order of
international relationships.

The second, and more serious, instance concerned the dispute
between Britain and Iran over the expropriation and eviction of
the Anglo-Iranian Oil Company (AIOC) from Iran. Very briefly
indeed,[109] the position early in 1951 was that the AIOC was faced
by the rejection by the Iranian Majlis of a Supplementary Agreement to the 1933 Concession,[110] by the passing of a bill for the

---

[107] This resolution had recommended Members to undertake the withdrawal
without delay of their armed forces stationed in the territories of Members
without their consent freely and publicly expressed in treaties or agreements
consistent with the Charter and not contradicting international agreements
(*GAOR*, 1st sess., pt. 2, Resolution 41(I)).

[108] *SCOR*, 2nd yr., 175th mtg., 5 Aug. 1947, pp. 1765-84.

[109] For background material and details of the dispute see Alan W. Ford,
The Anglo-Iranian Oil Dispute of 1951-1952 (Univ. of California Press, 1954);
S. H. Longrigg, *Middle East Oil* (London, OUP for RIIA, 1954), pp. 159-73;
RIIA *Survey, 1951*, pp. 299-337; J. Frankel, 'The Anglo-Iranian Dispute', in
YBWA, 1952; and G. Schwarzenberger, 'The Protection of British Property
Abroad', in *CLP, 1952*, pp. 308-21.

[110] The revelation, on 10 February 1951, of the conclusion of a 'fifty-fifty'
profit-sharing agreement between the King of Saudi Arabia and the Arabian-
American Oil Company (Aramco) helped to convince the Iranians that they
were being unfairly treated, despite the fact that the 1949 Agreement had previously been regarded as the most favourable one of its kind and that Iran had
rejected an earlier offer for a 'fifty-fifty' agreement which is said to have been
made by the AIOC (Ford, *Anglo-Iranian Oil Dispute*, p. 49).

nationalization of the oil industry, and by a demand for the eviction of the company from Iran. After proposals by the AIOC for arbitration (as provided for in the 1933 concession) had been rejected by Iran, the British Government, on 26 May 1951, brought the dispute before the International Court of Justice. In its application Britain asked the Court to declare, *inter alia*, that the execution of the Iranian nationalization laws would constitute a violation of international law for which the Iranian Government would be internationally responsible; that, by rejecting the AIOC's request for arbitration, the Iranian Government had denied the company the exclusive legal remedy provided in the concession and had thereby committed a denial of justice contrary to international law; and that, by thus treating a British national (AIOC) in a manner inconsistent with the norms of international law, the Iranian Government had committed a wrong against the Government of the United Kingdom.[111] The Iranian Government thereupon denied the competence of the Court to deal with the dispute, which, it asserted, was one within the exclusive domestic jurisdiction of Iran.

As the company's personnel and installations were being increasingly interfered with, the Court, on 5 July 1951, on application by Britain for the 'Indication of Interim Measures of Protection', ordered both parties to refrain from action which might prejudice the rights of either party or that might aggravate the dispute, pending a final decision by the Court.[112] The Iranian Government informed the Court that it rejected this order. After renewed negotiations had broken down, despite attempted mediation by Mr Averell Harriman and the visit of a British mission headed by the Lord Privy Seal (Mr R. R. Stokes), Dr Mussadiq, the Iranian

[111] The text of the United Kingdom's 'Application' is quoted in *Anglo-Iranian Oil Co. case (jurisdiction)*, *Judgment of July 22nd, 1952: ICJ Reports, 1952*, pp. 95-96.

[112] See *Anglo-Iranian Oil Co. Case, Order of July 5th 1951: ICJ Reports, 1951*, p. 89.

Prime Minister, announced that the British staff of the AIOC must leave Iranian soil by 4 October. On 27 September Iranian troops seized the Abadan refinery. On the 28th the British Government brought the matter before the Security Council on the grounds that a dispute existed which endangered international peace and security; the following day it submitted a draft resolution which would have had the Security Council call upon Iran to comply with the Court's Interim Measures and to permit the continued residence at Abadan of the staff whose expulsion had been ordered. The Council met on 1 October only to adjourn till 15 October, by which time British personnel had been evacuated from Abadan. A revised resolution was, therefore, tabled by Britain calling for the resumption of negotiations and for the avoidance of any action which might aggravate the situation. The Iranian delegation (headed now by Dr Mussadiq) continued to deny the competence of the Council in the matter, on the grounds that the dispute was clearly within the domestic jurisdiction of Iran and that Article 2, paragraph 7, of the Charter precluded intervention by the Security Council. Doubts about the Council's competence were so prevalent that the French delegate moved, with British support, that the Council should adjourn its debate until the Court had ruled on its own competence in the matter. The motion for adjournment was adopted by a vote of eight to one (the Soviet Union), with two abstentions.[113] The Council's eagerness to disembarrass itself of the Anglo-Iranian dispute was certainly not calculated to enhance its prestige or to encourage the belief that recourse to it might provide an effective remedy against illegal acts.

---

[113] China and Yugoslavia abstained on the grounds that the competence of the Council and that of the Court did not rest on identical foundations; since the powers and functions of the two bodies differ so radically, this view would seem to have much to commend it. (See Ford, *Anglo-Iranian Oil Dispute*, pp. 146-53.) That the Security Council is not deterred from intervening in a dispute which it considers a threat to the maintenance of international peace and security, despite a claim of domestic jurisdiction, is borne out by the Council's action over Indonesia. See pp. 113-15 below.

With the breakdown of attempts by the International Bank to achieve a compromise,[114] interest shifted to the International Court of Justice. But the Court was prevented from pronouncing upon the merits of the case by its decision, on 22 July 1952, by 9[115] votes to 5, in favour of a preliminary objection by Iran to the Court's jurisdiction. This majority judgment was based on the interpretation to be given to the wording of an Iranian declaration of 19 September 1932 accepting the compulsory jurisdiction of the Court. The Court held that this wording must be interpreted with due regard to the intention of the Iranian Government at that time. This interpretation excluded various treaties entered into by Iran before 1932 the breach of which had been cited by Britain as falling within the jurisdiction of the Court. The consideration of alleged breaches of these treaties being thus ruled out, there remained the 1933 Concession Convention signed between the Iranian Government and the AIOC. Although this had been concluded through the good offices of the League of Nations, the Court found that it was 'nothing more than a concessionary contract between a government and a foreign corporation', to which Britain was not a party.[116]

The Court's finding did not, of course, affect the validity of the United Kingdom's contention that the actions of the Iranian Government constituted a denial of justice and so an internationally illegal act.[117] The AIOC did, in fact, successfully take action to defend its legal rights and to establish its ownership of oil left in the storage tanks at Abadan refinery.[118] But the failure of either

[114] See *Review of the International Bank's Negotiations Concerning the Iranian Oil Problem*, Press Release No. 285, Washington, D. C., 3 Apr. 1952.

[115] Judge Arnold McNair (United Kingdom) concurred in the majority decision, but for reasons other than those of the other eight judges.

[116] *Anglo-Iranian Oil Co. case (jurisdiction)*, *Judgment of July 22nd, 1952: ICJ Reports, 1952*, p. 112.

[117] Ford, *Anglo-Iranian Oil Dispute*, pp. 180-90. See also statement by the Prime Minister (Mr Churchill), 23 July 1952, H. C. Deb., vol. 504, col. 533.

[118] For instance, the *Rose Mary* case before the Aden Supreme Court (Longrigg, *Middle East Oil*, p. 170).

the Security Council or the International Court to uphold the company's rights was naturally adversely commented upon in Britain. With the downfall of Dr Mussadiq in August 1953 the prospects for a settlement brightened,[119] but the United Nations played no part in the negotiations which opened in April 1954 between the Iranian Government and a consortium of oil companies, made up of AIOC (40 per cent. share), five American companies (40 per cent.), Shell (14 per cent.), and the Compagnie Française des Pétroles (6 per cent.). On 5 August 1954 it was announced in Teheran that agreement had been reached to restore the operation of the oil industry and on a settlement of the AIOC's claims for compensation.[120]

Without going into the merits of the dispute, so far as Britain's relations with the United Nations are concerned two main points emerge from this rather dismal story. The first is that the eventual decision of the British Government not to use force to protect either British lives or British property in Iran resulted to an important extent from a genuine reluctance 'to take any action which might have the effect of weakening the authority of the United Nations on whose principles their policy is based'.[121] No doubt the Government was anxious that its decision not to use force should appear in the best possible light; at the same time the knowledge that the use of British troops[122] would inevitably have resulted in an Iranian complaint to the Security Council, and that Britain would almost certainly then be faced with an adverse recommendation from the Council, strongly influenced the Government's attitude. Of course, this was by no means the only consideration. No less significant was the fact that President Truman made it clear that the United States could not support Britain in the use of force. Other con-

---

[119] Diplomatic relations, which had been broken off in October 1952, were restored in December 1953.

[120] *The Times*, 6 Aug. 1954.

[121] From a Foreign Office statement of 28 Sept. 1951.

[122] Perimeter defence of Abadan was perfectly feasible militarily.

siderations militating against the use of force were fears that the Soviet Union might think she could put up a good enough case under the Soviet-Persian Treaty of 1921 to justify intervention in the north; that Iranian nationalism might be further exacerbated, so making ultimate reconciliation even more difficult; that the Commonwealth would be sharply divided on the issue; and, finally, that it would be impossible to run the oil installations in the face of obdurate Iranian non-co-operation. If the United Nations had not existed, Britain would probably still have been induced to take the course she did by these considerations, and by the reluctance of an important section of the Labour Government to do anything which might be construed as imperialistic. But the view that the Charter in Article 2(4) positively prohibited the unilateral use of force, together with the distasteful prospect of Great Britain's being put in the dock at the Security Council, were certainly of appreciable importance in persuading Britain to rely on legal arguments and procedures[123] rather than, as occasionally in the past, on naval or military action.

The second is that the Anglo-Iranian dispute pointed up the dilemma with which the Charter confronts law-abiding states. The Charter, in Article 2(4), in effect enjoins Members to refrain from the *unilateral* threat or use of force to protect the lives and property of their nationals in foreign lands. Partly for this reason Britain stayed her hand. But what *collective* means of protection or of redress does the Charter provide as an alternative? Virtually none. The Security Council may intervene if it considers peace is endangered, but it may well be in doubt whether measures of confiscation and eviction by themselves constitute such a danger. Even if, in the most unlikely event of all the permanent members being in agreement and a sufficient majority being forthcoming, the Council did

---

[123] A reliance that was no doubt also fostered by the hope that negotiations would eventually lead to a solution and by the fact that the British 'found the established legal principles much more congenial to their position than did the Iranians' (Ford, *Anglo-Iranian Oil Dispute*, pp. 219-20).

call upon a state to rescind such measures, it would still have to rely on one or more members to exercise the necessary compulsion under its authority. Similarly, even if the International Court were in a position—which is highly improbable, given the reluctance of states to accept the compulsory jurisdiction of the Court and their insistence on their own exclusive domestic jurisdiction—to pronounce against the appropriation of the property of aliens without prompt, adequate and effective compensation, there is unfortunately no certainty that its decision would be respected. There is, therefore, a real danger that the United Nations may encourage the belief that legal obligations can be set aside with impunity and that the Charter may serve as a bulwark for the law-breakers rather than for the law-abiding. Is this a situation to be acquiesced in?

chapter four

The Far East[1]

Most Far Eastern problems of the period following the Second World War, such as the Japanese peace treaty, the accession to power of the Communist régime in China, and the civil war in Indo-China, have fallen outside the cognizance of the United Nations. Moreover here, as elsewhere, the West's system of defence rests on regional security arrangements, especially the South East Asia Collective Defence Treaty, concluded in September 1954 under Article 51 of the Charter, rather than on the Charter's own collective security system. Nevertheless, the United Nations played a notable part in the creation of the Republic of Indonesia, while up to December 1955 United Nations action in Korea was not only called the first 'war for collective security' but, for good or ill, it was more important for the United Nations than any other

---

[1] Including South and South East Asia.

single event in the post-war period; and it also provided the one issue on which the content of British policy, as distinct from its conduct, was strongly and directly influenced by the United Nations.

The general objective of British policy in the Far East, as elsewhere, may be defined as the preservation of external peace and internal tranquility. But the means adopted to further this end have of necessity been affected by two major considerations. In the first place, British policy must take into account interests in Western Europe and the Middle East which are more vital to her security and to which Far Eastern desiderata have often, therefore, to be subordinated. The fact that, of recent years, Britain's commitments nearer home have absorbed a much larger proportion of her total strength than hitherto and the diminution in her armed strength through the recognition of India's independence have further limited the commitments she can undertake in the Far East. In the second place, the preponderant position of the United States in the Far East and Pacific, marked by her predominant share in the defeat of Japan, has made Britain disposed to defer to American views, especially since these views have often been shared by Australia and, to a lesser extent, by New Zealand. These different conceptions of the priorities to be accorded to Far Eastern matters were of considerable importance in the differences in policy that at one time developed between Britain and the United States over Korea.

INDONESIA

The part played by the United Nations in bringing the Republic of Indonesia into being is often accounted one of the Organization's principal successes. It will be recalled that the British forces sent to Java in September 1945 to take the Japanese surrender and to release internees came into conflict with the forces of the Indonesian Republic, which had been set up towards the end of the Japanese occupation. This faced the British Government with a very delicate situation. It still regarded the Netherlands as the *de jure* sovereign, but the Republicans were in *de facto* control of much of the country. Accordingly, the British Commander in Java endeavoured to promote a pacific settlement between the returned Dutch officials and the Republican leaders, which would satisfy the more moderate nationalist ambitions and at the same time preserve some element of Dutch influence.

In the meanwhile, however, on 21 January 1946, the Ukrainian delegate to the United Nations had lodged a complaint with the Security Council about the activities of British forces in Java and had proposed that a commission should investigate the matter. This was a shrewd riposte to British support of the Iranian charges against the Soviet Union,[2] but an investigating commission could hardly have failed to unsettle the negotiations. However, the Ukrainian proposal was successfully opposed by Mr Bevin, as was a draft Egyptian resolution aimed at limiting the use of British troops and at securing their early withdrawal. The question was then dropped from the Security Council's agenda. The conclusion on 25 March 1947 of the Linggadjati Agreement, in which the Dutch Government recognized *de facto* the authority of the Indonesian Republic and agreed to the establishment by 1 January 1949 of a United States of Indonesia and a Netherlands-Indonesian Union, relieved Britain of any further direct concern in the matter.

When the breakdown of negotiations and the first Dutch 'police action'[3] again brought the Indonesian question before the Security Council on 30 July 1947, Britain's main concern was with the domestic jurisdiction issue. Thus she expressed her sympathy— though with some qualifications—with the Netherlands' claim that the question essentially fell within her domestic jurisdiction and

---

2 See above, p. 68.
3 For details of these and later events see RIIA, *Survey 1947-48*, pp. 388 ff., and *Survey, 1949-50*, pp. 384-400. A useful summary of the Security Council's deliberations is given in *Repertoire of the Practice of the Security Council*, pp. 315-25.

that the Council was, therefore, not competent to deal with it.
Two main points were at issue.[4] The first was whether the last
phrase of Article 2(7) authorized the Council to take action under
Article 39 of the Charter even if the Indonesian question fell within
the domestic jurisdiction of the Netherlands. The second was
whether resolutions by which the Security Council tendered its
good offices to the parties to a dispute, or called upon them to
cease hostilities and to settle the dispute by peaceful means, constituted intervention within the meaning of Article 2(7). The
inclination of many members of the Council, led by Australia and
the United States, was to deal with the substance of the question in
an effort to stop the fighting, whilst attempting, rather ingenuously,
to evade the question of the Council's competence. Accordingly,
although a French amendment explicitly reserving the question of
the Council's competence was rejected, no reference was made
to the provisions of the Charter in the Council's resolution of
1 August 1947, in which it called upon the parties (*a*) to cease
hostilities forthwith, and (*b*) to settle their dispute by arbitration
or by other peaceful means.[5] Similarly, the United States delegate
claimed that the question of the Council's competence was unaffected
by the Council's two resolutions of 25 August 1947.[6] In the first
of these the Council requested the Governments of members of
the Council which had career consular representatives in Batavia
to instruct them to report on the situation in Indonesia.[7] In the
second the Council expressed its readiness to set up a tripartite
Committee of Good Offices. This offer was accepted and a Committee of Good Offices, consisting of representatives of Australia,

---

[4] ibid. pp. 429-34.

[5] *SCOR*, 2nd yr., 173rd mtg., S/459.

[6] ibid. 194th mtg., 25 Aug. 1947; for consolidated text see S/INF/2, pp. 29-30,
S/525, I and II. A Belgian proposal to request the International Court of Justice for an Advisory Opinion concerning the Council's competence was rejected
the following day.

[7] An earlier Soviet proposal for a Commission of the Council—the Soviet
Union having no consul in Batavia—had been vetoed by France.

Belgium, and the United States, was constituted. Britain abstained from voting on the first resolution but supported the second.

As a result of negotiations conducted by the Committee of Good Offices a truce agreement was signed on 17 January 1948.[8] On 18 December 1948, however, the Netherlands Government denounced the agreement and resumed 'police action'. When on 22 December the matter came before the Security Council, the British position had shifted slightly. Thus the United Kingdom delegate (Mr Dening) on 24 December considered that 'the Indonesian situation is surely one which, in the terms of the Charter, may lead to international friction' and 'that the state of the world is too serious for a conflict of . . . [this] nature . . . to be allowed to continue with all its incalculable consequences.'[9] Accordingly, while not committing herself on the legal issues involved, the United Kingdom supported the Council's resolution[10] calling for an immediate cessation of hostilities and for the release of the President of the Republic and other political prisoners, in the belief that the Council would thus 'avoid the reproach either . . . of washing its hands of a situation which cries out for remedy, or of exceeding its power in matters which are solemnly protected by the domestic jurisdiction clause of the Charter.'[11] This call was reiterated in a resolution of 28 January 1949, which also supported the establishment of 'a federal, independent, and sovereign United States of Indonesia at the earliest possible date'.[12] The Committee of Good Offices was transformed into the United Nations Commission for Indonesia[13]—its membership remaining unchanged—and was charged with giving effect to the resolution.

---

[8] Text in *SCOR*, 3rd yr., special suppl. no. 1, app. xi, p. 72.

[9] ibid. 392nd mtg., pp. 6-7.

[10] ibid. suppl. for Dec. 1948, S/1154.

[11] ibid. 3rd yr., 392nd mtg., p. 7.

[12] ibid. 4th yr., suppl. for Feb. 1949, S/1234.

[13] The Commission was assisted by teams of military observers appointed by the Consular Commission.

Sporadic fighting continued for some time, but on 4 August 1949 the United Nations Commission for Indonesia, as a result of negotiations conducted under its auspices, was able to report that both parties had agreed to (1) the restoration of the Republican Government to its capital; (2) the cessation of hostilities; and (3) the holding of a Round Table Conference at The Hague.[14] The Round Table Conference opened on 23 August. It ended on 2 November with formal agreement on the transfer of sovereignty[15] to the Republican Government by 30 December 1949 and on the establishment of a Netherlands-Indonesian Union, based on equal status and rights, for the promotion of co-operation on matters of common interest in international affairs, defence, and, to a lesser extent, economic and cultural questions.[16] The General Assembly welcomed and approved the outcome of the Conference, but the Security Council was prevented from doing so by a Soviet veto. On 27 December 1949 sovereignty was formally transferred to the Republic, which was admitted to the United Nations on 28 September 1950.

British policy in the matter was shaped primarily by the desire to avoid conflict in the East Indies and to promote a compromise arrangement between the Netherlands and the Indonesian Republic. While not wanting to antagonize a friendly nation, co-signatory of the Brussels Treaty, Britain was anxious not to alienate opinion in Australia and the new Asian members of the Commonwealth, where there was strong support for the Republican cause.[17] As the situation deteriorated, this last consideration became the governing one, especially since it was reinforced by the general tendency of the Labour Government to sympathize with the aspirations of colonial peoples. And although this underlying

---

14 *SCOR*, 4th yr., special suppl. no. 5, S/1373 and S/1373/corr. 1.

15 Western New Guinea was to remain under Dutch rule pending a settlement.

16 *SCOR*, 4th yr., special suppl. no. 6, S/1417.

17 Twenty states (including five Commonwealth countries) participated in a three-day conference in Delhi in January 1949 at which Dutch policy was condemned in very forthright terms.

sympathy was closely circumscribed by the force of Article 2(7), the success of Communism in China seemed to underline the need to come to terms with Asian nationalism and to hand over authority to a moderate nationalist movement, rather than to continue a struggle which would almost certainly bring extremist and probably Communist leaders into power.

As in the case of Palestine, United Nations action in Indonesia was favoured by the absence of direct and open conflict between the United States and the Soviet Union. But, as they were not in the case of Palestine, Britain and the United States were in accord on the need for the Dutch to come to terms with the Republicans.[18] This accord, and their diplomatic pressure on the Netherlands Government, probably led most directly to the modification of Dutch policy which permitted the final settlement. However, an important contributory factor was the evident isolation of the Dutch at the United Nations. The Netherlands Government, though convinced of the strength of its case, appears to have been genuinely concerned about its country's reputation in the eyes of the world. Its consequent desire to placate criticism—whether bilateral or collective—helped to make United Nations intervention effective. And Dutch 'police action' would almost certainly have brought about the demise of the Republic—at least temporarily— had it not been curbed by the Security Council's successive calls for a cease-fire and a resumption of negotiations.

To sum up, the existence of the United Nations enabled the Republic of Indonesia to draw universal attention to what might otherwise have remained a local dispute and so to mobilize far wider support for its cause. Though of only marginal importance, this may well have proved decisive. The efforts at mediation by the Committee of Good Offices met with some criticism, chiefly from the Dutch, on the grounds that its members were not sufficiently impartial. But this is not an unusual fate for mediators;

---

[18] Though they frequently differed on details of the terms.

some of Count Bernadotte's proposals produced bitter resentment on the part either of the Israelis or of the Arabs, while in Kashmir the United Nations Commission was strongly criticized by both parties. In fact the Committee of Good Offices played quite a useful role in mediating between the two parties and in helping the United Nations to prevent the growth of a running political sore which might have grievously affected the attitude of the whole of South and South East Asia towards the West.

CHINA

In Britain the part played by the United Nations in Indonesia was soon overshadowed first by the Korean War and then by Chinese intervention in that war. The importance of these events was forcibly driven home to the general public by the threat that they might set off a general conflagration and by their impact on Anglo-American relations; for it is in their attitudes towards the People's Republic of China that British and American policies have been most at variance. To many Americans the British attitude has smacked of 'appeasement', whereas in British eyes the American approach has at times appeared to be tinged with an emotional intransigence which, though understandable after Chinese intervention in Korea, has nevertheless been generally regretted. There were also at one time renewed stirrings of the fear that American involvement in the Far East might weaken her interest and influence in Western Europe.

Up to the fall of the Chinese Nationalist Government in 1949, Britain took her stand upon the agreement reached at the Conference of Foreign Ministers in Moscow in December 1945, under which the three Powers agreed *inter alia* on the need for a 'unified and democratic China under the National Government' and 'reaffirmed their adherence to the policy of non-interference in the internal affairs of China'.[19] In line with this declaration, Britain continued

[19] U. S. Dept. of State, *Treaties and other International Acts Series*, no. 1555, p. 8.

to accord recognition to the Chinese Nationalist Government and to avoid official contacts with the Chinese Communist authorities. At the same time, while general concurrence was expressed with American efforts at mediation, this did not go beyond moral support.[20] British policy as late as 26 April 1949 continued to be governed by the Moscow Declaration.[21] In this policy of cautious aloofness the British Government enjoyed the general support of all parties. There were, indeed, individual exceptions, but there has been no equivalent in Britain to the 'great debate' on China policy which has been conducted with so much passion in America. Several reasons may be adduced for this. Britain did not share the somewhat emotional American attitude to China,[22] and the sanguine belief that China might in the near future replace Japan as the Great Power of the Far East. It was on American insistence, against British misgivings, that China had been made one of the sponsors of the Moscow Declaration of 1943 and later had obtained a permanent seat on the Security Council.[23] Therefore civil strife in China and the collapse of Chiang Kai-shek's régime could be regarded with more detachment by Britain than was possible in the United States. Nor on the commercial side had British relations with the Nationalist Government run so smoothly that any keen regret could be felt at its downfall. Indeed, British business circles were inclined to favour British recognition of the Chinese Communist Government as soon as there was one to recognize.

The establishment of the Communist Government at the beginning of October 1949 placed the British Government in a quandary. The Communist régime indicated its unwillingness to accept *de facto* diplomatic relations, while refusal of, or prolonged delay in, *de jure*

---

[20] See, for example, the statement by the Lord Chancellor (Lord Jowitt), H.C. Deb., vol. 145, col. 156.

[21] The Prime Minister (Mr Attlee), ibid. vol. 464, col. 26.

[22] Based partly on the strong missionary connexions and the traditional friendship between the two countries.

[23] See above, p. 7n.

recognition might well have reacted adversely upon British interests in China. It might even have encouraged a Chinese attack upon Hong Kong; and American assistance in the defence of that colony could not be expected with any confidence. Judicial authorities of the highest standing also contended that Britain had traditionally regarded recognition as simply the admission of a fact from which approval of a régime should not be inferred. And there could be little doubt that the new régime was in effective control over the whole or nearly the whole of Chinese territory.[24] Nor was the British Government inclined to regard China as necessarily and permanently a satellite of the Soviet Union; and recognition might assist in its detachment. These were important reasons for prompt recognition. On the other hand, the British Government was anxious not to get out of step with the United States, or to create a situation in which some Members of the United Nations recognized the Communist régime and others the Nationalist, with all the consequent vexatious difficulties which this would entail in respect of Chinese representation in the United Nations, especially in the Security Council. And it was clear that Congressional and public opinion in the United States precluded, at all events for the time being, American recognition of the Chinese People's Government.

Initially, therefore, the British Government would have preferred to wait upon American action.[25] Similarly, the older Dominions, though not unalterably opposed to recognition, made no secret of their anxiety not to get out of step with America. The situation was transformed, however, when on 30 December 1949 India accorded *de jure* recognition to the Chinese People's Government, an action which was quickly followed by Pakistan and Ceylon. In this situation, for Britain to have delayed recognition would

[24] According to one's view of the status of Formosa. Britain's view is that *de jure* sovereignty over Formosa is 'uncertain or undetermined' (4 Feb. 1955, H. C. Deb., vol. 536, col. *159* (Written Answers)).

[25] Mr Bevin recorded his preference for a 'combined decision' (16 Nov. 1949, ibid. vol. 469, col. 2013). Mr Churchill expressed much the same view for the Opposition (ibid. col. 2226).

have given the appearance of a split in the Commonwealth along racial lines. This factor appears to have tipped the balance and to have decided the British Government to accord *de jure* recognition to the Chinese People's Government on 5 January 1950, even before the meeting of Commonwealth Foreign Ministers which opened in Colombo a few days later. As Mr Bevin told the House of Commons on 24 May 1950,[26] it was evident that no agreement could be reached at the Colombo meeting, and he may well have hoped that the rest of the Commonwealth would follow the lead of Britain and the Asian members without much delay; indeed, until Chinese intervention in Korea it seems to have been anticipated that general recognition would be accorded to the Communist régime within a few months. There were good grounds for this belief. At the beginning of 1950 it appeared likely that the Nationalist régime would before long be driven from its last refuge in Formosa. Even if it held together afterwards, it would only be an *émigré* Government. This could hardly fail to influence the attitude of the United States Government and of others who were still holding aloof from Peking. As one authority has written:

> It is fairly safe to say that had the former Nationalist Government of China simply disappeared, recognition of the right of the Peking Government to represent China in the United Nations could scarcely have been withheld, whatever view was taken as to the political behaviour of that Government: at most, a certain delay might have occurred.[27]

The British Government evidently hoped, therefore, that the course of events would operate to bring about general recognition. The Sino-Soviet military alliance of 14 February 1950 and then

---

[26] ibid. vol. 475, col. 2083. It was in this debate that Mr Bevin also recorded his view that British interests in China had been hurt more by the Nationalist blockade than by anything the Communists had done (ibid. col. 2086).

[27] G. G. Fitzmaurice (then Second Legal Adviser and now Legal Adviser to the Foreign Office), 'Chinese Representation in the United Nations', in *YBWA, 1952*, p. 38.

the North Korean attack on South Korea were setbacks, but they did not finally blight these hopes.[28]

The United Nations' organs have been concerned not with the issue of recognition *per se*, but rather with the question of *which* China's representatives shall sit in China's seat, those of the People's Republic or those of the Nationalist Government in Formosa. In other words the question is: which set of credentials shall be accepted?[29] Despite her own recognition of the People's Republic, Great Britain at first (January 1950) abstained from voting for acceptance of the credentials of its representatives, partly because its Government was not recognized by the majority of members (nor had diplomatic relations with it yet been established by Britain), partly in her desire not to present a divided Anglo-American front or to offend American opinion.[30] However, the United States Government, in the spring of 1950, was reported to have signified its readiness to accept representation by the People's Republic on the Security Council should a majority of the Council decide in favour of this step.[31] Accordingly, during this period Britain used her influence, albeit unsuccessfully, to secure such a majority, though she continued to favour postponement of the issue in the meantime. During September 1950, however, Britain voted in favour of Soviet and other proposals that a representative of the People's Republic should be invited to attend the Council's discussions in

---

[28] After the start of the Korean War United States recognition of Communist China might have brought some very embarrassing results, for the Nationalist régime could then have been represented as in revolt against the legitimate Government of China, and American protection and aid to Formosa as a distinctly unfriendly act against that Government.

[29] It is the prerogative of each United Nations organ (with the assistance of its own Credentials Committee) to reach a decision concerning the credentials presented to it.

[30] On the defeat of a Soviet motion of 10 January to unseat the Nationalist representative, the Soviet delegate absented himself from the Security Council, not to return until 1 August 1950 (*SCOR*, 5th yr., 459th mtg., 10 Jan. 1950, pp. 3-4).

[31] H.C. Deb. vol. 475, col. 2085.

connexion with their complaint of the armed invasion of Formosa.[32] When the situation was transformed by Chinese intervention in Korea in November 1950, it was on United Kingdom initiative that the Security Council agreed on 8 November to 'invite, in accordance with rule 39 of the rules of procedure, a representative of the Central Government of the People's Republic of China to be present during discussion by the Council' of General MacArthur's report on Chinese intervention.[33] Only with the failure of all efforts to bring the war and Chinese intervention to a rapid end did the British attitude change. On 11 June 1951 the Minister of State, Mr Kenneth Younger, informed the House of Commons that, while there was no change in the policy of extending diplomatic recognition to the Chinese People's Government, the British Government considered that the question of the representation of that Government in the United Nations should be postponed for the time being.[34] This still appears to be the official British view.

Strictly speaking, the questions of recognition and representation at the United Nations are quite distinct.[35] Unfortunately, in practice this distinction is apt to become blurred if only because many countries, and especially the United States, consider that a willingness to carry out the obligations of the Charter (which is a qualification required for the admission of a state) should also be required of a

---

[32] In the course of the discussion on an Ecuadorian resolution to this effect the President (Sir Gladwyn Jebb) ruled that the vote on the resolution was procedural, which could not, therefore, be vetoed by a permanent member. His ruling was upheld, despite the strenuous objections of the delegate of Nationalist China, and the resolution was declared adopted (*SCOR*, 5th yr., 507th mtg., 29 Sept. 1950, pp. 4-8).

[33] ibid. 519th mtg., p. 16.

[34] H. C. Deb., vol. 488, coll. *159-60* (Written Answers). The United Kingdom representative on the General Assembly's Credentials Committee stated, however, that Britain's willingness to postpone discussions on the question implied neither recognition of the Chinese Nationalist Administration nor acceptance of the right of this Administration to represent China at the United Nations.

[35] See Secretary-General's memorandum on the legal aspects of representation in the United Nations, 8 Mar. 1950, *SCOR*, 5th yr., suppl. for Jan.-May 1950, S/1466.

government for accreditation. In Britain's view, however, just as recognition of another government implies no approval, either moral or political, of that government but is merely recognition of a fact, so a government's right to represent a state in the United Nations is merely a consequence of that fact. Similarly, recognition of that right in no way implies approval of the character or conduct of the government. Thus, at the nineteenth meeting of the *Ad Hoc* Political Committee on 23 November 1950, Britain submitted a draft resolution, which recommended that

> where the question of the representation of a Member State arises in consequence of internal processes or changes which have taken place in that State the right of a government to represent the Member State concerned in the United Nations should be recognized if that government exercises effective control and authority over all or nearly all the national territory, and has the obedience of the bulk of the population of that territory, in such a way that this control, authority and obedience appear to be of a permanent character.[36]

These views were not shared, however, by a majority of members of the *Ad Hoc* Political Committee, and the General Assembly could do no more than try to secure some measure of uniformity in the practice of United Nations bodies by recommending that 'the attitude adopted by the General Assembly or its Interim Committee concerning any such question should be taken into account in other organs of the United Nations and its specialized agencies'.[37]

Many delegates have evidently considered that the conduct of an applicant for accreditation has a direct bearing on the strength of its application and have felt most strongly that Communist China should not be allowed to 'shoot its way into the United Nations'. Yet it is, to say the least, an anomaly that China is still

---

[36] *GAOR*, 5th sess., Annexes, agenda item 61, p. 6.

[37] ibid. 5th sess., suppl. no. 20, Resolution 396(V), 14 Dec. 1950; for a summary of the preceding discussion in the *Ad Hoc* Political Committee see *Repertory of United Nations Practice*, i. 269-72.

represented in the United Nations not by the Government that exercises effective control over almost the whole of the national territory but by a Government which is in control of only a tiny fragment of that territory,[38] which is totally devoid of any control over the actions and policies of the state it purports to represent, and which is, therefore, incapable of implementing any recommendations which the United Nations or any of the specialized agencies may make. Nor is this all. In January 1954 Sir Gladwyn Jebb (then permanent United Kingdom delegate to the United Nations) contended that the absence of the effective Government of China

> imposes a considerable strain upon the Organization. The difficulty of negotiating with such a power outside the United Nations is indeed only too apparent at the present time, when we are trying to build something more solid on the basis of the existing armistice agreement. It could indeed even be argued with some force that had the Government of Peking been represented in the United Nations at the beginning of 1950, the North Korean aggression might never have occurred at all.[39]

Mr (now Sir Gerald) Fitzmaurice has also recorded his view that 'had the Peking Government been permitted to occupy China's seat in the summer of 1950, and to be present in the Assembly the same autumn, Chinese intervention in Korea in November 1950 might have been wholly averted.'[40] If the United Nations' chief task is to serve as a centre for 'harmonizing the actions of nations',[41] the *main* test for accreditation should be the representative character of an applicant rather than whether its conduct is in strict accord with the Purposes and Principles of the Charter, which, it may be remarked, is a test that not all existing members would pass successfully. If the United Nations is to be representative of the

---

[38] Even assuming that Formosa is part of China (but see note, p. 120).

[39] In a speech at Johns Hopkins University on 13 Jan. 1954. For text see Central Office of Information, appendix 1 to *International Survey*, no. 145, 28 Jan. 1954.

[40] *YBWA, 1952*, p. 50.

[41] Art. 1(4) of the Charter.

society of states and not merely a club for the like-minded, there is little to be said for continuing to exclude the People's Republic of China from the United Nations.

THE KOREAN WAR

In Britain the most common view of United Nations action in Korea is that, despite its obvious imperfections, it was an encouraging vindication of the principle of collective resistance to aggression which acted as a real deterrent to similar aggression elsewhere, and that the area of armed conflict might have spread had not United States action been taken within the framework of the United Nations. On the other hand, a not inconsiderable minority have claimed that in Korea the West became involved, through the United Nations, in a major war over an area of minor strategic significance, and that in attempting to unify the whole of Korea the United Nations made Chinese intervention inevitable and so drove Communist China irretrievably into the Soviet Union's arms. Adequately to assess the validity of either point of view would require, however, a far more detailed study of the Korean War than is possible in a single chapter.[42]

Before 25 June 1950 Britain's direct interest in Korea was small and she confined herself to general support of the American position in the impasse which resulted in the *de facto* division of Korea along the 38th parallel. When, in September 1947, the United States Government laid the Korean question before the General Assembly, the United Kingdom supported the General Assembly resolution of 14 November 1947[43] which, *inter alia*, established a United Nations Temporary Commission on Korea (UNTCOK),

---

[42] For a brief but informative study of the Korean War see Guy Wint, *What Happened in Korea* (London, Batchworth Press, 1954). United Nations decisions are examined more critically by Marc Frankenstein, *L'Organisation des Nations Unies devant le conflit coréen* (Paris, Pedone, 1952).

[43] *GAOR*, 2nd sess., Resolution 112(II).

and the resolution of the Interim Committee of February 1948, authorizing UNTCOK to proceed with its work in such parts of Korea as were accessible to it, which meant in effect the holding of elections in South Korea only. Both Canada and Australia, which were represented on the Commission, opposed this decision,[44] but Britain was content to follow the American lead. On 12 December 1948 the Temporary Commission was replaced by the United Nations Commission on Korea (UNCOK).[45] On 18 January 1949 Great Britain recognized the South Korean Government established by the previous year's elections, and appointed a chargé d'affaires in Seoul, its capital.

From 1947 until 1950 the United States seems to have regarded Korea as strategically expendable; this view was reflected, for instance, in the passage in the Secretary of State's (Mr Acheson) statement of 12 January 1950 to the National Press Club which implied that Korea as well as Formosa was outside the perimeter of the American line of defence in the Pacific, and that it would have to rely for its defence upon its own efforts backed by 'the commitments of the entire civilized world under the Charter of the United Nations'.[46] As late as May 1950 Senator Connally, Chairman of the Senate Foreign Relations Committee, implied that Korea was of little strategic importance to the United States.[47] Nevertheless, when they crossed the 38th parallel in the early hours of the morning of 25 June 1950, the North Koreans were not only committing a clear act of aggression but they were assailing a Government which had been sponsored by the United Nations.

---

[44] A/AC. 18/SR. 7, 28 Feb. 1948.

[45] *GAOR*, 3rd sess., Resolution 195(III).

[46] RIIA, *Documents, 1949-50*, pp. 103-4. On 2 November 1952 President Truman made public a memorandum of the Joint Chiefs of Staff of 26 November 1947 expressing the view that the United States had 'little strategic interest in maintaining' the existing 'troops and bases in Korea'.

[47] See report of an interview with Senator Connally in *Christian Science Monitor*, 2 May 1950.

The events of the next few days can only be summarized very briefly.[48] On receipt of reports from the United States Ambassador in Korea and from UNCOK that North Korean forces had launched attacks in strength along the 38th parallel, the Security Council (less the Soviet member who had walked out earlier in the year) met, at the United States request, in the afternoon of Sunday, 25 June, and passed a resolution calling, *inter alia*, for the immediate cessation of hostilities and the withdrawal of North Korean armed forces to the 38th parallel. All United Nations Members were, in addition, called upon to render every assistance to the United Nations in the execution of the resolution and to refrain from giving assistance to the North Korean authorities.[49] The resolution was adopted by a vote of 9 (China, Cuba, Ecuador, Egypt, France, India, Norway, the United Kingdom, and the United States) in favour, none against, with 1 abstention (Yugoslavia) and 1 absent (Soviet Union). The next day a further telegram from UNCOK was received which is worth quoting in full:

> North Korean advances have created dangerous situation with possibilities of rapid deterioration. Impossible [to] estimate situation which will exist tomorrow in Seoul. In view [of] Commission's past experience and existing situation Commission [is] convinced [that] North Korea will not heed Council resolution nor accept UNCOK good offices. Suggest have Council give consideration [to] either invit[ing] both parties [to] agree on neutral mediator to negotiate peace or requesting Member Governments undertake immediate mediation. Commission decided [to] stand by in Seoul. Danger is that critical operations now in progress may end in matter of days and question of cease fire and withdrawal [of] North

---

[48] For a more detailed account of these events see RIIA, *Survey, 1949-50*, pp. 466-515. The main documents are conveniently brought together in Cmd. 8078 [Korea No. 1 (1950)], *Summary of Events relating to Korea;* and Cmd. 8366 [Korea No. 2 (1951)], *Further Summary of Events relating to Korea, October 1950 to May 1951.*

[49] *SCOR*, 5th yr., 473rd mtg., 25 June 1950, pp. 7-8.

Korean forces suggested [in] Council resolution prove academic.[50]

In another message the same day (26 June 1950), UNCOK reported that it had considered the latest reports on hostilities and the results of direct observation along the 38th parallel by its military observers over a period ending forty-eight hours before hostilities began:

> [The] Commission's present view on [the] basis [of] this evidence is first that, judging from actual progress of operations, [the] Northern Regime is carrying out [a] well-planned, concerted and full-scale invasion of South Korea; secondly, that South Korean forces were deployed on [a] wholly defensive basis in all sectors of the parallel; and thirdly, that they were taken completely by surprise as they had no reason to believe from intelligence sources that invasion was imminent.[51]

From these and other reports it was abundantly clear by Tuesday morning (27 June 1950) that South Korea was in grave danger of succumbing to the invaders if assistance were not immediately forthcoming. At noon, therefore, President Truman announced that the United States would not only furnish arms and other aid to the South Koreans, as had been decided on the 25th, but that United States air and sea forces had been ordered to give the South Korean Government troops cover and support.[52] A few hours later the United States delegate informed the Security Council of this decision. The Council thereupon endorsed it and recommended that Members of the United Nations 'furnish such assistance to the Republic of Korea as may be necessary to repel the armed attack and to restore international peace and security in the area'. The resolution embodying this recommendation was adopted by 7 votes

---

[50] S/1503. See *SCOR*, 5th yr., 474th mtg., 27 June 1950, p. 2.

[51] S/1507. ibid.

[52] He also announced that the United States navy would 'neutralize' Formosa.

(China, Cuba, Ecuador, France, Norway, the United Kingdom, and the United States) with 1 abstention (Yugoslavia), 1 absent (Soviet Union), and 2 not voting (Egypt and India).[53] Three days later, on 30 June, President Truman announced that the United States would send ground forces to support the South Koreans and that the United States navy would blockade the Korean coast. On 7 July the Council, by a vote of seven to none, with three abstentions (Egypt, India, Yugoslavia) adopted a resolution proposed jointly by Britain and France, welcoming the prompt and vigorous support which governments and peoples of the United Nations had given to its resolutions of 25 and 27 June. The resolution[54] recommended that all Members providing military forces and other assistance pursuant to these resolutions should make such forces and other assistance available to a Unified Command under the United States; requested the United States to designate the commander of such forces; authorized the Unified Command at its discretion to use the United Nations flag in the course of operations against North Korean forces concurrently with the flags of the various nations participating; and requested the United States to provide the Security Council with reports on the course of action taken under the Unified Command. On 14 July 1950 the Secretary-General stated that he had received favourable replies from fifty-two countries (other than the United States) to the Security Council resolution of 27 June 1950.

The British Government was convinced that the North Korean invasion constituted an unmistakable case for United Nations

---

53 *SCOR*, 5th yr., 474th mtg., 27 June 1950, p. 4. At the 475th meeting, on 30 June 1950, the representative of Egypt, who had not participated in the voting, stated that had he received instructions in time, he would have abstained. The President, speaking as the representative of India, who also had not participated in the voting, informed the Council that his Government had accepted the resolution. By cablegram (S/1517) dated 29 June 1950, the Soviet Union stated that the resolution of 27 June had no legal force since it had been passed in the absence of two permanent Members, the Soviet Union and China, the latter not having been duly represented.

54 S/1588. See *GAOR*, 5th sess., suppl. no. 2, pp. 25-26.

action; if this armed Communist aggression were not resisted, similar aggression elsewhere would be encouraged. But it was also evident that the extent of that action would depend upon the response of the United States and that Britain would be unable to undertake any commitments in Korea unless the United States were willing to do so. In addition, from the British point of view (as no doubt from the American also) the desire to uphold the authority of the United Nations was reinforced by the determination to avoid the disintegration of the Western defensive system initiated only the previous year in the North Atlantic Treaty, and by a realization of the need to demonstrate to the free world generally that they could count upon external help in the event of Communist aggression. Yet even if these latter reasons had been thought sufficient to call for intervention irrespective of the existence of the United Nations, intervention might not have been possible. The experience of the inter-war years had driven home the lesson that even if the national interest required that aggression should be met by force, a democratic government might be hamstrung if public opinion were hesitant. It was only after a 'toughening-up course' of experience of successive German aggressions that opinion in Britain hardened sufficiently to rally united opposition to further appeasement of Germany. The United Nations' connexion in Korea provided, in a sense, a substitute for this experience, for the North Korean aggression seemed to strike at the whole basis of the United Nations, the preservation of which commanded the support of all parties in a way that the League had never done. Moreover, without the United Nations' connexion the Commonwealth would probably not have displayed its striking initial unity of view; and any backsliding within the first few days might well have been an additional reason for caution on Britain's part, as in 1938. The risk of the conflict spreading was not overlooked, but there was a widespread feeling that if this direct challenge to the United Nations were ignored, 'the United Nations would set their Organization on the ruinous slippery slope, down which the League of Nations ha d

k

slid after the Japanese invasion of Manchuria in 1931'.[55] And most people in Britain were prepared to take action in the name of the United Nations which they might have shied away from if it had been represented as merely part of a policy of containment. Of course, this is not the whole story. The flagrancy of the attack; the fear that if it were successful morale in Japan, and possibly in South East Asia also, might collapse; the misgivings that, if the United Kingdom did not co-operate whole-heartedly in Korea, American commitments under NATO might come to be questioned; all these helped to commend intervention to Britain. But the belief that the future of the United Nations was at stake seems to have been of no less importance. That the fear of the United Nations sharing the fate of the League was part of a necessary moral framework of action by Britain was indeed illustrated by her refusal to support that element in United States policy which was not endorsed by the United Nations, namely the neutralization of Formosa. On the contrary, the British Government on a number of occasions specifically dissociated itself from this policy.

It is, of course, the case that had there not been an American strategic reserve near at hand in Japan, the United Nations would have lacked a secular arm, while had the Soviet Union not been absent and had China not been represented by a rump Nationalist Government, it might have been difficult to represent the collective action in support of South Korea as a United Nations operation.[56] As will be seen in a later chapter,[57] the 'Uniting for Peace' machinery set up in November 1950 was designed to meet situations in which the Security Council may not be favoured by such good fortune. This anomalous situation provided the basis for some rather legalistic charges which were levied—and not by Communists or fellow-travellers only—against the validity of United Nations action.

---

[55] RIIA, *Survey, 1949-50*, p. 483, where a further discussion of these considerations is given.

[56] Although action could quite legitimately have been taken under Art. 51.

[57] Chapter 8.

Four main charges were cited: (1) that the Security Council's decisions were invalid because of the Soviet Union's absence and the non-representation of Communist China; (2) that South Korea was the aggressor; (3) that the war was a civil war in which the United Nations had no right to intervene; and (4) that the United States had 'jumped the gun' by the President's commital of American naval and air forces a few hours *before* the Security Council's resolution of 27 June. The British Prime Minister (Mr Attlee), in condemning the North Korean aggression in the House of Commons on 5 July,[58] combated the first charge by pointing out that the practice of not counting abstentions as negative votes had been accepted by the Soviet Union; if

> a member of the Security Council, and in particular a permanent member, chooses to refrain from exercising its right of voting, not by failing to vote when present, but by refraining from attending the meeting at all, that member must be regarded as having deliberately abstained from voting.[59]

Furthermore, the right of the Chinese Nationalist Administration to represent China had been endorsed by a majority of members of the Council. Though the United Kingdom dissented from this view, she recognized that the majority decision was perfectly valid. The second charge, that South Korea was the aggressor, was refuted by the reports of the United Nations Commission on Korea, and especially by the fully considered report submitted to the General Assembly in September 1950 in which the Commission said:

> The invasion of the territory of the Republic of Korea by the armed forces of the North Korean authorities, which began on 25 June 1950, was an act of aggression initiated without warning and without provocation, in execution of a carefully prepared plan. This plan of aggression, it is now clear, was an essential part of the policy of the North Korean

---

[58] When a motion supporting the Government's decision to support the United Nations and applauding American action was carried without a division.

[59] H. C. Deb., vol. 477, col. 489. See also Goodrich and Hambro, p. 223.

authorities, the object of which was to secure control over the whole of Korea.[60]

Of course, the sporadic skirmishing on each side of the 38th parallel which had taken place for many months certainly contributed to the outbreak of war; and there were no doubt those in South Korea who would willingly have attempted to subdue North Korea if they had had the power to do so. But, despite the imprudent utterances of some of their countrymen, the American authorities had denied the South Koreans the arms without which they could not seriously contemplate launching a war and had warned them that if they did so all military and economic aid from the United States would cease. The very considerable body of evidence that is now available points almost conclusively to the fact that a premeditated act of aggression was committed by North Korea on 25 June 1950. Whether or not the Soviet Union knew in advance of the North Korean intention to attack, either in general or on a particular day, it is as yet impossible to say.[61]

The third charge, that it was a civil not an international war, had an element of truth in it. Nevertheless, North Korea and South Korea were organized as separate states and both had applied for membership of the United Nations; there were in fact two quite distinct legal personalities on each side of the 38th parallel, one of which—South Korea—had been nurtured by the United Nations. The fourth charge, that the United States 'jumped the gun', again had some substance. But a perfectly legitimate basis for United States action was to be found in the paragraphs of the resolution of 25 June 1950 calling upon all Members of the United Nations to render every assistance to the United Nations in securing the immediate cessation of hostilities and the withdrawal of North Korean armed forces, and in Article 51 of the Charter. In fact Article 51 had been inserted at San Francisco partly to make quite

---

60 *GAOR*, 5th sess., suppl. no. 16 (A/1350), p. 32.
61 Max Beloff, *Soviet Policy in the Far East, 1944-51* (London, OUP for RIIA, 1953), p. 183.

explicit the inherent right of Members to go to the aid of a victim of aggression pending action by the Security Council;[62] and, as Mr Attlee said in the House on 5 July,

> It is true that Article 51 only mentions in this connection an armed attack against a member of the United Nations, and the Korean Republic is not a member. But the purpose of Article 51 is not to create a new right but merely to make it clear that an inherent right vested in every State is not prejudiced.[63]

The case against the legal basis of United Nations action was, therefore, rather thin. Few in Britain today doubt that the United States response was in conformity with the Purposes and Principles of the Charter, and that had President Truman not acted so resolutely, South Korea would quickly have been subjugated and the United Nations would have gone the way of the League.

In the early period of the Korean War no substantial difference of view arose between Britain and the United States, apart from American 'neutralization' of Formosa which continued to be regarded rather askance by Britain. Britain perhaps showed more eagerness to seek a negotiated settlement than the United States and made representations to this effect in Moscow and Peking, but she dispatched considerable naval, and (later) ground forces to the area and was the joint sponsor with France of the Security Council's resolution of 7 July providing for the Unified Command in Korea. Britain was also among the sponsors of the General Assembly's resolution of 7 October, which looked to the establishment of a 'unified, independent and democratic government' for the whole of Korea and set up a seven-Power Commission for the Unification and Rehabilitation of Korea to give effect to this plan.[64]

---

[62] See above, p. 32-33.

[63] H. C. Deb., vol. 477, col. 492.

[64] *GAOR*, 5th sess., suppl. no. 20, Resolution 376(V). The members of the Commission were Australia, Chile, Netherlands, Pakistan, Philippines, Thailand, and Turkey.

The references to the reunification of Korea did not add anything to earlier resolutions; for the most part they were no more than a logical development of previous United Nations policy. But they did appear to give tacit assent to the case that was currently being made out for the crossing of the 38th parallel by the now victorious United Nations forces.

The wisdom of crossing the parallel was questioned in some circles in Britain. The United Nations victories had secured the independence of South Korea and the withdrawal of North Korean forces. The prime aim now should be to negotiate a settlement lest hostilities spread outside Korea. The risk that they might do so was made more real by the Chinese Foreign Minister's statement on 30 September that China 'cannot remain indifferent to the fate of its neighbours'[65] and by the warning conveyed to the Indian Ambassador in Peking that if American forces crossed the 38th parallel 'China would be forced to intervene'.[66] Those in favour of crossing the parallel regarded these warnings as mere bluff, however, and argued that a decision to halt on a line of no strategic (or economic) importance would prevent the total destruction of the North Korean forces which seemed imminent. To leave these forces intact and Korea divided was to leave a transgressor unpunished and to invite renewed aggression when the North Korean forces had recovered. These latter views prevailed with the British Government, as they did with President Truman. Indeed, although certain sections of British opinion have sometimes claimed the virtue of foresight, there is little evidence either of any marked hesitation on the part of the British Government about crossing the parallel or that they were much attracted by proposals for stopping slightly north of the 38th parallel at the so-called 'waistline'. On the contrary, on 29 September Mr Bevin expressed the view that the time had come to unify Korea.[67] At Lake Success the political implications

[65] Beloff, *Soviet Policy in the Far East*, p. 193.
[66] K. M. Panikkar, *In Two Chinas* (London, Allen & Unwin, 1955), p. 110.
[67] *New York Herald Tribune*, 30 Sept. 1950.

of crossing the parallel seem to have received very little consideration until a few days before the event, and even then it was only too evident that the crucial decisions were being taken in Tokyo or in Washington. Consequently, on 9 October United Nations troops crossed the parallel and, in spite of a further warning from the Chinese Government, they continued to advance northwards. On 5 November General MacArthur reported contact with Chinese forces. Various attempts were made to reassure the Chinese Government of the United Nations limited objectives in Korea,[68] and for a time the inactivity of Chinese forces encouraged hopes that their intervention would be limited. However, on 24 November United Nations forces began a new forward movement which precipitated a violent Chinese counter-offensive.

In supporting United Nations policy for the unification of Korea, if necessary by force, Britain jeopardized her policy in respect of China—which was to establish peaceful relations with the new régime in Peking and to further its admission to the United Nations. Moreover, the massive Chinese intervention on 24 November now changed the whole character of the war. Instead of being a collective operation under the aegis of the United Nations to discipline a single unruly but relatively weak aggressor, it became a conflict between two major Powers which threatened to touch off a third world war. In response to this new situation, the major preoccupation of the British Government became to endeavour to promote a peaceful settlement. From then on Britain tried to conciliate and reassure Peking and to add her weight to those elements in Washington and at the United Nations who were opposed to any extension of the war to Chinese territory. Britain, like many in the Pentagon, would have regarded such an extension as provoking the wrong war, in the wrong place, with the wrong enemy. Also, in addition to fears that United Nations (and, of course, especially United States) forces might become involved in Asia on such a

---

[68] See Cmd. 8366, para. 4.

scale as to facilitate Soviet designs in Europe, there were growing doubts about the moral basis of such a war. After Chinese intervention public opinion became steadily more dubious about the rights and wrongs of the conflict. Consequently, as 1950 approached its end, there was almost undivided support for the British Government in its firm opposition to the bombing of Manchurian bases or to the use of atomic weapons. The visit of the Prime Minister (Mr Attlee) to Washington in December 1950 marked the peak of British anxiety in this respect. Unhappily, the subsequent restraint shown by United Nations forces and the efforts to convince the Chinese Government that no harm was intended to its legitimate interests proved of no avail, and the British Government had reluctantly to agree that the Chinese conditions for a withdrawal of their forces, which they put forward on 28 November 1950 and 17 January 1951, could not be accepted as they stood.

Here agreement ended. A discouraging but not wholly negative Chinese reply to the three-man Cease-Fire Group's proposals for a cease-fire led the United States to put forward on 20 January 1951 a draft resolution stating that the Central People's Government had engaged in aggression in Korea and requesting a committee composed of members of the Collective Measures Committee to consider additional measures to meet this aggression. Britain did not support this resolution. On 23 January Mr Attlee told the House of Commons: 'We have not lost hope of a negotiated settlement of the Korean war . . . . We are, therefore, of the opinion that the United Nations should not at this stage take a new and important decision.'[69] At Lake Success on 25 January the United Kingdom delegate (Sir Gladwyn Jebb) agreed that China should be condemned for supporting the aggressor in Korea, but he declared that a punitive policy might well prove to be a remedy worse than the disease and urged that further efforts should be made to reach

---

[69] H. C. Deb., vol. 483, col. 41.

a settlement.[70] In spite, however, of the Indian delegate's (Sir Benegal Rau) warning that his Government had been informed that the adoption of a resolution branding China as an aggressor would remove all hope of further negotiation,[71] and in spite of a not wholly negative response from Peking to proposals presented by the Cease-Fire Group and the reported acceptance by Peking of proposals by twelve Asian and Arab countries as a basis for a peaceful settlement,[72] a slightly weakened version of the original American resolution was adopted by the General Assembly[73] on 1 February 1951 by 44 votes to 7 (Soviet bloc, India, and Burma) with 9 abstentions (Afghanistan, Egypt, Indonesia, Pakistan, Saudi Arabia, Sweden, Syria, Yemen, Yugoslavia).[74] This resolution found that the Central People's Government had engaged in aggression in Korea, but it reaffirmed the desire of the United Nations to attain its objectives in Korea by peaceful means and provided for the setting up of a Good Offices Committee for that purpose, which should try its hand before a committee to study additional measures to meet Chinese aggression reported. Britain supported the resolution (which she had successfully tried to soften) with very considerable misgivings and only on the understanding that in future the emphasis should be on negotiations with China and not on sanctions against her, which, Sir Gladwyn Jebb claimed, would only be 'dangerous, double-edged, or merely useless'.[75] On

---

[70] *GAOR*, 5th sess., 1st Committee, 431st mtg., *SR*, pp. 544-47; the texts of the speeches on this issue by Sir Gladwyn Jebb between 18 January and 1 February 1951 and of the statement by the Prime Minister in the House of Commons on 1 February 1951 are given in Cmd. 8159.

[71] *GAOR*, 5th sess., 1st Committee, 435th mtg., *SR*, pp. 579-80.

[72] For a convenient summary of these interchanges see Cmd. 8366, p. 11; also Panikkar, *In Two Chinas*, pp. 120-24.

[73] On 31 January the Security Council, at the instance of the United Kingdom, removed from its agenda the 'Complaint of Aggression against the Republic of Korea', the retention of which might, under Art. 12(1) of the Charter, have cast doubts on the competence of the General Assembly to make recommendations on the subject.

[74] *GAOR*, 5th sess., suppl. no. 20A, Resolution 498(V).

[75] ibid. 5th sess., Plen., 327th mtg., 1 Feb. 1951, p. 692.

12 February Mr Attlee declared, in the course of a debate in the House of Commons on foreign affairs, that although British policy was to vindicate the authority of the United Nations, it was also desired to bring the hostilities to an end as soon as possible and to confine the fighting as narrowly as possible. 'We did not think', he added, 'that a motion condemning China as an aggressor and calling for sanctions was likely to promote the object we had in view'.[76] Later in the same debate the Minister of State (Mr Younger) told the House 'we see no alternative to a negotiated peace in the Far East, which would not be a disaster both for China and for ourselves'.[77] But by then the damage was done. Admittedly some of the sting had been taken out of the resolution, but it was still regarded by Peking as 'illegal, slanderous, null and void' and 'an insult to the Chinese people';[78] for the time being its adoption by the Assembly effectively put an end to any hope of a negotiated settlement.

Although watered-down, the resolution only papered over very thinly a deep-seated rift between the United States and Britain, which was indicative of a fundamentally different approach to the part to be played by the United Nations. On the British side the need for collective action to resist aggression was generally accepted, but most people were also convinced that the United Nations should do its utmost to reach a negotiated settlement with China. Moral issues could not be disregarded, but the United Nations should proceed not 'by the method of penalties' but 'by that of attempted reform'.[79] Once aggression had been defeated, reconciliation rather than retribution should be the aim. Naturally, opinion was not unanimous, but there was far less support for the

---

[76] H. C. Deb., vol. 484, coll. 59-63.

[77] ibid. col. 153.

[78] RIIA, *Documents, 1951*, pp. 548-51.

[79] United Kingdom delegate (Sir Gladwyn Jebb), *GAOR*, 5th sess., 1st Committee, 431st mtg., 25 Jan. 1951, *SR*, p. 546.

contrasting view, so prevalent in the United States, that the prime need of international society was to rebuild standards of international morality. Had not the United Nations been set up for that specific purpose and to assert the sanctity of treaties? If every violation—as Chinese aggression clearly was—was to pass uncondemned, how was respect for such morality to be promoted? The aggressor should be punished and the risks involved were merely part of the growing pains in the development of a true comity of nations in which the rule of law would prevail. On the domestic level a violator of the law was branded as a criminal and brought to justice; the same treatment should now be meted out to China—whatever the cost. The realization that the United Nations effort in Korea rested so heavily on American power and the anxiety lest United States policy in Europe might be adversely affected by any apparent back-sliding on the part of her allies in Korea no doubt induced the United Kingdom to defer, in the last resort, to the American point of view. But to some at least there seemed for a time to be little to choose between Chinese truculence and American inflexibility. Only as America's difficulties with President Syngman Rhee came to be better appreciated and the hollowness of Chinese germ warfare charges[80] was exposed did opinion in Britain come to sympathize more fully with United States policy. The process was fairly effectively completed by the later exposure of Chinese 'brain-washing' methods.

The most acute phase of British anxiety over American policy ended with the recall of General MacArthur on 11 April 1951 and the subsequent victory of the American school of thought that adhered to the policy of 'limited objectives'. However, on other matters, for example, Formosa and Chinese representation, American policy stiffened when overtures to Peking for a cease-fire continued to be rebuffed. On the eve of Mr Malik's proposal, on 23 June 1951,

---

[80] For a refutation of the charges see speech by the Minister of State (Mr Selwyn Lloyd), *GAOR*, 8th sess., 1st Committee, 649th mtg., 6 Nov. 1953, *SR* pp. 119-20; also Wint, *What Happened in Korea*, pp. 83-98.

for an armistice in Korea,[81] Washington and London were agreed
on no immediate extension of the war; on which of the two claimants
were to be regarded as the legitimate Government of China they
were as far apart as ever, but they were ready to leave the question
in abeyance for the time being. On economic matters Britain was
adamantly opposed to American suggestions for a blockade of the
Chinese coast, and she was not prepared to follow the American
example in imposing a complete embargo upon trade with China,
not so much on account of the value of the trade itself, but because
of the repercussions such a step would have upon Hong Kong,
and because it was feared that this Wilsonian desire to excommunicate
a pronounced evil-doer by a total embargo—a view then fashionable
in the United States—might prejudice the chances of reaching a
reasonable settlement with China.[82] But exports to China of
'strategic' materials were stopped immediately after the outbreak
of the Korean conflict, and exports of rubber, which had not
hitherto been listed as a 'strategic' commodity, were halted in
May 1951. Britain also supported an American draft resolution
of 7 May 1951 (submitted to the Additional Measures Committee),[83]
proposing an embargo on shipments to China and North Korea
of all commodities of military or 'strategic' importance. This was
accepted by the General Assembly on 18 May 1951.[84]

The advent to office of the Conservative Government under
Mr Churchill in November 1951 did not produce any substantial
change in British policy, the basis of which continued to be the
determination to avert an all-out war with China, and the desire
to avoid a serious rupture with the United States. The Left might
attach rather more importance to the former and the Right to the

---

[81] RIIA, *Survey, 1951*, p. 440.

[82] See statements by the President of the Board of Trade (Sir Hartley Shawcross)
on 7 and 10 May 1951 (H. C. Deb., vol. 487, coll. 1589-93 and 2170-88).

[83] Set up by the resolution of 1 Feb. 1951 with the same membership as the
Collective Measures Committee, though Yugoslavia and Burma refused to serve.

[84] *GAOR*, 5th sess., suppl. no. 20A, Resolution 500(V).

latter, but the prime aim, since Chinese intervention, of what was substantially a bipartisan policy was to fend off a situation in which it might become necessary to choose between the two. Thus the British Government continued firmly to oppose the imposition either of military sanctions or of a blockade[85] upon China. During the prolonged truce negotiations Britain supported the United States in upholding the principle that prisoners of war should not be forcibly repatriated, both because the repatriation of prisoners against their will was felt to be deeply repugnant and because of the risk that to yield to the Communist demand might be to discourage mass desertions from Communist forces in any future conflict.[86] But Britain warmly welcomed, and played a prominent supporting role in, Indian efforts to secure a compromise which would preserve the principle but be acceptable to the Chinese. Indeed, throughout these and later negotiations the British Government adopted a more sympathetic attitude towards Indian views and India's policy of non-alignment (if only in the hope that India's influence in Peking might be enhanced thereby) than did the United States, where the alleged ambivalence of India's attitude over Korea and her criticisms of American policy towards Communist China were construed as evidence of unrealism or even of sympathy for the Communist cause.

The abandonment by the Soviet Union and China, shortly after the death of Stalin on 5 March 1953, of their insistence on the forcible repatriation of prisoners was welcomed by the British Government as a 'most significant deed' which justified 'cautious optimism' on the possibility of Great Power co-operation. In the Armistice Agreement signed at Panmunjom on 27 July 1953[87] (shortly after the failure of a major Chinese offensive), provision was made for the immediate repatriation of those who desired it,

---

[85] See statements by the Foreign Secretary (Mr Eden) on 5 and 16 Feb. 1953 (H. C. Deb., vol. 510, col. 2062 and vol. 511, col. 874).

[86] See Wint, *What Happened in Korea*, pp. 72-83.

[87] S/3079, 7 Aug. 1953; or Cmd. 8938.

and for the handing over of all others to a Neutral Nations Repatriation Commission,[88] under whose guidance 'explanations' extolling the benefits of repatriation were to be given within a specified time-limit by representatives of the nations to which the prisoners belonged. The disposition of those refusing repatriation was to be decided by a political conference to be held within three months of the signing of the armistice; but, as the Indian commander of the custodian force (General Thimayya) put it, the explanations 'went agley', and no agreement on the political conference was reached. Out of some 23,000 prisoners in the hands of the Repatriation Commission only some 350 exchanged the custody of their Indian guards for that of the Communists. The remainder were handed back to the United Nations command on 20 January 1954 and released by them three days later.[89]

In the discussion at the United Nations on the arrangements for the political conference to settle 'the questions of the withdrawal of all foreign forces from Korea, the peaceful settlement of the Korean question, etc.',[90] Britain did not share the American desire to confine it to representatives of the two contending sides. In the British view the conference should not be an occasion for some straight talking across the table at the 'aggressors' but a round-table conference for the purpose of reaching a negotiated settlement not only on purely Korean issues but on other questions affecting the Far East generally; therefore membership should be extended to allow room for mediation by 'neutral' Powers like India. Consequently, when the reconvened seventh General Assembly met in August 1953, Britain supported a resolution for the participation

---

[88] Sweden, Switzerland, Poland, Czechoslovakia, and India. The Chairman (with a casting vote) and the custodian force were provided by India.

[89] Previously the United Nations had handed back 75,000 North Koreans and nearly 6,000 Chinese who had opted for immediate repatriation. Some 27,000 North Koreans were also released without warning by the South Korean Government on 18 June 1953 and were quickly assimilated by the South Korean people.

[90] Korean Armistice Agreement, Art. IV(S/3079 and Cmd. 8938).

in the political conference of the Soviet Union, and (with Canada, Australia, and New Zealand) pressed unsuccessfully against American opposition a motion to invite India to the conference.[91]

The Geneva Conference of Foreign Ministers on Korea and Indo-China (27 April-15 June 1954), though held at the Palais des Nations and serviced by the United Nations Secretariat, retained only a rather tenuous link with the United Nations and so falls outside the scope of this study. At the conference Communist claims that the United Nations had acted illegally in Korea and that it had lost its moral competence to deal with the Korean question, especially with the question of all-Korean elections, were firmly rejected by the sixteen countries whose forces had fought under the United Nations flag.[92] To have acquiesced in the Communist claim would have been to deprive their effort of a great deal of its significance. Similarly, to have entrusted Korean elections to the supervision of a so-called Neutral Nations Supervisory Commission (especially if half of its members were to consist of Communist Powers), whilst giving an all-Korean Commission (in which North Korea would be represented on equal terms with South Korea) primary responsibility for their preparation and organization, would have been to guarantee deadlock and to ensure that the 'elections would never be held, or that they would not be free'.[93] The Neutral Nations Supervisory Commission (consisting of Czechoslovakia, Poland, Sweden, and Switzerland) had attempted to perform a somewhat similar function under the Korean Armistice. Its task was to control and report on all military movements on both sides and to prevent any build-up of military strength. In practice its activities were so curtailed by both the North and the South

---

[91] When it appeared that the proposal would not quite receive the necessary two-thirds majority, it was withdrawn on India's request.

[92] Australia, Belgium, Canada, Colombia, Ethiopia, France, Greece, Luxembourg, Netherlands, New Zealand, Philippines, South Africa, Thailand, Turkey, United Kingdom, United States.

[93] Speech by Mr Eden at the Geneva Conference, 11 June 1954, Cmd. 9186, p. 88.

Korean Governments, and by the singularly unneutral conduct of its Polish and Czech members, that the Commission very soon ceased to serve any useful purpose.[94] The Western Powers were naturally not anxious to repeat this experience. When the conference ended in stalemate they declared[95] that in the negotiations they had been guided by the following two fundamental principles:

> 1. The United Nations, under its Charter, is fully and rightfully empowered to take collective action to repel aggression, to restore peace and security, and to extend its good offices to seeking a peaceful settlement in Korea.
> 2. In order to establish a unified, independent and democratic Korea, genuinely free elections should be held under United Nations supervision, for representatives in the National Assembly, in which representation shall be in direct proportion to the indigenous population in Korea.[96]

During the political and military stalemate that followed the Armistice Agreement, attention turned to the manifold and perplexing problems of bringing relief to the millions of South Korean 'war victims' and of restoring the country's shattered economy. The people of South Korea could not be expected to find much comfort in the defeat of aggression if victory perpetuated the widespread misery and distress which war had brought. After rather a hesitant start, complicated by organizational difficulties and by the not altogether helpful attitude of the South Korean Government, reconstruction work (under the United Nations Korean Reconstruction Agency, UNKRA) started to make fairly rapid progress in 1954-5.[97] The main burden has been borne by the United States,

---

94 'In two years the Republic of Korea Army has doubled in size, and the North Korean Air Force, which was practically non-existent at the time of the armistice, is said to have about 600 aircraft, including 400 jets, operating from about 30 airstrips built or reconditioned since 1953' (*The Times*, 13 Nov. 1955).

95 'Declaration by the Sixteen Nations, June 15, 1954', Cmd. 9186, pp. 100-1.

96 South Korea has a considerably larger population than North Korea.

97 *GAOR*, 10th sess., suppl. no. 18 (A/2936): *Report of the Agent-General of the United Nations Korean Reconstruction Agency for the period 1 Sept. 1954 to 30 June 1955.*

both in the form of direct aid for relief and as a contributor to UNKRA; but as on 30 June 1955 Britain had pledged $28 million to the Agency,[98] while business firms and non-governmental organizations in Britain have been enlisted by the Agency for several of its projects. Although the circle of contributors could have been much wider, this further test of collective action yielded not unimpressive results.[99]

It is too early to write with any confidence of the 'lessons' of the Korean War. These will emerge only gradually in the perspective of history. Yet there are one or two aspects of this first 'war for collective security' which deserve brief mention. It is said, for instance, that as an enforcement agency in Korea, the United Nations did not prove very effective in widening the circle of those willing to share the military burden,[100] despite the fact that so many Members of the United Nations endorsed the initial decision to resist North Korean aggression. Yet is this particularly surprising? In any system of collective resistance to aggression the decision as to when such action shall be taken may be collective, but the main burden is bound to fall on those one or two Powers whose interests are most directly affected and whose armed forces are near at hand. In Korea by far the main burden was borne by South Korea and by the United States, but the role of the forces sent by the other fifteen Members of the United Nations[101] should not be too hastily discounted. Even on military grounds the contribution of, for example, the Com-

---

[98] For a list of country pledges as on 30 June 1955 see ibid. Annex 1, p. 25.

[99] UNKRA's work is described by Sir Arthur Rucker in 'Korea—the Next Stage', *International Affairs*, July 1954.

[100] This view is forcibly expressed by General Mark Clark (who succeeded General Ridgway as Commander-in-Chief of the United Nations forces in Korea) in *From the Danube to the Yalu* (London, Harrap, 1954), pp. 209-17.

[101] Australia, Belgium, Canada, Colombia, Ethiopia, France, Greece, Luxembourg, Netherlands, New Zealand, Philippines, Thailand, Turkey, South Africa, United Kingdom. Medical units were sent by Denmark, India, Italy, Norway, and Sweden. For further details see ibid. p. 211, or *YBUN*, 1950, pp. 226-28. Supplies of various kinds were contributed by a number of other countries, some of which also offered military assistance; for various reasons these offers were not accepted by the Unified Command.

L

monwealth division was far from negligible. And if some countries sent national contingents primarily to ensure American support if they themselves became the victims of aggression, is this not the very essence of the dictum 'hang together or hang separately'? Moreover, the presence of these national contingents and of the United Nations flag, under which they fought, at least gave further substance to the claim that this was in a real sense a United Nations effort and not simply an American-led alliance of *status quo* Powers fighting to contain an expansionist Communist bloc.

The war did show, however, that if collective measures are to be taken in the name of the United Nations, more effective machinery and procedures need to be developed for laying down the broad political principles for the conduct of these measures and for giving continuing political guidance to the military commander. This problem is not peculiar to the United Nations. It is almost bound to face any coalition of sovereign states; NATO continues to be greatly perplexed by it. But if similar measures again become necessary, some attempt will have to be made to guard against the pitfalls which the United Nations encountered at the time of the crossing of the 38th parallel. Although the resolution of 7 October 1950 involved a political decision of great importance, the General Assembly was not kept *au courant* with the course of events, and delegates at Lake Success found it almost impossible to get adequate reports from General MacArthur. Nearly all the important decisions were taken in Tokyo, or between Tokyo and Washington, or, occasionally, between Tokyo, Washington, and London; but very rarely at Lake Success.

It is probably the case that this was not due primarily to defects in the actual machinery of the United Nations. When General Ridgway took over, relations between Lake Success and Tokyo immediately improved. Also, the unique character of United Nations action needs to be remembered. Given that the system envisaged in Article 47 of the Charter had not come into existence, there was no ready-made system of United Nations control; experiment and improvisation were inevitable. Nor is Article 47 ever likely to operate. Yet it is doubtful whether there is any middle way between the full United Nations control envisaged in that article and the arrangements that operated in Korea, whereby a leading Member of the United Nations was asked to assume control on the condition that it accounted regularly to the United Nations on the exercise of that control. But Korean experience suggests that everything possible needs to be done to keep alive the notion of collective responsibility and that there might be some advantage in having any officer appointed to command United Nations forces resign his national command. It might also be desirable for some procedure to be evolved which would limit the operational use of national contingents except with the specific consent of their governments.[102] Unless, however, the national contingents concerned form an appreciable part of the combined force, the problem of securing more effective control of the policies of those Powers on whom the main military responsibility falls will most probably turn chiefly on their sensitivity to the advice proffered by other Members of the United Nations. There is no ready-made prescription for ensuring such sensitivity or, indeed, that the advice is good advice.

It has been contended that the conciliatory functions of the United Nations were weakened by the fact that the Korean War forced it to take sides in the cold war. How could it be expected to act simultaneously as policeman and mediator? Evidently, by acting as a moral authority purporting to pronounce on the rights and wrongs of a dispute and intent on condemning and punishing an aggressor, the United Nations may run the risk of weakening its role as an 'honest broker'; there was in fact too marked an inclination in many quarters to believe that the United Nations purpose

---

[102] For instance, the British naval forces in Japanese waters were placed under American command only for the support of South Korea and not for the defence of Formosa; see reply by Mr Ernest Davies (Under-Secretary of State for Foreign Affairs), 10 July 1950, H. C. Deb., vol. 477, col. 957.

in Korea could only be achieved by the 'unconditional surrender' of the 'criminal' aggressor. As a result, Communist China's refusal to regard 'United Nations' supervision of Korean elections as sufficiently 'neutral' to be acceptable was at least understandable. On the other hand, Korean experience suggests that this duality of function is not incapable of being resolved in an Organization as loosely knit as the United Nations. For instance, India's membership of the United Nations—and her initial support of United Nations action—might have been expected to reduce her ability to mediate successfully. In practice, however, India's leadership at the United Nations of the Arab-Asian bloc may well have strengthened her influence in Peking. Similarly, the United Nations character of the war gave India a *locus standi* in Washington which she probably would otherwise not have enjoyed, while the participation of Indian delegates in discussions at Lake Success gave them an insight into Western policies which, on several occasions, gave greater point to India's representations in Peking. Thus India's ability to secure acceptance of the eventual compromise on the prisoners-of-war question was almost certainly enhanced by her membership of the United Nations.

So far as Britain was concerned, it is arguable that in the later months of the war the United Nations played a significant part in enabling her to avoid choosing between an all-out war with China and a serious rupture with the United States, not only by affording greater scope for mediation but also by strengthening the hands of those intent on limiting the fighting. It is true that the return to limited objectives in Korea, the acceptance of a negotiated peace and of a continuation of the division more or less along the 38th parallel, was imposed chiefly by the fear of extending the war and by the realization that an effort to push the Chinese out of North Korea would have required the commitment of more troops and air power than could safely be spared from other possible theatres of war. Yet United Nations discussions also reinforced the belief that any such attempt might have led to the disintegration of the

Western alliance and to the alienation of nearly all the Arab-Asian Powers. While due regard must be given to the opposition of the American Secretary of Defence and of the Chiefs of Staff to military measures involving Chinese territory, it is open to doubt whether, had action against North Korean aggression been a purely South Korean and American concern, and had the United Nations not existed to point up the dangers of a general conflagration, the area of armed conflict would still have remained confined to Korea. And how long would the United Kingdom have been able to stand aside?

Perhaps the most difficult question of all is the effect of United Nations action in Korea on the overall balance of power between the Western and Communist camps.[103] On the debit side, it is arguable that through the United Nations the West became involved in a far from minor war over an area of minor strategic importance and that the campaign proved an unwelcome drain on the strength of the free world, a source of strain in Anglo-American relations, and an encouragement to neutralism in Asia and elsewhere. And although against Chinese military successes must be set the fact that American forces were fighting, as it were, with one arm tied behind their back, the war did bring the People's Republic of China considerable military prestige and enable it to forge, with Soviet assistance, a modern, self-confident, and well-equipped army which is an important new factor on the Asian scene. Furthermore, although the Sino-Soviet alliance was concluded well before the outbreak of the Korean War (in February 1950), the war helped to consolidate an alliance which might otherwise have been subjected to considerable strain. Above all, it provided Communist China with a strong irredentist grudge against the United States over Formosa and with a legitimate source of grievance over her continued exclusion from the United Nations.

On the credit side, however, United Nations action may have

---

[103] This question is discussed by Coral Bell, 'Korea and the Balance of Power', *Political Quarterly*, Jan.-Mar. 1954.

yielded some slight strategic benefit in that it retained a foothold for the West on the mainland of North Asia.[104] Moreover, as has been seen, the unresisted conquest of South Korea could hardly have failed to weaken morale in Japan and probably throughout the whole of South East Asia. Above all, failure to act would have cast serious doubt on the West's determination to face up resolutely to aggression on the same pattern in Europe. Instead, the decision to resist in Korea brought a new sense of urgency both in Western Europe and North America, which made possible a rapid build-up of NATO and set in train the slow process of Western Germany's integration into the Western camp. By serving as a testing ground for NATO,[105] and by giving it new meaning and momentum, the Korean War may be said to have played an appreciable part in redressing the balance of power in the West's favour.

The war has not, of course, led to the attainment of the eventual United Nations objective, namely, the creation of a unified, democratic, and independent Korea. Nor has it shown that collective security can be an 'automatic rule of thumb procedure, guaranteeing peace in the foreseeable future'.[106] On the contrary, the war tended not only to confirm the difficulties confronting any collective security system, but also to revive the criticism, frequently heard in League days, that action in the name of collective security may turn what might otherwise remain a local war into a general war, thus bringing about the very eventuality which it is the aim of a collective security system to prevent. Admittedly, even before Chinese intervention, United Nations action in Korea was not an unqualified example

---

104 Although, writing in the American magazine *Newsweek* of 1 July 1953, the former commander of the United States Eighth Army in Korea, General Robert L. Eichelberger, claimed that if President Syngman Rhee provoked a successful Communist invasion of South Korea and was left to his fate, the loss 'would not do us any great harm in the strategic sense'.

105 To argue that direct action by the NATO Powers under Art. 51 would have been preferable to working through the United Nations is to overlook the crucial fact that the United Nations provided the necessary moral framework for action.

106 Wint, *What Happened in Korea*, p. 144.

of collective security, both because of the significance attached to the political complexion of the aggressor[107] and because of the consciousness of Soviet (and, to a lesser extent, Chinese) power lurking in the background. Indeed, it might perhaps be more accurately described as an example of collective resistance to Communist aggression. And although the United Nations provided the necessary moral framework for such resistance, it did in the first months of the war strengthen the disposition, especially in the United States, to believe that no war fought in the name of the United Nations could 'end rightly . . . except by the unconditional surrender of the aggressor nation and by the overthrow and transformation of its political regime'.[108] This flavour of 'unconditional surrender' in United Nations policy was in no small part responsible for the events which led to Chinese intervention.

However, these rather sobering facts do not obscure the importance of the Korean campaign as a vindication of the concept of collective resistance to aggression and as an assertion of the determination of the Western world to resist the 'little-by-little' method of its own subversion. It may be many years before the lasting significance of the campaign can be grasped, but at present it seems justifiable to construe it as a relatively successful attempt to uphold the Purposes and Principles of the Charter, which may have helped to strengthen the deterrents not perhaps to aggression anywhere but at least to Communist aggression elsewhere. For, if the impact of the experience on the men in the Kremlin and in Peking is not calculable, they could hardly have failed to note that the West avoided the insidious sapping of the will to resist that accompanied the progressive losses of the 1930's and the slow demise of the League. Had it not been for courageous American leadership, the

---

[107] As Arnold Wolfers implies, the situation would have been very different if the aggressor had been South rather than North Korea ('Collective Security and the War in Korea', *Yale Review*, Summer 1954, p. 488).

[108] See Walter Lippman, *Public Opinion and Foreign Policy in the United States* (London, Allen & Unwin, 1952), p. 26, where this attitude is more fully described.

United Nations would almost certainly have suffered the same fate. In a very real sense the Korean War was a local war which was fought to prevent a world war.

chapter five

Disarmament

Britain's stake in the 'establishment of a system for the regulation of armaments',[1] conventional or atomic, is clear enough. Apart from any moral considerations, her difficulties in attaining and maintaining economic solvency in the post-war world have been, and still are, appreciably aggravated by the burden of having to turn so large a part of her industrial resources over to the production of armaments and of having to maintain larger armed forces than have ever been necessary before in peace-time. As regards weapons of mass destruction, Great Britain's closely concentrated population and her exceptional dependence on imports of food and raw materials make her peculiarly vulnerable to atomic, bacteriological, or chemical attack. Yet the prolonged and tortuous disarmament negotiations at the United Nations have been viewed with considerable scepticism by most people in Britain. Four main reasons may be adduced for this. In the first place, the disillusioning

---

[1] Art. 26 of the Charter makes the Security Council, with the assistance of the Military Staff Committee, responsible for formulating the necessary plans. Under Art. 11 (para. 1) the General Assembly has the right to consider 'the principles governing disarmament and the regulation of armaments'.

experience of the League of Nations disarmament discussions is still vivid, while the encouragement the totalitarian Powers drew in the 1930's from Britain's military weakness is also well remembered. Despite the shadow of the hydrogen bomb, there is little or no inclination to indulge in any form of unilateral disarmament. In the second place, in contrast to the British thesis of the 1920's that disarmament was a necessary prelude to an increased sense of security, the orthodox view for most of the past decade has been that the armaments race is a consequence, not the cause, of international tension. Accordingly, the inauguration of a water-tight system for the regulation of armaments must, it is argued, await, though it could contribute to, a settlement of the major outstanding political issues, especially that of a divided Germany; and few believe that such a settlement is near. In the third place, not only do the very complexity of the problem and the intricacies of a decade of argument at the United Nations baffle the lay eye, but the negotiators' evident concern with the reactions of both domestic and world public opinion has led many to conclude that the real issues have become obscured in a propaganda battle, the essence of which is to appear more eager for disarmament than the other side without giving up any present or potential military advantage. In the fourth place, although the advent of the hydrogen bomb gave renewed impetus to the discussions, they subsequently became overshadowed by the great debate on the shape of wars to come, and especially on the issue of 'Massive Retaliation or Graduated Deterrence';[2] the curious divorce between this debate and the disarmament negotiations also endowed the latter with a certain air of unreality, while the growing belief in the last year or so that mutual possession of the 'Great Deterrent'

---

[2] There is an abundance of literature on both sides of the Atlantic on this issue, but the main arguments heard in the United Kingdom are conveniently summarized in a discussion between Rear Admiral Sir Anthony Buzzard, Marshal of the R.A.F. Sir John Slessor, and Richard Lowenthal, which is recorded in 'The H-Bomb: Massive Retaliation or Graduated Deterrence?', *International Affairs*, Apr. 1956.

may usher in a 'Pax Atomica' has now cast some doubt on the desirability as well as on the feasibility of atomic disarmament.

Chronologically, the disarmament discussions fall into three fairly distinct periods. The first, 1945-9, was the period of the American monopoly in atomic weapons and of the Soviet Union's overwhelming superiority in conventional armaments. It was the period, on the Western side, of the 'Baruch Plan' for an international agency which would own and operate all atomic energy facilities and materials, and, on the Soviet side, of proposals for the unconditional prohibition of atomic weapons and for the one-third reduction of conventional forces. This period actually ended in 1949 with the signature of the North Atlantic Treaty and the first Soviet atomic explosion, but the second period, 1950-3, did not really get under way until the outbreak of the Korean War. This was the period in which the West sought to rebuild its strength in conventional armaments and the Soviet Union to make up its leeway in atomic weapons. Against this background the disarmament negotiations naturally made little progress. The third period, 1954 to the time of writing, was ushered in in 1953 by the Korean Armistice and by the explosion by the United States (in November 1952) and by the Soviet Union (in August 1953) of thermo-nuclear devices. The revelation in March 1954 of the destructive capacity of the hydrogen bomb gave new urgency to the negotiations and contributed to a more flexible attitude on the part of the negotiators. The technological developments which in this period have produced the beginnings of 'nuclear plenty' in weapons also focused increasing attention on the peaceful uses of atomic energy, a field in which the United Nations has been able to play a constructive part.

THE PERIOD 1945-9

When the General Assembly first met in London in January 1946 agreement had already been reached between the United

States, the Soviet Union, Britain, and Canada that the international control of atomic weapons should be tackled separately from the regulation and reduction of conventional armaments.[3] Accordingly, the General Assembly on 24 January 1946 set up an Atomic Energy Commission, to consist of a representative of each member of the Security Council together with a representative of Canada (if she were not already on the Council).[4] When the Commission first met, on 14 June 1946, it was presented with American and Soviet proposals. The American (or Baruch) proposals[5] became, with minor amendments, the majority plan. This contemplated the creation of an International Control Agency which would *own* all uranium and thorium which was mined, and would *operate* and *manage* plants using nuclear fuel in dangerous amounts. Only 'safe' activities would be permitted to Member Governments, and these would be subject to a strict system of licensing and inspection. There would be a transition period during which information would be gradually disclosed and facilities transferred to the Agency. When the system of control was established, the manufacture of atom bombs would be prohibited and existing stocks destroyed. The plan envisaged a far-reaching system of inspection and control designed to ensure the use of atomic energy for peaceful purposes only and to provide effective safeguards against the dangers of violations and evasions. The Baruch plan also insisted, unlike the Acheson-Lilienthal Report, that the Security Council should not be prevented by the veto from inflicting sanctions on a transgressor.

The Soviet Union proposed[6] an international agreement which

---

[3] See McNeill, *America, Britain and Russia*, pp. 710-11.

[4] *GAOR*, 1st sess., 1st Pt., Resolution 1(I).

[5] *AECOR*, 1st mtg., 14 June 1946, pp. 10-13. The Baruch proposals were based on the Acheson-Lilienthal Report; see *The Truman Memoirs*, ii. 6-12. Opinion in America and Britain was not unanimous in supporting these proposals and there were reservations about some of the details, but if they had been accepted in principle by the Soviet Union in 1946, it is probable that the United States would have been prepared to implement them.

[6] *AECOR*, 2nd mtg., 19 June 1946, pp. 26-30.

would prohibit the production or use of atomic weapons and would require the destruction within three months of those already in existence. In 1947 the Soviet Union expanded her proposals for control and inspection and for the imposition of penalties on those violating the agreement. An international authority, acting within the framework of the Security Council, would control the mining of raw materials and the successive stages in production through a system of inspection and control, but it would not have the power to manage or license undertakings. Although the routine inspection and control operations would not be subject to the veto, the authority would not be able to set in motion sanctions against wilful transgression; it would merely have the duty to report the facts and to make recommendations to the Security Council. An attempt by Britain to secure Soviet acceptance of the proposition that minor sanctions should be imposed by a majority vote of the international authority or of the Security Council was firmly rejected.[7]

From this much condensed outline of the two sets of proposals, it will be seen that they were at variance on four main points. The first was whether international ownership and/or management of large-scale installations was essential, as the majority proposals claimed, to prevent the clandestine diversion of fissile material. This may well have been so, but the categorical rejection by the Soviet Union of any form of international ownership or management, together with doubts about its practicability short of the institution of a system of world government, subsequently led to the virtual abandonment of this proposal; international ownership is no longer, therefore, a live issue.[8] The second difference arose from the Baruch plan's insistence that the Security Council should be empowered to enforce sanctions against a transgressor by a simple majority vote, while the Soviet Union insisted on the

---

[7] AEC/31/Rev. 1., *Third Report of the Atomic Energy Commission*, Annex 3(c), p. 29.

[8] See Cmd. 9205, pp. 101 and 104.

retention of the unanimity rule. The American negotiators who succeeded Mr Baruch are said to have 'more or less disowned in a quiet fashion' the Baruch proposals on this point;[9] but it is one which still seems to divide the two sides. The third difference centred on the question of the timetable: should atomic weapons be outlawed and destroyed *before* (as the Soviet Union contended) or *after* (as the West insisted) the coming into operation of an effective inspection system? On this point a considerable measure of agreement was reached by 1953. The fourth and crucial issue concerned the nature and powers of the control organ and the pre-requisites of an effective system of inspection. The importance of this issue can hardly be exaggerated. The West has constantly stressed the folly of trusting verbal declarations or paper formulae unless they are accompanied by a system which can guarantee that they are being meticulously observed. As Mr Bevin once said: 'If a country will not open its doors for inspection, what is the use of entering into agreements when you do not know whether they are being kept or not.'[10] In later negotiations the Soviet Union has gone a good way towards meeting the West's requirements but a number of uncertainties still remain.

By the end of 1947 the prospects of bridging the gulf between the two sets of proposals had dwindled almost to vanishing point. In Western eyes the Soviet proposals did not provide the water-tight and enforceable system of inspection and control (including, at that stage, ownership and management), which could prevent the Soviet Union from evading her undertakings and secretly building up her own atomic arsenal. In their stress on the total prohibition of the use, manufacture, and stockpiling of atomic weapons, the Soviet proposals looked like an attempt to deprive the West of the one weapon which could redress the Soviet Union's clear margin of superiority in conventional weapons, a superiority

9 Robert W. Frase, 'International Control of Nuclear Weapons', *American Academy of Political and Social Science, Annals*, Nov. 1953.
10 22 Mar. 1950, H. C. Deb., vol. 472, col. 1951.

which would in no way be reduced by the all-round percentage reduction proposed by the Soviet Union. In Soviet eyes the majority proposals could be represented as an attempt by the West to set up an international control authority on which the Soviet Union would be in a permanent minority, unprotected by the veto, and through which her carefully guarded military secrets might be exposed to Western intelligence services. In addition, the allocation of large-scale installations to achieve a strategic balance could be represented as an attempt to hamper the Soviet Union's development of the peaceful uses of atomic energy and so to slow down the future rate of growth of her economy.

In its Third Report (17 May 1948)[11] the Atomic Energy Commission concluded that no useful purpose would be served by further discussion. Only the news of an atomic explosion in the Soviet Union (September 1949) and the pressure of the smaller Powers kept the Commission in being until it was merged into the Disarmament Commission in January 1952.

Likewise the Commission on Conventional Armaments set up by the Security Council in February 1947 had reached a state of substantial deadlock by the middle of 1948. In a resolution of 12 August 1948 a majority of nine to two declared that 'a system of regulation and reduction of armaments and armed forces can only be put into effect in an atmosphere of international confidence and security'.[12] The resolution also stressed the need for effective international supervision to ensure observance of any such system. In reply the Soviet Union, at the third session of the General Assembly, reiterated her call for an immediate reduction by one-third of existing land, naval, and air forces. The very simplicity of this proposal gave it considerable propaganda value, especially as Soviet spokesmen could cite a similar proposal made by the United States in the days of the League. But its manifest absurdity was fairly soon accepted by most delegates. As the Minister of State

11 AEC/31/Rev. 1.
12 S/C. 3/25.

(Mr Selwyn Lloyd) said at a later session 'A cut by one-third . . . would produce an arbitrary and quite inequitable redistribution of strength, even if we could be sure, without some kind of supervision, that such a reduction would be made in fact by all, or even if we knew from what existing strength the reduction would take place.'[13]

THE PERIOD 1950-3

The next full-scale disarmament debate took place at the sixth session of the General Assembly in Paris (1951), at a time when fighting was still going on in Korea and when the West's rearmament drive was rapidly gathering momentum. However, the news, in early October 1951, that the Soviet Union had succeeded in exploding another atomic bomb persuaded delegates to make a further effort to check the atomic armaments race. A new set of proposals was tabled by the Western Powers[14] and, as a result of private discussions between representatives of the United States, the Soviet Union, Britain, and France, some of the main issues were clarified. These were outlined by the Minister of State (Mr Selwyn Lloyd) in a speech to the First Committee on 11 December 1951.[15] Disagreement persisted on the timetable; on the use of the veto; and on the West's insistence on disclosure and verification on a progressive basis. On the other hand, agreement had been reached on the constitution of a Disarmament Commission to consider both conventional and atomic armaments,[16] and some convergence of views could be reported on the setting up of an international control organ; on the need for a 'continuous' system of inspection; and on the

13 *GAOR*, 8th sess., Plen., 443rd mtg., 24 Sept. 1953, p. 125.

14 See speech by the Foreign Secretary (Mr Eden), ibid. 6th sess., Plen., 339th mtg., 12 Nov. 1951, p. 56.

15 ibid. 6th sess., 1st Committee, 463rd mtg., *SR*, pp. 61-62.

16 ibid. 6th sess., suppl. no. 20, Resolution 502(VI) of 11 Jan. 1952. The initial singling out of atomic disarmament, though an understandable reaction to Hiroshima and Nagasaki and a useful way of exploring a novel, complex, and highly technical subject, was soon shown to be quite unreal.

necessity for the leading Powers to adhere to any disarmament agreement before it could be considered binding.

The Disarmament Commission held its first meeting on 14 March 1952, and continued to meet fairly regularly until the end of August of the same year. However, it made little progress, its work being impeded not only by the familiar irreconcilability of Soviet and Western proposals but also by Soviet efforts to use it as a platform for charges of bacteriological warfare in Korea. Otherwise, the Soviet Union adhered for the most part to her previous proposals, apart from moving slightly nearer the Western position by conceding that effective international control should 'be instituted simultaneously' with the prohibition of atomic and other weapons of mass destruction. The Western Powers maintained, however, that this formula would result in a period of mere paper prohibition without any control, since prohibition was an instantaneous act, whereas some considerable time was bound to elapse before the system of control could be brought into operation. On their side they elaborated, as an essential first step to the institution of any system of international inspection, their proposals for the progressive disclosure and verification of all armed forces and armaments, proceeding from the less secret to the more secret weapons. They also proposed that numerical ceilings should be established for all armed forces, ranging from between 1 and $1\frac{1}{2}$ million for China, the Soviet Union, and the United States, and from between 700,000 and 800,000 for Britain and France, with ceilings for other nations in proportion. After the completion of the disclosure and verification operations the Great Powers would reduce their armed forces to these levels, which would leave their forces in balance and so help to relieve them of any fear of attack.[17] But these proposals met with a stony response from the Soviet Union.

> Underneath the surface of the formal proposals and the specific criticisms of them, each side accused the other of

17 Cmd. 8589.

m

wanting to disarm it in the field where it was strongest. The Western plan involved the following sequence: first, the establishment of control; secondly, the reduction of conventional armaments and armed forces; and thirdly, the prohibition of nuclear weapons. The Soviet Union claimed that this sequence would give the West access to all Soviet secrets, both military and economic, before any measure of disarmament took place; furthermore, it would reduce Soviet armed forces and conventional armaments while permitting the existence of nuclear weapons, in which the West regarded itself as having an advantage, until some remote and indefinite final stage which might never be reached.

On the other hand, the effect of the Soviet plans for disarmament was to create the exact reverse sequence: first, prohibition; second, reduction; and third, control. The Western Powers claimed that this time-table of disarmament was designed to strip them of nuclear weapons, which they regarded as their main defence or deterrent against the possibility of aggression, while preserving the Soviet preponderance in armed forces and conventional armaments; moreover, neither measure would be subject to really effective control under the Soviet plan, and no country could be assured that the others were living up to their obligations.[18]

The disarmament discussions at the second half of the seventh session of the General Assembly (April 1953) reflected the apparently somewhat softened Russian attitude of the period immediately following Stalin's death. Nevertheless, the Disarmament Commission, which had been asked to continue its work, met only once in 1953 to draw up its Report, in which no progress could be recorded.[19] At the following Assembly, which opened in November 1953, Mr Vyshinsky reasserted the standard Soviet demand for a one-third cut in armaments, the prohibition of atomic weapons, and the elimination of foreign bases. But he appeared to have moved closer to the Western position by conceding that 'the decision on

---

[18] 'Disarmament Proposals and Negotiations, 1946-1955', *World Today*, Aug. 1955, pp. 336-37.
[19] DC/32.

prohibition should enter into force simultaneously with the *entry into operation* of the control organ'.[20] And he did not oppose a Western resolution taking up an idea first mooted by M. Moch and then formally proposed by Mr Krishna Menon that the Disarmament Commission should set up a Sub-Committee of Canada, France, the Soviet Union, Britain, and the United States, which should meet in private and so, it was hoped, in an atmosphere more conducive to serious negotiation.[21] A few days later, on 8 December 1953, President Eisenhower presented his proposals for an atom 'pool'.

THE PERIOD 1954 TO JULY 1956

Discussions from 1954 onwards have taken a new turn. Not only have they become even more complex than before but they have recaptured some of that sense of urgency which prevailed in the United Nations' earliest days. The main reason is obvious enough. As the 1955 Defence White Paper said: 'Overshadowing all else in the year 1954 has been the emergence of the thermo-nuclear bomb.'[22] The devastating effects of the hydrogen bomb exploded in the Bikini-Eniwetok area of the Marshall Islands on 1 March 1954 shocked a hitherto rather apathetic British public into the realization that one such bomb could destroy the greater part of London and that the fall-out of radio-active ash might cause casualties hundreds of miles from the scene of the explosion. On 13 May 1954, at Britain's instigation, the Disarmament Sub-Committee met again in London to see whether these new developments might not impel some way out of the disarmament impasse.

---

[20] *GAOR*, 8th sess., 1st Committee, 658th mtg., 6 Nov. 1953, *SR*, p. 174 (italics added). Mr Vyshinsky's clarifications on this point did not satisfy the Western Powers; Mr Selwyn Lloyd said that he had mastered the problem of how to make a thing simultaneous and non-simultaneous simultaneously (ibid. 665th mtg., 13 Nov. 1953, p. 215).

[21] ibid. 8th sess., suppl. no. 17, Resolution 715(VIII).

[22] Cmd. 9391.

The advent of the hydrogen bomb did more than refocus attention on the problem of atomic disarmament, however; it also triggered off a debate on the shape of wars to come which is still in progress and the outcome of which is bound to affect the outlook for disarmament. This is an exceedingly involved and controversial issue and only the barest outline can be given of those features of it which bear most directly on the disarmament problem. Before the Sub-Committee met, Mr Dulles had already propounded, in his speech of 12 January 1954, the doctrine of 'massive and instant retaliation';[23] and although this doctrine was reformulated by the end of the year as one of 'measured retaliation' or 'graduated deterrence', America and Britain were evidently agreed not only that full atomic retaliation would follow atomic attack, but that it would follow any *major* overt aggression, even with conventional forces. Lord Montgomery, indeed, disclosed in a series of speeches that SHAPE was basing all its operational planning on using atomic and thermo-nuclear weapons.[24] Proposals for 'the elimination and prohibition of atomic, hydrogen and other types of weapons of mass destruction'[25] appeared rather out of step, therefore, with declared Western strategic policy.

The disarmament discussions also had to take into account the unexpected rapidity of Soviet progress both in the output of hydrogen weapons and in the capacity to deliver them. Soviet achievements were, of course, very much a matter of conjecture. Although the United States had lost her monopoly of atomic and nuclear weapons, she almost certainly retained a clear quantitative lead in them. On the other hand, the Soviet Union had already accumulated a considerable atomic stockpile, she had developed a long-range and medium-range bomber of advanced design, and she was thought to have discovered—as had the United States—a

---

[23] *The Times*, 13 Jan. 1954.
[24] *Manchester Guardian*, 6 Apr. and 22 Oct. 1954; see also F.-M. Lord Montgomery, 'A Look through a Window at World War III', *Royal United Services Institution Journal*, Nov. 1954.
[25] *GAOR*, 8th sess., suppl. 17, Resolution 715(VIII).

process which would greatly facilitate the production of hydrogen bombs. By the time the Sub-Committee met, therefore, there were already indications that 'saturation point' in these weapons—or an 'atomic stalemate'—would be reached within not very many years. Since it was also already becoming apparent that there were at present no 'foolproof' methods of detecting existing stockpiles, or, it appeared, of preventing the rapid conversion of fission-able materials and atomic reactors used for peaceful purposes to war purposes, the outlook for the eventual elimination of atomic weapons seemed bleak in the extreme.

Another development also tended to confirm this view. In the field of so-called conventional weapons, the build-up of NATO forces had gone some way to correct the Soviet preponderance; and although these forces were still substantially inferior in man-power, there was now a reasonable prospect that this inferiority might be offset in the not too distant future not only by the addition of twelve divisions from Western Germany but also by the supply of tactical atomic weapons. But dependence on these weapons meant that in the event of anything more than a frontier sortie, even if nuclear weapons were not used, tactical atomic weapons almost certainly would be.

To set against these disquieting considerations, however, was the doctrine of the 'Great Deterrent' and of the 'Pax Atomica', which was just beginning to take shape. As 'saturation point' was neared and passed, might not the knowledge of the colossal destructive power which would be brought to bear on an aggressor prove such an awesome deterrent that no country would run the risk of major aggression for fear that even victory would bring obliteration? Sir Winston Churchill on 28 April expressed the hope that nuclear weapons might 'lead not to general annihilation but to the outlawry of war which generation after generation has hitherto sought in vain' and that 'our peril will prove our salvation'.[26] The Defence White

---

[26] *The Times*, 29 Apr. 1954. The dangers of fanaticism and accident were not ignored, however.

Paper of February 1955 gave official blessing to this view when it explicitly claimed that 'the knowledge that aggression will be met by overwhelming nuclear retaliation is the surest guarantee that it will not take place'.[27]

It was against this background that the Sub-Committee met in private in Lancaster House on 13 May 1954. It is impossible here to do more than pick a few of the main threads out of the tangled skein of the ensuing eighteen months' negotiations.[28] Very briefly, the chronological sequence was as follows. On 11 June 1954, after a desultory start, a joint Anglo-French memorandum[29] was tabled which was to serve as the main basis for future negotiation. In outlining a 'phased' disarmament programme in three stages, the memorandum, in effect, abandoned the concept of disclosure and verification prior to any disarmament measures, which it replaced with that of a 'freeze' (in the first stage) on armed forces and military budgets, to be followed (in two successive stages) by the reduction of conventional armaments and armed forces *pari passu* with, first, the prohibition of the production of nuclear weapons and, second, their elimination; of crucial importance was the proviso that each phase would only come into operation when a control organ reported that it was able effectively to enforce it. These proposals were not at first received with any favour by the Soviet delegate, Mr Malik, but in the following September Mr Vyshinsky startled delegates to the General Assembly by proposing that the Disarmament Commission should be instructed to draft a treaty on disarmament and nuclear weapons 'using as a basis' the Anglo-French plan.[30] The subsequent debate revealed substantial differences on a number of issues, especially

---

27 Cmd. 9391, para. 19.

28 Though the meetings were private, a report and a verbatim record were published afterwards; see *Report of the Proceedings of the Sub-Committee of the United Nations Disarmament Commission*, Cmd. 9204; also *Verbatim Records of the Meetings of the Sub-Committee*, Cmd. 9205.

29 Cmd. 9204, pp. 31-32 (or DC/53).

30 *GAOR*, 9th sess., Plen., 484th mtg., 30 Sept. 1954, pp. 126-27.

on the timing of the various phases of disarmament, on the functioning and powers of the control organ, and on the balancing of
atomic with conventional disarmament. But prospects of a break in
the eight-year-old deadlock were strengthened when on 4 November
1954 the General Assembly unanimously adopted a resolution
initiated by Mr Paul Martin, the Canadian delegate, and co-sponsored
by both the Western Powers and the Soviet Union, restating the
basic principles of disarmament and suggesting that the Sub-
Committee should be reconvened in another effort to seek agreement.[31]

The Sub-Committee met again at Lancaster House on 25 February
1955. After rather an awkward start and the restatement by both
sides of their earlier positions, Mr Nutting (now the United Kingdom
representative) and M. Moch suggested two major modifications
to the original Anglo-French proposals of 11 June 1954.[32] The
first was to reduce the ceiling for the armed forces of France and
Britain to 650,000 men each; the second sought to balance atomic
and conventional disarmament in a manner more acceptable to
the Soviet Union by proposing that the prohibition of the use of
nuclear weapons should occur after 75 per cent. of the reductions
had been completed (instead of after 100 per cent. as previously
proposed), and that the final 25 per cent. of the reductions should
commence simultaneously with the process of elimination of
nuclear weapons, with both processes ending together. At first
these compromise proposals evoked no marked response from
Mr Malik. However, on 10 May 1955 he introduced comprehensive
new Soviet proposals set out in three draft resolutions to be adopted by the General Assembly—the first a declaration on the relaxation of international tension, the second outlining an international

---

[31] ibid. suppl. no. 21, Resolution 808(IX). This was the first important resolution on disarmament to be adopted unanimously since 1946.

[32] Cmd. 9636, pp. 28 and 30-31 (or DC/71, Annexes 9 and 13). The verbatim
records of the meetings of the second session of the Sub-Committee have been
published in Cmds. 9648-9652.

disarmament treaty, and the third outlining the principles of international control.[33]

The Western and Soviet proposals on the Disarmament Treaty as then elaborated can best be studied in juxtaposition with each other.

COMPARATIVE TABULATION OF THE SEQUENCE OF DISARMAMENT MEASURES [34]

WESTERN POWERS

Preliminary Steps

1. All states possessing nuclear weapons should regard themselves as prohibited from the use of such weapons except in defence against aggression.

2. The Disarmament Treaty should include an immediate and explicit acceptance of this prohibition by all signatory states pending the total prohibition of nuclear weapons.

Phase I

3. The control organ is to be constituted and positioned, and is to report that it is ready to enforce the measures of Phase I.

4. Conventional armaments and overall military manpower are to be limited to levels of 31 December 1954, and overall military expenditures to the amount in 1954.

Entr'acte

5. The control organ is to make preparations and report it is ready to enforce the measures of Phase II.

SOVIET UNION

First Stage-1956

Note: An International Control Organ is to be instituted by the General Assembly to carry out its allotted tasks.

1. Within one month, the United States, Soviet Union, China, Britain, and France shall furnish full official figures of their armed forces, conventional armaments, and military expenditures.

2. Within two months, conventional armaments and armed forces are to be limited to levels of 31 December 1954 and military appropriations to the amount in 1954.

---

33 Cmd. 9636, pp. 33-42 (or DC/71, Annex 15).

34 This tabulation is taken (with a number of minor modifications) from *World Today*, Aug. 1955, pp. 346-48.

Phase II

6. One-half of agreed reductions of conventional armaments and armed forces and consequent reductions in military expenditures.

7. On completion of (6), the production of nuclear and other weapons of mass destruction shall cease.

Entr'acte

8. The control organ is to make preparations and report it is ready to enforce the measures of Phase III.

3. One of the first measures shall be an undertaking by states to discontinue tests of nuclear weapons. An International Commission is to supervise this measure.

4. The five Powers shall, within the one year, reduce their armaments and armed forces by 50 per cent. of the agreed reductions (the difference between the 1954 level and the agreed ceiling levels), and correspondingly reduce their military appropriations.

5. No later than 30 June 1956, a World Conference of all states is to be convened to determine reductions for other states and to prohibit atomic weapons.

6. Simultaneously with the commencement of (4), states shall assume a solemn obligation not to use nuclear weapons except in defence against aggression when so authorized by the Security Council.

7. States possessing foreign military bases shall undertake to liquidate them and agreement shall be reached on those to be liquidated during this stage.

Phase III

(Franco-British Compromise of March 1955)

9. The third quarter of the agreed reductions of conventional armaments and armed forces shall take effect.

Second Stage-1957

8. The production of nuclear weapons shall be discontinued, with a corresponding budgetary reduction.

9. The five Powers shall, within one year, reduce their armed forces and armaments by the remaining 50 per cent., with a corresponding budgetary reduction, and other states are to carry out their reductions.

10. On completion of (9), the following shall take place simultaneously:

(a) A complete prohibition on the use of nuclear and other weapons of mass destruction shall come into force;

(b) The elimination of these weapons shall begin;

(c) The final quarter of the agreed reductions of conventional armaments and armed forces shall begin.

Both (b) and (c) shall be completed within the time-limit fixed in the treaty.

All atomic materials shall thereafter be used only for peaceful purposes.

Further Reductions

11. After the completion of the above measures, it was hoped that the armaments and armed forces of the Powers would be further reduced to the levels necessary for internal security and the fulfilment of United Nations Charter obligations.

10. After armed forces and conventional armaments have been reduced by 75 per cent. of the total reduction, the following shall take place simultaneously:

(a) A complete prohibition on the use of nuclear and other weapons of mass destruction shall come into force;

(b) The elimination and destruction of these weapons shall begin;

(c) The final 25 per cent. of the agreed reduction shall begin.

Both (b) and (c) are to be completed within the time-limits in 1957.

All atomic materials shall thereafter be used only for peaceful purposes.

11. The liquidation of all foreign military bases shall be completed.

Further Reductions

12. After the completion of the above measures, it was hoped that the armaments and armed forces of the Powers would be further reduced to the levels necessary for internal security and the fulfilment of United Nations Charter obligations.

As will be seen, the proposals had many similarities; especially significant was Soviet acceptance of the need for the establishment of a single permanent control organ. But this was accompanied by the frank admission that the production of atomic energy for peaceful purposes could also be used for atomic weapons, and that no known system of international control could prevent the clandestine manufacture of nuclear weapons.[35] The proposals therefore made much of first-stage measures to guard against a surprise attack.

---

[35] Cmd. 9636, p. 40.

The control organ would have the right to demand any necessary information from states and have unimpeded access to military budget records. During the second stage of the disarmament programme the control organ would also have the right of permanent inspection, through its own staff of inspectors 'having, within the bounds of the control functions they exercise, unimpeded access at all times to all objects of control'.[36]

These proposals were welcomed by the United Kingdom and by other Western spokesmen as an encouraging step forward. But a number of doubts remained. If the Soviet disarmament proposals were dependent on acceptance of the measures covered in the first resolution, especially the withdrawal of 'occupation forces' in Germany and the liquidation of foreign military bases, the West would be placed at a severe strategic disadvantage. Precisely what 'objects of control' would be open to inspection and when would the control organ come into operation? Would the control organ itself be able to take interim measures to deal with violations? And if the control organ was to report violations of the Disarmament Treaty to the Security Council (instead of to the General Assembly as proposed by the West), would not the Soviet Union use her veto to frustrate any remedial action?

None of these doubts was cleared up in the ensuing six months. On the contrary, the picture became still more confused as a result of the various striking, but seemingly rather ill-considered, proposals presented at the Geneva 'summit' conference on 21 July 1955. The most notable was President Eisenhower's 'open sky' plan for the exchange of military blueprints between the United States and the Soviet Union and their verification by mutual aerial reconnaissance, the prime object of which appeared to be to provide against the possibility of a massive suprise attack.[37] Marshal Bulganin elaborated early Soviet proposals with the main additional suggestion that,

---

[36] ibid. p. 41.
[37] ibid. pp. 48-50.

pending the conclusion of the Disarmament Treaty, the four Great Powers should declare that they would not be the first to use nuclear weapons.[38] For Britain Sir Anthony Eden proposed a pilot inspection project of the forces now confronting one another in Europe, in the belief that a practical test on a limited scale of methods of international inspection would, if successful, establish a sense of security in Europe and so facilitate the institution of a more far-reaching system of inspection and control.[39] Not to be outdone, M. Faure proposed budgetary controls on military expenditure, any savings that resulted being used, in full or in part, to help under-developed areas, a special international fund being set up for this purpose.[40]

Faced with this mixed bag of proposals, which the 'summit' conference refrained from elaborating or exploring, the Sub-Committee spent most of the next session in New York (29 August until 7 October) in listening to each other's explanatory statements and to pointing out the flaws in their opponents' proposals. Mr Nutting elaborated Sir Anthony Eden's proposal for a 'curtain-raiser' to disarmament. Although it could be tried out anywhere in the world where armed forces confronted each other, Europe offered the most logical testing ground.

> It was envisaged that joint inspecting teams, with suitable rights, representing both the North Atlantic Treaty Organisation Commander in Chief and the Soviet Commander in Chief in East Europe, should inspect military units and installations in the agreed area. It was not intended that the scheme should enforce limitations on armaments or man-power, although it might be that ceilings on forces and armaments could be agreed. The plan should operate in an area of equal depth on either side of the line at present dividing Europe. It was intended to be without prejudice to any arrangements which might be made for German reuni-

---

[38] ibid. pp. 50-53.
[39] ibid. pp. 53-55.
[40] ibid. pp. 56-58.

fication or European security. It would, nevertheless, help to reduce tension in Europe, and hence between the Great Powers. Its operation would afford invaluable experience in working out a disarmament control organ's rights and powers. The simplicity of the plan enabled it to be put into immediate effect; this would demonstrate that the Great Powers were ready at last to take some practical steps together towards disarmament.[41]

In addition, Mr Nutting explained that the United Kingdom was not prepared to subject her right to use nuclear weapons in defence against aggression to the decision, and possibly the delays and veto, of the Security Council, and he intimated that his Government was prepared to contemplate a ban on nuclear test explosions only as part of a comprehensive disarmament plan and provided methods were found for effectively enforcing it. He also argued that, though the Soviet proposals of 10 May 1955 might provide an adequate safeguard against a surprise attack by conventional forces, they would be helpless against a nuclear attack launched by air or guided missiles.

The 1955 meetings of the Sub-Committee were conducted in a more amicable atmosphere than hitherto. But the beneficent effects of the 'Geneva spirit' seem to have been more than offset by the element of uncertainty posed by the fluid strategic picture and by the knowledge that existing techniques for the detection of nuclear materials could not guarantee that existing stocks of nuclear fuel would not be misused. Despite, therefore, the convergence of Western and Soviet views on inspection and control, attention during the year appears to have shifted away from comprehensive disarmament towards schemes designed to guard against surprise attacks by either nuclear weapons or conventional forces. The Sub-Committee was unable to make much headway on such

---

[41] ibid. p. 12.

schemes, however; nor did it receive any guidance from the Geneva meeting of the four Foreign Ministers in November 1955.

When the General Assembly met for its tenth session (September 1955) it was presented with a report from the Disarmament Commission transmitting the second report of the Sub-Committee and the verbatim records of its own meetings.[42] This massive document proved no great aid to the General Assembly's discussions, which were not marked by the unanimity and cordiality of the previous session's discussions. But in the debates the shift away from comprehensive towards partial disarmament was apparent, and a Western draft resolution was modified in order to meet widespread misgiving that too great a stress on the 'summit' proposals might distract attention from the regular and methodical work of the Sub-Committee. The amended resolution calling for a continuation of the Sub-Committee's work was adopted against Soviet opposition on 16 December 1955 (53 votes for, 5 against, no abstentions).[43]

Developments since this resolution can be noted only in very summary fashion. The Sub-Committee met from 19 March to 4 May 1956, but without any significant result.[44] At the first meeting Britain and France tabled a revised version of the original Anglo-French plan of June 1954, intended to meet some of the outstanding points at issue. This modified version did not provide for the *elimination* of nuclear stockpiles—on the grounds that it was technically impossible to control existing stocks—but the *manufacture* of nuclear weapons was to be prohibited at the beginning of the third stage. Two concessions were made to the Soviet point of view. The first provided for the limitation of nuclear test explosions in the second stage, and for the prohibition of tests in the third stage. The second provided for the initial reduction of conventional forces during, and not after (as hitherto), the first stage of dis-

---

[42] A/3047; this report, together with the attached documents, totalled over 3,000 pages and weighed 12½ lb.

[43] *GAOR*, 10th sess., suppl. no. 19, Resolution 914(X).

[44] See Cmd. 9770 (also DC/83).

armament.[45] The Soviet counter-proposals of 27 March[46] conceded that the control organization should be formed and established before the processes of disarmament began and the 'objects of control' were roughly defined. On the other hand, the proposals represented a retrograde step in that they provided solely for the reduction of conventional forces and they looked to full-scale conventional disarmament within three years regardless of progress towards the solution of outstanding political problems. Soviet reticence on nuclear disarmament probably reflected her determination to build up her nuclear stockpile to a level comparable with that of the United States, her belief that the political map of Europe was at present drawn to Soviet advantage, and her recognition of the unlikelihood of the Western democracies indulging in a surprise 'preventive' attack. On the Western side some restraint on the manufacture of atomic weapons was obviously to their advantage but was probably impossible; the reunification of Germany still figured high amongst their foreign-policy objectives, and mistrust of Soviet ambitions and of Soviet secrecy remained acute. Consequently, the Soviet proposals were at variance with the trend in the Western (and specially the United States) proposals, namely, to concentrate on partial disarmament in the first stage, which would include an initial reduction of conventional forces (in which the Soviet Union still held a clear lead) and the institution of safeguards against surprise nuclear attack (which was more likely to come from the East than from the West), and to make progress on subsequent stages more dependent on 'the necessary conditions of confidence', that is, on progress towards the settlement of outstanding political issues (as well, of course, as on the effective functioning of the control organ).

Since the Sub-Committee met, the Soviet Union is said to have

---

[45] ibid. pp. 26-29 (or DC/83, Annex 4). See also the United States Summary Memorandum setting out eight basic principles of United States Government policy on disarmament, ibid. pp. 46-47 (or DC/83, Annex 9).

[46] ibid. pp. 31-35 (or DC/83, Annex 5).

accepted,[47] though only with qualifications, the United States
suggestion that the level of armed forces at the end of the *first*
phase of disarmament should be 2.5 million for the three largest
Powers and 750,000 for France and Britain.[48] But in other respects
the Soviet attitude seems to have hardened, while in a letter to
President Eisenhower, Marshal Bulganin has alleged that 'the
activity of the Disarmament Sub-Committee retards progress in
this matter'.[49] The prospects of future progress are bleak, therefore.
Two serious bones of contention persist; both concern the functions
and powers of the control organization. The Western Powers insist
that a system of aerial inspection is an essential component of
control. Although the Soviet proposals of 27 March made brief
mention of aerial surveys as one of the methods of control, Soviet
spokesmen still seem to look upon aerial reconnaissance as a
'Baedeker for bombing missions', to which they are adamantly
opposed. There have been hints that President Eisenhower's 'open-
skies' plan is open to revision if Soviet acceptance can be secured
thereby.[50] And it is true that even air reconnaissance can probably
not provide a cast-iron safeguard. For instance, the United States
Strategic Air Command is said to be ready for instant retaliation
against an aggressor;[51] and presumably the same could be said
of its Soviet counterpart. It might not always be easy to distinguish
between preparations for an ordinary training mission and preparations for a full-scale nuclear attack. Yet it still remains the

---

[47] *The Times*, 13 July 1956.

[48] See American Draft Working Paper for the First Phase of a Comprehensive
Agreement for Disarmament, Cmd. 9770, pp. 35-39 (or DC/83, Annex 6).
The United Kingdom and France had previously been criticized for accepting
the American 'ceiling' figures, even though they had earlier suggested lower
ones. This criticism was based on a misunderstanding. The latest American
figures referred to the first stage, the earlier British and French figures to the
last stage, of disarmament.

[49] *Soviet News*, 12 June 1956.

[50] *Christian Science Monitor*, 10 July 1956.

[51] *Manchester Guardian*, 2 Sept. 1955.

case that, given the conditions of secrecy with which the Russians surround their every activity in this field, no warning system can be effective unless the control organ possesses very wide freedom of access and movement in the air as well as on the ground. This is not an issue on which there is much room for compromise.

The other main issue, which harks back to the Baruch proposals, is Britain's belief that the officials of the control organ must be able to give instructions in the case of breaches of the disarmament agreement if the effective functioning of control is not to be hamstrung by a veto in the Security Council. Military action or sanctions would be a matter for the Security Council. But the Foreign Secretary (Mr Selwyn Lloyd) has recently contended that no control organ can function effectively

> if its actions are subject to the veto of the Security Council; if the only thing its agents can do is to send in a report that something is being done. I have always believed that the control organ must have some right to stop some malpractice.[52]

It is not clear, however, from their Working Paper on Control of 3 May 1956,[53] precisely what kind of 'instructions' (Section V) Britain and France have in mind. Nor would the control organ's 'right' to stop a deliberate and substantial malpractice (other than an unwitting violation or one committed by an individual without his Government's knowledge) be of much moment if it lacked the *capacity* to enforce that right; and it is not easy to think of any control organ possessing such capacity unless it were well on the way to becoming a system of world government. In other words, the main function of the control organ would be to detect and report deliberate violations. If these were committed by a less-than-Great Power, that is by a so-called 'fourth country', the Great Powers could probably, if agreed, bring sufficient pressure to bear

---

[52] 24 July 1956, H. C. Deb., vol. 557, col. 260.
[53] Cmd. 9770, pp. 40-45.

n

on the transgressor to persuade it to mend its ways. If the transgressor were a Great Power, any form of military sanctions would be impossible without a global war; the most the control organ could do would be to provide a warning system which might prevent the transgressor from obtaining a decisive lead. There might well be room for negotiation on this point, therefore.

From this necessarily brief account of the manoeuvrings of the Powers the disarmament problem does indeed seem to 'boil down to the question of control and inspection'.[54] And as M. Moch has very pertinently remarked, the problem of control is the most difficult not only for

> scientific and technical reasons . . . [and] because it encroaches on the internal sovereignty of States [but also] because we all have the idea at the back of our minds that at bottom control cannot be properly exercised unless there is confidence between States—in which case it would be unnecessary and superfluous—whereas it must be put into operation at a time when such confidence does not exist, so as to create confidence.[55]

Certainly, whatever techniques are discovered for detecting nuclear stockpiles, there is little hope of the institution of a comprehensive disarmament scheme while the problems of a divided Germany or of Formosa's future remain unsettled and the ideological divide persists. The prospects for some form of partial disarmament[56] may not be quite so sombre, but the Soviet Union is unlikely to accept any restraint on the manufacture of atomic weapons under

---

[54] Statement by Marshal Bulganin to the Supreme Soviet on 4 Aug. 1955.

[55] Cmd. 9652, pp. 959-60.

[56] The Foreign Secretary (Mr Selwyn Lloyd) has advocated a partial disarmament scheme that 'should include the reduction of conventional forces and armaments, it should include the control of those limited reductions, it should also incorporate the Russian ideas about precautions against surprise attack, and it should certainly include some provision for air reconnaissance . . . Without that, there cannot be satisfactory control even in this limited field. Such an agreement should also include provisions for limiting and controlling nuclear test explosions, unless this has already been arranged by other means' (24 July 1956, H. C. Deb., vol. 557, coll. 258-59).

any such scheme until her own stockpile is such as to enable her to obliterate any possible opponent or combination of opponents. When 'saturation' point is reached she may be more ready to give her attention to the problem of the 'fourth country'. But may it not be too late by then? What if this terrible weapon should in the meantime fall into the hands of a state with powerful irredentist ambitions or into the grasp of a megalomaniac dictator? It is to schemes for partial disarmament that immediate attention should be directed. But little less urgent is the need for the present 'H-Bomb Powers' to agree on a system which will retain the monopoly of the manufacture of nuclear weapons for themselves and deny it to 'fourth countries'; given the increasing use of plutonium for peaceful purposes throughout the world, this will not be easy, but it should not be impossible.

There is also a strong case for limiting, if not prohibiting, test explosions of nuclear weapons. The effects of atomic radiation have been the subject of much alarmist, and often ill-informed, speculation in the last few years. It is clearly a subject that requires more study, preferably on an international basis. The General Assembly at its tenth session wisely decided to establish a fifteen-nation Scientific Committee[57] which is to receive and assemble radiological information; to recommend uniform standards for assessing background level of radiation; to review, collate, and evaluate reports submitted by national scientific bodies or by authorities of national Governments; to make yearly progress reports and to develop by 1 July 1958, or earlier if the assembled facts warrant it, a summary of the reports received on radiation levels and radiation effects on man and his environment.

Since this resolution, the *Report of the Medical Research Council on the Hazards to Man of Nuclear and Allied Radiation* has been published.[58] The *Report* emphasized the tentative nature of its conclusions. On the whole these were reassuring, but there was

[57] *GAOR*, 10th sess., suppl. no. 19, Resolution 913(X).
[58] Cmd. 9780.

a significant and disquieting qualification. Thus, in discussing the
fall-out from test explosions of nuclear weapons the *Report* stated:

> *a*) The present and foreseeable hazards from *external* radia-
> tion due to fall-out from the test explosions of nuclear
> weapons, fired at the present rate and in the present proportion
> of the different kinds, are negligible.

> *b*) Account must be taken, however, of the *internal* radiation
> from the radioactive strontium which is beginning to accu-
> mulate in bone. At its present level, no detectable increase
> in the incidence of ill-effects is to be expected. Nevertheless,
> recognising all the inadequacy of our present knowledge,
> we cannot ignore the possibility that, if the rate of firing
> increases and particularly if greater numbers of thermo-
> nuclear weapons are used, we could, within the life-time of
> some now living, be approaching levels at which ill-effects
> might be produced in a small number of the population.[59]

Until mid-1956 Britain argued that the prohibition or limitation
of test explosions of nuclear weapons must form an integral part
of any disarmament agreement. She has since modified her position.
On 12 July 1956 the Prime Minister (Sir Anthony Eden) stated:

> Her Majesty's Government are prepared to discuss methods
> of regulating and limiting test explosions which take account
> of their own position as well as that of other Powers. It would
> no doubt be preferable that this matter should be pursued
> within the context of a comprehensive agreement on dis-
> armament. For our part, however, we should not exclude other
> methods of discussion acceptable to those concerned.[60]

The United Kingdom has still to test her own nuclear weapons
and the technical, as well as the political, difficulties of controlling
the testing of, for instance, inter-continental ballistic missiles with
nuclear warheads, may turn out to be far greater than is generally
realized. But the attempt desperately needs to be made.

---

[59] ibid. p. 80.

[60] H. C. Deb., vol. 556, col. 586. On 23 July the Prime Minister (Sir Anthony
Eden) said, 'we are quite ready now to discuss that matter separately from the
disarmament convention' (ibid. vol. 557, col. 47).

SOME GENERAL REFLEXIONS

The prospects of the eventual elimination of nuclear weapons in a comprehensive disarmament scheme are at present extremely remote, and are bound to remain so until a reliable method of detecting existing stockpiles of nuclear material has been discovered. But even if this technical difficulty is overcome—as no doubt it will be in the course of time—and the political climate becomes more propitious, is the elimination of nuclear weapons necessarily desirable? Whatever their cost in terms of human and material resources, the fact is that the deterrent value of nuclear weapons has in the past few years undoubtedly been the main safeguard against aggression. Unless there is a radical transformation in the political scene, would it not be folly to remove this deterrent, or, indeed, to call into question NATO's right to use its tactical atomic weapons? An agreement (or an understanding) between the 'H-bomb' Powers that they would forbear from the strategic use of nuclear weapons except in the event of a major aggression might serve some useful purpose. But this is very different from advocating their total elimination.

In the field of conventional disarmament the reductions in conventional forces announced during 1956[61] will, if implemented, probably bring their levels within or very near the ceilings suggested in the Sub-Committee's recent discussions (that is, 2.5 million for the United States, the Soviet Union and China, and 750,000 for Britain and France). The conventional armed forces of both sides would then be more nearly in balance and some kind of agreement registering and 'freezing' this balance may be possible. The actual reductions will, of course, result from unilateral decisions and not from collective agreements. And in the Soviet Union

---

[61] The Soviet Union announced reductions of 640,000 in 1955 and of 1.2 million in May 1956; the United States has indicated her willingness to reduce her forces to 2.5 million as part of a partial disarmament agreement; and the United Kingdom is, over a period of five years, to reduce hers from 870,000 to 700,000 (the Foreign Secretary, 24 July 1956, H. C. Deb., vol. 557, col. 257).

—as elsewhere—the decisions may be assumed to reflect not only reduced fears of a global war, but also the desire to devote more resources to the production of the most advanced types of military equipment, including guided missiles and bombers; the technological race is, in fact, likely to grow more, rather than less, keen. It may yet prove possible to institute a joint inspection scheme on either side of the present dividing line in Europe, but further conventional disarmament on any scale is unlikely to prove either feasible or desirable. Indeed, reductions much beyond those already announced might merely place a great strain on NATO. A reduction of conventional forces below 2.5 million would probably make it very difficult for the United States to meet her NATO commitments. Also Britain's own capacity to meet her European commitments and to deal with local 'brush-fire' wars in other parts of the world would almost certainly be seriously weakened if her conventional forces were reduced much below the figure already announced—there is already not a very great margin to spare. Accordingly, further reductions might so cripple the West's capacity to fight local wars with conventional forces as to render impossible a policy of 'measured retaliation' and to encourage either the West's piecemeal dissolution or a hasty resort to the ultimate weapon of the hydrogen bomb. These are very large issues on which it would be foolish to dogmatize. But they need to be faced up to in any realistic discussion of disarmament.

In concluding this necessarily rather cursory examination of an immensely complicated problem two points need to be made. The first is that the disarmament issue even today tends to become highlighted out of all proportion to its intrinsic importance. The prime international problem is the preservation of peace, not the curtailing of the means of waging war. The prolonged disarmament negotiations have succeeded in clearing up some of the very difficult technical problems involved and in considerably narrowing the gulf between the parties, at least on partial disarmament. And it may well be that 'disarmament and the settlement of outstanding disputes must proceed *pari passu*.[62] But the clarity with which the negotiations have mirrored the political climate in the world at large suggests very forcibly that the regulation and limitation of armaments, atomic or conventional, partial or comprehensive, is far more likely to be the consequence rather than the cause of a relaxation of international tension. The second is that if delegates to the Sub-Committee are to be encouraged to concentrate on the substance of disarmament rather than on shadow-boxing aimed at winning the plaudits of the uncommitted Powers and of their own domestic public opinion, their meetings need to be held in far greater privacy than at present prevails. Delegates must, of course, be free to correct misrepresentations of their governments' positions, but the decision to publish the verbatim records of the Sub-Committee's discussions induces the suspicion that some delegates are more interested in scoring propaganda points than in reaching agreement. This is a travesty of private negotiation and a positive encouragement to verbal duelling.[63]

THE PEACEFUL USES OF ATOMIC ENERGY

The peaceful and the military uses of atomic energy are intimately related. One of the great question-marks that hangs over the future of the civilized world is whether the tremendous energy resources released by science will be used for 'the destruction, not of man himself, but of the enemies of man: the real, abiding, deep-rooted enemies, hunger and famine, poverty and disease'.[64] President Eisenhower's proposals of 8 December 1953 for an International Atomic Energy Agency were also designed, in part, to break the

---

62 The Foreign Secretary (Mr Selwyn Lloyd), 24 July 1956, H. C. Deb., vol. 557, col. 262.

63 In which, incidentally, the West has not shown up particularly well.

64 The Minister of State (Mr Nutting) in a speech to the First Committee at the General Assembly's tenth session, describing the United Kingdom's achievements in the development of atomic energy for peaceful purposes, Cmd. 9716, p. 62.

deadlock in negotiations about the control of atomic weapons. In other respects, however, the proposals represented what might be called an extension of technical assistance to the atomic field. And it is on this aspect of atomic energy that the United Nations has been able to make considerable progress.

During 1954 the proposal made on 8 December 1953 to the General Assembly by the President for an atomic 'pool' out of which 'fissionable material would be allocated to serve the peaceful pursuits of mankind'[65] became whittled down to a clearing house for information and for bilateral arrangements; a 'broker' rather than a 'bank', as the United Kingdom delegate said. In spite, however, of the rather diminished enthusiasm shown for the proposal at the General Assembly's ninth session, it was resolved not only to continue negotiations on the Agency but also to convene a technical conference on the peaceful uses of atomic energy in Geneva the following year.

The 1955 International Conference on the Peaceful Uses of Atomic Energy in Geneva must be accounted one of the United Nations' major successes; indeed, as a result of the extensive release of classified information and the freedom of the discussions, of all the manifestations of the Geneva 'spirit' it is perhaps the only one which is destined to have a lasting effect.

> It also provided . . . a remarkable example of the capacity of groups of highly qualified professional intellectuals to co-operate regardless of national origins, and the total objectivity and lack of political bias which characterized its proceedings was extremely encouraging.[66]

At the tenth session of the General Assembly the achievements of the Conference were warmly praised, and Anglo-American proposals for a second international scientific conference on nuclear power in three years' time and for the promotion of separate

---

65 *GAOR*, 8th sess., Plen., 470th mtg., p. 452.
66 'The Tenth Assembly of the United Nations', *World Today*, Feb. 1956, p. 70.

conferences on specialized aspects of atomic energy were very well received. The revised proposals for a permanent International Atomic Energy Agency, contained in a draft statute circulated in August 1955, had a rather different reception. The main functions proposed for the Agency, which were to promote research and the interchange of scientific information on the peaceful uses of atomic energy and to receive and allocate fissionable materials and fuels for peaceful purposes, were not the subject of much criticism, partly because they were something of a reversion to the original idea of an atomic 'pool'. But the proposal that the Agency should be directed by a Board of Governors on which the atomically most advanced states would be in a permanent majority was not to the liking of the atomic 'have-nots', who sought to bring the Agency into a closer relationship with the United Nations, where they could themselves command a majority. In this they were supported by the Soviet Union, who wanted the Agency to be closely tied to the Security Council. In order to meet these criticisms, Brazil, Czechoslovakia, India, and the Soviet Union were invited to participate in negotiation of the statute, provision was made for a conference of all Members of the United Nations and the specialized agencies to decide on the final text of the statute, and the question of the Agency's relationship to the United Nations was referred to the Secretary-General to study, with the help of his Advisory Committee on the Scientific Conference. In this amended form the proposals were adopted unanimously.[67]

The growth of bilateral and regional atomic arrangements and the extensive declassification of scientific information which has taken place since the start of the Geneva Conference, have pushed the proposed Agency out of the limelight. Nor is it either desirable or feasible that these existing arrangements should eventually be brought within the framework of the Agency. But in providing a 'pool' of fissionable materials, in giving technical assistance and advice,

---

[67] *GAOR*, 10th sess., suppl. no. 19, Resolution 912(X).

and in promoting the exchange of scientific information, the Agency may yet come to play a useful complementary, albeit secondary, role.

THE 'DE FACTO'
REVISION
OF THE CHARTER

PART THREE

chapter six

The Growth of Regionalism

Considering the kind of world in which it had to operate, the record of the United Nations is neither as disappointing nor the part it has played in shaping British policy as insignificant as is sometimes alleged. The collective action taken under United Nations auspices to resist aggression in Korea is a landmark in the history of international co-operation. The states of Indonesia, Israel, and Libya owe their creation, at least in part, to the intervention of the United Nations, while both in Indonesia and Palestine the Security Council was instrumental in limiting the fighting. When bilateral negotiations have reached deadlock, the Council has more than once been influential in restraining the disputants from precipitate action and in preventing an irreparable and possibly disastrous rupture (Berlin and Kashmir), in spite of the fact that several of these disputes were outcrops of conflicts so deep-seated that they still defy peaceful solution. Through the Assembly the United Nations has also brought succour to the South Korean people devastated by war, to the Arab refugees, and to refugees in all parts of the world, while it has given states such as India invaluable opportunities for mediating between the main Power blocs (Korea and the prisoner-of-war issue). Moreover, whereas in the past an international misdemeanor might threaten armed conflict, the modern practice of complaining—or threatening to complain—to the Security Council or the General Assembly has sometimes served as a useful 'safety-valve' or 'cooling-off' period.[1] Both bodies have rarely been able to secure redress for the wrong done, but they have made for forbearance in the face even of acute provocation. When tension is high and tempers are easily aroused, this is no small service.

The collective principle has, therefore, had its successes. But there can be little doubt that, except during the early days of the Korean War, there has been a steady loss of confidence in the United Nations, as an instrument both of collective security and of pacific settlement. Thus the San Francisco picture of the Security Council as the organ of an armed Concert was soon shattered by the vituperative wrangling which marked its first meetings and by the Soviet Union's ready resort to the veto, while the Council's sudden access of vigour in June 1950 was short-lived. The General Assembly might at first have been regarded as the embryo of a world government, but before long it came to be viewed chiefly as a form of diplomatic machinery whereby disputes that did not yield to bilateral treatment could be considered collectively. And many were ready to point out that the babel of propaganda and the skilful manoeuvring for votes made the outcome of such collective consideration highly unpredictable. Nor did the realization that United Nations recommendations could be flouted with relative

---

[1] The best-known instances are the American threat in August 1946 to arraign Yugoslavia for shooting down an American plane, the United Kingdom complaint against Albania in the Corfu Channel case (January 1947), and the American complaints in September 1954 against the Soviet Union for shooting down an American plane over the Sea of Japan and against Communist China for the retention of American airmen serving with the United Nations in Korea.

impunity (Palestine), or the feeling that British rights were apt to be overlooked (Corfu Channel case and Anglo-Iranian oil dispute), help to mitigate this deepening scepticism. In more recent years, with the solution through traditional diplomatic channels of such knotty questions as Trieste, the Anglo-Iranian oil dispute, the Anglo-Egyptian dispute over the Canal Zone (all of which had previously been unsuccessfully brought before the Security Council), the collective approach—multilateral diplomacy—has lost much of its appeal. Traditional diplomacy—private negotiations between directly interested parties—has returned to favour.

The reasons for the steady diminution in the authority of the United Nations are complex and varied, but four closely inter-connected facts stand out. The first is that in a deeply divided world the collective security system of the Charter has remained little more than a paper formula, of interest to international lawyers and political theorists but virtually ignored by most governments. The dominant motif of the past decade has been the coalescence of states into systems of mutual defence, centred for the most part on either the Soviet Union or the United States. With the exception of a fairly small band of uncommitted states, almost every country in the world has gravitated towards the camp of one or other of the chief protagonists in the cold war. The main result for the United Nations has been to upset the delicate balance achieved at San Francisco between the Charter system of collective security—the 'League against an unknown enemy'—and the 'escape' clause articles (51 and 107). These articles have served to legalize the creation of a series of military alliances of collective defence against a known potential enemy, the 'particular' has superseded the 'general', 'regionalism' has ousted 'universalism', and the United Nations has been elbowed off the centre of the international stage.

The second is that the United Nations itself has been inextricably caught up in the realities of world politics and in the manoeuvrings of the cold war. The San Francisco presumption of an overriding unity of purpose and a community of interests was soon shattered and the policies pursued by most governments at the United Nations have tended—though not uniformly so—to be motivated primarily by the needs of the particular alliance to which they belong. Thus the Soviet Union from the start has used the United Nations to foster dissension within the Western world, while early American attempts to salvage something from the wreckage of the Charter's collective security system reflected as much a disposition to turn the United Nations into an anti-Communist alliance as a loyalty to the collective security idea. It is true that even in this early period United Nations meetings afforded some scope for mediation and conciliation, but they were usually plagued by a verbal warfare in which the protagonists seemed more preoccupied with singing their own praises and drawing attention to their opponents' short-comings, or currying favour with 'uncommitted' Powers, than with arriving at an accommodation. In this propaganda contest even the most 'technical' questions were apt to become bones of political and ideological contention. Indeed, at one time the only common interest the West and the Soviet Union seemed to have in the continued existence of the United Nations was 'the common interest of rival hucksters in their freedom to advertise their wares in the market place'.[2] With the temporary relaxation of international tension after Stalin's death this aspect of the United Nations has become less pronounced, but its effects have persisted, for it gave rise not only to second thoughts about the merits of 'open diplomacy' and 'majority voting', but it was instrumental in re-shaping the Organization.

Thus the third fact and perhaps the most striking change in the United Nations is that, of the two main elements in the original concept of the Organization, namely, the Great Power 'Concert' or 'Grand Alliance' idea (embodied in the Security Council) and the 'town forum of the world' idea (represented by the General

---

[2] Martin Wight in *Scotsman*, 23 Oct. 1946.

Assembly), the former has suffered an almost total eclipse whilst the latter has far outgrown the rather limited role of expressing public opinion assigned to it at Dumbarton Oaks. Indeed, in view of its impotence as an enforcement agency (except initially over Korea) and its atrophy even as an instrument of pacific settlement, the Security Council may be said to have lapsed into virtual desuetude. By contrast, because of the absence of the veto, its wider membership, and its greater potentialities as a propaganda platform, the General Assembly now overshadows the Security Council in almost every sphere of the United Nations' political activities.

The fourth and rather distinct fact is that the modest place given to 'peaceful change' in the Charter and the intended limiting effect of Article 2(7) have not prevented the growth of strong anti-colonial pressures, frequently directed against the United Kingdom. Nationalism may be on the wane in the Western world, but elsewhere it is more vocal than ever. The United Nations provides a handy forum for publicizing nationalist grievances and for proclaiming the principle of self-determination. As the cold war issues have tended increasingly to be tackled outside the United Nations, the clash between the colonial and anti-colonial Powers has come to divide the Organization almost as deeply as the East-West conflict.

The growth of regionalism (and the prominence given to the 'escape' clause articles of the Charter), the uses—or misuses—to which the United Nations has been put in the cold war, coupled with the new relationship between the Security Council and the General Assembly and the growth of strong anti-colonialist pressures in the latter, have not resulted in the formal amendment, or the *de jure* revision, of the Charter. But they have so radically transformed the role of the United Nations and its machinery, practices, and procedures, that it is scarcely misleading to speak of the *de facto* revision of the Charter.[3] The most notable features of this process

---

[3] G. Schwarzenberger, *Power Politics*, 2nd ed. (London, Stevens for London Institute of World Affairs, 1951), p. 744.

of revision and the British attitude thereto will be discussed in this and the following three chapters.

THE 'ESCAPE CLAUSES'

There is no need to dwell on the stillbirth of the Charter collective security system except to recall that the lack of unanimity among the permanent members of the Security Council, which has so often prevented the Council from reaching a decision, was also reflected in the failure of the Military Staff Committee[4] to agree on the size and nature of the forces which members were to make available to the Security Council under Article 43.[5] As a result, none of the agreements provided for under Article 43 has been concluded. But at San Francisco the United Kingdom delegate gave an assurance, on behalf of the Sponsoring Powers, that Members were under no obligation to employ 'armed forces, assistance, and facilities' in excess of those specifically provided for in the agreements.[6] Consequently Members are under no obligation to take military action under Article 42[7] and the Security Council has no authority to *call upon* them to do so. Thus, on the outbreak of the Korean War, although the Security Council was not obstructed by the veto, it was unable to rely on the provisions of Articles 43-7; it could only 'recommend', not 'call upon', Members to assist the Republic of Korea. Of course, in practice this difference is unlikely

---

[4] A useful analysis of the Military Staff Committee's Report on this failure (S/336 of 30 Apr. 1947) is contained in Goodrich and Hambro, pp. 283-85. See also Sir Alexander Cadogan, 'The United Nations: a Balance Sheet', in *YBWA, 1951*, pp. 4-5.

[5] Art. 43, para. 1, reads: 'All members of the United Nations, in order to contribute to the maintenance of international peace and security, undertake to make available to the Security Council, on its call and in accordance with a special agreement or agreements, armed forces, assistance, and facilities, including rights of passage, necessary for the purpose of maintaining international peace and security.'

[6] UNCIO, xii. 508. The precise legal status of this assurance is rather uncertain.

[7] Which empowers the Security Council to 'take such action by air, sea, or land forces, as may be necessary to maintain or restore international peace and security'.

to be of cardinal importance. In case of aggression the crucial question is not whether states have earmarked forces for use by the Security Council, but whether they are ready to take part in collective action under the United Nations; if they are, they can be expected to make the necessary forces available. Nevertheless, it is as well to recall that the failure to conclude any military agreements deprived the Charter system of the teeth it was originally intended to have.

The failure of the Military Staff Committee testified to the inability of the United Nations to assure its Members a reasonable sense of security. As suspicion grew, inevitably those sharing common fears and, for the most part, common traditions and beliefs, gathered together in limited systems of mutual defence, organized on a regional basis. Regionalism alone seemed to offer something of that sense of security which the United Nations had failed to provide. But it was not the regionalism of Chapter VIII of the Charter (Arts. 52-4), under which regional agencies are explicitly subordinated to the Security Council. The texts of the treaties through which the Communist and Western defence systems are organized are liberally—even carefully—supplied with references to the Charter, but the most notable references are to the 'escape clause' Articles 51 and 107, and to the 'loophole' in Article 53.[8] These Charter provisions have one important feature in common. Action under them, unlike enforcement action by a regional agency under Article 53, does not require the prior authorization of the Security Council[9]—an authorization which the veto could be expected to preclude. They are, therefore, substitutes for the Security Council system rather than sub-systems under the Council as the regional agencies were intended to be. Thus the treaties of mutual assistance between the

---

[8] See above, pp. 31-32.

[9] For a valuable discussion of this point see Andrew Martin, *Collective Security* (Paris, UNESCO, 1952), pp. 175-77. On Art. 51 see also Sir W. Eric Beckett (former Legal Adviser to the Foreign Office), *The North Atlantic Treaty, the Brussels Treaty and the Charter of the United Nations* (London, Stevens for London Institute of World Affairs, 1950).

Soviet Union and her satellites and the Sino-Soviet Treaty of February 1950 are based on the 'loophole' in Article 53 and on Article 107, since they purport to be directed exclusively against ex-enemy states. The North Atlantic defence system, together with its offshoots in the Baghdad Pact (April 1955) and in the South East Asia Collective Defence Treaty (September 1954), is based on Article 51.[10] The only limitation on the right of collective self-defence under this article is that it can be exercised solely in the event of an armed attack[11] and only until the Security Council has taken the necessary measures to restore peace—an improbable contingency. Therefore, much as one might wish that these security arrangements should underpin rather than bypass the United Nations system, it would be disingenuous not to recognize that, at present, their formal subordination to the United Nations rests not altogether easily on their Member Governments' obligation to act in accordance with the Purposes and Principles of the Charter.

However, in Britain NATO's defensive character is considered to be such as to make it fully compatible with these Purposes and Principles. The firm resolve that it should remain so partly explains the criticism of suggestions, happily long discarded, that NATO should become an instrument of 'liberation', and of the distinction drawn by the United States, in a protocol to the South East Asia Collective Defence Treaty, between Communist aggression and aggression generally.[12] In short, British obeisance to the Purposes and Principles of the Charter is not merely formal. Some may be held more highly in regard than others, but they are still widely regarded as the standard of international propriety, the flagrant violation of which would deeply divide public opinion.

---

[10] As are the Inter-American Treaty of Reciprocal Assistance (Rio de Janeiro, 1947) and the Arab League Treaty of Mutual Defence (1952).

[11] This does not, of course, preclude states from building up their individual and collective capacity to meet an attack. On the question whether the right is limited only to the occurrence of an armed attack against a Member of the United Nations, see Chapter 5, p. 135.

[12] See speech by the Rt Hon. Kenneth Younger, 8 Nov. 1954, H. C. Deb., vol. 532, col. 944.

REGIONAL AGENCIES AND THE
PACIFIC SETTLEMENT OF DISPUTES

Despite the stress laid at San Francisco on the value of regional agencies in the pacific settlement of disputes, in practice they have played a minor part since, with few exceptions, the disputes which have threatened or involved bloodshed have not lent themselves to regional settlement. Partly for this reason, and subject to two important reservations, Britain has generally been concerned to foster the authority of the United Nations, and especially that of the Security Council, as an instrument of pacific settlement. The first reservation stems from the fear that recourse to the United Nations may give the Soviet Union and others opportunities for playing upon differences within the Western camp. Britain has, therefore, often preferred to settle differences through direct negotiations, especially when reference to the United Nations might merely have encouraged meddling by third parties. The second reservation is to be inferred from the disposition to defer to an apparent American preference for dealing with Latin American and, to a lesser extent, Far Eastern matters outside the United Nations. That Britain may sometimes have to tread warily between her interest in the authority of the Organization and a disinclination to offend the United States or play the Soviet game is illustrated by the Guatemalan 'dispute'.

The rather unsavoury story of the Guatemalan 'civil war' need not be examined here. But the submission of the dispute to the Security Council by Guatemala in June 1954 revealed interesting differences of attitude between the United States and Great Britain on a constitutional conundrum of some significance,[13] namely the precise relationship between the Security Council and regional agencies in the pacific settlement of disputes. The issue was whether

---

13 The debate was not primarily concerned with legal niceties. One commentator has aptly remarked that 'the loudest noise was the unmistakable yelp of the Monroe Doctrine when the Soviet Union stepped on its tail' (Alistair Cooke in the *Manchester Guardian*, 22 June 1954).

members of a regional agency (in this case the Organization of American States) are under an *absolute* obligation to 'make every effort to achieve pacific settlement of local disputes . . . by such regional agencies before referring them to the Security Council',[14] or whether they are entitled to ask the Security Council to deal with local disputes in the first instance. If the former view is taken, as it was by all members of the Security Council at the time except the Soviet Union, the Security Council is a body of last resort and paragraph 4 of Article 52—which states that the Article 'in no way impairs the application of Articles 34 and 35'—does no more than reaffirm the ultimate authority of the Security Council and the right of a state to refer the matter to the Security Council if no settlement can be reached through regional means. Indeed, as was pointed out in the *Report of the Sub-Committee on International Co-operation in the Political Field to the Interim Committee*,[15] Article 20 of the Charter of the Organization of American States provides that 'all disputes that may arise among the American States shall be submitted to the peaceful procedure set forth in the Charter before being referred to the Security Council of the United Nations.' Moreover, although it can be contended that a state cannot be deprived of the right to bring a matter before the Security Council in the first instance,[16] the Security Council itself is still required, under paragraph 2 of Article 52, to 'encourage the development of pacific settlement of local disputes . . . by such regional agencies'. Therefore, the majority proposal to refer the Guatemalan complaint to the Organization of American States was legally correct.

---

[14] Art. 52. Guatemala appealed to the Council under Art. 39 as well as under Art. 35, but the Council evidently considered there was no threat to international peace.

[15] A/AC.18/114, 5 July 1950, pp. 12-13. See also Goodrich and Hambro, p. 315.

[16] As argued by the Rt Hon. P. J. Noel-Baker, 14 July 1954, H. C. Deb., vol. 530, col. 580. This was also the British view at Dumbarton Oaks and San Francisco.

Nevertheless, when a few days later Guatemala appealed again to the Security Council, there was some criticism, particularly in British Liberal and Labour circles, of the United Kingdom's action in abstaining on the Security Council's decision (by 5 votes to 4 with 2 abstentions) not to reopen the discussion. No brief was held for the Guatemalan Government and it was realized that the Soviet Union was taking full advantage of the opportunity to stir up muddy waters. The Organization of American States could also rightly claim that the dispute fell within its jurisdiction. But when this Organization seemed to be acting with a dilatoriness amounting almost to premeditated prevarication, had not Guatemala a clear right of appeal to the Security Council? Did not the Security Council's decision suggest that the right of a small Power to be heard, instead of applying to all and sundry, as was the obvious intention of the Charter, now turned on its ideological complexion?

Interest in the issue was confined to a relatively small circle, within which criticism of American policy was for the most part[17] tempered by the desire to preserve Western unity. But dissatisfaction was keen enough for the Conservative Minister of State (Mr Selwyn Lloyd) to admit some disquiet at the way in which the matter had been handled by the Organization of American States.[18] The overriding need in the present times is the relaxation of tension by whatever means rather than over-zealous adherence to the strict doctrine of the Charter. Moreover, the role of the Organization of American States in the Costa Rican incident (January 1955) showed 'how useful regional organization can be in damping down the first sparks of what might grow into a dangerous fire,'[19] But the Guatemalan incident confirmed that there is a widespread desire in Britain not to undermine the authority of the United Nations and that a

---

[17] There were also those, of course, who are always ready to criticize the United States.

[18] 14 July 1954, H. C. Deb., vol. 530, col. 588.

[19] *Manchester Guardian*, 27 Jan. 1955.

seeming attempt to manipulate its machinery to stifle the right of a small Power to appeal to it[20] may arouse considerable resentment.

REGIONALISM: ITS MERITS AND LIMITATIONS

In 1948 Field-Marshal Smuts foresaw a world in which security rested upon what he called a 'triangle of power', the three angles of which would be formed by the Atlantic Community and the Commonwealth, the Communist bloc, and a third or 'middle Power' group of the uncommitted states of South Asia. It is towards this pattern, which is not so unlike that advocated by Sir Winston Churchill in 1943,[21] that post-war groupings have tended.

That states might have to fall back on this alternative to the universalism of the Charter was not far from the minds of delegates at San Francisco. Governments might hope for the best but they prepared for the worst. Thus the Foreign Office commentary gave explicit warning that if Great Power unanimity were undermined: 'the Members will resume their liberty of action'.[22] Accordingly, the 'escape clause' articles of the Charter were made sufficiently broad to enable a system of collective defence to be organized in the West if Soviet opposition resulted in the breakdown of the Charter's own security system. Article 51 might not have been tailor-made to fit the North Atlantic Treaty, but it was a close enough fit to still doubts as to the Treaty's legality.

This is not to argue, however, that regionalism was, or is, looked upon as a mere second best. On the contrary, right from the early days of the League of Nations there has been a powerful school of thought in Britain which has argued that strictly limited and care-

[20] The Greek complaints over Cyprus at the ninth (1954) and tenth (1955) sessions of the Assembly were regretted and the competence of the United Nations denied. But few questioned the right of the Greek Government to raise an issue which divided the two countries at the United Nations rather than at NATO, so long as that issue was proper for international discussion.

[21] See above, p. 7.

[22] Cmd. 6666, para. 88.

fully defined agreements (on the model of Locarno), to deal with the specific sources of mistrust, are more efficacious than abstract and general undertakings, if only because the latter may appear to have no obvious relation to the national interest or to be beyond the nation's capacity to meet them. This view has been, and is, more commonly held on the Right than on the Left. Yet Mr Bevin himself seems to have shared Mr Churchill's preference for regional arrangements with their more precise and limited commitments, and his belief that they alone were sturdy enough to bear the weight of a more universal system. As has been seen, the Charter itself went some way to accepting this view when it explicitly recognized (in Chapter VIII) the role of regional agencies in resolving local disputes and in acting as enforcement agencies. Moreover, in the political conditions that have obtained since 1949 NATO has come to be regarded in Britain as the main guardian of the Purposes and Principles of the Charter, on the grounds that it alone is capable of taking 'effective collective measures for the prevention and removal of threats to the peace, and for the suppression of acts of aggression or other breaches of the peace', and that only a strong NATO system can secure that balance of forces within the world which may enable the United Nations to become a more effective 'center for harmonizing the actions of nations'. In the non-political field, in which there are no formal obstacles to the growth of regionalism, the sprouting of regional bodies within both the United Nations (for example, regional economic commissions) and the specialized agencies also testifies to the recognized merits of limiting discussion to the small number of countries with a common interest in the problems peculiar to a single region and of excluding loquacious or obscurantist outsiders.

On the other hand, the events which preceded the Second World War are generally considered to have shown up the grievous defects of the doctrine of 'limited liability', while today the United Kingdom is made well aware of the limitations of regionalism by the fact that her world-wide interests tend to outrun her capacity to defend

them single-handed and by her position as the centre of a Commonwealth which might be irrevocably split by a too thorough-going
regionalism. It is also the case that regional bodies have not been
very successful in resolving local quarrels, and that the United
States Government has at times appeared to be able to negotiate
more freely and to be less trammelled by domestic pressures within
the framework of the United Nations. Above all, the constant
influence that the United Nations has exercised in favour of peaceful
negotiation rather than the use of force is a powerful argument
for upholding its authority. Thus, in political matters the United
Nations has still an important role as a body of last resort, as a
convenient 'cold storage' for unresolved disputes, and, occasionally,
as a restraint on hot-headed action by the Great Powers. Last,
but by no means least, regionalism cannot supplant the abiding
interest of the Great Powers in those issues of peace and war which
transcend all regional groupings. The development of nuclear weapons
and of a more or less stable balance between the rival camps may
serve as the most effective deterrent to major aggression, but, if
the armaments race is to be checked and the risk of accidents
inherent in a two-sided balance is to be reduced, the need for
re-establishing a Great Power 'Concert' is no less great than it was at
the time of San Francisco.

chapter seven

The 'New Diplomacy' and the Cold War

Although the 'Concert' function of the Security Council was very much in the minds of the permanent Members at San Francisco, most delegations (including the United States) laid more stress on the importance of the General Assembly as the deliberative assembly —the 'town meeting'—of the world, in which the sanction of world public opinion would have full rein. Majority voting—a good democratic device—would make it easier than it had been in the League to register this world public opinion, while the impact and representative character of that opinion would be enhanced by 'open diplomacy' and by the admission, within the near future, of all respectable members of international society.

The preoccupation of the protagonists in the cold war with strengthening their own alliance system has had a crippling effect on these expectations. The United Nations has become as much a scale for weighing the strength and merits of the competing alliances as an instrument for mobilizing and expressing world public opinion. Despite occasional tactical flexibility, the paramount aim of the Soviet Union seems to have been to sap the strength and unity of the Western world and to manoeuvre for support from the uncommitted Powers. United Nations organs have been used by the Soviet Union mainly as propaganda forums for weaning the masses from their bourgeois loyalties and as points of observation for locating and playing upon the sources of dissension within the West.

The Western Powers have been less single-minded. The main issue which for a time divided them, whether the United Nations should be reshaped as an additional arm of Western defence or retained as a centre for conciliation and mediation, will be discussed in the next chapter. But hardly less important has been the difference in attitude towards the 'new diplomacy'. All the Western Powers have been concerned to show up the hollowness of Soviet pretensions and have seen in the United Nations a valuable instrument for upholding principles of justice and fair dealing. But whereas the United States has hardly questioned, at least until recently, the merits of 'open diplomacy' as a means of bringing pressure to bear on recalcitrant states, Britain has been more conscious of its perils. In contrast to the American disposition to use the United Nations to enforce civilized standards on delinquent states, and as a place for public intimidation, condemnation, and coercion, Britain has for the most part sought to develop the Organization as a centre for private diplomatic agreement and negotiation.[1] It is mainly for this reason that Britain has viewed such characteristic features of United Nations meetings as 'open diplomacy' and 'majority' and 'bloc' voting with considerable distaste.

---

[1] Regular meetings of the Foreign Ministers at the Security Council (as Britain proposed at Dumbarton Oaks and as is made possible by Art. 28, para. 2) might have considerably facilitated such negotiation.

'OPEN DIPLOMACY'

In Britain the argument that the collective pressure exerted by the United Nations on the occasions mentioned earlier in this study would have been less effective had it not been brought to bear quite openly is not dismissed out of hand. But in other respects, and despite the early inclination towards 'open diplomacy', the Wilsonian precepts of 'open covenants . . . openly arrived at' and that 'diplomacy should proceed always frankly and in the public view'[2] now find little support. The excesses of 'diplomacy by loudspeaker' and 'diplomacy by insult' are unsympathetically contrasted with what is held to be the moderation, discretion, and continuity of traditional diplomacy. It can hardly be denied that the glare of publicity in which United Nations meetings are held has aggravated most delegates' preoccupation with wooing public opinion at home and abroad—by demonstrating the propriety of their own point of view and by showing up the pretensions and alleged obscurantism of their opponents—rather than with exploring the possibilities of an accommodation. Some delegates seem more concerned with hitting the headlines in their national press or with their showing on the television screen than with contributing constructively to the debates. As Sir Harold Nicolson has, with some justice, pointed out, 'it would be incorrect to suppose that these [i.e. United Nations] meetings are intended to serve the purpose of negotiation: they are exercises in forensic propaganda and do not even purport to be experiments in diplomatic method'.[3]

In this propaganda contest Soviet delegates have indulged most consistently in the more scurrilous forms of abuse—'diplomacy by insult'—but wilful misrepresentation and 'talking tough', either

---

[2] President Wilson himself does not appear to have meant that the actual negotiations should be conducted in public, but that is the interpretation put upon 'open diplomacy' by many of his supporters.

[3] Sir Harold Nicolson, *The Evolution of Diplomatic Method* (London, Constable, 1954), p. 91. Though it can be argued that in the modern world this cultivation of public opinion is itself a 'diplomatic method', just as it was in the ancient Greek world.

for the record or perhaps to stifle charges of appeasement or from a sense of personal affront, have by no means been a Soviet monopoly. And, as the United Kingdom delegates concluded towards the end of 1947, wilful misrepresentation can strike home all too effectively unless the more telling points are quickly rebutted. But the consequent interminable wrangling has placed a heavy strain on delegates' patience and has strongly militated against that mutual exploration of interests which is the corner-stone of true negotiation. As Mr Lester Pearson has said, 'open diplomacy tends to become frozen diplomacy'. Some debates seem merely to have succeeded in arousing slumbering suspicions and passions and in adding 'to the sum of human tension and bewilderment'.[4] Instead of acting as a safety-valve, United Nations meetings are just as likely to rub a small sore spot into a dangerous and spreading infection. In addition, the task of looking after, in public, the national interest in an Organization which purports to safeguard the collective interest, has made for a 'double talk' in which real motives and intentions are cloaked by protestations of high-mindedness and respect for the Charter. This kind of protestation was far from uncommon in the League of Nations;[5] it may occasionally have some genuine content (though usually in inverse proportion to the force and frequency with which it is made), but more often than not its prime aim is to placate domestic opinion or to win over uncommitted countries.

This 'verbal' war is an almost inevitable concomitant of the cold war, in which the struggle for the minds of men permeates every facet of international life. Indeed, most extra-United Nations diplomatic exchanges also have a strong propaganda flavour. Moreover, the readiness of some delegates to identify the collective interest with their own national interest and their indignation at the

---

[4] ibid. p. 91.

[5] It is probably unavoidable in any international institution which models itself on parliamentary practices but which lacks a well developed sense of community.

obscurantism—even wickedness—of their opponents may but testify to their capacity for self-righteousness and to the power of contemporary ideologies rather than to the corrupting influence of 'open diplomacy'. Moralizing about another country's iniquities is not confined to the United Nations.

'Open diplomacy' has also its compensations.

> Nowhere but in the United Nations where the protagonists are face to face in debate can it better be shown that the Western Powers are taking their stand on principles of freedom and respect for the individual, principles common to the vast majority of the countries of the free world; and that they have at heart the interests not only of themselves but of small countries also.[6]

In this respect the debates have enabled the differences between the Western and Soviet world to be displayed clearly and dramatically for everyone to see. Soviet pretensions and the carefully concealed flaws in the Soviet system have been shown up in all their nakedness (for example, forced labour)[7] both for the peoples of the Western world and for those in the uncommitted countries. Indeed, the United Nations debates—and the intemperate language used by Soviet delegates—have played a vital part in educating the British and American peoples in the realities of international life and in the extent of Soviet ambitions. Or again, the dexterity with which Soviet propaganda bubbles have been pricked may have helped to convince 'marginal' delegates of the hollowness of Soviet charges (for example, the Communist 'germ warfare' campaign) and to quieten stirrings of self-doubt within the Western world. Nor, from the start, has 'open diplomacy' been quite unqualified. The need for the Great Powers to meet in private on such questions as the veto, disarmament, and the appointment of a Secretary-General, is generally accepted. And, whatever the shortcomings of

---

[6] 'Can the United Nations keep the Peace', *Round Table*, March 1954, p. 133.
[7] *ESCOR*, 16th sess., suppl. no. 13: *Report of the Ad Hoc Committee on Forced Labour* (E/2431, 1953).

'open diplomacy', Sir Harold Nicolson himself has admitted that 'confidential negotiations that lead to secret pledges are worse even than the televised diplomacy we enjoy today'.[8]

There have, therefore, been occasions, particularly in the earlier days of the United Nations, when the public airing of issues was welcome. But this does not substantially detract from the conclusion that 'open diplomacy' commonly makes for a rigidity of view and an impassioned demagogy—a 'playing to the gallery'—which is detrimental to the prime diplomatic task, the reconciliation of conflicting interests. The worst acerbities of 'open diplomacy' will have to be tempered if the United Nations is to become a diplomatic instrument of first importance. This will not be easy. For instance, most Americans have an almost pathological suspicion of 'private' meetings, a suspicion that is all too readily (but understandably) played upon by press correspondents, who seem to regard denial of access to a meeting almost as the infringement of some inviolable human right. Fortunately, a number of developments over the last few years point in the right direction. Firstly, most delegates have realized that demagogy is a two-edged weapon, as likely to reap disapproval as applause; the merits of moderation and brevity are increasingly recognized. Secondly, a wide range of techniques have grown up both in the Security Council and in the General Assembly for bringing disputants together or for reconciling conflicting views in private; ample provision is now made for conciliators, mediators, Committees of Good Offices, and the like.[9] Thirdly, the unfortunate effects of the feverish atmosphere of New York are more openly admitted, as are the merits of Geneva (or London or Paris), as is witnessed by the Geneva Conference

---

8 Nicolson, *Diplomatic Method*, p. 78. It was this dislike of secret treaties which led to the insertion in the Charter of Art. 102 (modelled on Art. 18 of the Covenant) which stipulates that every treaty and every international agreement entered into by any Member of the United Nations shall as soon as possible be registered with the Secretariat and published by it.

9 H. Field Haviland, Jr., *The Political Role of the General Assembly* (New York, Carnegie Endowment for International Peace, 1951), pp. 68-72.

on Korea and Indo-China and the meetings of the Sub-Committee of the Disarmament Commission in London. Fourthly, much stress is now laid on the importance of informal and personal contacts between delegates in the lounges and corridors, in the leading delegations' offices and hotel rooms, and at the innumerable receptions which mark every major United Nations meeting. Such contacts can afford much greater scope than public debates for the practice of the diplomatic arts. Partly as a result, and fifthly, most of the real business of the United Nations is now conducted in relative privacy outside the formal meetings.[10] Indeed, the main function of plenary meetings and committees of the whole, particularly in the Security Council, is to let off propaganda steam or to discuss, and usually to endorse (perhaps with some drafting amendments), recommendations privately reached between interested delegates.

These changes reflect a marked shift away from 'open diplomacy'; they do not result from, and their further elaboration does not require, formal amendment of the Charter (which is silent on the question), or even of the various Rules of Procedure. But this does not diminish their significance. In the British view, they herald a welcome step forward towards the desired goal of *open* covenants, *privately* arrived at.

'MAJORITY' RULE

In both the League of Nations and the United Nations voting was based on the principle of 'one state, one vote'. But whereas in the League the rule of unanimity obtained (with minor qualifications), in the United Nations organs other than the Security Council[11] majority voting is the rule. 'Decisions of the General

---

[10] Sub-committees can make for repetition and irrelevancy (if their terms of reference are not clearly defined) but they are a useful means of bringing directly interested parties together in private.

[11] Where the rule of unanimity, or qualified unanimity, of the permanent members obtains for all but procedural questions.

Assembly on important questions shall be made by a two-thirds majority of the members present and voting',[12] while 'decisions on other questions, including the determination of additional categories of questions to be decided by a two-thirds majority, shall be made by a majority of the members present and voting'.[13] The implications of this change[14] are very little remarked and probably little understood. Yet they are far-reaching and not altogether encouraging.

The main consequence is the introduction into most United Nations organs of what has been fittingly called 'voting-power' politics, the aim of which is to muster the number of votes (either a two-thirds or simple majority) required to secure the passage of a resolution. If the prescribed majority can be secured, the minority can then be voted down. In the League, on the other hand, although much of the work was done in committees which used majority voting, neither the Council nor the Assembly could, as a rule, come to a final decision of any importance unless at least the acquiescence of the minority could be obtained. But this presupposed a certain amount of 'give and take', a willingness on the part of the majority to compromise and to take account of the wishes of the minority. It called for negotiation, not steamroller voting tactics.

Majority voting in the United Nations owes its introduction partly to the analogy so often drawn between majority rule within a parliamentary democracy and majority rule in an international institution. Were the institution in question the embryo of a world government and accepted as such by all its members, the analogy would have some point, especially if voting were weighted. But in radically different circumstances it is basically misleading, firstly,

---

12 Art. 18(2).

13 Art. 18(3).

14 Which was agreed at Dumbarton Oaks with less consideration than was given to any other important aspect of the Charter.

because the exis.ence of a democratic state is predicated on a degree of political agreement as to ends and means which does not exist in the international context. In other words, majority voting 'presupposes an ability and willingness to compromise on certain points of issue and an agreement on "fundamentals"', whereas 'in all the organs of the UN there is a continuous contention between the Western Powers and the Soviet Union over the nature and significa ice of the assumptions underlying the organization'.[15] Secondly, the dissentient minority within the state is constitutionally compellable. If it cannot be convinced, it can be voted down, and if necessary made to conform, since the state has a mcnopoly or near monopoly of the means of coercion. But this is manifestly not the situation in the United Nations. Consequently, as Sir Hartley Shawcross pointed out as early as 1947:

> It is an over-simplification of the complex relationships between the nations of the world to suppose that every-thing can be settled by the simple device of a majority vote. Majority rule is the appropriate institution in a society the individual members of which are subordinate to one sov-ereign legislature. That is not yet the position amongst the nations of the world.[16]

Yet each session the General Assembly's agenda has included a wide range of questions upon which the opinions of a majority of Member States carry no authority in the eyes of the minority, and concerning which it is clear in advance that the minority is both determined and able to defy the majority will. Thus the Soviet Union and her satellites have often been voted down; but to little effect. The reasons are not far to seek. In the first place, even if the majority were entitled to impose conformity—which they are not, for a

---

[15] Kenneth H. Dawson, 'The United Nations in a Divided World', *World Politics*, Jan. 1954, p. 230.

[16] Speech on the Interim Committee delivered by Sir Hartley Shawcross to the Political Committee of the second session of the General Assembly, Cmd. 7320, p. 55.

majority vote gives no legal power to coerce the minority[17]—they would not have the capacity to do so, short of a third world war. On the contrary, the majority and the dissentient minority are fairly evenly matched in terms of real power; and whatever their respective voting strength, votes cannot do the work of bullets. In the second place, the moral authority of the majority's recommendations is not universal. In Communist eyes they are more probably regarded as capitalist moves to weaken the defences of the 'home of the proletariat'. Only fear of diplomatic isolation, of a loss of sympathy in uncommitted countries, is likely to induce even a modicum of outward conformity. And it might in fairness be admitted that if the roles were reversed a not dissimilar attitude would probably be taken by a minority West.

Nor is this situation limited to the issues that divide the West and the Soviet Union. Any number of states, both within and outside the Organization, have shown themselves both willing and able to ignore United Nations recommendations. They have been able to do so with impunity and—it might seem—in good conscience. Some such instances have already been alluded to earlier in this study. Another classic example is the total failure of the General Assembly's recommendations for the withdrawal of Ambassadors (or Ministers) from Madrid and for Spain's exclusion from the specialized agencies (December 1946).[18] In fact, in this instance the net effect was probably the opposite of that intended; certainly the Assembly's action in no way contributed to the formation of an acceptable alternative government. On the contrary, General Franco

---

[17] Not only is the Security Council not entitled to take enforcement action against a permanent member, but except when additional powers have been specifically conferred upon them (for example, the Italian colonies), the General Assembly and other United Nations organs are only empowered to make recommendations on the analogy of a 'vœu' in the League.

[18] *GAOR*, 1st sess., pt. 2, A/64/Add. 1, Resolution 39(1). Mr Bevin was caught between the fervour with which British trade unionists denounced Franco and the desire of his official advisers not to involve an already overburdened United Kingdom in unlawful intervention. In the event the United Kingdom reluctantly supported and complied with the recommendations, but mainly lest worse befall.

was able skilfully to exploit the xenophobic inclinations of most Spaniards to consolidate his position, whilst the technical work of several of the specialized agencies suffered from Spain's enforced absence. Four years later the Assembly's decision had to be reversed; Spain is now a member of most of the specialized agencies and she was admitted to the United Nations itself in December 1955. Similarly, the constant pressure of the Assembly on the South African Government appears to have acted as an irritant rather than a solvent. Nor have most of the recommendations of the anti-colonial majority carried real 'moral' authority in the eyes of the colonial minority, since they are often thought to be based on little more than irrational prejudice. Britain, France, Belgium, and other colonial Powers have more than once had occasion to warn the majority that further pressure might lead to their 'non-co-operation'.[19]

Against the defects of majority voting, however, must be set the fact that a perpetuation of the unanimity rule of the League would almost certainly have stultified the Assembly as surely as has the veto the Security Council. The present voting system does at least prevent the Assembly from being hamstrung by the vagaries or calculated obstructionism of a small minority and enable the majority to act with United Nations backing. Were it not for majority voting, the Assembly would have been unable to 'decide' on the future of the Italian colonies, to appoint the Balkan Committee or the United Nations Mediator in Palestine, or to channel aid to Korea and to Arab refugees, whilst its work in the economic field would have been severely limited. Nor would the Western Powers have been so well placed to arraign the Soviet Union and her satellites on such issues as forced labour, the denial of human rights in the ex-enemy satellites, and the Soviet refusal to allow Russian wives of British and other non-Soviet nationals to leave the Soviet Union to rejoin their husbands. It is improbable that United Nations condemnation touched off any stirrings of conscience amongst Soviet leaders, but at least it threatened them

---

[19] See below, pp. 354-55.

with diplomatic isolation and helped to impress on the non-Soviet world the contumely in which Communist leaders hold the individual. And it is not impossible that a number of non-Communist states have held their hand for fear of similar condemnation. Above all, in several countries, and especially in the United States, domestic opinion is acutely sensitive to world opinion. In so far as the General Assembly is able to focus and crystallize, formulate and express that opinion, it can occasionally exercise a beneficent influence on policy in these countries, whether by prodding it into action or by exercising a friendly restraint.

On balance, therefore, majority voting in the Assembly is to be preferred to the rule of unanimity. The real need is for the majority to appreciate the limitations of their arithmetical preponderance and to explore the possibilities of an acceptable compromise to the full before proceeding to vote down the minority. There have been signs recently of a more general recognition both of this need and of the desirability in some instances of postponing discussion in order to allow the parties directly concerned more time to negotiate. Unfortunately such restraint is rendered more difficult by the practice of 'bloc' voting.

'BLOC' VOTING

Many in Britain who are well versed in United Nations' affairs consider that what has come to be known as 'bloc' voting, and the swapping of votes between blocs, makes for a degree of manoeuvring and not always entirely relevant negotiation that tends to obscure the main issues and to produce results of dubious merit (for example, Libya). This dislike is no doubt partly to be explained by the fact that Britain is at a disadvantage (since there is no Commonwealth bloc) in 'bloc' voting as compared with the Soviet Union, that has commanded five, and now commands nine votes,[20] and the

20 The Soviet vote was weighted from the start by the concession of full membership to the Ukraine and Byelorussia. In addition, Czechoslovakia and Poland automatically follow the Soviet lead, and the recently admitted Albania, Bulgaria, Hungary, and Roumania can be expected to follow suit.

United States that can usually (except on economic aid) count upon the support of some sixteen Latin American republics. Until the admission of sixteen new Members in December 1955 the United States was in a particularly powerful position. The seventeen votes she could normally mobilize were only four short of the twenty-one votes then necessary to block any resolution on an important issue.[21] These four votes were almost always forthcoming on political issues, giving the United States what amounted to a veto in the General Assembly (witness American opposition to inviting India to the Geneva Conference on Korea).[22]

There are, of course, a number of countries which do not belong to any bloc. Much of the manoeuvring at the United Nations is designed to secure these floating votes. The composition and alignments of the different blocs also vary considerably according to the issue involved, be it the cold war, colonialism, or economic aid. None of the three major 'free world' groupings (the NATO bloc, the Latin American bloc, and the Arab-Asian bloc) is as monolithic as the Soviet bloc. On cold war issues the first two cluster together almost unanimously, with a varying number of members of the Arab-Asian bloc standing aloof (accompanied occasionally by Argentina, Sweden, and Yugoslavia). On colonial and race rivalry issues, the Latin American and Arab-Asian blocs tend to act together, with the United States (and occasionally Canada) taking a rather equivocal position within the NATO camp. This combination has been a powerful one for it has normally been able to muster sufficient Arab-Asian (including Ethiopia) and Latin American votes, to achieve, with the Soviet bloc, the two-thirds majority (40) until recently required for 'important' questions. And even if there were a few defaulters, there were others outside these groups who would often vote the same way (for example, Israel and Yugoslavia). This combination is likely to be strengthened by the

---

[21] Such resolutions required 40 votes if all the then 60 Members were present and voting.

[22] See above p. 145.

adherence of several of the sixteen new Members. Its weakness in the past has lain in the strong inclination of the Latin American countries to follow the lead of the United States. In the early years of the United Nations the United States took an anti-colonial line; in the last few years the Americans seem to have been torn between, on the one hand, their traditional anti-colonialism and, on the other hand, their desire not to weaken the unity of a West which includes the major colonial Powers, and their recognition of the bad effects which may be produced by too great encouragement of the principle of self-determination. Of late the latter considerations have usually predominated (except on race questions), and the United States and Latin American votes have usually been cast in favour of moderation—much to Britain's relief, since the attitude of the United States is usually decisive. Thus, although the less seemly side of 'bloc' voting is the 'horse-trading' of votes, often irrespective of the merits of a question, Britain's irritation at its vagaries and irrationalism has come to be tempered by the success of the United States' moderating counsels. It is also now more readily granted that 'bloc' voting not only signifies an attempt by the medium and small Powers to exercise a greater influence in the counsels of the United Nations than their individual stature allows, but that it also marks a real if inchoate community of ideas and interests within the blocs. In short, 'bloc' voting is, to some extent, the United Nations' counterpart of regionalism. It has, therefore, probably come to stay.

WEIGHTED VOTING

Much of the inequity of 'bloc' voting stems from the egalitarianism of the 'one state, one vote' principle. This principle seems firmly entrenched,[23] but it is in fact quite absurd that, for instance, the smallest Central American republics should have the same voting

---

[23] Despite its modification in the International Bank and the International Monetary Fund. See below, p. 276.

strength as the Great Powers. This discrepancy between voting weight and diplomatic weight has led to the advocacy of various forms of 'weighted' voting, based on such criteria as population, national income, diplomatic weight, &c.[24] Britain, as one of a small minority of European colonial Powers, was for a time much attracted by the merits of weighted voting,[25] but the agitation in its favour has now rather died down. Five main reasons may be adduced for this. Firstly, the more moderate temper of the debates on colonial issues has, at least temporarily, relieved the pressure on Britain. Secondly, where the Assembly is able in fact to 'decide' (e. g. the Italian colonies or the setting up of subordinate bodies), weighted voting might make for less opportunist decisions. But the Assembly is usually only able to 'recommend'; and although Assembly recommendations may carry considerable 'moral' authority, they are not binding. Governments are free to decide whether to implement a recommendation or not. In doing so they are likely to take more notice of the composition of the majority than of its size and to 'weight' the individual votes in their own minds. Thirdly, this 'mental weighting' is also reflected in the disposition of the smaller states to look to the Great (and some medium) Powers to take the initiative on major policy questions and in the more frequent representation of these Powers on the *ad hoc* committees and sub-committees of the General Assembly and other United Nations organs.[26] These practices greatly narrow the gulf between real power and voting power. Fourthly, 'weighted' voting is most frequently pressed by those who hope to give the Assembly the power to arrive at decisions binding on its members. Britain,

---

[24] Elizabeth McIntyre, 'Weighted Voting in International Organization', *International Organization*, Nov. 1954. Britain unsuccessfully proposed a system of weighted voting for the International Trade Organization.

[25] Cmd. 6666, para. 85; also report of statement by Sir Hartley Shawcross, *The Times*, 12 Dec. 1949, and similar statements quoted in Alan de Rusett, 'Large and Small States in International Organization', *International Affairs*, Oct. 1954.

[26] Field Haviland, *Political Role of the General Assembly*, p. 79.

in common with all the other permanent members of the Security Council and probably the vast majority of United Nations Members, would strongly resist any such proposal. Lastly, whatever the intrinsic merits of 'weighted voting', it would be extremely difficult to obtain agreement on the precise weighting. Which criteria should be used in computing voting strength? Population? National or per capita income? Territorial area? Literacy? If the weighting were based on a single factor only it would give an entirely false picture of the relative importance of states. If, on the other hand, several factors were taken into account, how much importance should be attached to each? And should the weighting not vary according to the issue on which the vote was being taken, for most states are bound to be more interested in some issues than others. Quite clearly, at every turn there are not only difficult technical problems but delicate questions of prestige are also involved. These would inevitably lead to long and acrimonious discussions which could hardly fail to threaten the new-found moderation and sense of responsibility which has marked recent sessions of the General Assembly. All things considered, therefore, 'mental weighting' is not at all a poor substitute.

MEMBERSHIP[27]

A more serious handicap than voting-power politics to the use of the United Nations as a diplomatic instrument has been the exclusion for the first decade of its existence of a large number of states, including several of considerable diplomatic standing and influence. At San Francisco original membership was made the exclusive privilege of those who had participated in the struggle

[27] There is a voluminous literature on this topic. See especially A/AC.64/L.1 (*Memorandum on the Historical Background to the Question of the Admission of New Members*); A/2400 (*Report of the Special Committee on Admission of New Members*); *Repertory of United Nations Practice*, i. 165-213; L. C. Green, 'Membership in the United Nations', in *CLP, 1949*; and Leo Gross, 'Election of States to United Nations Membership', in *Proceedings of the American Society of International Law, 1953*.

against the Axis Powers, while in order to preclude the admission of ex-enemy (or 'Fascist') states until they had repented of their ways, criteria of eligibility were set out which subsequent applicants were expected to satisfy, namely, that they must (*a*) be states, (*b*) be peace-loving, (*c*) accept the obligations of the Charter, (*d*) be able, and (*e*) be willing, to carry them out. The major obstacle, however, to the admission of a new Member into the United Nations is that it requires not only the approval of two-thirds of the General Assembly but also a favourable recommendation from the Security Council, so enabling a permanent member to veto the admission of any state.[28]

In an Organization in which majority voting is the rule, the permanent members are bound to have a heightened interest in the admission of states with whom they have special ties or on whose loyalties they think they can count and to be predisposed to prevent the admission of any state that is likely to vote in the opposite camp. For most of the period under review this latter consideration has prevailed, with the result that, despite the lip-service paid to the principle of universality, to making the Organization fully representative of the diplomatic society of states, up till the tenth session (1955) of the General Assembly only 9 new Members had been admitted[29] and 21 states had had their applications for admission rejected.

The feeling of impatience at the exclusion of so many states was for a time somewhat mitigated by the freedom with which non-Member States have been invited to take part in discussions on matters of direct concern to them. Article 32 of the Charter requires that 'any state which is not a Member of the United Nations, if it is a party to a dispute under consideration by the Security Council,

---

28 Art. 4 of the Charter. Compare Art. 1, para. 2 of the Covenant, under which any fully self-governing state, Dominion or Colony could become a Member of the League if its admission were agreed to by two-thirds of the Assembly.
29 In chronological order: Afghanistan, Iceland, Sweden, Thailand, Pakistan, Yemen, Burma, Israel, Indonesia.

shall[30] be invited to participate, without vote, in the discussion relating to the dispute'. The conditions laid down for such participation—for example, those in Article 35(2)—have not been very onerous and in cases of doubt (for example, whether a dispute exists or whether a country is a 'state'), a representative has been invited to furnish the Council 'with information or to give other assistance in examining matters within its competence'.[31] The decisions to issue such invitations are also instanced in the Joint Statement on Voting Procedure, and have in fact been treated, as procedural matters and so not subject to the veto. Occasionally, the Security Council has refused to invite an obviously interested party (for instance, North Korea), but on the whole invitations have been issued fairly liberally.[32]

Despite the lack of provision in the Charter or in its Rules of Procedure, the General Assembly has also frequently invited states not Members of the United Nations (for instance, Italy, Jordan, and the Republic of Korea) to participate, without a vote, in the discussion of issues in which they are directly interested. The Assembly usually requires applicants for a hearing to accept the obligations of pacific settlement in the Charter as a condition of participation, but if they refuse, as did Albania and Bulgaria during discussion of the Greek question, they can still be invited to 'make statements'. Similarly, Italy has been invited to attend meetings of the Trusteeship Council when Italian Somaliland has been under discussion, while the Economic and Social Council has allowed certain non-Member States to participate in the work of its regional commissions either as full members or in a consultative capacity. And, of course, many states which have been, or are

---

[30] Italics added.

[31] Rule 39 of the Security Council's *Provisional Rules of Procedure* (S/96/Rev. 4). The invitation of 8 November 1950 to the People's Republic of China was based on this rule; see above, p. 123.

[32] This is a much condensed version of the practice of the Security Council in issuing invitations; for further details see *Repertoire of the Practice of the Security Council*, Chapters III and IV.

still, excluded from the United Nations, are members of one or more of the specialized agencies.

The pressure in favour of universality has persisted, however, and it was evident at the eighth (1953) and ninth (1954) sessions of the General Assembly that some resentment was felt at United States lukewarmness towards it. American reservations reflected genuine doubts about the eligibility of some of the applicant states, both as regards their status as sovereign states and as regards their acceptance of the basic concepts of the United Nations. But to some at least the American attitude seemed to betray a disposition to treat admission as an award for meritorious conduct in the cold war and to interpret the criteria of Article 4 in such a way as to turn the United Nations into a club of like-minded (that is, anti-Communist) states. This attitude was coming to be contrasted unfavourably with the Soviet Union's fairly consistent support, both in the Security Council and in the General Assembly, for the collective admission of a balanced 'slate' of Soviet and Western applicants. It is true that on the rejection of these 'package' proposals the Soviet Union used her veto in the Security Council to prevent the admission of the Western applicants. Moreover, the Soviet insistence on the admission of her own candidates as the price of her acquiescence in the admission of those supported by the West was directly contrary to an Advisory Opinion of the International Court,[33] to the effect that a Member State was not judicially entitled to make its consent to the admission of a state dependent upon conditions not expressly provided for in Article 4, para. 1, and, in particular, that it was not entitled to subject its affirmative vote to the additional condition that other states must be admitted together with that state. In other words, it was the view of the Court that the criteria of Article 4, para. 1, 'constitute an exhaustive enumeration and are not merely stated by way of guidance or example'.

---

[33] *ICJ Reports, 1948*, p. 65.

The Court's opinion was only reached by a narrow majority,[34] however, while many delegates were ready to point out that the criteria of Article 4 were not only far from clear but were almost bound to be interpreted in a highly subjective manner. Furthermore, despite Outer Mongolia's uncertain international status and Albania's persistent refusal to carry out a decision of the International Court, were there not a number of existing Members whose international status was equally uncertain,[35] or whose respect for the obligations of the Charter was also in serious doubt? As the tenth session of the General Assembly approached, therefore, there was a growing body of opinion in favour of some kind of bargain in which controversial applicants would be balanced against each other and admitted simultaneously.

Britain sympathized with this view. In the past her reluctance to vote for applicants (such as Albania and Outer Mongolia) which, by any reasonable standard, did not match up to the requirements of Article 4, or to indulge in the kind of 'horse-trading' deprecated by the Court, led her to abstain on most of the Soviet 'package' proposals. Nor has she been in favour of the extreme thesis of universality, namely, that an applicant only has to be a state in order to secure more or less automatic admission to the United Nations. On the other hand, from the start Britain has been strongly influenced by the concept of universality, and by the belief 'that the United Nations should include countries with different ideologies and different systems of government.' And Sir Gladwyn Jebb went on to explain,

> in our view . . . the greatest value of the United Nations is
> that it should be a meeting place in which views can be

---

[34] By 9 votes to 6. The minority (which included Sir Arnold McNair) held that a Member in voting for the admission of a state 'is participating in a political decision and is therefore legally entitled to make its consent to the admission dependent on any political considerations which seem to it to be relevant'; and that was precisely what it would be doing if it desired 'that the admission of the State should involve the contemporaneous admission of other States'.

[35] Byelorussia and the Ukraine; India's status before independence in 1947 was also certainly not that of a fully independent sovereign state.

exchanged and the differences between countries or groups of countries, however serious they may be, can be hammered out and, if possible, reconciled. We would not, therefore, wish to exclude any applicant State simply because its internal structure or the position of its Government in regard to foreign affairs is different from our own.[36]

Accordingly, at the tenth session (1955) of the General Assembly, in an effort to break the deadlock and to secure the admission of Ceylon and other friendly states, Britain supported, though with some reservations, a Canadian initiative to secure the admission of all those applicants (eighteen in number)[37] in regard to which no problem of unification arose. A resolution requesting the Security Council to consider these applications favourably was passed on 8 December 1955 by 52 votes in favour to 2 against (China and Cuba), with 5 abstentions (including Belgium, France, and the United States).[38] When the Security Council considered this 'package' proposal, the United Kingdom delegate (Sir Pierson Dixon) reiterated his Government's reservations about Outer Mongolia and Albania, but he intimated that the United Kingdom was nevertheless willing to vote in their favour.[39] Subsequently, the whole proposal seemed in danger of collapse when the Nationalist Chinese delegate, having skilfully manoeuvred the Soviet delegate into casting the first veto by suddenly requesting the inclusion of South Korea and Vietnam in the 'package', himself vetoed Outer Mongolia. The Soviet delegate retaliated by casting a veto against all thirteen Western candidates, and the meeting ended in angry accusation and counter-accusation. On the following day, however, the Council was unexpectedly recalled at the request of the Soviet delegate, who declared that, as a temporary expedient, the Soviet Union was prepared to accept

---

[36] *SCOR*, 7th yr., 573rd mtg., 6 Feb. 1952, pp. 16-17.

[37] Albania, the Mongolian People's Republic, Jordan, the Irish Republic, Portugal, Hungary, Italy, Austria, Roumania, Bulgaria, Finland, Ceylon, Nepal, Libya, Cambodia, Japan, Laos, and Spain.

[38] *GAOR*, 10th sess., suppl. no. 19, Resolution 918(X).

[39] See Cmd. 9716, Annex VIII, for an extract from his speech.

the exclusion of Outer Mongolia if Japan also was dropped from the list. Whilst resenting the exclusion of Japan, this solution was accepted by the Western Powers with some relief; it was subsequently endorsed at a late night plenary session of the General Assembly,[40] and sixteen of the applicants thus became Members of the United Nations.

This broadening of the membership of the United Nations is welcome, but it is not altogether an unmitigated blessing. Apart from the danger that the General Assembly is likely to become even more unwieldy (and perhaps volatile) than at present, the balance of voting power has been modified very much to the disadvantage of the colonial Powers; of the 16 new Members at least 10 are likely to vote with the anti-colonial Powers.[41] Moreover, although several of the new Members are states of considerable diplomatic standing, they cannot fill the gap left by the exclusion of Japan, by the absence of Federal Germany, and by the continued refusal to accept the credentials of the People's Republic of China.[42] The United Nations is now more representative, but it is still not fully representative.

It will be apparent that United Nations organs have shown considerable ingenuity and flexibility in adapting their procedures to meet changing needs. The British attitude towards these procedures has been shaped by the belief that the United Nations is essentially a diplomatic meeting place, a centre for harmonizing conflicting national interests, which should be animated by the spirit and forms of traditional diplomacy and appreciative of diplomatic moderation and punctilio. The growing acceptance of this view in the last few years reflects the new-found doubts about the importance, even the very existence in a world in which a common morality

---

[40] *GAOR*, 10th sess., suppl. no. 19, Resolution 995(X), 14 Dec. 1955.

[41] The voting power of the anti-colonial group will also be further increased when other newly independent states are admitted.

[42] Strictly speaking, the problem of Chinese representation is not one of admitting a new Member, but of deciding which 'China' should be represented at the United Nations (see above, p. 122).

is lacking, of 'world opinion', and, therefore, about the merits of 'open diplomacy' and 'majority voting' on which, at San Francisco, the ability of the United Nations to express that opinion was predicated. Few in Britain now believe that the 'world opinion' which is said to crystallize during United Nations debates either includes the Communist world or is likely to convince the Communist leaders of the error of their ways. So-called 'world opinion' is, in fact, almost always 'free world opinion', the mobilization of which is usually designed to attract the uncommitted Powers to the West, to reassure the peoples of the West of the propriety of the policies their leaders are pursuing, and, occasionally, to check hot-headed action by one of their own number or to bring pressure to bear on the Communist Powers by indicating that continued intransigence might alienate the uncommitted Powers. This is not wholly to discount the role of public opinion as expressed at the United Nations. There are still a few countries, especially the newly independent ones, that can be persuaded to mend their ways in order to avoid public arraignment at the United Nations, while the principles of justice and morality to which the free world subscribe are, in a sense, the very lifeblood of the United Nations. Were it to close its eyes to their violation, what remaining claims would the United Nations have on people's loyalties?[43] How could it hope to combat the diminishing respect for international law and order? Condemnation may occasionally threaten to exacerbate rather than to relieve tension, but the greater risk is that persistent silence might not only stifle the sense of moral purpose which, however imperfectly and intermittently, still animates the great majority of United Nations delegates, but also that it might induce powerful states to take the law into their own hands. The real need, therefore, is for 'open diplomacy' and 'majority voting' to be used with moderation and discrimination rather than for either to be rejected out of hand.

---

[43] Compare the conduct of Members of the League of Nations in the years immediately preceding the Second World War.

chapter eight

The Security Council
and the General Assembly

The outstanding *de facto* revision of the Charter is to be found
in the virtual eclipse of the Security Council by the General Assembly.
The General Assembly has now come to overshadow the Security
Council in the field of peace and security as in everything else.[1]
One reason for this shift, that has already been discussed, has been
the use of the United Nations as a 'propaganda platform, occasional
arbitrator . . . convenient shelf for awkward problems . . . mediation
board or Delphic oracle';[2] in these respects the General Assembly
had obvious advantages over the Security Council. But a more
important reason was the apparent American determination, up

---

[1] A comprehensive and authoritative account of the evolving legal relationships between the Security Council and the General Assembly is to be found
in F. A. Vallat (Deputy Legal Adviser to the Foreign Office), 'The General
Assembly and the Security Council of the United Nations', in *BYIL, 1952*.
See also *Repertoire of the Practice of the Security Council*, Chapter VI.

[2] Article by Sebastian Haffner, *Scotsman*, 13 Dec. 1948.

till a few years ago, to reshape the United Nations as an additional arm of Western defence and to circumvent the veto on the Security Council by developing new collective security machinery within the General Assembly.

In Britain, this trend aroused considerable disquiet. The United Kingdom recognized that, subject to the primary responsibility of the Security Council, the Charter conferred upon the General Assembly broad responsibilities for international peace and security. She was not unsympathetic to the argument that, if the Security Council could not function effectively, more responsibility, particularly for investigating and publicizing the facts of a dispute, could properly devolve on the General Assembly.[3] Nor was the vital importance of retaining American support for the United Nations or for the collective security idea—the two being, in many American eyes, virtually synonymous—lost sight of. But the wisdom of refashioning the Charter collective security system by 'putting teeth' into an Assembly-centred United Nations was doubted. British security could best be ensured by the development of regional systems of collective self-defence under Article 51. The United Nations should be kept alive and oecumenical as a centre for mediation and conciliation, especially between the Great Powers, in the hope that, on the threshold of a major *détente*, its organs or (more likely) its corridors, might facilitate the process. Clearly the Security Council was better fitted for this function than the General Assembly. Moreover, the strong anti-colonial pressure in the General Assembly made it possible to conceive of issues on which a majority might be mobilized against Britain. The United Kingdom was, therefore, concerned to preserve the authority of the Security Council or at least to prevent its total eclipse. And since the stultification of the Security Council was ascribed chiefly to the Soviet Union's abuse of the veto, Britain's earlier efforts were directed to limiting that abuse.

[3] For the legal arguments see speech by Sir Hartley Shawcross to the First Committee at the second General Assembly, Cmd. 7320, pp. 52-53.

THE VETO

It is as well to remember that not only was there never really any chance of having a United Nations in which the permanent members could be outvoted on security matters, but at no time since have any of them shown any sign whatsoever of willingness to forgo their right to prevent the Security Council from taking or recommending action under Chapter VII.[4] Indeed, although Britain shared in the general dismay and resentment evoked by the Soviet Union's abuse of the veto, she consistently opposed early attempts, mainly on small Power initiative, to amend the Charter in order to whittle down the veto rights of the permanent members; such attempts were, in the British view, not only futile but a threat to the 'Concert' function of the Council. Moreover, from the start United Kingdom delegates argued that the importance of the veto was greatly exaggerated, that its existence was no more than recognition of one of the basic facts of international life, and that its excessive use was a *symptom*, not a *cause*, of the 'suspicion among the great Powers and their tendency to take sides according to political ideologies'.[5]

On the other hand, it is the British contention that the Soviet Union's abuse of her veto powers has been the most important single obstacle to the more effective functioning of the Council. This is not to deny that there may be more than a grain of truth in the Soviet Union's contention that her frequent use of the veto has been a necessary protection against a hostile majority. But in Britain's view the Soviet Union has abused her veto powers by her readiness to cast her negative vote against almost any draft resolution which does not accord precisely with her own wishes and by her scant regard for the undertaking in the Joint Statement on

---

[4] Action with respect to threats to the peace, breaches of the peace, and acts of aggression.

[5] Sir Hartley Shawcross, *GAOR*, 1st sess., pt. 2, 1st Committee, 33rd mtg., 1 Dec. 1946, *SR*, pp. 212-13. See also pp. 440-42 below for an analysis of the Soviet Union's use of the veto.

Voting Procedure by the permanent members that they would not 'use their "veto" powers wilfully to obstruct the operation of the Council'. At least the undertaking might reasonably be held to preclude the Soviet practice of casting a negative vote merely on the grounds that a draft resolution does not go far enough, a practice in which they alone have indulged.

The United Kingdom's aim, therefore, has been not to limit the permanent members' veto rights, but to limit their abuse. That this was more likely to be achieved through agreement among the permanent members than through amending the Charter or attempting to bludgeon the Soviet Union into changing her ways seemed to be confirmed by the Soviet Union's introduction of the practice of 'abstention'. By this is meant the practice of not counting the abstention (or absence) of a permanent member as a negative vote. The practice is clearly against both the strict letter of Article 27(3) and the intention of the framers of the Charter, but it complies with the literal meaning of the veto, which is to say 'no'. The Soviet Union initiated the practice in April 1946 when she abstained on a resolution to consider whether Franco's Spain constituted a threat to international peace.[6] And although the Soviet delegate specifically stated that his abstention was not to be taken as a precedent, he did not challenge the statement of the President of the Security Council during the Indonesian debate, in August 1947, that

> It is now jurisprudence in the Security Council—and the interpretation accepted for a long time—that an abstention is not considered a veto, and the concurrent votes of the permanent members mean the votes of the permanent members who participate in the voting. Those who abstain intentionally are not considered to have cast a veto.[7]

The legal consequences of absence, as opposed to abstention, are not so clear. The Soviet Union has strongly denied the Council's

[6] *SCOR*, 1st yr., 1st ser., 39th mtg., 29 Apr. 1946, p. 243.
[7] ibid. 2nd yr., 173rd mtg., 1 Aug. 1947, pp. 1711-12.

right to treat absence as having the same legal effect, so far as voting is concerned, as abstention. The Security Council's recommendations on the Iranian question in 1946 (during the Soviet Union's absence) and on Korea in June 1950 were denounced by the Soviet Union as invalid. The remaining members of the Council, however, took the logical line that absence was intentional abstention and not, therefore, to be regarded as a veto.[8] This view can now be regarded as the accepted practice of the Council.

Acceptance of the practice of abstention is one of the most notable *de facto* revisions of the Charter. Although it may occasionally encourage 'sitting on the fence' tactics, it has introduced a useful element of flexibility into the voting procedures of the Security Council.

> By abstaining a permanent member avoids responsibility for supporting a proposal of which it does not approve in full, while at the same time he permits a decision to be taken if there is the necessary support for it by other members of the Council.[9]

For instance, the United Kingdom's abstention on Israel's application for membership did not prevent Israel's election. On the other hand, the practice of abstention in no way restricts the veto powers of the permanent members. It is merely a mark of their willingness to use those powers with restraint. This is an achievement, but a permanent member is under no compulsion to abstain, nor is the Soviet Union likely to absent herself again.

In 1946, however, the Soviet Union's lead on abstention encouraged those who sought to breathe new life into the Security Council without alienating the Soviet Union. Consequently, at the second part of the first session of the General Assembly, Mr Bevin sought to secure the agreement of the Soviet Union to a 'code of conduct' which would, in the spirit of the Joint Statement, make the veto a weapon of last resort rather than one of persistent obstruction.

[8] See *Repertoire of the Practice of the Security Council*, Chapter IV, pt. III.
[9] Goodrich and Hambro, p. 223.

Mr Bevin's proposals,[10] though modest, met with little immediate response from the Soviet Union, but the substance of them came up for consideration again in 1948-9 by the newly appointed Interim Committee.

The Report of the Interim Committee[11] indicates what could be done, given better relations between the permanent members, to rob the veto of some of its sting without formally revising the Charter. The Committee's major recommendations were adopted by the General Assembly, at the second half of its third session, in two resolutions.[12] The first recommended that:

(*a*) the Council should deem procedural a number of decisions which included, *inter alia*, the establishment of subsidiary organs of the Council, the deletion of a question from the list of matters of which the Council was seized[13] (so allowing it to be considered by the General Assembly), and the approval of representatives' credentials.[14]

(*b*) the unanimity rule should be excluded 'to the greatest extent feasible' from agreements conferring functions on the Security Council;[15]

(*c*) the permanent members should agree among themselves upon decisions with regard to which 'they might forbear to exercise

---

[10] The proposals were made privately to the other permanent members on 15 November 1946. Later they were tabled at the First Committee (*GAOR*, 1st sess., pt. 2, 1st Committee, Annex 7f (A/C.1/95), pp. 327-28). See also statement by the Minister of State (Rt Hon. P. J. Noel-Baker), ibid. pp. 114-16. Mr Noel-Baker also called for agreement to set up 'commissions of enquiry as a matter of principle in order to obtain the true facts of a dispute for the Security Council'. But this was not pursued, possibly because it would seem to run counter to para. 4 of the Joint Statement. See ibid. pp. 348-51 for Canadian proposals to which the United Kingdom gave general support.

[11] *GAOR*, 3rd sess., pt. 1, suppl. no. 10 (A/578).

[12] ibid. 3rd sess., pt. 2, Resolutions 267(III) and 268(III) of 14 and 28 Apr. 1949.

[13] This was already the practice of the Council, e.g. the removal of the Greek question, 15 Sept. 1947.

[14] A point of importance in the context of the representation of the People's Republic of China.

[15] Doubtless with atomic energy and Trieste in mind.

their veto [i.e. to abstain], when seven affirmative votes have
already been cast in the Council, giving favourable consideration
to the list of such decisions contained in conclusion 2 of part IV
of the report of the Interim Committee'. The most important of
these decisions were: the admission of new Members; the determination of whether a matter was procedural within the meaning
of Article 27(2);[16] and the determination of whether a question
was a 'situation' or a 'dispute' for the purposes of Article 27(3).
The purpose of the first of these is self-evident; the veto has been
exercised by the Soviet Union to exclude new Members more
than on any other issue. The other two need a word of explanation.

In their Joint Statement the Sponsoring Powers stated that 'the
decision regarding the preliminary question as to whether or
not . . . a matter is procedural must be taken by a vote of seven
members of the Security Council, including the concurring votes
of the permanent members'. Accordingly, in cases where it is not
clear whether a matter is a procedural or a substantive one,[17]
a permanent member can exercise what is commonly called the
'double veto'. That is to say, a permanent member can first veto
a proposal that a matter should be regarded as procedural, and,
since the matter has then to be treated as a substantive one, it can
exercise a second veto in the normal way under the terms of
Article 27(3).[18] The Interim Committee's recommendation was
designed to do away with this 'double veto'. The recommendation
was in flat contradiction to the Joint Statement. But, irritated no

---

[16] So requiring only the affirmative vote of any seven members.

[17] e.g. the appointment of a sub-committee of the Council or a request to the
General Assembly to make a recommendation on a matter of which the Council
remained seized.

[18] See, for instance, the Soviet Union's exercise of the double veto on a proposal
to appoint a sub-committee to hear evidence on the Czechoslovak coup d'état
(*SCOR*, 3rd yr., 288th mtg., 29 Apr. 1948, pp. 19-29; also Goodrich and Hambro, pp. 221-22). For a more detailed analysis of this issue see *Repertoire of the
Practice of the Security Council*, Chapter IV, pts. I and II; also Leo Gross,
'The Double Veto and the Four Power Statement', *Harvard Law Review*, Dec.
1953.

doubt by Soviet obstructionism and comforted by the knowledge that the United States would rarely be faced by an adverse majority, the American delegate claimed that the passage in the Joint Statement had been rendered inoperative by the Soviet Union's misuse of it. Britain also deplored the Soviet Union's misuse of the double veto, but declared her continued adherence to the Joint Statement and refused to be associated with the recommendation.

The significance of the rather subtle distinction[19] between the handling of a 'dispute' and the handling of a 'situation' stems from the fact that, under the terms of Article 27(3), a permanent member of the Security Council is required to abstain from voting only when it is a party to a 'dispute', not when it is a party to a 'situation'.[20] In practice the distinction has not been important, since members of the Council have normally abstained from voting in such cases. The Council was, therefore, able to avoid taking decisions on whether it was dealing with a dispute or a situation and also on whether such decisions were to be regarded as procedural or substantive questions.[21] However, the Interim Committee tried to forestall any future difficulties by recommending that the decision (on whether a question was a situation or a dispute) should be treated as a procedural, not a substantive one. There was also, on the basis of a United Kingdom draft, agreement on a liberal, if somewhat artificial, definition of the word 'dispute'[22] to the effect that a dispute existed if (i) the states concerned agreed there was a dispute; or (ii) a breach of an international obligation was, or was likely to be, involved; or (iii) the maintenance of international peace and security was, or was likely to be, endangered.

---

[19] For legal comments on the distinction see Yuen-li Liang, 'The Settlement of Disputes in the Security Council: the Yalta Voting Formula', in *BYIL, 1947*, p. 330; also Goodrich and Hambro, pp. 224-26. For a case study see *Repertoire of the Practice of the Security Council*, Chapter IV, pt. III.

[20] Under Art. 35 the Security Council can have before it either a 'dispute' or a 'situation'.

[21] See above, p. 73.

[22] For the purpose of Art. 27(3) only.

Given the irritation aroused by the Soviet Union's frequent resort to the veto, the General Assembly's recommendations were exceptionally modest. The Interim Committee's discussions showed not only that none of the permanent members was willing in any way to limit its veto rights under Chapter VII, but that neither Britain nor France nor the Soviet Union was prepared to go as far as the United States in limiting its veto rights under Chapter VI.[23] The main aim of the Committee's proposals, in the British view, was not to transform the practice of the Security Council by drastically modifying the veto, but merely to ease its functioning by encouraging the permanent members, and especially the Soviet Union, to exercise their veto rights with the greatest possible forbearance. Thus, even if all the recommendations had been put into practice, probably the most significant result would have been to open the door to those applicants for United Nations membership not opposed by the Western Powers. In the event, virtually all the recommendations (where not already the accepted practice of the Council) were rejected or ignored by the Soviet Union. Interest in the Assembly's proposals may revive if and when a conference is held to review the Charter, but in retrospect the Interim Committee's efforts appear well-intentioned but rather pointless. Despite Mr Bevin's earlier initiative, the main task of the United Kingdom delegates on the Committee was to inject a sense of realism into its deliberations and to curb the enthusiasm of the more fervent critics of the veto. In this they were not unsuccessful.

THE COUNCIL AS A POINT OF CONTACT

Britain attached more importance to the General Assembly's second resolution[24] based on the report of the Interim Committee,

---

[23] The Vandenberg Resolution, approved on 11 June 1948 by the United States Senate, called for voluntary agreement among the permanent members of the United Nations not to use their veto powers either to prevent the admission of new Members or on questions covering the pacific settlement of disputes (Chapter VI of the Charter).

[24] *GAOR*, 3rd sess., pt. 2, Resolution 268(III) B, 28 Apr. 1949.

which aimed at increasing the scope for diplomatic negotiation by taking disputes out of the public limelight. Thus the resolution recommended that parties to cases brought before the Council should try to agree upon a representative on the Council (either the President or his appointee) to act as a rapporteur or conciliator, and that the Council should refrain from further action whilst efforts at conciliation were in progress.[25] However, despite its acceptance in principle by the Council,[26] this procedural device was never to be put to the test because of the Council's subsequent decline. In any case, far more significant in British eyes was the vindication, by the *démarche* in January 1949 which led to the settlement of the Berlin dispute, of the British view that the Council's main value was as a point of contact between the Great Powers.

The events leading up to, and during, the Soviet blockade of Berlin (which began on 24 June 1948) and the subsequent Western airlift have been recounted elsewhere.[27] Very briefly, diplomatic negotiations having failed to secure the raising of the blockade, the dispute was referred by the Western Powers to the Security Council on 27 September 1948, under Article 39.[28] After it had been decided that the Security Council was competent to consider the matter,[29] the neutral members on the Council tried to find a formula acceptable to both sides. When this attempt failed, the President

---

[25] The resolution also provided for the revival of the General Act of September 1928 and for the creation of a panel for inquiry and conciliation under the General Assembly.

[26] *SCOR*, 5th yr., 472nd mtg., 24 May 1950, p. 15. The Council had already followed a similar practice, e.g. the appointment of General McNaughton in December 1949 to mediate between India and Pakistan.

[27] RIIA, *Survey, 1947-8*, pp. 343-52 and *1949-50*, pp. 62-64; also Trygve Lie, *In the Cause of Peace* (New York, Macmillan, 1954), pp. 199-218.

[28] The United States took the initiative; the United Kingdom (and France) followed rather reluctantly, fearing that open discussion in the Security Council might exacerbate the situation. See James Forrestal, *The Forrestal Diaries* (London, Cassell, 1952), p. 458.

[29] The Soviet Union contended that Art. 107 required reference of the matter to the Council of Foreign Ministers.

of the General Assembly[30] and the Secretary-General made an appeal to the four Powers to resolve their differences in conference. On the failure of this move, the neutral members again tried to find a way out, with the result that a committee of experts was set up. This committee discussed the problem in Paris and Geneva until February 1949, when it, too, had to report failure. The first hint that the Soviet Union might be thinking again about her terms for ending the blockade came in an interview which Marshal Stalin gave to an American journalist, on 27 January 1949, in the course of which he indicated his terms for a Berlin settlement without referring to the currency question, which had previously proved the main stumbling block. Was this omission intentional, and if so, was it significant? Dr Jessup, then deputy American representative on the Security Council, informally approached Mr Malik in the delegates' lounge at Lake Success to find out. After consulting Moscow, Mr Malik was able to reply that it was 'not accidental'. Out of this informal, even casual, *démarche* grew the negotiations which led to a settlement.

It is improbable that the Soviet Union's readiness to modify her position in order to achieve a settlement was greatly influenced by negotiations at the United Nations. Far more important was the success of the Western Powers' air lift, the shortage of raw materials in East Germany brought about by the West's counter-blockade, and the refusal of the Western Powers to call a halt to the formation of a West German Government in Bonn. Indeed, the failure of the efforts both of the 'neutral' Powers and of Dr Evatt and the Secretary-General had a chastening effect on hopes that the United Nations might be able to mediate between the Great Powers. Moreover, the intervention of Dr Evatt and the Secretary-General met with some criticism in official circles in Britain, partly because of the British view that a Secretary-General should work behind the scenes rather than play the lead, but chiefly on the grounds that their intervention cut across the efforts of the 'neutrals'

[30] Dr Evatt.

and neglected to place responsibility for the impasse fairly and squarely on the Soviet Union. Nevertheless, although all these efforts at mediation bore no direct fruit, in retrospect they appear to have played a not unimportant part in putting a check on precipitate action. All the Great Powers wanted to avoid a general conflagration, but without the steady mediatory pressure at the United Nations an accidental spark might well have set it off. Although a settlement might eventually have been reached through normal diplomatic channels had the United Nations not existed, not only was there a risk that a formal diplomatic approach to elicit Marshal Stalin's intentions might have been misconstrued, but at this time the doors of the Kremlin were rarely opened to Western diplomats, while Soviet envoys abroad shunned all but the most formal contacts with their colleagues. Thus the United Nations appeared to have hastened a settlement by providing a readily available point of contact—a diplomatic meeting place—between East and West where, at the opportune moment, the possibilities of a settlement could be discreetly explored.

Two main lessons were drawn from the part played by the United Nations over Berlin. In the first place, the relative failure of the various mediatory efforts strengthened the view that when, as in the case of Berlin, an issue was of vital importance to the disputants, solutions advocated by supposedly disinterested third—or 'neutral'—parties were likely to fall on deaf ears. As always, the readiness of the disputants to compromise mattered more than the ingenuity of the solutions proposed. Such readiness was more likely to result from the hard facts of the situation than from reminders to the disputants of their obligations under the Charter. The Council's role in mediation was not altogether discounted. Palestine, Indonesia, and, to a lesser extent, Kashmir, had demonstrated its potentialities. But its impotence in face of a refusal to make concessions confirmed the view that machinery was secondary to the will of the parties to negotiate, and that, given the breakdown of the Charter's enforcement system, direct diplomatic pressure would often accomplish more than, or at least be an essential concomitant to, action by the Council.

In the second place, the Berlin settlement confirmed that the Council's main value was as a point of diplomatic contact, particularly but not only between the Soviet Union and the West, through which negotiations could be initiated whenever the situation allowed. In this view private contacts and negotiation mattered more than the formal meetings and public debates of the Council. And the preservation of the Council's representative character was more important than the strengthening of its machinery.

THE REPRESENTATIVE CHARACTER
OF THE SECURITY COUNCIL

Britain's concern to preserve and enhance the representative character of the Security Council has been illustrated by her desire not only to secure a seat for Communist China and the admission of states such as Italy and Japan, but also by her opposition to American-led efforts at the annual elections by the Assembly to pack the Council with 'friendly' Powers.

Article 23 of the Charter attempts to give some guidance regarding the election of the six non-permanent members of the Council by stipulating that regard shall be 'specially paid, in the first instance to the contribution of Members of the United Nations to the maintenance of international peace and security and to the other purposes of the Organization, and also to equitable geographical distribution'. These criteria are, of course, liable to conflict, but it has become the general practice for one seat to go to an Eastern European country, one to a Western European or Scandinavian country, one to a Middle East country, two to Latin American countries, and one to a member of the British Commonwealth. And although the extent of the commitment is obscure, it is said that an understanding—a 'gentlemen's agreement'—was reached at the first session of the General Assembly whereby 'the candidates supported by these groups of nations should receive general support'.[31]

There has, however, been a great deal of squabbling over the Eastern European seat. The United States has denied the right of the Soviet Union to say which country shall fill the seat, on the grounds that the Soviet-sponsored candidates do not satisfy the first requirement of Article 23, that alternative candidates can be found who will ensure equitable geographical distribution (in any case a secondary criterion), and that the Council's slender majority for its recommendations over Korea show how important it is to exclude 'unfriendly' Powers. It has also been claimed on both sides of the Atlantic that the so-called 'gentlemen's agreement' was no more than a declaration of general intention which has been outmoded by events, or that it was limited to the 'slate' for the 1946 elections to the various organs and committees of the United Nations. By contrast, and very largely out of a desire not to endanger the 'Commonwealth seat', Britain has generally argued against giving the Soviet Union legitimate cause for grievance at the exclusion of her protégés, has upheld the continuing validity of the 'gentlemen's agreement', and has sought to preserve the 'non-denominational' character of the Council.[32] Despite strenuous and often successful American lobbying in favour of non-Communist candidates for

---

[31] See statement by the Parliamentary Under-Secretary of State for Foreign Affairs (Mr C. Mayhew) of 23 Nov. 1949, H. C. Deb., vol. 470, col. 349.

[32] The rivals were Czechoslovakia and Yugoslavia (recently weaned from the Cominform) in 1949, Byelorussia and Greece in 1951, and Poland and Turkey in 1953. Turkey's candidature in 1953 was particularly surprising since she had been elected to the Council in 1950 as a Middle Eastern country. Her contribution to United Nations action in Korea was notable, but her election in 1953 as an Eastern European country seemed 'a little too adroit' (*The Times*, 6 Oct. 1953). On this occasion the British vote was not disclosed (voting is by secret ballot), but it is generally thought to have been cast in favour of Poland. At the 1955 elections to fill the seat vacated by Turkey, the United Kingdom supported Yugoslavia against the candidature of Poland and the Philippines. Poland later withdrew and, after a very hotly contested election, a solution was at last found by sharing the two-year period between Yugoslavia and the Philippines.

the Eastern European seat, Britain has usually[33] supported the Soviet-sponsored candidate.

Anglo-American differences over elections to the Security Council once again illustrate the contrast between the British desire to preserve the oecumenical character of the Council—and to 'keep faith' with the Soviet Union—and the American tendency to treat election to the Council as an award for 'good conduct'. The irritation aroused by the public airing of these differences and the unseemly wrangles which so often occur between competing candidates and their supporters suggest the continuing need for some kind of 'gentlemen's agreement', or at least for an agreed 'slate' of candidates, before the elections start. A matter of much greater importance, however, and more harmful to the 'Concert' conception of the Council (apart from the absence of Communist China), is the under-representation of Asia. One seat is kept by the 'gentlemen's agreement' for the Commonwealth, but the Asian members (India, Pakistan, and now Ceylon) have to compete with those of Anglo-Saxon stock, while, under the present practice, it is very difficult for any of the many other Asian countries to secure election at all. In 1954, when Asian problems were the centre of international attention, apart from Nationalist China there was not a single Asian member of the Security Council. Strong resentment has been expressed in some Asian countries at this omission;[34] this resentment is likely to grow as a result of the recent admission of several more Asian countries. One result of Asian under-representation has been that India's mediatory efforts have mostly been made in the General Assembly, which, if only because of its size, is less well adapted to mediation and conciliation than the Security Council. If the Security Council is to revive in importance, increased Asian representation is called for, either by increasing the Council's

---

[33] In 1947 the United Kingdom supported India against the Ukraine even though Canada had already been elected to the 'Commonwealth seat'.

[34] See, for instance, Mr Nehru's speech to the Council of States, *The Times*, 24 Sept. 1953.

membership so as to allow of an Asian seat, or by giving India some special status on the Council, even perhaps that of a permanent member. In view of the very substantial contribution they have made to the United Nations, there is also a strong case for giving preferential treatment to such 'middle' Powers as Canada and Brazil.[35] One method would be to make such Powers immediately re-eligible for election (as in the League) by rescinding the present provision (Art. 23, para. 2) whereby 'a retiring member shall not be eligible for immediate re-election'.

THE INTERIM COMMITTEE

British efforts to prevent the eclipse of the Security Council by limiting the abuse of the veto and by preserving its oecumenical character have not, therefore, been particularly successful. Of greater significance have been the American-led attempts to circumvent the veto by devolving the Security Council's responsibilities on to the General Assembly. Britain has viewed this trend with some misgiving.

The first move was taken by General Marshall (then United States Secretary of State) on 17 September 1947, when, in addition to suggesting a study of how the Security Council's voting procedures under Chapter VI might be liberalized, he also proposed the creation (under Art. 22) of an Interim Committee on Peace and Security, which would in effect put a 'reserve team' General Assembly in continuous session like the Security Council.[36] General Marshall was careful to explain that the Interim Committee should not infringe upon matters which were the primary responsibility of the Security Council. His aim was to assist the Assembly to discharge its unexpectedly heavy responsibilities. Nevertheless, it

[35] As the United Kingdom urged at Dumbarton Oaks and after.

[36] *GAOR*, 2nd sess., Plen., 82nd mtg., pp. 24-26. Britain had no foreknowledge of these proposals nor was she consulted in their formulation. See statement by the Minister of State (Rt Hon. Hector McNeil), ibid. 88th mtg., 22 Sept. 1947, p. 207.

r

was suspected, with some reason, that his prime motive was to surmount the deadlock in the Security Council by developing the General Assembly as the United Nations' main instrument for the maintenance of peace and security.[37]

Britain accepted the legality of these proposals, but questioned their expediency. Apart from their threat to the authority of the Security Council, Mr Vyshinsky's bitter attack on them seemed to foreshadow a Soviet withdrawal from the United Nations as a prelude to setting up a rival organization. This would have been a singularly unhappy prologue to the forthcoming meeting of the Council of Foreign Ministers (London, November-December 1947), to which great importance was attached. And might not other Powers accompany the Soviet Union for fear that, by remaining members of an attenuated and Western-dominated United Nations, they might appear to be committing themselves to the Western camp?

Consequently, the United Kingdom delegates sought to restrict the powers of the proposed Interim Committee and to preserve the primary responsibility of the Security Council for the maintenance of peace and security.[38] In this they were partially successful, for the General Assembly resolution[39] limited the Committee's functions of preparatory consideration and report to questions relating to Articles 11(2), 14, and 35 of the Charter and to any other questions specifically referred to it. It also stipulated that a question could be discussed by the Committee only if it were not on the Security Council's agenda, while all important decisions (e.g. the dispatch of a Commission of Inquiry) required a two-thirds majority. Nevertheless, the United Kingdom's efforts to soften the Soviet Union's opposition by affirming Britain's continued adherence to the principle of the unanimity of the permanent members were

---

[37] A more detailed account of the setting up of the Interim Committee is to be found in L. C. Green, 'The "Little Assembly"', in *YBWA*, *1949*.

[38] *GAOR*, 2nd sess., Plen., 110th mtg., 13 Nov. 1947, pp. 789-90.

[39] ibid. Resolution 111(II).

unavailing; the Soviet Union and other Eastern European countries voted against the resolution and later carried out their threat to boycott the Committee.

The subsequent activities of the Interim Committee (or Little Assembly) were limited mainly to consideration of the problem of the veto and of ways and means of strengthening the procedures of the Security Council and of the General Assembly in the pacific settlement of disputes, the more important of which have already been discussed. The growth in the powers of the General Assembly resulted from the reference to it of such questions as disarmament, Greece, Palestine, and the Italian colonies, and from its use as a propaganda forum. The Interim Committee's importance lay not in its achievements but in the signpost it gave to future developments.

'UNITING FOR PEACE'

The General Assembly's 'Uniting for Peace' resolution of 3 November 1950,[40] which was based on proposals presented early in the fifth session by Mr Acheson, marked a more decisive step in the *de facto* revision of the Charter and the main turning-point in the relations between the Security Council and the General Assembly. Though it reaffirmed the primary responsibility of the Security Council, the resolution was based on the postulate that the stultification of the Security Council did not release Members of the United Nations from their obligations under the Charter, or the United Nations of its responsibility to maintain international peace and security. The resolute response to North Korean aggression had lifted the United Nations out of the morass of petty squabbling which had threatened to engulf it; it could not be allowed to sink back again merely because the Security Council was paralysed by Soviet obstructionism.[41] If the Security Council could not act, the

[40] *GAOR*, 5th sess., suppl. no. 20, Resolution 377(V).

[41] The prompt action of the Security Council in June-July 1950, in the absence of the Soviet delegate, had been followed by complete deadlock on his return in August.

General Assembly must, and could properly, do so. The very *ad hoc* and hastily improvised measures taken over Korea were also thought to show the need to put into more explicit and coherent form the powers which the General Assembly might exercise in any future emergency. For at this time many feared that North Korean tactics might be repeated in Germany, or at least that the Soviet Union would not stop at 'all mischief short of war'.

The 'Uniting for Peace' resolution was adopted by an impressive majority.[42] It is interesting to note that, in line with Korean experience, the machinery it set up was closer to the decentralized system of the Covenant (Art. 16) than to the centralized system of the Charter, whereby Members pledged themselves to carry out the instructions of the Security Council. Thus the General Assembly can only *recommend*, not 'call upon', its Members to take part in collective measures. Its recommendations may carry considerable moral authority, but they are in no way binding upon Member States. Each state is entitled to decide for itself whether an act of aggression has taken place, and, if so, whether to take part in, and what contribution to make to, the measures recommended to meet it. The effectiveness of any action under the resolution rests, therefore, on the majority's sense of solidarity and mutual obligation, not on the existence of precise and automatically binding legal obligations.[43]

The resolution was divided into four sections. Under Section A, if the Security Council failed to exercise its primary responsibility, the Assembly was immediately to consider any threat to the peace, breach of the peace or act of aggression, with a view 'to making appropriate recommendations to Members for collective measures, including in the case of a breach of the peace or act of aggression the use of armed force when necessary'. It also provided for the calling of an emergency special session of the General Assembly

---

[42] 52 votes in favour, 5 against (Soviet bloc), and 2 abstentions (India and Argentina).

[43] Martin, *Collective Security*, p. 129. The importance of this distinction should not be overrated; it is the readiness to take part in collective action, not the sense of legal compulsion, that matters most.

within twenty-four hours upon request by the Security Council (on the vote of any seven members) or by a majority of the Members of the United Nations. Section B established a Peace Observation Commission which, by stationing United Nations observers at potential trouble spots, might be able to provide the United Nations with reasonably accurate and objective information about any threat to, or breach of, the peace, and so fulfil the same useful verificatory function as had the Korean and Balkan Commissions.[44] Section C was intended to fill the gap left by the failure to conclude the special agreements of Article 43. Member States were invited to survey their resources to determine the assistance they might be able to render in support of recommendations by the Security Council or the General Assembly for the restoration of international peace and security. Each Member was also recommended to maintain within its national armed forces elements that could promptly be made available 'in accordance with their respective constitutional processes'[45] for service with the United Nations.[46] The earmarking of forces for United Nations action was, however, to be 'without prejudice to the use of such elements in exercise of the right of individual or collective self-defence recognized in Article 51 of the Charter'; so safeguarding NATO requirements. The Secretary-General was also asked to appoint a panel of military experts to advise Member States on these matters. Section D established a Collective Measures Committee (of fourteen members) to report on methods, including those of Section C of the resolution, that might be used to maintain and strengthen international peace and security. The position of NATO (and the Inter-American defence system) was again safeguarded by the instruction to the

---

[44] The Commission would be available to the Security Council as well as to the General Assembly and its Interim Committee.

[45] The conventional Congressional safeguard.

[46] The provision of armed forces for United Nations action under this resolution would be entirely voluntary, whereas under the special agreements it was to have been obligatory.

Committee to take account of collective self-defence and regional arrangements.[47]

One of the main aims of the 'Uniting for Peace' resolution was to encourage states to stand up to pressure in the knowledge that they would receive aid if attacked. Although in Britain it was realized that, in a world divided between two Power blocs of more or less equal weight, collective security had lost much of its meaning, the resolution might help to diminish their sense of insecurity by organizing collective resistance to aggression. Furthermore, the new machinery and procedures would enable the NATO Powers to obtain the moral backing of the United Nations if war should come. The main burden of resistance to further aggression would inevitably fall on the NATO Powers. But, apart from Germany, most of the trouble spots lay outside the NATO area. Greece and Turkey were not yet members of NATO, Yugoslavia was out of the Soviet camp but not in the Western orbit, the idea of a 'northern tier' in the Middle East was only just beginning to take shape, and SEATO was still no more than a hope for the future. What link, then, would there be between a non-NATO state which was attacked and the power of the Western world? The NATO Powers could properly come to the aid of a state under Article 51. But Article 51 only gave legal sanction; it could not give moral backing. And however clear the need to defend Western outposts might seem to ministers and officials, on an issue that might easily appear both obscure and remote to the electorate, the moral backing of the United Nations might well be instrumental in rallying the necessary public support—as the Security Council's endorsement of American action in Korea had been. Moreover, United Nations endorsement of military action by the NATO Powers might secure the sympathy and even support of those countries who might otherwise be inclined to call 'a plague o' both your houses'. The military power commanded by these countries was slight, but in

---

[47] A final Section E consisted of a rather pointless general exhortation.

some cases their economic resources, particularly in strategic raw materials, were considerable. At least these materials might more easily be denied to the enemy.

The resolution was strenuously opposed by the Soviet bloc. Mr Vyshinsky protested that it was quite illegal and that the General Assembly was trying to usurp powers which belonged exclusively to the Security Council, his main contention being that the last sentence of paragraph 2 of Article 11[48] placed a limitation on the powers of the Assembly under Article 10.[49] The ambiguity of Article 11(2) was such, however, that Western spokesmen were able to interpret it in a way which satisfied the vast majority of delegates as to the legality of the resolution.[50]

At first the American initiative was welcomed by Britain.[51] Mr Bevin's own faith in the United Nations had been awakened by the reaction of the vast majority of its Members to the Korean aggression. The new-found unity in resistance to aggression had to be consolidated. In addition to the moral backing they might offer, the proposals might also encourage a wider sharing with other states of the burden of any future United Nations action and afford the United Kingdom a more direct voice in control of United Nations military operations without seriously fettering her freedom of decision. Nevertheless, the misgivings about the trend set in train by the original Interim Committee proposals persisted. The chief fear was again that the concentration on the Assembly's role as an instrument of collective resistance to aggression and the draining away of the Security Council's authority might weaken

---

48 'Any . . . question [relating to the maintenance of international peace and security] on which action is necessary shall be referred to the Security Council by the General Assembly either before or after discussion.'

49 *GAOR*, 5th sess., 1st Committee, 364th mtg., 16 Oct. 1950, *SR*, p. 133; and ibid. 366th mtg., 17 Oct. 1950, *SR*, pp. 143-44.

50 For an outline of the legal arguments of both sides see *YBUN, 1950*, pp. 185-87. The British view is summarized by Vallat in *BYIL, 1952*, pp. 96-100.

51 See Mr Bevin's speech on 25 Sept. 1950, *GAOR*, 5th sess., Plen., 283rd mtg., pp. 87-88.

the conciliatory and mediatory role of both. And to no great gain, for, whatever its psychological value, the new machinery was both clumsy and makeshift and in practice could hardly prove of more than marginal importance. Nor was it impossible to envisage cases in which a two-thirds majority hostile to Britain might be mobilized. On the other hand, not only might the machinery serve to cover those parts of the world not yet defended by regional organizations, but it would have been extremely difficult not to support Mr Acheson's initiative at a time when the United Kingdom delegation was pre-occupied with securing more effective United Nations control of American military leadership in Korea. Active United Kingdom opposition or even her open hesitancy would have struck at the unity of the Western world when that unity was more vital than ever. It could scarcely have failed to strengthen the hands of the 'go it alone' school in America. Certainly if, after Korea, the Assembly had been left without any power to act when the Security Council was stalemated, the reaction of most Americans would probably have been that the United Nations might as well be scrapped altogether. But then the more important possibilities of pacific settlement through the Organization might also have vanished. Far better, therefore, to be a party to the proposals and so in a position to preserve the possibilities of mediation and conciliation in the United Nations and the prime importance of NATO (and similar arrangements yet to come) as instruments of collective self-defence.

In the more sober—and private—atmosphere which prevailed when the Collective Measures Committee got to work,[52] British misgivings became more explicit. At once a basic point of principle was at stake. Should the Committee plan quite specifically against the possibility of further Communist aggression—as the Americans desired—or should it—as Britain argued—concentrate on setting

---

[52] The 'Uniting for Peace' resolution was passed a few days before overt Chinese intervention; when that intervention transformed the military situation, the United Kingdom's main aim became to secure an armistice. See above, p. 137.

out general principles for United Nations action under United Nations auspices, leaving the more important, delicate, and detailed work of planning against Communist aggression to NATO? The British view mainly prevailed, and in its three reports[53] up to the time of writing the Committee has concentrated on setting out general principles looking to the mobilization of the maximum support for collective measures on behalf of the United Nations and to the effective co-ordination of national and international action. The reports are long and detailed; only the salient features can be mentioned here.

Korean experience suggested that the most difficult question was the control of military operations undertaken in the name of the United Nations. On this point the Committee recommended that, in the event of a decision to take collective military action, the United Nations should apply to the Assembly the same principle which Article 48 applies to the Security Council, that is, that a state or group of states should be authorized to act on its behalf as its Executive Military Authority. The latter should be responsible for the co-ordination, strategic direction, and control of military operations within the framework of the objectives and general policies adopted by the United Nations. In the event of the failure of the Executive Military Authority to carry out its responsibilities to the satisfaction of the United Nations, the appropriate United Nations body should determine whether the mandate should be continued or brought to an end. The Executive Military Authority should designate the United Nations Commander-in-Chief. The latter's authority should be defined by, and his instructions received direct from, the Executive Military Authority, which should also have the right to replace him. The senior military representatives in the theatre of operations of each state contributing military forces should have direct access to the United Nations Commander-in-Chief on national matters and matters of major policy affecting

53 For the first report see *GAOR*, 6th sess., suppl. no. 13, A/1891; for the second see ibid. 7th sess., suppl. no. 17, A/2215; for the third see ibid. 9th sess., A/2713.

the operational capabilities of their forces. They should also have the right to communicate directly with, though not to take orders from, their governments on these matters and others of an administrative nature. In order to ensure joint consideration of questions of common interest, the Executive Military Authority should develop procedures, both at its seat of government and in the theatre of operations, for consultation on a regular basis with participating states.

This pattern is very similar to that evolved during the Korean War.[54] Of interest is the provision whereby a 'group of states' can be appointed as the Executive Military Authority, so allowing NATO to become the instrument of United Nations action. Otherwise it is difficult to detect anything of special significance, apart from the explicit recognition that, in any future action under United Nations auspices, the picture would probably be one of national forces acting with the sanction of the United Nations, but under the wing of one Power—or a group of Powers; the real problem would then be how to secure as effective a political voice as possible in the decisions taken by that Power. And the solution of this problem was more likely to turn on the sensitivity of that Power to advice than on the threat to terminate its mandate to act on behalf of the United Nations. In short, although the reports of the Collective Measures Committee probably outline the maximum agreement that could be secured as to 'techniques, machinery, and procedures', they also demonstrate how unrewarding and difficult it is to lay down general principles when practically everything depends on what kind of war is being waged, where, and by whom.

Even less impressive were the replies to pointed inquiries from both the Secretary-General and the Committee about the measures taken by Member States to earmark forces for United Nations

---

[54] As were the Committee's recommendations for underlining the United Nations character of military operations conducted on its behalf, e.g. the flying of the United Nations flag and the awarding of United Nations service medals.

action. Despite the gloss put on these replies in the Committee's report, they read more like excuses for not attending the wedding feast.[55] Section C of the 'Uniting for Peace' resolution has remained, therefore, virtually a dead letter,[56] an outcome that has not unduly distressed Britain, any more than the vast majority of other states. Nor did Britain respond at all sympathetically to a proposal by the Secretary-General for a United Nations Volunteer Force designed to help smaller states to contribute to United Nations forces and to enlist the services of individual volunteers.[57]

On the military side, the Committee stressed the need for an equitable sharing of the burden of any future United Nations action—a thrust at some of the less active supporters of United Nations action in Korea—and suggested that, instead of direct negotiation between the Executive Military Authority and governments (as had been the practice over Korea), there might be set up an *ad hoc* Negotiating Committee.[58] The task of such a committee would be to obtain from the Executive Military Authority specifications of its requirements and by direct negotiation with states to elicit contributions from them to fulfil these requirements. Such a United Nations 'go-between' might possibly be able to persuade 'waverers' to contribute, but the experience of similar committees in other fields is not encouraging.

Of greater significance was the work of the Committee on an arms embargo list and a list of strategic materials.[59] These lists

---

55 See A/2215, Annex G and A/2713, Annex 2 for a summary of replies. Most NATO members affirmed that their NATO forces might, in *appropriate circumstances*, become available for use under United Nations command. Britain's diplomatic reply was that 'H.M.G. will continue to consider its responsibilities under the "Uniting for Peace" Resolution in the light of future circumstances'.

56 The panel of military advisers has not, therefore, been called upon for advice.

57 This proposal was soon shelved. See A/2713, p. 4.

58 A/2215, Chapter III. This Committee would be analogous to the Negotiating Committee for Extra-Budgetary Funds, which obtains contributions for relief operations in Korea and Palestine and for the Expanded Programme of Technical Assistance.

59 ibid. Annexes H and I.

were modelled closely on, and probably added little to, the work of the Consultative Group Co-ordinating Committee in Paris.[60] But the discussions thereon may have helped to initiate a larger number of states into the problems of an economic blockade. The friction which usually arises between blockading countries and non-belligerents might perhaps be reduced by the Committee's success in fashioning measures which take careful account of the needs and susceptibilities of both.

In the first flush of enthusiasm for United Nations action in Korea, and the irritation aroused by the subsequent Soviet obstructionism on the Security Council, it seemed only right and proper to regularize and systematize the new methods which the United Nations had so hastily improvised. If the Organization was not shown to be capable of development and of adaptation to its political environment, it could not expect to remain a potent force. Moreover, the new machinery had possibilities. Not only might it provide moral backing for action by the NATO Powers, but it might help to guard some of the vulnerable spots outside the NATO area which were not yet covered by regional arrangements. Also at one time in the Anglo-Egyptian negotiations over the withdrawal of British troops from the Canal Zone, Britain is said to have 'proposed an idea given to them by the Egyptian Foreign Minister that the decision to re-enter should depend upon a resolution of the United Nations'.[61] Nevertheless, almost from the start, and especially as the regional arrangements began to take shape, Britain came to fear that the Collective Measures Committee might prove little more than an unwelcome distraction from the far more important task of building up the strength of NATO; and it was still not impossible to conceive of circumstances in which the machinery might be invoked for use against a colonial

---

[60] Commonly known as COCOM. This Committee meets to co-ordinate controls on exports of strategic goods and materials. Its members are the NATO Powers plus Western Germany and Japan.

[61] *World Today*, May 1954, p. 195.

Power, even against the United Kingdom herself.[62] As the terrifying prospects of nuclear warfare burst upon the public consciousness and underlined the need for coexistence without bloodshed, informed opinion in Britain perceptibly hardened against the 'Uniting for Peace' machinery and against what seemed to be an accompanying tendency to turn the United Nations into a pliable instrument of an American-dominated world, a tendency which seemed more likely to frighten off the 'uncommitted' Powers than to win their sympathy and friendship. Britain might deem it imprudent publicly to belittle the new machinery or to press for the Collective Measures Committee to be wound up, for such a step might alienate American opinion and remove an instrument of potential value in strengthening both the concept and the practice of collective measures. But behind the scenes the United Kingdom representatives successfully sought to limit the Committee's scope, to secure first place for NATO and similar regional arrangements in the Committee's proposals for collective action, and to keep the scales of the United Nations itself weighted in favour of the Organization's conciliatory and mediatory role. As a temporary expedient the Committee was not without value, but the deep slumber into which it fairly soon settled was greeted with relief rather than regret.[63]

---

[62] Not all members of the United Kingdom delegation shared this misgiving.
[63] Especially as most of the vulnerable spots were by then covered by regional arrangements.

chapter nine

The United Nations and Anti-Colonialism[1]

The attempts to adapt the United Nations to the exigencies of the cold war have provided the main focus of interest at the United Nations. But with the growth of regionalism and the cessation of fighting in Korea, a second conflict has moved to the centre of the stage at the United Nations which has proved little less important. This conflict, in which the whole system of relationships—political, economic, and racial—which grew up between Europe and the non-European world over the past three centuries is being called into question, closely concerns Britain, as one of the leading 'imperialist' or 'colonial' Powers. It has been well described by the Foreign Minister of Israel, Moshe Sharett, at the sixth Assembly (1951) as comprising

> deep and far-reaching antagonisms, sometimes latent and
> smouldering, sometimes flaring up in violent disputes, be-

[1] This chapter follows closely the argument in Coral Bell, 'The United Nations and the West', *International Affairs*, Oct. 1953.

tween Occident and Orient, between the more fully developed and the so-called backward countries, between nations accustomed to domination and races still [*sic*] recently subject, between the high industrial civilization of the West and an East only just awakening from age-long lethargy.[2]

These antagonisms[3] should not be exaggerated. They do not preclude a real community of outlook on many cold war issues or the development of close bonds of sympathy between delegates from the opposing camps. And, as on other issues, perhaps the main value of the Commonwealth is that it has helped to foster mutual respect and tolerance between the protagonists. But the antagonisms do reflect what, in the perspective of history, may come to be called the 'contraction of Western Europe': the mopping-up of those pools of European domination and influence left by the 'Expansion of Europe' in the eighteenth and nineteenth centuries. Their roots are to be found in the growth of national self-consciousness and self-assertiveness among non-European peoples at a time when Western Europe's power and influence are diminishing. In Western Europe, nationalism—or the more blatant forms of national self-consciousness—seems to be on the wane, but the Asian and Arab worlds are bursting with an aspiring and effervescent nationalism which regards national self-determination as the panacea for most of the world's ills. Inevitably, this attitude is mirrored in discussions at the United Nations. One result is that the United Nations, unlike the League, has tended to function in this important area of conflict much less as a defence of the *status quo* than as an incitement to peaceful—or relatively peaceful—change.

The growth of extra-European nationalism and the contraction of Western Europe are, of course, long-term phenomena which

---

[2] *GAOR*, 6th sess., Plen., 364th mtg., 15 Nov. 1951, p. 154.

[3] Their most familiar guise is the friction between the Administering and non-Administering Powers in the Trusteeship Council and the perennial tussle in the Assembly over the Committee on Information from Non-Self-Governing Territories. This side of the picture is examined in detail in Chapter 14. In this section the wider context will be sketched in.

preceded the creation of the United Nations. Indeed, perhaps the most important single example—the British withdrawal from the Indian sub-continent—was quite independent of the United Nations and was adumbrated by Britain herself as long ago as the First World War. But elsewhere the United Nations, at least in its early days, has functioned as a powerful instrument in speeding up the process by which the destinies of non-European peoples have passed from European hands. It has served as a focus of discontents, a standard by which to measure the shortcomings, real or imaginary, of the colonial Powers. In Indonesia it intervened directly in a contested transition from colonial to independent status. In two instances, Palestine and the Italian colonies, the United Nations helped to fashion new political entities when the Powers which would otherwise have had to make and enforce the decisions had, for one reason or another, renounced the responsibility. In a number of cases the United Nations has provided an instrument for bringing pressure to bear on European Powers (the French and British withdrawal from Syria and Lebanon and the Soviet withdrawal from Iran) or for imposing restraints against 'self-help' by these Powers (the Anglo-Iranian dispute). The possibility that the United Nations might be used in this way was foreseen at San Francisco and was one reason for the care with which the powers of the Assembly were limited and defined. But the strength and persistence of the anti-colonial forces at the United Nations has come as something of a shock to the West.

The spearhead of this movement is formed by the 'Bandung' Powers, usually with considerable support from the Latin American bloc. One especially disturbing feature is that, although the attack was originally directed against the status of 'tutelage' or 'clientship' rather than race discrimination as such, the fact that the ex-'tutor' states are European and the ex-'client' states non-European makes it almost inevitable that the conflict should at times take on the appearance of a tension between peoples of European stock and the rest of the world, not only in the geographical sense but in the racial sense also. Thus, not only may the Arab-Asian Powers be expected to interest themselves in any situation that can be construed as European oppression of a non-European people, but, as India's complaints against the treatment of persons of Indian origin in South Africa[4] and the annual discussions on race conflict in South Africa[5] indicate, the United Nations has become a mechanism through which race relations are apt to be transformed into international relations. It is a transformation that Britain cannot contemplate with equanimity, for, although the impotence of the United Nations in these matters has been shown up by South Africa's flat denial of its competence, there are one or two disquieting signs that racial policies in East Africa and the Central African Federation may lay a rather more sensitive[6] United Kingdom open to attack.

The use of the United Nations to put pressure on colonial Powers, or the ruling strata of plural societies, may seem a perversion of its purposes to the Western countries or peoples concerned, but it is part of the nature of an international organization that its members should tend to identify its aims with national objectives and should use the organization to pursue not only the general interest in the avoidance of war but their own particular interest in bringing to an end the last vestiges of European overlordship. The statement of the Egyptian delegate at the Security Council in 1947 (presenting his country's case for the withdrawal of British troops): 'We are here to challenge the basic assumptions of nineteenth-century imperialism',[7] is indicative of an attitude towards the United Nations which is neither lightly held nor likely to be easily dropped. It is all the stronger because those in power not

---

[4] Britain has expressed doubts about, but has not explicitly denied, the Assembly's competence in the matter (except when comment has been passed on the Union Government's internal legislation).

[5] Britain's insistence that her denial of the United Nations' competence to consider this question does not imply approval of the policies under attack has fortunately been generally accepted.

[6] Since opinion in Britain is on the whole strongly critical of any form of racial discrimination.

[7] *SCOR*, 2nd yr., 175th mtg., 5 Aug. 1947, p. 1749.

s

infrequently play upon the latent xenophobia of their countrymen to perpetuate their own rule. And although schemes of economic aid and technical assistance may do something to mollify this attitude, as Mr Hourani has pointed out: 'The essence of imperialism is to be found in a moral relationship—that of power and powerlessness—and any material consequences which spring from it are not enough to change it'.[8] Arguments that a people have benefited, or may benefit, materially from Western rule are unlikely, therefore, to carry great weight. Nor are appeals to reason, for the yearning for self-determination springs from the depths of the human heart and is not founded on cold reason or political logic.

In this conflict Britain, like the other 'colonial' Powers, is at a disadvantage. The 'colonial' Powers are in a voting minority. The United States is traditionally anti-colonial and, although some Asian leaders are increasingly aware of the Soviet Union's own brand of imperialism, and occasionally at the United Nations compare it unfavourably with the West's recent change of heart, such criticism is still infrequent. In any case it is most unlikely to reach the Soviet people's ears or substantially to influence the attitude of their leaders. But in Britain a considerable body of opinion in the early days of the United Nations was, and to a lesser extent still is, acutely sensitive to charges of 'imperialism', even when they may be quite ill-founded. The reason is not far to seek. The 'anti-imperialist' campaign is being fought to a very large extent under banners borrowed from the West: the preamble to the Charter and the Declaration of Human Rights, to which the Arab-Asian countries so often refer, are, in a sense, the distilled essence of Western political liberalism. As Mr Hourani has observed: 'If we look in the eyes of the Eastern nationalist, we shall see there a distorted image of ourselves: we have shaped the form as well as provided the object of his reaction.'[9] When the Egyptian delegate said that between the 1936 Treaty and the Charter,

8 'The Decline of the West in the Middle East', *International Affairs*, Jan. 1953, p.31.
9 ibid. Apr. 1953, p. 183.

Egypt had chosen the Charter, he was using an argument which found a response in some circles in Britain. The passion, hypocrisy,[10] and occasional malevolence which colour many of the attacks have naturally aroused keen irritation, as has the impression that far too little credit is given to the good intentions of British policy.[11] Nevertheless, these attacks may often be echoed in domestic opinion, while to some extent at least the arguments which are used in their rebuttal tend to lack conviction.

This is apt to be particularly true of the orthodox legal defence, namely that these matters (e.g. South African racial policy, French policy in North Africa, Greek claims on Cyprus) are expressly excluded from the competence of the United Nations by Article 2(7) of the Charter, the 'domestic jurisdiction' article.[12] Yet this is a sound, though not perhaps watertight, defence, on which United Kingdom delegates have understandably laid great stress. Two points are, in the British view, central to the domestic jurisdiction issue: firstly, when is a matter 'essentially within the domestic jurisdiction' of a state; secondly, what constitutes 'intervention'? International lawyers are not of one mind as to the correct answers, which in any case will be relative to, and dependent upon, the existing state of international law and relations.[13] But the present

---

[10] When, for instance, the Egyptian Government in 1947 based its plea for the withdrawal of the British troops from the Canal Zone on the principle of self-determination, but was most reluctant to apply the principle to the Sudanese people. Similarly, the Greek Government's advocacy of self-determination for the people of Cyprus might be more accurately described as an attempt to secure sovereignty over Cyprus for Greece.

[11] See below, p. 432.

[12] 'Nothing contained in the present Charter shall authorize the United Nations to intervene in matters which are essentially within the domestic jurisdiction of any state or shall require Members to submit such matters to settlement under the present Charter; but this principle shall not prejudice the application of enforcement measures under Chapter VII.'

[13] For argumentation which in principle supports the United Kingdom interpretation of Art. 2(7) see L. Preuss, 'Article 2, Paragraph 7 of the Charter of the United Nations and Matters of Domestic Jurisdiction', *Académie de Droit International*, vol. 74 (1949), pp. 553-653. For different interpretations see H. Lauterpacht, ed., *International Law* by L. Oppenheim, 7th ed., i. 376-81; also Hans Kelsen, *The Law of the United Nations* (London, Stevens for London Institute of World Affairs, 1950), pp. 769-91.

official British view appears to be that, with one important qualification, a matter is essentially within the domestic jurisdiction of
a state if, in respect of that particular matter, that state is not subject
to any precise and definite international obligation (whether it be
derived from an existing general principle of international law or
from a treaty to which the state is a party). Thus the argument
that a matter is of 'international concern' is, in the United Kingdom's
view, irrelevant. A country's commercial policy is often of direct
concern to other states but it is generally accepted that legally it
has full freedom of action except in so far as a particular aspect
of commercial policy is subject to a precise international obligation
to which the country is a party. Thus the general obligation of
United Nations Members to promote respect for, and observance of,
human rights (Art. 55) does not denote a derogation from the domestic
jurisdiction provision, not only because in this as in other respects
Article 55 is qualified by Article 2(7), but also because human rights
have not yet been defined; indeed, their precise nature is still a
subject of much controversy.[14] Similarly, the Declaration of Human
Rights imposes at the most a general moral obligation, not a precise
legal one, as would be the case for those states that ratified a
covenant, or as was placed upon the ex-enemy countries in the
peace treaties.

The qualification is, of course, that mentioned in the Charter,
namely, that the principle of domestic jurisdiction 'shall not prejudice the application of enforcement measures under Chapter VII'.
In practice, Britain does not stand on legal pedantry, for she concedes
that the Security Council is entitled to intervene if it can properly
discuss enforcement measures; in other words, a matter which is
considered to give rise to a genuine threat to *international* peace
and security thereby ceases to be covered by the domestic jurisdiction

---

[14] See speech by the Minister of State (Rt Hon. Selwyn Lloyd), *GAOR*, 7th
sess., 1st Committee, 6 Dec. 1952, *SR*, p. 202. For full text see Cmd. 8747,
pp. 39-42.

provision.[15] But it must be a threat to *international* peace, not merely to internal tranquillity (as is the case, it is claimed, in Cyprus or French North Africa). In Britain's view, events within an overseas territory under British sovereignty are as much an internal affair as would be similar events within Britain itself.

The second question is: what constitutes 'intervention'? By some authorities 'intervention' has been broadly interpreted in such a way as not to preclude discussion of, or even the passing of a resolution addressed to an individual state on, matters acknowledged to be essentially ones of domestic jurisdiction. In support of this view, it is argued that the term must be read in its traditional legal sense as involving 'dictatorial, mandatory interference intended to exercise direct pressure upon the State concerned. It does not rule out action by way of discussion, study, enquiry and recommendation falling short of intervention.'[16] It is also claimed that Articles 10 and 14 clearly confer on the Assembly the right to discuss questions within the scope of the Charter even though they be essentially domestic in character. And any matter is 'within the scope of the Charter' that is mentioned in the Charter, even if it only be in general terms in Articles 1 or 55.

The British view is that the General Assembly is entitled to discuss in terms of *general* principle and to make *general* recommendations addressed to *all* its Members on, for example, the matters mentioned in Articles 1, 55, or 73. But it is not entitled to single out, either for discussion or for comment in a resolution, the specific practices of a particular state in relation to these matters. It is also claimed that the San Francisco discussions show conclusively that Article 2(7) was intended both to preclude discussion (or consideration) of

---

[15] A distinction is sometimes drawn between the actual threat to international peace and security and the domestic situation out of which this threat may have arisen. It is argued that the United Nations can properly intervene to preserve or restore international peace but that it can only intervene in the domestic affairs of a state if the threat to peace cannot be countered by other means. This distinction is entirely in accordance with the Charter, but in practice (for example, Indonesia) it is apt to be disregarded.

[16] Lauterpacht, ed., *International Law* by L. Oppenheim, 7th ed., i. 378.

matters of domestic jurisdiction and to limit the scope of Article 10.[17] Again, although Article 14 empowers the General Assembly to 'recommend measures for the peaceful adjustment of any situation, regardless of origin', in the context of the Charter 'any situation' clearly means 'any *international* situation'; in any case, the scope of Article 14 is also limited by Article 2(7). Finally, Article 103, which is sometimes quoted by the anti-colonial school, does not look to the *revision* of treaties; it is only concerned to remove any possible conflict between Members' obligations under the Charter 'and their obligations under any other international agreement'.

It cannot be said that these arguments have carried much weight with the vast majority of delegates. This disrespect for the strict law of the Charter is regrettable. But even Britain has on at least one occasion (Indonesia) recognized the need for the Security Council to act without first satisfying itself as to its competence to do so, while United Kingdom delegates do not seem to have been greatly troubled by the domestic jurisdiction issue during the debates on forced labour in the Soviet Union or the complaint at the General Assembly's third session against the Soviet Union's refusal to allow the Soviet wives of foreign nationals to leave the Soviet Union. In short, the question whether the 'domestic jurisdiction' issue is to be taken seriously or not is not primarily a legal but a political one. Legal considerations may enter in, but they are unlikely to deter delegates from seizing opportunities to make effective propaganda either in the cold war or to extend the operation of the principle of self-determination. Britain has increasingly stressed, therefore, the imprudence—the 'political folly'—rather than the impropriety of United Nations discussion of domestic issues. This line of argument has proved more effective. Warnings that discussions such as those on French policy in Morocco and Tunisia tended to promote rather than allay unrest and friction and were 'fraught with grave dangers for the future of the Organization' have had a decidedly sobering

---

[17] See UNCIO, Verbatim Minutes, 15th mtg. of Committee II/2, 29 May 1945; also Preuss, in *Académie de Droit International*, vol. 74, p. 583.

effect on many delegates, as had the French delegation's withdrawal from the tenth session of the Assembly, when the latter, rather to its own surprise and disquiet, decided by one vote to include the Algerian question on its agenda. The United States' change of front in 1953 in favour of the French case and the efforts by the French Government to arrive at an accommodation have also resulted in a slight relaxation of pressure. But the lull may well prove only a temporary one.

Similarly during the Assembly's discussions at its ninth and tenth sessions on whether to include the Greek complaint about Cyprus on the agenda, United Kingdom delegates concentrated on the grave dangers that such discussion might presage rather than on the limiting effect of Article 2(7). Not only would Britain boycott any substantive discussion, but she might be forced to reconsider her willingness 'to co-operate fully and freely with those bodies of the United Nations which are concerned with the affairs of Non-Self-Governing Territories'. If the principle of self-determination were accepted

> the way would be open to foment discord, to agitate for territorial adjustments, to cause racial and religious discord, and to use this Organization for these purposes . . . There is scarcely a treaty defining territorial frontiers which accords in every detail with the corresponding ethnic frontiers, which does not leave ethnic groups outside the frontier in question. If the self-determination of an ethnic group is a reason for revising treaties, then there would be hardly one of them which would not be in conflict with the provisions of the Charter, according to the interpretation given to the Charter by Mr Kyrou.[18]

And might not a protracted debate intensify communal strife in Cyprus, jeopardize the still tenuous friendship between Greece

---

18 The Minister of State (Rt Hon. Selwyn Lloyd), *GAOR*, 9th sess., Plen., 477th mtg., 24 Sept. 1954, p. 53. See also speech by the Minister of State (Rt Hon. Anthony Nutting) in the General Committee on 21 September 1955, the full text of which is given in Cmd. 9716, Annex II.

and Turkey, and, last but not least, embarrass Great Britain in the exercise of her strategic responsibilities in the region? Britain was resolved to assist the 'people of Cyprus to develop their own political institutions and to proceed in an orderly and peaceful manner towards self-government',[19] but outside interference would impede rather than hasten the process.

These arguments made a notable impression on most delegates. The Latin American bloc and some Asian countries quickly appreciated that self-determination, if pressed *à l'outrance*, could not fail to upset precariously balanced frontiers and foment unrest. The Moslem Arab countries shared Turkey's acute and very evident concern about the possible plight of 100,000 Moslems under the Greek Orthodox Church, while the United States and other NATO Powers feared, *inter alia*, that Cyprus might not be quite so secure a strategic asset in Greek as in British hands and deplored the public squabble between two NATO members. It is true that even if these more sober counsels had not prevailed, any Assembly recommendations would almost certainly have been regarded by the United Kingdom as invalid and would, therefore, have been quite ineffectual.[20] But to the British Government the Assembly's decision to postpone discussion of the issue was welcome evidence of the Assembly's new-found caution—even if it was and still is only 'for the time being'.[21]

The Arab-Asian countries are well aware of the bargaining power conferred upon them by the West's eagerness to obtain, or retain, their support in the cold war, and by their control both of one of the great strategic cross-roads of the world and of a large part of its oil reserves. They have already shown considerable diplomatic skill in their use of these assets, and it would be unwise to assume

---

[19] The Minister of State (Rt Hon. Anthony Nutting), *GAOR*, 9th sess., Plen., 514th mtg., 17 Dec. 1954, p. 539.

[20] Except in the improbable contingency of their successful use by the Opposition to secure a reversal of the present United Kingdom Government's policy over Cyprus.

[21] See *GAOR*, 9th sess., suppl. no. 21, Resolution 814(IX), 17 Dec. 1954.

that they will not continue to use the United Nations as an instrument for exerting the pressure of majority opinion to secure the ending of European overlordship in Asia and Africa. Even at Dumbarton Oaks it was suspected that, whatever limitations were proposed, there was really no way of preventing the Assembly from discussing anything it had a mind to discuss. And it is arguable not only that the United Nations is a useful safety-valve for these pressures, but also that the metropolitan Powers need to be reminded of the great force of Arab and Asian nationalism and of its determination both to throw off the last vestige of European dominance and to hasten the emancipation of colonial peoples from European rule. Nevertheless, the crucial test is whether unrest and friction between the territories concerned and the West are likely to be promoted rather than allayed, and the orderly progress of colonial peoples towards self-government impeded rather than assisted, by United Nations intervention. There can be no certain answer to this question, but there are some grounds for suspecting that the hope of United Nations intervention has tended to exacerbate rather than to relieve nationalist feeling and to put a premium on insurrection and the use of violence. The smouldering embers in Cyprus and North Africa may well have been fanned into flickering flames precisely in order to strengthen the case for United Nations intervention on the Indonesian model.

If the United Nations were to continue to operate in this way, Britain might be forced seriously to reconsider her whole attitude to the Organization. The need may not, of course, arise. In the last few years many delegates seem to have become aware of the complexity of issues to which previously they had thought application of the principle of self-determination would give the complete answer, and to be more ready to listen to moderating counsels. The glimpse of the chaos and violence which the too rapid application of the principle of self-determination would almost certainly bring has also helped to persuade them of the merits of orderly progress. Some at least have grasped the need to strike a balance between their desire for change and the reasonable preservation of established rights and treaty obligations. But the clear warnings given by the United Kingdom (and other colonial Powers) that persistent ill-advised intervention might threaten the United Nations' very existence, together with the United States' recent disposition to side with the colonial Powers in order to preserve Western unity, have probably been of chief moment in dampening down anti-colonial pressure. The more colourful and vocal personalities in the attack will no doubt continue their verbal sorties, but at long last delegates seem to be tumbling to the fact that strengthening the United Nations is not synonymous with arrogating to it powers to which it is not entitled.

BRITAIN
AND THE
BRETTON WOODS SYSTEM

PART FOUR

chapter ten

Planning for Multilateralism

The United Nations constellation of specialized agencies is now
so extensive that it is only possible in this study to examine the
three economic agencies the activities of which bear most directly
on the content and conduct of British foreign economic policy,
namely, the International Monetary Fund, the International Bank
for Reconstruction and Development, and the General Agreement
on Tariffs and Trade (GATT).[1] This limitation is imposed almost
wholly by considerations of space, not by any desire to belittle
the importance of the practical achievements of agencies such as
the ILO, WHO, and FAO. Indeed, it is evident that even the work
of the economic agencies cannot be described within the space of

---

[1] Strictly speaking, the term 'Bretton Woods system' applies only to the IMF
and the International Bank, the Articles of Agreement of which were negotiated
at the Bretton Woods Conference (July 1944). But in practice GATT forms
part of the system, and the Economic and Social Council is a close appendage.
Both these latter bodies will be considered in this Part.

a single chapter without sliding over often highly controversial questions. Yet the contribution these agencies have made, and can make, to the material welfare and political well-being both of the people of the free world in general and of the British people in particular is not to be ignored. It is, of course, the case that in the long-drawn-out 'transition' period they have been overshadowed by the massive annual injections of American bilateral aid and by the more limited groupings of the sterling area and the Organization for European Economic Co-operation (OEEC). But, by contributing to an expanding volume of world trade, they have already materially assisted Great Britain in her struggle towards economic solvency, while by providing a forum for the discussion of the effect of one country's actions in the economic sphere (and especially those of the United States) on the economic fortunes of other countries, they have helped to ease economic strains which might also have proved a serious source of political friction. Furthermore, the future prospects for convertibility may well turn on whether the Bretton Woods system can be so imbued with new life and vitality as to enable it to fulfil the kind of role marked out for it in 1944.

A word or two must first be said about the background to Bretton Woods.[2] Just as the Dumbarton Oaks negotiations were concerned to fulfil President Roosevelt's promise of 'Freedom from Fear' in the post-war world, so the chief aim of the United Nations Monetary and Financial Conference, which opened in Bretton Woods (New Hampshire, U.S.A.) on 1 July 1944, was to ensure 'Freedom from Want'. It was not alone in this aim. Not only was UNRRA already in existence, but the United Nations Conference on Food and Agriculture had held a successful meeting in Hot Springs, Virginia, in May 1943, while the ILO was meeting

---

[2] For background material see, *inter alia*, R. F. Harrod, *The Life of John Maynard Keynes* (London, Macmillan, 1951), Chapters XIII ff.; E. F. Penrose, *Economic Planning for the Peace* (Princeton University Press, 1953); and especially Richard N. Gardner, *Sterling-Dollar Diplomacy* (Oxford, Clarendon Press, 1956), which became available after the completion of this study.

concurrently in Philadelphia. Moreover, in spite of their differing spheres of action, underlying all these meetings was a common determination to avoid the economic chaos and distress of the 1930's, memories of which were still vivid in the minds of the chief negotiators. Nor did they recall only the human degradation and economic waste of mass unemployment or the economic damage caused by the growth of autarkic policies. Many on both sides of the Atlantic considered that the 'Great Depression' had also been instrumental in creating psychological conditions conducive to the growth of militarism and totalitarianism; that the spread of economic nationalism in the 1930's had helped to exacerbate international relations; and that the failure to heed the pleas of the economic 'have-nots' had encouraged them to turn to military means to attain their ends. In short, the failure of members of the League of Nations to grapple with the root causes of the economic stresses and strains of the inter-war period had not only led to great human misery but it was held, rightly or wrongly, to have contributed to the holocaust in which all were now engaged. What those causes were had been revealed—or so it was widely supposed—by Keynesian analysis, so making it possible to evolve an economic system for the post-war world which, while preserving the advantages of the international division of labour, would put an end to the booms and slumps, the economic inequalities, and the barriers to trade which had caused so much trouble in inter-war years. In addition, the vital importance of continued close collaboration with the United States and the fear that she might repeat her 'back-to-normalcy' policies of 1919 made early agreement on the post-war system highly desirable, as did the need to hold out both to the Allied peoples and to the hungry and oppressed peoples of a Europe on the threshold of liberation an invigorating prospect of a peace worth fighting for.

Thus, apart from the problem of relief and reconstruction, which was regarded as a temporary problem to be dealt with mainly by UNRRA (with some help from the International Bank) and

by an American grant or loan to Britain, attention was concentrated
in the negotiations leading up to Bretton Woods on three kinds
of post-war international economic problems: (1) economic stability
at a high level of employment; (2) economic development; and (3)
the reduction of barriers to trade. These problems were, of course,
closely interconnected; but on the whole it was anticipated that
the Fund would provide the main answer to the first (although
Keynes himself seems to have expected commodity stabilization
schemes to play an important part also), the Bank (within limits)
to the second, and some kind of trade organization to the third.

The IMF and the International Bank, the Articles of Agreement
of which were agreed upon at Bretton Woods, are of virtually
unsullied Anglo-American parentage, a fact which reflects the
belief, both then and now, that the prime need was to establish
a fruitful relationship between the 'key currencies', namely, the
dollar and sterling; most other currencies, it was thought, would
then conveniently fall into line. The form that this relationship
was expected to take was indicated in Article VII of the Mutual
Aid Agreement (February 1942) between the two countries, which
looked in principle to the eventual 'elimination of all forms of
discriminatory treatment in international commerce, and to the
reduction of tariffs and other trade barriers'. It is true that on
the British side several of the negotiators had serious reservations
as to the feasibility of this goal; indeed most prognostications at
the time suggested that the plethora of controls Britain had developed
during the war might have to be retained well into the peace. Lord
Keynes himself was so conscious of the magnitude of Britain's
post-war economic task as to be attracted at first by Schachtian
ideas. Gradually, however, both he and most others of a like mind
came to the conclusion that for a country in Britain's position
they would be inappropriate. Not only had Britain traditionally
practised a free-trade policy, but unrestricted economic nationalism
in the post-war world would clearly frustrate all efforts to build
up her export trade, on which her very livelihood would depend.

Moreover, it would almost certainly foster dissension within the Commonwealth, while by antagonizing the United States it would be bound to prejudice both a favourable settlement of lend-lease and the prospects for continuing Anglo-American co-operation in the economic field.

The main outcome of this change of view was Lord Keynes's plan for a 'Clearing Union',[3] which was to take the form of a world central bank upon which each member would have a substantial overdraft right in an internationally acceptable currency. Total overdraft facilities of the order of $25,000 million were suggested, but these were to vary with the monetary value of world trade; the Clearing Union was also to have the power 'should an occasion, such as a severe world depression, demand it, to create credit without obtaining additional subscriptions from anyone'.[4] The American, or Harry Dexter White, proposals, like those of Lord Keynes, contemplated more or less fixed rates of exchange in the short run, with a fair degree of flexibility in the long run,[5] so as to allow exchange-rate variations to serve as the main means of maintaining a balance between the national economies; but in other respects they differed considerably. They envisaged a 'Stabilization Fund', analogous to the British Exchange Equalization Fund and the American Stabilization Fund, which was to have the limited function of providing a pool of currencies upon which members would have the right to draw in an emergency. The most disturbing feature, however, was that the total assets of the Fund were to be set by the amounts subscribed in the first instance. These were expected to be only about $5,000 million; no provision was made either for their expansion or for the creation of additional credit to meet a world depression.

---

[3] Cmd. 6437.

[4] R. F. Harrod, *The Dollar* (London, Macmillan, 1953), p. 107.

[5] Lord Keynes's formula was the more flexible since it allowed a country to depreciate by not more than 5 per cent. in a single year without the leave of the Fund, whereas in the White proposals the consent of the Fund would be needed for any adjustment, however small.

t

The 'Clearing Union' was in almost every respect a more spacious and flexible scheme than the 'Stabilization Fund'; but by the summer of 1943 it became clear that the Americans were firmly opposed to the virtually 'unlimited liability' it would impose on a persistent creditor and that they were determined, largely for Congressional reasons, to limit their liability to a fairly small once-and-for-all contribution. From about July 1943 onwards, therefore, Britain concentrated on obtaining a modification of the White plan to fit it more closely to British needs. The Americans, having obtained a victory for the principle of 'limited liability', subsequently made considerable concessions, so that although the 'Joint Statement by Experts for the Establishment of an International Monetary Fund' (April 1944) was based mainly on the White proposals, a great many of its details were Keynesian in origin. Thus the British plea for a greater degree of exchange flexibility and more liberty of action was partly met since a once-and-for-all right to depreciate by 10 per cent. without leave of the Fund was granted, while special facilities were accorded for obtaining leave for a further 10 per cent.; further depreciations were, however, to be made subject to the Fund's consent. The total assets of the Fund were also to be raised to $8,000 million, but to ensure that the use to which they were put did not run directly counter to the wishes of the chief contributors a system of weighted voting was proposed, based on the size of contributions.[6] At the Bretton Woods Conference the Joint Statement, with no substantial changes, became the Articles of Agreement of the IMF,[7] which secured the support of forty-four countries, including the Soviet Union.

Up till this time interest had centred on the Fund, but at Bretton Woods the Articles of Agreement of the International Bank were also approved.[8] These were but a pallid reflection of the far more

---

[6] At present the United States has 28 per cent. of the total votes, Britain 13 per cent.

[7] Cmd. 6546, Annex A. pp. 16-45.

[8] ibid. Annex B, pp. 46-68.

ambitious plans first mooted by Harry White. The Bank's task was now to be confined to encouraging the flow of 'untied' capital from the creditor countries to the underdeveloped areas by 'priming the pump' for the private, especially the American, foreign investor and by guaranteeing him against exceptional risks. This task was of very direct interest to Great Britain. In the first place, she was very conscious both of the lag in development during the war in many of her dependent territories and of the general need to encourage the appreciable and steady flow overseas of American investment upon which the attainment of an expanding and balanced world economy would so greatly depend. In the second place, bearing in mind past difficulties over the 'tied' loans of the United States Export-Import Bank, it was a particular British interest to secure a flow of 'untied' capital, in the hope that borrowers would spend in Britain a proportion of the dollars they received. The Bank might also, it was hoped, be able to allay the suspicions of some borrowing countries as to the possible political consequences of foreign investment by channelling it through an international institution in which they would have a voice, whilst at the same time the Bank would relieve donor countries of the need to make invidious—and politically embarrassing—distinctions between rival claimants for their limited resources. The scope of the Bank was further limited by the stipulation that it should only finance 'economic' projects. Even so some feared that the Bank's initial resources might prove too small; but the general view was that if they were used prudently the Bank would have little difficulty in raising more.

On British initiative discussions on commercial policy were held in 1943 at the official level, first with the Dominions and then with the United States. Mainly because of differences of view in the War Cabinet[9] the negotiations were not very far advanced, however, by the time of Bretton Woods. It was not until December

---

[9] W. K. Hancock and M. M. Gowing, *British War Economy* (*History of the Second World War*, UK Civil Series, 1949), p. 545.

1945 that they finally bore fruit in the Anglo-American *Proposals for Consideration by an International Conference on Trade and Employment*.[10] These will be discussed later. Their main aim was to obtain agreement on a code of commercial conduct which, by eliminating (after a brief transition period) nearly all forms of quantitative and discriminatory restrictions and by securing a general reduction in tariff barriers, would limit the more virulent forms of economic nationalism and make it easier for countries to correct a persistent deficit in their balance of payments by exchange-rate (or price and income) variations; doubts about the efficacy of the latter were reflected, however, in the British insistence that a country with an adverse balance of payments should be entitled to impose quantitative restrictions without having to obtain the permission of an international authority. The proposals also looked to the creation of an International Trade Organization, which would be an integral part of the Bretton Woods system—the 'third leg of a three-legged stool'—dealing not only with commercial policy but also with full-employment policies, commodity agreements, and so on. Finally, to round off the picture, although the Economic and Social Council, which had been set up at San Francisco as a 'principal organ of the United Nations', was not regarded by most of those who had been at Bretton Woods as of great importance, its role in co-ordinating the activities of the growing constellation of what were later to be known as the 'specialized agencies'[11] was recognized.

Fundamentally, the Bretton Woods 'picture' was of a non-discriminatory, multilateral, 'world economy', in which a high degree of international specialization, based on the relatively unimpeded operation of the law of comparative advantage, would make for the greater prosperity both of the whole and of the national parts. An underlying assumption was that some sort of equilibrium in the international economy could be restored after a

10 Cmd. 6709, 6 Dec. 1945.
11 The IMF and the International Bank are, of course, 'specialized agencies'.

transition period of about five years and that subsequently, if all went well, the main problems would be how to deal with a world economy which only occasionally got out of balance, with an economy, that is, in which there was a tendency towards, rather than away from, overall stability. By relying on controlled and orderly exchange-rate variations as the chief means of keeping the national parts in balance with each other, the Bretton Woods system would, it was hoped, enable countries to overcome a chronic deficit in their balance of payments ('fundamental disequilibrium') without resorting to deflationary policies, which might bring mass unemployment, or to quantitative restrictions, which might threaten a return to the 'beggar-my-neighbour' policies of the 1930's. Thus the Fund, which was to be the hub of the system, was to have four main functions. Firstly, by providing short-term credits for countries in temporary balance-of-payments difficulties, it would give them a breathing space in which to work out what measures were necessary without immediately resorting to deflation or to quantitative and probably discriminatory controls. Secondly, by confining the right to depreciate to countries faced by a chronic deficit in their balance-of-payments position,[12] as well as by providing a forum for consultation on proposed exchange-rate variations, the Fund could help to prevent competitive depreciations. Thirdly, the 'scarce-currency' clause[13] could serve to discipline persistent creditor countries, it could afford a loophole for debtor countries, and, perhaps above all, it could act as a symbol of the United States' duty to maintain a high level of aggregate demand. Fourthly, and not the least important, the Fund might serve as a framework for co-operation between national monetary authorities.

---

[12] The depreciation of the American dollar in 1934 still rankled.

[13] That is, the provision (Art. VII of the Articles of Agreement of the IMF) that if the Fund's holdings of a member's currency threatened to become exhausted, then that currency could be declared 'scarce'. All other members would then be entitled to discriminate against imports from the 'scarce currency' country, while continuing to trade as freely as before with each other.

With the advantage of hindsight, it is clear that an atmosphere of over-optimism attended the discussions at Bretton Woods. This was especially marked on the American side. The United Kingdom delegates were more conscious of the difficulties to be faced, especially in the immediate post-war period, but most anticipated that these would be met by UNRRA (and, to a lesser extent, by the Bank and the Fund themselves), by an American grant or loan to Britain, and by a 'robust' settlement of the sterling balances accumulated by a number of Middle Eastern and Asian countries mainly as a result of British military expenditure overseas. Also, apart from Mr R. G. Hawtrey, who consistently forecast the danger of inflation, most of the experts on the British side were chiefly apprehensive of a repetition of the 'Great Depression' and mainly intent on devising measures which would guard against the mistakes then made. The main problem was thought to be how to sustain aggregate demand in the United States rather than how to avoid inflation in the debtor countries; consequently, nearly all the safeguards written into the Articles of Agreement of the Fund, for example, the 'scarce-currency' clause, related to the disciplining of creditor countries.

When the Final Act of the Bretton Woods Conference was made public, many of its details were sharply criticized in Britain; most of these criticisms are not without their relevance today. For instance, the efficacy of the 'scarce-currency' provision was doubted, and there was a widespread concern lest membership of the Fund should prove an obstacle to the maintenance of full employment.[14] But perhaps the chief source of criticism[15] was the concentration on the long-term post-transition period before it could be seen with greater certainty how the immediate problems of relief and reconstruction could be overcome. Many feared that the struc-

---

14 *Employment Policy*, Cmd. 6527, was tabled on 26 May 1944.
15 Apart from the extreme fringes of 'Empire Free Traders', who strongly opposed the whittling-down of imperial preferences, and Socialist critics of anything that seemed to smack of the gold standard and *laissez-faire*.

tural changes in the international economy, especially the immense rise in the productive capacity of the United States, had been underestimated and that it would be a far longer uphill task to bring the dollar and sterling areas into balance with each other, free of all discriminatory controls, than the Bretton Woods negotiations allowed.

The reliance on exchange-rate variations as a means of remedying chronic deficits was also not to everybody's liking, mainly on the grounds that it presupposed too high an elasticity in the demand and supply of commodities entering into world trade. Sir Hubert Henderson, then in the Treasury, was a notably trenchant critic of the view that exchange-rate adjustments could form an adequate basis for an orderly international economy; he argued that it was

> extremely short-sighted to adopt an attitude which implies that quantitative import restrictions are an inherently objectionable expedient, the use of which can only be tolerated in exceptional cases and subject to a special procedure of international approval. They are far more rapid and effective than tariffs in stabilising the level of domestic production and minimising the effects of disturbances from world market fluctuations.[16]

Both then and subsequently his views found much support. The meagre size of the Fund's resources and the limitations on access to them also forced even many of those sympathetic to the general conception of the Bretton Woods system to the conclusion that it would be unable to play an effective part either in the reconstruction period or in safeguarding the rest of the world against the painful consequences of an American recession, which almost all believed would come within the not too distant future. Furthermore, the willingness of creditor nations to meet their responsibilities as wholeheartedly as would be necessary for the system to work seemed to demand a very exceptional degree of political foresight. According-

---

[16] *Oxford Economic Papers*, 1953, suppl.: *Sir Hubert Henderson*, p. 50. See also Henry Clay, ed., *The Inter-War Years and Other Papers; a Selection from the Writings of Hubert Douglas Henderson* (London, OUP, 1955), pts. iv and v.

ly, nearly all these critics anticipated that quantitative and discriminatory controls would form an integral part of United Kingdom
economic policy for a long time to come and several dwelt on the
benefits of the more limited multilateralism of a sterling area insulated
from the vagaries of a volatile and overbearing American economy.

Lord Keynes, and those who shared his general approach, were
not, of course, unaware of the weaknesses and uncertainties in
the system. The small size of the resources it could command
was a major disappointment; so was the very great detail into
which the Articles of Agreement of both the Fund and Bank entered,
making them indeed a 'lawyer's paradise'. Had it not been for
the American insistence that Congress and the business world should
be told precisely what arrangements they were being asked to
underwrite, a much shorter statement of principles would clearly
have been preferable, leaving their day-to-day interpretation to be
worked out in the light of developments in the world economic
situation. But the considerations which had led to the initial shift
away from Schachtian ideas now seemed to have been considerably
reinforced. Britain's bargaining position in the 'free for all' which
would ensue if the Bretton Woods system were rejected would almost certainly not be strong enough to enable her to restore her
balance of payments at a tolerable standard of living. Lord Keynes
himself had not only been encouraged by the American attitude in the negotiations but he had become convinced that the
alternative to Bretton Woods could only be to 'build up a separate
economic bloc which excludes Canada and consists of countries
to which we already owe more than we can pay, on the basis of their
agreeing to lend us money they have not got and buy only from us
and one another goods we are unable to supply.'[17] Moreover, the
urgent need to cement and perpetuate war-time Anglo-American
economic co-operation impressed itself on all concerned as the
gigantic nature of the reconstruction problem and of Britain's own
economic task was revealed; the rejection of the Final Act would

---

[17] 18 Dec. 1945, H. L. Deb., vol. 138, col. 790.

assuredly have dealt a severe blow to such co-operation and have had the most unfortunate political repercussions. For reasons such as these the British delegates went to Bretton Woods determined to get some kind of agreement with the Americans down on paper. Nor, apart from its meagre resources, was the Final Act agreed upon so very far from the original Keynesian proposals; almost every clause of the Fund's Articles of Agreement reflected British authorship. Finally, there was a strong feeling amongst both ministers and officials that it would be most impolitic to jeopardize a favourable settlement of Lend-Lease and the proposed American loan by rejecting the Final Act, and that even if the success of the system[18] were not altogether certain, it did at least hold out a real hope of proving superior to the pre-war system—or lack of system. In short, once the overriding need for Anglo-American agreement was conceded, there seemed little point in turning the system down, since it was evidently the best that could be obtained in the circumstances.[19] Despite the considerable body of criticism and the mental reservations of many of those sympathetic to the Bretton Woods Final Act, non-adherence was never, therefore, a real issue, and the Fund and the Bank came into being on 25 and 27 December 1945 respectively.

---

[18] Including, that is, the proposed trade organization and its 'code of conduct'.
[19] One powerful circumstance being the necessity of hitting upon a scheme that would have a good chance of acceptance by Congress.

chapter eleven

The International Monetary Fund

Any tentative assessment of the merits and shortcomings of the Bretton Woods system over the last ten years must distinguish between the weaknesses in the system, both of faulty design and of faulty execution, and the unexpected turn of events in the world in which it was expected to operate. The most obvious fact is, of course, that the whole political climate in which the system has had to operate is diametrically different from that envisaged at Bretton Woods. With one solitary exception the Communist world is outside, not part of, the system,[1] which has consequently tended

---

[1] The Soviet Union never became a member of either the Bank or the Fund; Poland and Czechoslovakia relinquished their membership of both in 1950 and 1954 respectively. The exception is Czechoslovakia's continued membership of GATT.

to become an instrument of the 'free' world, especially in the field of economic aid, rather than of the 'one world' dreamed of by its begetters. The benefits of the international division of labour and of many forms of international trade have also become less obvious to countries like Britain in which economic stability often seems to take precedence over economic growth and in which security considerations are held to demand a greater measure of self-sufficiency (especially in agriculture) and the strict control of any trade which might contribute to the military potential of unfriendly countries. Indeed in a great part of economic life the economics of power have taken precedence over the economics of welfare. In these circumstances, the hope in 1944 that the Fund and Bank would operate relatively uncontaminated by politics has been frustrated; on the contrary, economic and political considerations have become so closely interwoven that they are often difficult to disentangle. The central economic fact against which their operations must be viewed is, of course, that recovery has been so slow that the underlying equilibrium in the international economy which was the pre-condition of the system's functioning has not yet been fully realized. It is true that the application of Keynesian ideas in this and other countries has meant (so far) that there has been a much greater degree of economic stability than was anticipated in 1944, so that the economic climate, though unfavourable because of the slowness of recovery, has been very favourable because of the general maintenance of high levels of employment. Nevertheless, the frag-mentation of the international economy into more limited and discriminatory groupings has almost inevitably taken the Fund and, to a lesser extent, the Bank and the 'rump' General Agreement on Tariffs and Trade, out of the mainstream of international economic relations. Despite massive American aid, the notable growth in British exports, and the steady progress of recent years towards a freer international payments system, there still seems to be a 'hard core' to the dollar problem, while a great deal of the British effort in the last decade towards the liberalization of trade and payments has been through the sterling area, the **OEEC**, and the European Payments Union (EPU) rather than through the IMF or GATT.

The persistence of the 'dollar' problem is cited in some quarters in Britain as evidence of a continuing and deep-seated structural maladjustment in the international economy (as reflected, for instance, in the marked predominance of the American economy and the adverse—as compared with the 1930's—turn in Britain's terms of trade), which is considered to rule out all possibility of rehabilitating the Bretton Woods system. An unbridgeable 'chasm' rather than a bridgeable 'gap' is said to exist between the dollar and non-dollar worlds. The more orthodox view, however, at any rate in the last three years or so, is that the continuance of the dollar problem is to be attributed mainly to the heavy economic burdens imposed by the cold war, to failures in the realm of domestic economics in the debtor countries, and to the reluctance of creditor countries to make the necessary adjustments in their own domestic policies. Moreover it is pointed out that very considerable progress has recently been made towards a freer and less discriminatory system of both trade and payments between the dollar and non-dollar worlds.[2] And although it is true that the balance of payments of the non-dollar world is still supported by some $4,000 million of 'extraordinary' American aid, there is little sign that these annual disbursements will cease or even taper off within the near future. In short, although necessary, and, indeed, brilliant improvisations, neither OEEC nor EPU have so far been generally considered to provide a basis for an enduring world trade-and-payments system. For the most part the basic concepts of Bretton Woods are at the time of writing (December 1955) still thought to be valid, though it is generally conceded that the original institutional forms require to be modified and supplemented to meet the needs of the changing economic scene.

---

[2] For some examples see IMF, *Annual Report, 1955* (Washington, D. C.), pp. 1-11.

Nevertheless, it is the case that so far the world has turned out so different a place from that in which the IMF[3] was intended to function that the Fund has tended to drift along in a backwater. It has not been entirely inactive. It has helped to facilitate mutual understanding between its members; it has helped to give some useful advice on monetary matters to many of its Latin American members; and its research work has on the whole been of high quality. Up till 30 April 1955, however, its transactions amounted only to approximately $1,200 million, and in the previous twelve months demands on the Fund's resources were extremely light. In 1947-8 Britain was able to purchase $300 million for sterling as a stop-gap measure before the receipt of Marshall Aid,[4] but the Fund subsequently refused to allow the recipients of Marshall Aid to turn to it for assistance. This decision had the merit of keeping its limited resources intact for use after the end of the European Recovery Programme, but it accentuated the trend for monetary questions to be discussed at OEEC rather than at the Fund. For a long time, therefore, the Executive Directors were left without a great deal to do except to discuss administrative matters or hypothetical questions of little importance. This was mainly due to the fundamentally frustrating situation in which the Fund was placed. But flaws in the design were also partly responsible.

It will be readily appreciated that the Fund is in a most delicate position; the monetary matters with which it is concerned are not only ones on which governments are extremely sensitive to outside

---

[3] The Fund's membership (as on 30 April 1956) consisted of: Afghanistan, Australia, Austria, Belgium, Bolivia, Brazil, Burma, Canada, Ceylon, Chile, China (Nationalist), Colombia, Costa Rica, Cuba, Denmark, Dominican Republic, Ecuador, Egypt, El Salvador, Ethiopia, Finland, France, Federal Republic of Germany, Greece, Guatemala, Haiti, Honduras, Iceland, India, Indonesia, Iran, Iraq, Israel, Italy, Japan, Jordan, Republic of Korea, Lebanon, Luxembourg, Mexico, Netherlands, Nicaragua, Norway, Pakistan, Panama, Paraguay, Peru, Philippines, Sweden, Syria, Thailand, Turkey, Union of South Africa, United Kingdom, United States, Uruguay, Venezuela, Yugoslavia (58 in all).

[4] Britain's total quota is the equivalent of $1,300,000,000, but of this only just over $236 million had to be paid in dollars or gold.

interference, but they need to be handled with the utmost discretion if money markets are not to be adversely influenced. Unhappily in a Fund of so many members the necessary measure of discretion can hardly be expected, especially as several members are known to hold the basic premises of the Bretton Woods system in disdain and to have little interest in making the system work. Nor is this difficulty overcome by devolving the day-to-day work of the Fund on to a smaller number of Executive Directors. Indeed, perhaps the most serious defect in the Fund's structure is the virtual impossibility of discussing any question requiring secrecy with as many as seventeen Executive Directors. However discreet they may purport to be, 'leakages', inspired or otherwise, are almost inevitable. This difficulty is not peculiar to the Fund. Even in the smaller and more exclusive club of the Management Board of the EPU confidences are not exchanged at all freely. But the wider and more polyglot circle of the Executive Directors in the Fund both makes governments even less inclined to disclose their intentions and greatly aggravates the technical difficulty of discussing matters on which secrecy is crucial. Consequently, instead of the prior consultation required under Article IV, Section 5, of the Articles of Agreement on vital questions like devaluation (where prior knowledge of a decision can be disastrous), governments are forced to present members with a virtual *fait accompli*, by consulting them either an hour before the decision is made public or on a Saturday afternoon when places of business are closed. The way in which the devaluation of sterling took place in September 1949 is only a particularly striking example of this fact. Whether it can be overcome is extremely difficult to say. Weighted voting has certainly not proved the answer. A modification which allowed the everyday work of the Fund to be carried on by a 'standing group' (on the analogy of NATO) of four or five might go some way to meeting it. At least it should then be possible to have more sensible discussions; but the technical difficulties would almost certainly still remain. The provision for prior consultation on questions of devaluation must probably be regarded, therefore, as virtually a dead-letter.[5] The criteria by which the propriety of devaluation may be judged remain valid, however, and there can still be *post hoc* approval.

A related question is the status and role of the Executive Directors. Lord Keynes's view was that the Fund's staff should not confine itself to research and advice but should also be responsible for day-to-day routine activities, leaving policy decisions to be taken by part-time Executive Directors, who would be high officials in their national treasuries. At the first meeting of the Governors of the Fund and the Bank held at Savannah (United States) in 1946, the Americans insisted, however, that the Executive Directors (and their Alternates) should serve full-time. The wisdom of this decision was, to say the least, open to question, and it almost certainly aggravated the tendency in the Fund, which OEEC has happily avoided, to divorce international from domestic economic policy. In the early years of the Fund it was also an inducement to the Executive Directors to examine transactions in the minutest detail, with the result that what Lord Keynes had hoped would be virtually automatic drawing rights came to be hedged around with conditions which appreciably reduced the certainty of access to the Fund's resources and so induced a certain lack of confidence in the Fund's willingness to help members in times of crisis.

Fortunately the Fund has recently adopted a much more flexible attitude on the question of access to its resources. Members can now feel confident that the Fund will be sympathetic to requests for the purchase of other currencies, whether to meet temporary balance-of-payments difficulties or to support the establishment or maintenance of convertibility. As far back as February 1952 the Fund announced that it was

> prepared to consider requests by members for stand-by arrangements designed to give assurance that, during a fixed period of time, transactions up to a specified amount will be made whenever a member requests and without further

---

5 At least so far as sterling is concerned.

consideration of its position, unless the ineligibility provisions of the Fund have been invoked.[6]

The Fund has also shown itself willing to grant waivers under Article V, Section 4, so allowing countries to draw more than the 25 per cent. of their quotas, which is normally the maximum permitted in any one twelve-month period. Perhaps the most striking instances of this new-found flexibility are the intimation that a member which allows its exchange rate to fluctuate in response to market forces (as Canada at present does) will not necessarily be deprived of its right of access to the Fund, and the decision to restore France's eligibility to use the Fund's resources even though she has not yet reached agreement with the Fund on an official parity value for the franc.[7] These are encouraging moves in the right direction, and the greater certainty of access to the Fund's facilities has undoubtedly helped to counter most members' limited confidence in the Fund's *willingness* to help in time of need. However, an equally serious reason for concern is the uncertainty about the Fund's *capacity* to do so at all effectively. In the present state of national reserves[8] the present level of the Fund's resources is clearly insufficient to give the bulk of members the security they desire against, for instance, either an American recession or the risks of convertibility.

AMERICAN RECESSIONS

The 1949 American recession appeared to bear out the saying that 'America sneezes and Europe catches pneumonia', and to reinforce the belief that the dominance and instability of the American

---

[6] IMF, *Annual Report, 1953*, p. 95; see also pp. 49-53.

[7] ibid. *1955*, pp. 84-88.

[8] The value of the United Kingdom's reserves, in real terms, as measured by an index of prices of United Kingdom imports, is only about one-quarter of their pre-war level. See R. G. Opie, 'International Finance', *London and Cambridge Economic Bulletin*, Mar. 1956, pp. x-xi.

economy were such that Britain would be well advised to base its policy on an insulated sterling-area and EPU system. Since then Western Europe and the sterling area have survived with little difficulty the economic 'readjustment' in the United States of 1953-4, the main lessons of which seem to be that American administrations can be counted upon to take early remedial action to prevent an American recession either lasting very long or going very deep, and that there is no simple relationship between the level of economic activity in the United States and the flow of dollars to the outside world. Yet especially favourable circumstances existed in 1953-4 which might not perhaps be repeated. The proclivity of the American economy to depressions evidently needs reassessing, but it would be imprudent to assume too readily that a similar 'readjustment' on another occasion might not have serious repercussions in the non-dollar world. With the present low level of her national reserves Britain would very likely be unable to ride out even a fairly shallow recession on her own without reverting to further severe discrimination against the dollar.[9] An appreciable increase in national reserves is very desirable for this and other reasons. But an increase of the size necessary to rule out altogether the need to resort to national improvisations, which might be as harmful as the 'beggar-my-neighbour' policies of the 1930's, is most unlikely for some time to come. The Fund was intended to help out in circumstances such as these by supplementing national reserves. Yet not only were its resources generally considered inadequate in 1945 but their real value has been reduced by at least one-third by the rise in world prices. Their present level is pitifully small in relation to the need.

In an ideal world what would probably be desirable would be the institution of an international central bank which, by paying out freely in time of depression and contracting its issues at time of inflation, would exert the necessary stabilizing influence. In

---

[9] Assuming that the flow of dollars was not maintained by the Administration increasing the volume of extraordinary disbursements.

present circumstances, however, anything as ambitious as a central bank is out of the question and the practical choice seems to be between (*a*) increasing the resources of a reformed Fund, or (*b*) setting up an independent stabilization fund especially charged with the duty of lending freely to governments and central banks in times of depression on such terms as to secure rapid repayment in times of expanding trade. The latter proposal has the advantage of entrusting the task to an institution less administratively and politically unwieldy than the Fund. But, on balance, it would seem preferable to build on the basis of the Fund as a going concern and along the lines suggested in the United Nations report of 1951 on *Measures for International Economic Stability*.[10] This report proposed that the Fund should be prepared to use its resources boldly to prevent the spread of a recession, both by waiving freely the present limits on annual drawings by members, which, to a very great extent it has now done, and by borrowing from the country experiencing the recession if the Fund's resources turned out to be insufficient. In practice, of course, it would almost certainly be dollars that would be in short supply.

One method of increasing the Fund's resources to the necessary level would be an increase in the dollar price of gold; an increase of 50 per cent. would mean the addition of something like $5,000 million to the reserves of the non-dollar part of the free world. An increase of such a size could make a tremendous contribution to the latter's economic well-being. It could hardly fail to be in Britain's interest, especially since a high proportion of the additional annual income from the production of gold would accrue to the sterling area. The timing of such an increase would need careful consideration, however, since there is a real risk that it might re-stoke the fires of a world inflation. Moreover, not only has the United States consistently opposed such a step, but under present American legislation it would require Congressional

[10] U. N., Dept. of Economic Affairs, *Measures for International Economic Stability* (New York, 1951).

approval. Consequently, even if a favourable decision were reached, a degree of exchange speculation might take place beforehand which might almost negate its value. It would probably be more feasible, therefore, for the Fund to borrow dollars direct from the United States; and there is no technical reason why the Fund should not do so even before they are declared 'scarce'. It is extremely difficult to say precisely how great an increase in the Fund's resources is called for on this score.[11] An increase from its present holdings of gold and dollars of $3.3 thousand million (approx.)[12] to, say, $6,000 million, might be desirable were it not for the risk that countries might be encouraged to borrow too lavishly from the Fund when other, perhaps more painful, remedial measures of domestic policy might be more appropriate. Yet too timid an increase would do little to combat the present limited confidence in the Fund amongst even governments sympathetic to its general aims. The problem is essentially a psychological one, depending on a number of variables. Perhaps all that can usefully be said is that the Fund's resources should be increased to the point at which governments would be prepared to place more confidence in the Fund, and in the ability of the free world, with the aid of the Fund, to weather an American recession without reverting to large-scale restrictions.

The terms on which the Fund's resources could be drawn upon and the conditions of repayment would also be important. The former must naturally depend to a very large extent on the terms on which the Fund itself could borrow from the United States. Once again they should, on the one hand, be strict enough to encourage self-help, and, on the other hand, generous enough to discourage early resort to autarkic measures. Flexibility in the terms of repayment would be desirable since so much would turn on the course of economic activity after a recession; for this reason

---

11 An increase is also desirable to cushion the shock of convertibility; see the next section.

12 IMF, *Annual Report, 1955*, pp. 91-92.

it would be prudent to have some kind of waiver provision which could be invoked when the difficulties of repayment were peculiarly acute. If a recession were short-lived and followed by a boom, rapid repayment would be both appropriate and useful in combating inflation; in different circumstances it might have to be extended over several years. But there is something to be said for strengthening the determination of governments to repay promptly, as and when circumstances permit, by increasing the penalties for failure. The original Bretton Woods interest charges have already been revised in this direction; it is now difficult for a country to draw on the Fund and to leave the debt outstanding over more than five years.[13] This is a welcome step in the direction of making the Fund more like the revolving Fund it was intended to be.

One word of warning should be sounded on the question of repayment. Implicit in this kind of stabilizing operation is the belief that a 'downswing' will be followed by an equally marked 'upswing'; and, of course, this is necessarily so if the centre point is correctly defined. But will it be? The trouble is that countries which try to maintain activity at a higher level than the United States are apt to regard the 'upswing' as normal and to expect a recession to be followed by a further upswing which may never take place. There can in fact clearly be no guarantee that the *fall* in the American demand for imports, which would follow a recession in the United States, would be succeeded, once the recession were over, by a *rise* in the American demand for imports great enough to enable other countries to repay the dollars they had borrowed during the recession. This problem of repayment would be even more serious if, as at present, most non-dollar countries were finding it difficult to earn enough dollars even under reasonably favourable conditions, or were already labouring under a heavy burden of dollar debt. However, to set against these fears is the fact that so long as remedial action by the United States Administra-

---

[13] Britain was able to take longer over repayment of the 1947 drawing because it came under the old rules.

tion were reasonably rapid and effective—and there is every reason to expect that it would be—other countries might not need actually to draw on the Fund's resources. The knowledge that they could easily do so if necessary might enable them to run down their national reserves to a lower level without resorting to autarkic measures. In other words, in this context the main purpose of an increase in the Fund's resources would be to promote the kind of confidence which comes from the possession of adequate reserves rather than to encourage countries to use those resources.

CONVERTIBILITY

A matter of more immediate concern has been the extent to which the Fund might help to reduce the risks of convertibility. This is not the place to discuss the pros and cons of convertibility except to note that, for obvious reasons, the Chancellor of the Exchequer's statement at the Istanbul meeting of the Board of Governors of the Fund in September 1955, namely, that the British Government did not 'contemplate any early move on any (I repeat any) aspects of the exchange front' has recently been reaffirmed,[14] and that from the start the official approach has been fairly cautious and piecemeal through administrative measures which have been neither decisive nor irreversible. This continuing caution again springs very largely from the fact that reserves outside the United States are still, in general, inadequate to give support for a decisive move to convertibility. Considerable progress has been made towards *de facto* convertibility but a major danger still is that, if the pound were made more freely convertible into dollars, there might well be a 'run' on the pound which would gather momentum as the sterling area's reserves fell and confidence in sterling evaporated. A period of *de jure* convertibility might thus be as disastrously short-lived as it was in 1947. It is true that the Fund could provide

---

[14] Oral answer by Sir E. Boyle (Economic Secretary to the Treasury), 28 Jan. 1956, H. C. Deb., vol. 548, col. 353.

a useful supplement to the sterling area's reserves. Under stand-by credits Britain and other members of the sterling area could obtain automatic access to a specified amount of its resources if the sterling area's reserves declined dangerously. Again, they would not need actually to draw on the credits; their purpose would be to sustain confidence in, and so prevent a prolonged run on, sterling, thereby making a major convertibility move safer. But the present dollar resources that the Fund could make available (even if the 25 per cent. rule were waived) to meet the collective needs—and it is the collective approach that has constantly been emphasized—of all currencies to be made convertible almost certainly does not provide generous enough cover. Nor is it certain that the assurances of a two-year stand-by arrangement (which is at present the maximum period) would be sufficient; a longer period might well be necessary. There is a strong case, therefore, for supplementing the resources of the Fund and for introducing further flexibility into the stand-by arrangements in order to reduce the risks of convertibility. The United States Government is the obvious source of such supplementary credits; whether it would be better for Britain that they should be made directly to the sterling area or indirectly by augmenting the Fund's resources, is very largely a technical question. On balance the latter course seems the more desirable, if only because the need to augment the Fund's resources is not limited to the convertibility issue. If convertibility were successful there would still remain the need for some central stabilization fund to guard against the possibility of the spread of deflationary pressures from the United States.

With convertibility the 'scarce currency' clause might once again become important. In spite of some of the high hopes at first placed in the clause it has so far been of virtually no significance, except possibly as a symbol of the United States' recognition of its obligations as a creditor nation. Even in conditions of convertibility it would evidently be a great mistake to place too much reliance on the clause, if only because the Fund's main responsibility is to avoid the necessity of declaring a currency 'scarce' by persuading a persistent creditor to make more of its currency available. But the review conference of GATT[15] showed that the clause could serve as a useful basis for the regulation of discrimination. It is true that the wording of the present clause is not altogether satisfactory from this point of view,[16] but formal amendment would require Congressional approval, which would almost certainly not be forthcoming. Consequently, unless revision of the Articles of Agreement were desired on other grounds, what is probably needed is a gloss on, or an interpretation of, the present clause, which would allow whatever policies were most appropriate to be followed.

Two other points of considerable importance but highly esoteric and technical in nature can only be touched upon. The first is the rule that the maximum and minimum rates for exchange transactions should not differ from parity by more than 1 per cent. (Art. IV, sect. 3). Although intrinsically sound, there is a strong case for widening the present margin of variation in order to allow for periods of experimentation, since in times of economic change it is often difficult for governments to foresee the right rate. For instance, it might be desirable to introduce greater flexibility in order to test the strength of sterling before convertibility. A more intricate and delicate question is whether the Fund's system of pegged exchange rates with sudden and once-and-for-all adjustments as the means of correcting a fundamental disequilibrium in a country's balance of payments is preferable to a system of fluctuating exchange rates in which the value of national currencies would vary from day to day, or from hour to hour, in accordance with the forces of supply and demand for each currency on the money markets.[17] This is an issue of crucial importance to the Fund and there is an intimate connexion between it and the level of reserves required

---

[15] See below, p. 329.

[16] See *Financial Times*, 13 Jan. 1955, article by R. F. Harrod.

[17] The range of fluctuation could of course be limited by the intervention of an Exchange Equalization Account.

to make convertibility possible. If it were felt that the rate could take much of the initial strain, convertibility might be attempted with a lower level of reserves, while there would also probably be less incentive to perverse speculation.[18] In the longer run, there is certainly a great deal to be said for

> the method employed by the Exchange Equalization Account of tentative, provisional, reversible, small, stage-by-stage reductions, subject to trial and error and the power of the authorities to influence the movement by applying their resources in the market from time to time, rather than by the International Monetary Fund system of a once-over movement in the parity.[19]

And although fluctuating (or floating) rates would, strictly s peaking, be quite incompatible with the present provisions of the Fund's Articles of Agreement,[20] it is to be noted that Canada (and Peru) has had a floating rate for some years and yet has remained a member. Indeed, in June 1954 the Executive Board of the Fund adopted a set of rules to deal with such cases, and the Fund is formally on record to the effect that a 'member whose currency fluctuates [is not] necessarily deprived of its right to purchase the currencies of other members'.[21] On the other hand the strong arguments against a floating rate have evidently prevailed with the present United Kingdom Government. The Chancellor of the Exchequer categorically affirmed on 26 July 1955 that British policy 'has been, and will continue to be, the maintenance of exchange parity of 2.80 dollars to the £, either in existing circumstances or when sterling is convertible',[22] and this statement was confirmed by Sir E. Boyle (Economic Secretary to the Treasury) on 28 January

---

[18] The case for fluctuating exchange rates is persuasively argued by Professor J. E. Meade in *Three Banks Review*, Sept. 1955.

[19] Harrod, *The Dollar*, p. 134.

[20] Art. IV, sect. 3.

[21] IMF, *Annual Report, 1955*, p. 87.

[22] H. C. Deb., vol. 544, col. 1025.

1956.[23] Whether the issue is entirely dead remains to be seen, however.

To place the emphasis on building defences against the risks of convertibility or of an American recession is to obscure the extent to which inflationary over-spending in the non-dollar world in general, and in Britain in particular, has contributed to the persistence of the dollar problem. The major post-war problem has been inflation, not deflation. Access to the Fund's resources needs to be as free as possible for those in genuine need; but the Fund would almost certainly benefit if it were more free to 'take into account domestic policies when deciding on eligibility for credit facilities',[24] and so to bring pressure not only on chronic creditors but also on chronic debtors who may hope to avoid putting their own house in order by drawing on the Fund or relying on American aid. It is true that the Fund has the right to limit a member's use of its resources, or to declare it ineligible to use those resources, lest they be used 'in a manner contrary to the purposes of the Fund' (Art. V, sect. 5). But members are naturally extremely reluctant to impose sanctions against each other; indeed the whole trend has been to interpret them away. Therefore a more feasible approach might be to develop these techniques of mutual accountability and cross-examination which have proved so successful in NATO and OEEC. Whatever the means the end should be to break down the present divorce between international and national economic policies. A different question which can only be mentioned *en passant* is that of working out a satisfactory relationship between the IMF and the proposed European Fund, which is to replace the present EPU when convertibility is achieved. This is

---

[23] ibid. vol. 548, coll. 352-53.

[24] Lionel Robbins, 'The International Economic Problem', *Lloyds Bank Review*, Jan. 1953, p. 23. It appears that the European Fund, which is to form part of the European Monetary Agreement that is intended, with convertibility, to replace EPU, will have regard, in considering requests, 'not only to the needs of the country concerned, but also to the firmness of its domestic policy and to the interests of the organization as a whole' (*The Economist*, 19 Nov. 1955, p. 19). The EPU had no such right.

but another example of the difficulty of dovetailing a regional with a more universal system; it is natural that, as the hub of a sterling area which radiates out all over the globe, Britain should be more mindful than some of her European neighbours of the latter's virtues.

Finally, the rehabilitation of the IMF is of significance not only on economic but also on political grounds. By perpetuating present economic divisions within the Western world the indefinite postponement of convertibility might well give rise to serious political friction, while persistent fears (however unfounded) of the toll that an American recession might take of the delicately balanced British economy still provide fertile soil for incipient anti-Americanism. As always, the prime responsibility for economic policies that will avoid these dangers lies with member governments, and especially, may it be said, with the United States and Britain. But the Fund could serve as an important institutional aid if to the welcome flexibility it has shown in facing up to unforeseen circumstances could be added the vigour which a transfusion of additional resources alone can bring.

chapter twelve

The International Bank and Economic Aid

Discussion about the IMF is apt to centre on its defects and on methods of overcoming them. By contrast, the International Bank for Reconstruction and Development enjoys a more enviable reputation[1]. This is perhaps an unfair contrast. The economic environment has been far more favourable to the Bank; in a world in which there is an immense need for capital wisely laid out the Bank is almost bound to be both active and popular. Nevertheless, it is a fact that the Bank's administration is animated by a sense of purpose and orderly direction which for the most part the Fund has conspicuously lacked. Much of the credit for this must go to the management of the Bank, and especially to its present

---

[1] For an account of the Bank's operations see *The International Bank for Reconstruction and Development, 1946-1953*, prepared by the Staff of the Bank (Baltimore, Johns Hopkins Press; London, OUP; 1954). The membership of the Bank is the same as that of the Fund.

President, Mr Eugene R. Black; but it is also partly due to the sensible arrangement whereby the Bank's day-to-day operations are conducted by its staff, the role of the Executive Directors normally being limited to proffering advice on major questions of policy and to acting as a bridge between the Bank and member governments.

At first the Bank moved very cautiously in the field of development. Reconstruction needs had first call on its resources, which were in any case very limited. Nor was it easy for it to raise more by, for instance, the sale of its bonds on Wall Street, until its securities were qualified for institutional investment in the United States and until the initial mistrust of the investment community (which had burned its fingers badly in the inter-war period) had been overcome. It was, therefore, incumbent upon the Bank to build up a reputation for soundness. But this was not all. Even if the Bank had been prepared to adopt a less conservative attitude, its main difficulty would not have been so much the lack of funds as the scarcity of what by any reasonable standard could be regarded as well-conceived and carefully-thought-out projects.

However, in the last three years the scale of lending by the Bank for development purposes has steadily increased. In 1954-5 the Bank lent a total equivalent to approximately $410 million, the highest rate of lending in any fiscal year, while as on 30 June 1955 the amount (net of cancellations and refundings) lent by the Bank for *development* purposes since it began operations had reached the fairly impressive total of $1,777 million.[2] Of this total $579 million has gone to the Western Hemisphere, $432 million to Europe, $275 million to Asia, $259 million to Australasia, and $232 million to Africa; electric power and transport have claimed the major share, with agriculture (and forestry) and industry some way

---

[2] In addition the Bank lent a total of $497 million in 1947 to assist reconstruction in France, the Netherlands, Denmark, and Luxembourg. With the institution of the European Recovery Programme the Bank's lending operations in Western Europe diminished.

behind.[3] This increase in the Bank's lending activities in the field of development is mainly the result of three favourable developments. The first is that more 'sound' economic projects are now coming forward than in the past. Many governments are more experienced (frequently as a result of the Bank's own advisory services)[4] in drawing up and carrying through projects which match up to the fairly stringent requirements of the Bank. In addition, the rate of utilization of loans, which previously was apt to lag far behind authorizations, has been speeded up as management and administration have improved and some at least of the varied resistances to economic change have been overcome. Indeed, the Bank's achievement in countering the initial tendency to treat it as a kind of Santa Claus dispensing universal charity and its services in helping governments both to hammer out sound projects for financing and to use the money provided in the most effective way have probably been almost as important as the actual loans made. The second is that the Bank has been able to add very considerably to its resources through the sale of its bonds on the international capital markets, and especially on Wall Street, through the sale of parts of its loans to other investors, through the funds flowing back to it in repayment of earlier advances, and, to a lesser extent, through the releases of some of the 18 per cent. capital subscriptions[5] of non-dollar member countries.[6] The third, which

---

[3] For further details of loans made up to 30 June 1955 see IBRD, *Tenth Annual Report, 1954-5*, vol. 2, app. F and J.

[4] In addition to the fourteen Survey Missions which have surveyed the economic resources of member countries and have assisted governments to draw up and carry out development plans, the Bank has also recently set up an Economic Development Institute, the first Director of which is Professor A. K. Cairncross of Glasgow University. The Institute is to run six-month courses for senior officials concerned with economic planning.

[5] 18 per cent. of each member's subscription is payable in the currency of that member and can only be used with the member's consent; 2 per cent. is payable in gold or dollars; 80 per cent. is available on call (Art. IV).

[6] For details of resources available to the Bank on 30 June 1955, (estimated at the equivalent of $2,262 million) see IBRD, *Tenth Annual Report, 1954-5*, vol. I, p. 12. Loan commitments stood at $2,274 million.

is very largely consequential on the previous two developments and on the fact that Europe's reconstruction needs were met by Marshall Aid, is that the Bank is now ready not only to take rather less narrow a definition of what is a 'good risk' but also to interpret the 'specific projects' provision of Article III, section 4(7), more liberally. Thus it is now prepared to make general development loans and to finance the indirect foreign-exchange requirements engendered by general development programmes so as to help dampen down inflationary pressures set up by those programmes. It has also made known its willingness, in exceptional circumstances, to make loans which would not finance imports at all, but which would provide local currency for local expenditure.

In two important respects the Bank has a less impressive record, not because of mismanagement or misdirection but because the economic and political climate in which it has had to operate has been so different from that anticipated in 1944. In the first place, it has been singularly unsuccessful in stimulating the flow of private dollar investment into the underdeveloped countries, especially in South and South East Asia. It will be recalled that the original aim was for the Bank to act

> as a catalyst to private investment. It was thought that a few strategically-placed loans from the Bank would have a stimulating effect on private investment and that the granting of guarantees to private investors would create sufficient security to produce a large flow of capital. In the event the flow of private capital has been much smaller than was expected, obliging the Bank to turn to direct lending as its chief activity, and it now attempts to provide the maximum amount of capital 'consistent with sound banking principles'.[7]

It is true that although the Bank has been unable to overcome the reluctance of American investors to invest in underdeveloped countries which have no oil resources or are not politically 'sound', it has nevertheless indirectly contributed to the flow of dollars

---

[7] 'The International Bank', *Planning*, 13 Apr. 1953, p. 172.

overseas by raising rather over $600 million on Wall Street from the sale both of its bonds and of portions of loans from its portfolio. Had it not been for the Bank, it is improbable that these dollars would have been channelled into large-scale investment schemes in underdeveloped countries outside the American orbit. Another recent significant development in the revival of private international investment was the linking of two of the Bank's loans with a simultaneous offering of the borrower's bonds by private bankers in the United States. Otherwise there are not many signs that the Bank will become the catalyst for private dollar investment that it was intended to be.

Nor, in the second place, has an appreciable part of its dollar loans been spent outside the United States as was originally intended. Indeed, far from developing this kind of triangular trade, the Bank has probably to date only provided a few more dollars than borrowers have needed for buying dollar goods. Although under the Articles of Agreement the Bank's loans are formally 'untied' (Art. III, sect. 5(*a*)),[8] loans in fact tend to be made in accordance with the foreign-exchange needs of the particular project to be financed. Furthermore, it is probable that this tie between the place where a country buys and the currency in which it borrows is likely to persist; the more borrowers desire to satisfy their requirements outside the dollar area, the easier it should be for the Bank to increase its borrowing outside the dollar area to match, since non-dollar members will naturally be more willing to release their 18 per cent. contributions unconditionally if they know they will be spent on their own exports. It seems unlikely, therefore, that the Bank's loans can make any appreciable contribution in the foresee-

---

[8] Which reads: 'The Bank shall impose no conditions that the proceeds of a loan shall be spent in the territories of any particular member or members.' But compare *Loan Regulations no. 3*, applicable to loans made by the Bank to member Governments (rev. ed. Feb. 1955), Art III, sect. 3.01, 'Currencies in which proceeds of loans are to be withdrawn': 'The Borrower shall use reasonable efforts to purchase goods with the currencies of the countries from which such goods are acquired.'

able future to solving the dollar problem by enabling non-dollar countries to earn a portion of the dollars it lends.

The Bank is now also faced by the prospect that the increase in the number of sound projects coming forward and the greater flexibility in its lending terms may cause legitimate demands upon it to become too great for its resources; a further difficulty is that the requirement that the Bank shall only lend direct to governments, or to enterprises that can obtain a guarantee from their government or central bank (Art. III, sect. 4(1)), tends to limit its activities in the industrial field, as does its inability to make 'equity' investment. Yet if the widening gap between living standards in the industrial West and those in the underdeveloped areas is to be narrowed and the race against population growth is to be won, the volume of economic aid will have to be considerably stepped up, especially in the industrial field. Existing bilateral arrangements like those that have grown up under the Colombo Plan can serve as a very important channel for any such increase; but there is a strong case for expanding or supplementing the Bank's resources to enable it to play its full share.

Since currencies other than dollars are now in greater demand, one way of augmenting the Bank's resources would be the more liberal release of the 18 per cent. capital subscriptions of non-dollar members, for many of the releases already made are so hedged around with conditions as to make it difficult for the Bank to use them. Britain agreed in 1953 that £60 million of the Bank's sterling capital should be available to finance projects that might improve the sterling area's balance of payments; when the latter becomes healthier this stipulation might well be lifted. The proposed International Finance Corporation, which is to be an affiliate of the Bank, should also usefully supplement the Bank's operations. Unlike the Bank, the Corporation will be able to make loans to private enterprise without requiring government guarantees and will be able to hold securities bearing interest payable only if earned. It should, therefore, be of value in encouraging the flow of both foreign (particularly American) and domestic private investment into the numerous smaller projects in the industrial field which have up till now fallen outside the Bank's own sphere of operation. At one time Britain had some reservations about the need for such a Corporation and was in any case not prepared to anticipate United States action. But when American support was forthcoming she became markedly more sympathetic; the Economic Secretary to the Treasury (Sir Edward Boyle) has since said in a written answer that the proposed Articles of Agreement[9] are acceptable to Her Majesty's Government and that provision will be made for United Kingdom participation in the Corporation 'when we have assurance that the United States and other prospective members intend to proceed similarly.'[10] The United States has now formally accepted the Articles of Agreement of the Corporation,[11] which should come into existence in the near future. Britain is to subscribe rather over $14 million of the total $100 million capital proposed; and although the latter sum may at first sight seem but a drop in the ocean, the effective contribution of the International Finance Corporation will, through, for instance, its portfolio sales, be many times the size of its own capital.

In addition to the International Finance Corporation, the under-developed countries have been pressing for the creation of a Special United Nations Fund for Economic Development (SUNFED) of about $250 million, which would dispense grants-in-aid or low-interest long-term loans to assist schemes[12] which, on the one hand,

---

[9] See *Articles of Agreement of the International Finance Corporation and Explanatory Agreement*, as approved for submission to Governments by the Executive Directors of the International Bank, 11 Apr. 1955. Membership of the International Bank is to be a precondition of membership of the Corporation, the organizational structure and voting provisions of which are also to be very similar to the Bank's. See also *Statement on the International Finance Corporation*, by Robert L. Garner, Vice-President of the Bank, at the tenth annual meeting of the Board of Governors, Istanbul, 15 Sept. 1955.

[10] 4 May 1955, H. C. Deb., vol. 540, col. *145* (Written Answers).

[11] *The New York Times*, 6 Dec. 1955.

[12] For example, irrigation and drainage schemes, roads and canals, schools and hospitals.

though economically sound are not of the kind that the Bank can finance (because it is limited to financing on commercial principles) and, on the other hand, are beyond the limited resources of the specialized agencies (for example, WHO or FAO) most directly concerned. Any fund of this kind must be on a fairly large scale if it is to make a significant impact; generous and continuous American support is therefore essential. So far the United States has made it quite clear that, though sympathetic in principle, she is not yet willing to commit herself to active participation. Britain has strongly advised against trying to go ahead without the United States and has also argued (with the United States and others) that until the defence burden is appreciably reduced through the institution of an effectively supervised and world-wide system of disarmament, she has no margin of resources available for development finance through governmental channels over and above the very substantial sums already committed through the Colombo Plan[13] and colonial development schemes.[14] Certainly, under present conditions, with domestic investment and consumption running at such a high level, any British contribution to SUNFED might well lead to a diversion of resources from territories for which Britain has a special responsibility and, quite possibly, to the less effective use of those resources.

An important consideration is also indicated by the former Chancellor of the Exchequer's (the Rt Hon. R. Butler) remark that for development finance 'private funds are those upon which

[13] Mainly in the form of releases from the blocked sterling balances. By agreements concluded in 1951, India, Pakistan, and Ceylon are entitled to draw upon these balances up to £42 million annually until 1957. Up till the time of writing, annual drawings have in fact fallen far short of these figures but the balances provide a valuable 'nest-egg' for future development financing.

[14] There are three main channels: (*a*) the Colonial Development Corporation, which has authority to borrow up to £100 million for development schemes of a commercial nature; (*b*) the Colonial Development and Welfare Acts, under which Britain spent £100 million between 1945 and 1955 on development and welfare in her colonial dependencies and is to spend £120 million in the next five years; (*c*) the Commonwealth Finance Corporation, established in 1953 with an authorized share capital of £15 million net.

I think we should rely more than any other'.[15] The question is whether a sufficient volume of such funds will be forthcoming. Estimates of new long-term overseas investment (excluding intergovernmental lending but including British Government loans for commercial projects and borrowing by overseas governments in the London market) by Britain in the rest of the world are subject to a considerable margin of error, but in the four years 1952-5 it appears to have run at an annual average of the order of £150-75 million,[16] a not inconsiderable figure. But a high proportion went to the United States, Canada, Australia, and South Africa, not to the underdeveloped countries. Moreover, the amount Great Britain has been *lending* on long term to, for instance, British colonial territories has been in large measure offset by the amount she has been *borrowing* from the latter on short term in the form of additions to their sterling balances.[17] Put very simply, the future outlook for private British investment in the underdeveloped countries is likely to depend on two conditions. The first is whether internal demand in this country can be damped down so as to release resources for investment abroad; this is a *sine qua non* of any attempt by Britain to contribute more to the well-being of the Asian and African peoples. The second is whether the underdeveloped countries can offer more attractive opportunities for such investment than are offered by the developed countries. The policies of many underdeveloped countries are rarely such as to encourage the private foreign investor to believe that his investments will reap a fair reward. The International Bank can contribute to the necessary atmosphere of mutual confidence, as can institutions such as the recently created Industrial Credit and Investment Corporation in India. But the main onus rests on the underdeveloped countries them-

[15] IBRD, 9th Annual Mtg. of the Board of Governors, *Summary Proceedings*, p. 53.

[16] Cmd. 9731, p. 43.

[17] See P. W. Paish, 'Britain as an Exporter of Capital to Underdeveloped Countries', in United Nations Association, *Financing the Economic Development of Underdeveloped Countries* (1956), p. 24.

selves, remembering always that foreign investors have regard not to what governments say but rather to what they do. A possible danger is that their expectations from SUNFED may make them less inclined to meet the private investors half-way. Unless it becomes clear, therefore, that private investment will not be forthcoming to any appreciable extent even if and when these two conditions are satisfied, the only decisive arguments (failing a sharp reduction in the general level of defence expenditure) in favour of SUNFED are if American participation were to act as a further stimulus to the flow of dollars overseas or if open opposition or tepid support provoked acute resentment in countries whose goodwill Britain and the West are generally anxious to retain. These are powerful arguments to which Britain would be well advised to pay careful heed, but for the moment there is a lot to be said for the General Assembly's decision of 9 December 1955[18] not to force the issue until after the presidential elections and for using the interval in clarifying the kind of functions SUNFED could usefully perform if called upon to do so.

In conclusion, mention should be made of the criticism that the International Bank is not 'international' enough, as reflected, for instance, in the 'weighted voting' provisions which give the United States 30 per cent. of the votes, in the sensitivity of the Bank to the political moods and prejudices of both Wall Street and the National Advisory Council on International Financial and Monetary Problems in Washington,[19] and in the high proportion of American nationals on the Bank's staff and on its Operational Missions which, it has been said, tends to 'lead to orders for American equipment, where European methods and equipment would often be cheaper

---

[18] *GAOR*, 10th sess., suppl. no. 19, Resolution 923(X), which was adopted unanimously.

[19] Set up under the Bretton Woods Agreements Act of July 1945 and composed of the Secretary of the Treasury as Chairman, the Secretaries of State and Commerce, the Chairman of the Board of Governors of the Federal Reserve System, the Chairman of the Board of Directors of the Export-Import Bank, and the United States Executive Directors on the Bank and the Fund.

and more efficient'.[20] These criticisms are not without some substance. 'He who pays the piper calls the tune' at least to some extent, whether there be weighted voting or the kind of mental weighting that goes on in, for example, the United Nations itself and in GATT. The Bank's policies must necessarily be closely attuned to those of the United States and must be such as not permanently to alienate potential bond-holders on Wall Street. Nor is it surprising that the dichotomy posed in Article IV, section 10,[21] between economics and politics broke down almost from the start. How, indeed, could the Bank overlook the bearing of political and social resistances to change or the political record or stability of a régime in assessing the economic soundness of a loan? Nevertheless, although the Bank may not be as successful in 'de-politicizing' economic co-operation or as 'international' as the purist might wish, a Federation of British Industries group has commented very favourably on the Bank's 'impartiality of outlook' and on the way the Bank's staff has been built in only about eight years 'into a real international team'.[22] Moreover, the borrowing countries not only have a direct voice in the Bank's proceedings, but the Bank's international character helps to relieve its loans of the suspicion of political strings, to allay the natural restiveness of borrowers at the close supervision of the uses to which loans are put, and to induce in the major donor countries a degree of consideration for the interests—and vanities and prejudices—of their fellow members which is not always found in most bilateral arrangements. Possibly the international character of the Bank could be strengthened by, for instance, broadening the geographical composition of its staff and missions, but even

---

[20] *Times Literary Supplement*, 17 June 1955, p. 335. See also Federation of British Industries, *The World Bank* (London, 1954), p. 16.

[21] Which reads: 'The Bank and its Officers shall not interfere in the political affairs of any member; nor shall they be influenced in their decisions by the political character of the member or members concerned. Only economic considerations shall be relevant to their decisions, and these considerations shall be weighed impartially in order to achieve the purposes stated in Article I.'

[22] Federation of British Industries, *The World Bank*, p. 7.

as at present constituted, there can be little doubt that the International Bank is far more international than any possible alternative.

THE ECONOMIC AND SOCIAL COUNCIL

Problems of economic development, and especially of technical assistance, are also of major concern to the Economic and Social Council. By concentrating on these problems in the last few years the Council has shown some signs of acquiring a much needed sense of purpose and direction. Unfortunately, although the Council has had some success in reducing duplication of effort between the specialized agencies and in encouraging closer co-operation between them, it has fallen considerably short of early expectations that it could pull together and reinforce the work of the specialized agencies.[23] The educative value of debates on land reform, international investment, and, earlier, on full employment, has also been much reduced by the low level of representation on the Council, while the steady pressure to extend the activities of the United Nations in the field of development has provoked the United Kingdom delegate into pointing out that

> it was no part of the functions of the United Nations to act as a kind of international government, or even to plan for governments on an international scale: it should never remotely consider assuming responsibility for the general direction, economic or social, of any nation or region . . . The function of the United Nations was to provide a forum for international discussion of common problems and a channel through which help and advice could be sought.[24]

In the social field the efforts of the Council have been handicapped by the fact that social conditions vary so greatly from one region to another that the universal approach is rarely appropriate; even when it is, the Council often has to play second fiddle to the longer

23 See above, p. 39.
24 *ESCOR*, 22nd sess., 942nd mtg., 25 July 1956, p. 152.

established and more experienced ILO. The Council's work on human rights has received considerable publicity but without any obvious impact on the behaviour of states; universal declarations (or even conventions) elaborating specific human rights can have little impact when the basic condition of respect for the innate worth and dignity of the individual is so noticeably lacking in over half the world.

There is a credit side to the Council's record. The work of a number of the Council's functional commissions (for example, the Population Commission and the Narcotics Commission) has been of real value, and the regional Commissions (especially the Economic Commission for Europe[25] and the Economic Commission for Asia and the Far East) have served as useful meeting places for specialists and technicians and have published a number of informative and competent reports. The Council can also claim some of the credit for putting the United Nations' technical assistance work on a more efficient basis; it has also done something to pare down its own over-elaborate structure[26] and to stabilize its expenditure, though not to the extent desired by the United Kingdom.[27] Yet the credit side is still regrettably small for the amount of time and energy expended. With an amelioration in the political atmosphere the record of the Council may improve, but so far it can hardly be said to have justified its existence. There is a strong case for devolving its responsibilities on to other existing bodies,[28] such as the General Assembly's Second (Economic) and Third (Social)

[25] See David Wightman, *Economic Co-operation in Europe* (London, Stevens and Heinemann for Carnegie Endowment for International Peace, 1956).

[26] *ESCOR*, 18th sess., suppl. no. 1, Resolution 557(XVIII), 5 Aug. 1954; also ibid. 20th sess., suppl. no. 1, Resolution 590(XX), 5 Aug. 1955.

[27] At the Council's twenty-second session the United Kingdom delegate (Lord John Hope) warned the Council that 'if stabilization were not achieved and financial contributions continued to increase, Her Majesty's Government would be obliged to consider seriously whether it could continue to participate on the present footing in the programmes of the United Nations and the specialized agencies' (ibid. 22nd sess., 942nd mtg., 24 July 1956, p. 153).

[28] See A. Loveday, 'Suggestions for the Reform of the United Nations Economic and Social Machinery', *International Organization*, Aug. 1953, pp. 325-28.

Committees and especially the inter-governmental Technical Assistance Committee.

TECHNICAL ASSISTANCE

If capital can provide the 'brawn' for economic development, technical assistance can provide the 'brains'.[29] Already the United Nations Expanded Programme of Technical Assistance (in which the specialized agencies also take part) has made a substantial contribution to mitigating the crippling effect of the lack of 'expertise' in underdeveloped countries. After rather a difficult 'teething' period, due mainly to lack of experience, to a shortage (which still exists) of the right kind of experts, and to the suspicions of many recipient governments that the scheme was an ill-disguised form of colonialism or dollar diplomacy, the programme is now functioning quite efficiently; the appointment of Resident Representatives and the new system of basing allocations on country programmes has also made for more effective co-ordination with similar assistance from other sources, such as the Colombo Plan or Point Four. In accordance with Colombo Plan experience there has also been a welcome shift in favour of establishing training institutes and demonstration projects in the recipient countries as distinct from sending experts to, or training 'fellows' from, them. In spite of this encouraging progress, however, the programme is gravely handicapped by lack of finance, by the uncertainty resulting from the year-to-year basis of its budgeting and from the late receipt of many contributions, and by its inability to provide its experts with the supplies and equipment which they so often need to fulfil their tasks satisfactorily.[30]

---

[29] See 'Technical Assistance: I-Agencies and Programmes' and 'Technical Assistance: II-Policy and Method', *Planning*, 1 Sept. and 22 Sept. 1952; also 'Technical Aid after Three Years', ibid. 26 Oct. 1953.

[30] See *Seventh Report of the Technical Assistance Board on the Expanded Programme of Technical Assistance*, 29 June 1955 (*ESCOR*, 20th sess., suppl. no. 4). See also H. L. Keenleyside, 'The Financing of Technical Assistance', in United Nations Association, *Financing the Economic Development of Underdeveloped Countries*, p. 43.

Britain has gone some way to demonstrate her belief in the programme by increasing her contribution from £450,000 in 1952 to £800,000 in 1955.[31] Also, in addition to making three-quarters of her pledge available on 1 January each year, the Government has now guaranteed that it will, subject to the annual approval of Parliament, continue to make contributions for the next three years.[32] If more governments were to follow suit one of the programme's major problems would be resolved. The lack of finance would still be serious, however, especially in the field of public administration. Britain has heavy commitments under the Colombo Plan and now under the Baghdad Pact. But the United Nations programme can draw experts from a far wider range of countries (including a number of non-United Nations members), while every contribution from countries other than the United States is matched by an additional contribution from the United States. There is a strong case, therefore, for increasing the British contribution. Such an increase need not strain her balance of payments. On the contrary, over the past five years the amount of money flowing into Britain from the programme (by way of experts' fees, fellows' stipends, and payments for equipment) has been about double her contribution to the programme. There are also 'a good many instances . . . in which concerns in this country . . . have received contracts for development projects in underdeveloped parts of the world that are the direct result of the contributions that have been made to the Technical Assistance Programme'[33] —exports follow experts. The right kinds of experts, those who have both the technical skill and the personal qualities required, are not easy to find; but this difficulty could perhaps be reduced if British

---

[31] Contributions in 1955 totalled $28 million.

[32] Lord John Hope (Joint Under-Secretary of State for Foreign Affairs), 20 July 1955, H. C. Deb., vol. 544, coll. 355-56.

[33] Keenleyside, in *Financing the Economic Development of Underdeveloped Countries*, p. 53. See also Mr Dodds-Parker (Joint Under-Secretary of State for Foreign Affairs), 3 Feb. 1954, H. C. Deb., vol. 523, col. 362.

industry was brought into closer touch with the programme[34] and if recruitment was put on a rather more systematic basis.

The transplantation of Western 'know-how' into alien soil is a precarious operation. Not only are Western techniques often inappropriate, but not all experts commend themselves to those whom they have gone to help. External assistance is also often vitiated by mismanagement (or worse) or by the unwillingness of recipients to take the equally essential measures of self-help. In brief, technical assistance, whether through the United Nations or the Colombo Plan, is not a universal panacea; but it is a most valuable grafting operation which deserves rather more encouragement in Britain than it has so far received.

CONCLUSION

The economic development of backward areas is one of the great challenges of the second half of the twentieth century. In face of the strong prejudice in several of the underdeveloped countries against most forms of bilateral aid for fear that there may be political strings attached to them, it is a challenge which the United Nations and its specialized agencies are peculiarly well fitted to tackle. This challenge is at heart a moral one; and so it appears to not a few of the British people. If there be a moral objection to poverty in the midst of riches, why should it stop short at the waterfront?[35] These commendable and comparatively new found moral promptings are, of course, apt to be sluggish and restricted to a fairly small section of the population. But it is quite evident that they inform the work of many of those responsible for shaping and executing policy and that they frequently help to enrich and humanize policies based on harder-headed calculations of self-interest. That this moral impulse should be at work is of

---

[34] See Federation of British Industries, *United Nations Technical Assistance*, Feb. 1955.

[35] See 'The Strategy of World Development', *Planning*, 23 Apr. 1951.

no small importance. Aid that is administered in a patronizing manner rather than in a spirit of partnership, or that is doled out grudgingly as a kind of retaining fee, can do more harm than good. Yet it is mainly as a matter of self-interest that Britain would be well advised to do her utmost to expand even the considerable body of aid she is already giving. Economically, such aid can contribute to the growth of world trade, both by developing new sources of supply for the growing industrial machine in the West and by opening up new markets for manufactured goods. Politically, the growing awareness of the peoples of underdeveloped countries that their grinding poverty need not be their predestined lot may act as a serious incitement to unrest and violence if external help is paltry and intermittent and if democratic institutions on the Western model prove incapable of satisfying their yearnings for material betterment. And in a world in which global war may have been banished by the 'Great Deterrent', insurrection and subversion from within may become the orthodox way of softening up prospective victims of expansionist totalitarianism. Of course, political allegiances cannot be bought by economic aid; indeed much of the goodwill earned by such aid can be lost overnight by a maladroit political move or by an ill-considered speech. Moreover, economic aid to be effective must have its counterpart in the efforts of recipient régimes to remove such resistances to economic growth as maladministration, archaic land tenure systems, and unduly low levels of domestic savings. Nor should it be forgotten that empty minds—and spirits—may breed fanaticism and violence as certainly as empty stomachs. Nevertheless, the maintenance both of political stability and of a partiality for the Western way of life clearly requires the West to help on a scale and in a spirit which compares favourably with aid given behind or beyond the 'bamboo' curtain. The International Bank and the United Nations and the other specialized agencies are not the only channels for such help, but it would be most imprudent and short-sighted not to use their potentialities to the full.

#

chapter thirteen

The General Agreement
on Tariffs and Trade[1]

As has been seen, the Bretton Woods system was intended to be completed by an International Trade Organization, and by a commercial 'code of good conduct' which would foster the international division of labcur (by the elimination of quantitative and discriminatory restrictions and by the reduction of tariffs) without jeopardizing the maintenance of high and stable levels of employment.[2] This was the main aim of the Anglo-American proposals of 20 December 1945 and later of the Havana Charter for an International Trade Organization. However, the growing suspicion outside North America that the 'dollar problem' might be so deep-seated as to prevent the institution of the multilateral,

---

[1] For an expanded version of this section see G. L. Goodwin, 'GATT and the Organization for Trade Co-operation', in *YBWA, 1956*, pp. 229-55.

[2] See above, p. 278.

non-discriminatory, 'world' economy envisaged at Bretton Woods, together with the determination of underdeveloped countries to build protective barriers around their developing economies, led to the insertion of so many 'escape clauses' in the Charter that the United States Administration decided not to submit the emasculated version of the original Anglo-American proposals to Congress.

Fortunately, partly as a safeguard against such a contingency, the countries which were conducting tariff negotiations in Geneva in 1947[3] had carved out that part of the 'code of conduct' in the Havana Charter which dealt specifically with commercial policy, and had embodied it in a General Agreement on Tariffs and Trade. Designed ostensibly to tide over the interval till the Havana Charter came into effect, GATT, which began its provisional—or so it was hoped—existence on 1 January 1948, began to assume an air of permanency with the Charter's demise.

At first GATT was elbowed off the centre of the international economic scene by the OEEC's own trade-liberalization programme. It was not until 1953-4, when the return of more 'normal' economic conditions focused attention on preparing the stage for convertibility, that GATT came back into the limelight. Its future was then subjected to close and critical examination at the ninth session of the Contracting Parties which met in Geneva from 28 October 1954 to 7 March 1955. As a result of this prolonged review the principles of GATT were reaffirmed and proposals were made for an Organization for Trade Co-operation to administer it. Was this outcome a testimony to GATT's proven success, or was it an

---

[3] Namely, Australia, Belgium, Brazil, Burma, Canada, Ceylon, Chile, China, Cuba, Czechoslovakia, France, India, Lebanon, Luxembourg, the Netherlands, New Zealand, Norway, Pakistan, Southern Rhodesia, Syria, Union of South Africa, United Kingdom, and United States of America. Since then the following countries have acceded to the Agreement: Austria, Denmark, Dominican Republic, Finland, German Federal Republic, Greece, Haiti, Indonesia, Italy, Japan, Nicaragua, Peru, Sweden, Turkey, and Uruguay. China, Lebanon, and Syria have withdrawn.

attempt to patch up a rickety structure lest it founder in a world in which its 'rules of the game' threatened to become outmoded?

GATT IN OPERATION

Over the past eight years GATT has fulfilled three main functions. It has provided a 'code of good conduct' intended to limit the use, especially the discriminatory use, of quantitative restrictions; it has served as a framework for the reduction or 'binding' of tariffs; and it has acted as a forum for the discussion of trade disputes.

The code for the reduction of quantitative restrictions and the elimination of discriminatory treatment has been more honoured in the breach than in the observance. Most of the contracting parties to GATT have suffered in one form or another from balance-of-payments difficulties, which, by virtue of an 'escape clause' in the agreement, allow them to impose quotas and to discriminate against goods from dollar sources. The main progress towards the liberalization of trade has been made within the more limited area encompassed by the sterling area and Western Europe, through the multilateral payments system of the European Payments Union and through the fixing of percentage targets by the OEEC for the removal of quantitative restrictions. GATT's only substantial achievement in the field of quantitative and discriminatory restrictions has been to facilitate periodic consultations among its members about the possible relaxation of these restrictions. Occasionally these consultations have borne some fruit; but their efficacy has been greatly limited by their relative infrequency and the general reluctance of members to allow their domestic policies to be called into question, even when defects in these policies (for example, the failure to curb inflation) may be very largely responsible for the drain on monetary reserves and so for the need to impose restrictions. In this field, therefore, the 'escape clauses' and 'waivers' have figured more prominently than the code itself.

The General Agreement's main significance has been as a framework for the reduction of tariffs on a multilateral basis through negotiations on a bilateral level. The three marathon[4] sets of negotiations that have taken place at Geneva (1947), Annecy (1949), and Torquay (1950-1) have followed the pattern of the pre-war bilateral negotiations under the United States Reciprocal Trade Agreements Act. Pairs of countries have agreed to *quid pro quo* reductions in duties on imports from each other, and have 'bound' other duties against increase. In the past such concessions would normally have been extended to cover imports from only those third countries that enjoyed the special treaty right of 'most-favoured-nation' treatment. One of the main achievements of GATT has been to extend reciprocal concessions to all—or almost all[5]—its member countries. Most-favoured-nation treatment is thus no longer a right acquired by reciprocal treaty; it automatically accompanies membership of an international institution. In addition, by conducting negotiations at the same time and place an immense amount of time has been saved and concessions have tended to be granted more readily since the reciprocal advantage can be perceived more easily.[6]

However, from the start three important exceptions were made to this principle of generalized most-favoured-nation treatment. In the first place, in spite of the State Department's obsessional dislike of imperial preference, permission was given for the retention of *existing* rates of imperial preference between members of the Commonwealth. In the second place, contracting parties which had formed, or were in process of forming, a customs union (for instance, Benelux) were permitted to eliminate tariffs on trade *inter se* and to establish a common outside tariff. In the third place, underdeveloped countries were allowed a certain latitude in the

---

[4] A fourth session took place at Geneva in the spring of 1955 to provide Japan with an opportunity to negotiate her way into GATT. A further session opened in January 1956, mainly in order to take advantage of the new powers given to the President of the United States to reduce American tariffs.

[5] Under Art. XXXV a contracting party has the right to refuse to apply the agreement to another contracting party. This is the article the United Kingdom and others have invoked with regard to Japan; see below, p. 334.

[6] For further details see *The Attack on Trade Barriers, progress report on the operation of the General Agreement from Jan. 1948 to Aug. 1949*, pp. 10-11.

observance of their obligations so that they might protect their 'infant' industries or further the development of their agriculture.

In addition to these waivers written into the General Agreement itself, a number of waivers have been granted under Article XXV (para. 5a),[7] which provides that 'in exceptional circumstances' the Contracting Parties may waive an obligation imposed upon a contracting party by the agreement. The most notable waiver is that accorded in November 1952 to the six governments[8] belonging to the European Coal and Steel Community, which exempted them from GATT rules against discrimination so that duties and quantitative restrictions on products covered by the Community might be abolished *inter se* even though they were retained on similar products of outside countries. The dissatisfaction subsequently expressed at the alleged failure of members of the Community to comply strictly with its terms illustrates the difficulty of fitting a closely-knit group of limited membership into the wider framework of GATT; if the movement for closer economic integration within Western Europe should obtain a new lease of life, additional waivers of this kind may go far to demolish the principle of equality of treatment upon which GATT is based.

A waiver from the 'no new preference' rule was granted to Britain in October 1953 to enable her to raise duties on horticultural imports from non-Commonwealth countries, while continuing to grant free entry to similar imports from Commonwealth countries. The waiver was basically of a technical nature, but the persistent suspicion of imperial preference was reflected in the conditions attached to it and in the accompanying declaration that it should 'in no circumstances' be construed as impairing the ban on increases in preferential margins.[9]

---

[7] References in this section are to the text of the General Agreement before revision; see Cmd. 7258.

[8] Belgium, France, German Federal Republic, Italy, Luxembourg, and the Netherlands.

[9] GATT, *Basic Instruments and Selected Documents*, 2nd suppl. (Jan. 1954), pp. 20-22.

The economic effects of the tariff negotiations are difficult to assess with any precision. It is probable that GATT schedules, whether for tariff reductions or for the stabilization or 'binding' of tariffs, now cover about 80 per cent. of world trade, about four-fifths of the import trade of the United States, and between 40 and 45 per cent. of British exports. And it has been estimated that the United States tariff level of 1945 was reduced by one-third by the negotiations undertaken in the succeeding six years.[10] These are quite impressive figures, but the major concessions were achieved at the initial Geneva negotiations in 1947. A number of factors have made it extremely difficult to sustain the initial momentum. Outside the United States the most decisive has been the general movement in the last two or three years towards the liberalization of trade through the progressive dismantling of quantitative restrictions; this has made governments reluctant to embark on further reductions in their tariff levels, since tariffs may soon come to constitute their principal means of protection.

Critics of GATT in Britain have argued that the reductions in United States' duties on imports from Commonwealth countries have proved an inadequate *quid pro quo* for the reductions or even elimination of preferential margins. But perhaps the main criticism is that GATT deals primarily with tariff levels, whereas the main impediment to increased trade with the United States is the continued uncertainty surrounding the latter's foreign economic policy generally. It is true that the initial binding of the concessions negotiated under GATT until 1 January 1958 has ensured an almost unprecedented degree of stability in United States tariff levels. But the occasional resort by the United States to the 'escape clause' in GATT (Art. XIX), which allows an obligation to be suspended or withdrawn if its application results in a product being imported 'in such increased quantities and under such conditions as to cause or threaten serious

---

[10] U.S. Tariff Commission, *Effect of Trade Agreement Concessions on United States Tariff Levels based on Imports in 1952* (Washington, Sept. 1953).

w

injury to domestic producers', is not calculated to persuade exporters of, for example, bicycles, of the efficacy of GATT. Moreover, in spite of the principles set out by GATT with the aim of simplifying 'customs formalities', the right of contracting parties to deviate from these principles whenever they are not consistent with 'existing legislation' has deprived them of much of their value. Thus the extreme complexity, and occasionally perverse use, of American customs procedures continues to be a major obstacle to dollar-hungry exporters. The removal of these obstacles and uncertainties and the more liberal application of the 'Buy American' Act is of little less moment, therefore, than the reduction and stabilization of American tariff levels; it still remains to be seen whether collective pressure through GATT for their removal can offset protectionist pressure within the United States for their retention.

The role of GATT in helping to open up the dollar market to European exporters is perhaps the chief touchstone of its success or failure. But it is not the only one. Its part in reducing tariff barriers within Europe is little less significant. Here GATT encountered a serious difficulty. The procedure of the bartering of 'concessions' solely on a strict *quid pro quo* basis has tended to perpetuate existing disparities and to weigh heavily against the low-tariff countries, chiefly the Benelux countries, Denmark, and Sweden, which, having bound their low duties in three successive negotiations, find they have little left to bargain with on the present GATT formula. The Torquay (1950) conference focused attention on this difficulty and initiated a search for a new bargaining formula. The result is described in a pamphlet entitled *A New Proposal for the Reduction of Customs Tariffs* published by the GATT Secretariat in January 1954. The bare substance of the plan was that the multilateral character of the GATT tariff conferences should be retained, but that, in place of bilateral negotiations between countries on a product-by-product basis, each government should accept an obligation to reduce the protective incidence of its tariff in accordance with a common standard. Customs tariffs would be divided into about ten sectors and the common standard would require each government to reduce the incidence of the duties in each sector by 30 per cent. in three years, or by less than that in the case of countries having a comparatively low level of duties; thus the effort required of each country would be proportionate to its existing tariff level. In addition, each government would accept the obligation to reduce to certain maximum levels any rates of duties which were in excess of these ceilings. In spite of the initial flurry of interest which these proposals aroused they were fairly soon shelved. The inadequacy of the present bargaining formula is continually stressed by most West European countries, but for the present there seems to be no acceptable alternative. However, the main threat to GATT in the near future is the possibility that the gradual dismantling of quantitative controls may lead to an upward revision of tariffs and to the withdrawal of many of the concessions already negotiated. The best testimony to the value of the negotiations undertaken under GATT's aegis will be the continued strict observance of existing GATT schedules.

One of GATT's most important functions is to provide a forum for the discussion and settlement of trade disputes. Not only do the annual meetings allow differences of interpretation to be thrashed out, but they also provide a unique opportunity for the discussion and settlement of trade disputes and for the airing of grievances against a state that is alleged to be defaulting on its obligations. A large proportion of these disputes are settled through direct negotiation between the parties concerned; only when direct negotiation has temporarily failed is a dispute formally placed on the agenda.[11] Interesting techniques have been developed for the handling of these disputes. At first they usually went to working parties, composed of the disputants themselves and a cross-section of supposedly disinterested neutrals, the task of which was to agree upon a statement both of the facts and, if possible, of the

---

[11] For examples of such disputes see GATT, *International Trade 1954*, July 1955, pp. 132-36.

application of the relevant provisions of GATT to those facts.[12] As the number of complaints and experience in their handling grew, however, a more streamlined method became necessary. At the seventh session in 1953 a small Panel on Complaints, composed of representatives of countries not directly affected by the complaints to be examined, was set up. The disputants present their cases to the Panel and are consulted by it during the drafting of its report; but the Panel meets *in camera* and its findings and recommendations are its responsibility alone. Frequently disputes are settled during the course of its deliberations; otherwise its recommendations are usually incorporated in resolutions by the contracting parties 'inviting' or 'recommending' appropriate action by the transgressing state. Not only is there a high rate of compliance with these recommendations, but the Panel has already built up a valuable body of 'case law' on the interpretation and application of the provisions of the General Agreement.

Of course some disputes have become hardy perennials. The most serious is the complaint of a number of European countries, together with Canada and New Zealand, against the United States' quota restrictions on imports of dairy products. The annual recommendations emanating from GATT for the removal of these restrictions seem to have made virtually no impression on Congress. In these circumstances all that the contracting parties have been able to do is to authorize retaliatory action (under Art. XXIII) against imports from the United States into the countries affected. Were real reciprocity to exist in the agreements between these countries and the United States, the threat of such retaliatory action might serve as an effective restraint on Congress; as it is, it is no more than a pin-prick.

GATT is also precluded by Article XXI (Security Exceptions) from pronouncing upon disputes which arise out of the imposition

---

12 See, for instance, the working party report on a complaint by Chile against Australia's subsidy on ammonium sulphate; GATT, *Basic Instruments and Selected Documents*, vol. ii, (Geneva, May 1952), pp. 188-96.

of discriminatory measures based on security considerations. The scope of this 'escape clause' is worthy of remark. It could hardly have been made any broader; for example, under the article each contracting party is entirely free to decide for itself whether an 'emergency' exists which entitles it to take 'any action which it considers necessary for the protection of its essential security interests', and which of its exports fall outside the scope of the agreement on the grounds that they might contribute 'indirectly' to the war potential of an unfriendly Power.[13] In 1945 economic disputes were widely thought to be a significant source of political friction, and there was much talk about providing adequate machinery for their settlement. Today the Economic Commission for Europe's inability to discuss strategic controls, the Economic and Social Council's denial of its competence to discuss disputes between individual nations, and the loophole of Article XXI of GATT, testify to the existence of a kind of economic 'no man's land', events in which are not even discussed, let alone regulated, by any international body.[14] The regulation and limitation of armaments is apparently a fit subject for negotiation between the two Power blocs, but economic disarmament is not.

In spite of these and other limitations, the merits of GATT's complaints procedure should not be underestimated. Collective pressure exercised through GATT cannot always offset the pressure of domestic interests, especially when an election is in the offing, while it cannot be expected to dissuade its members from giving security needs precedence over welfare considerations—especially

---

[13] The article was successfully invoked by the United States in rebutting a charge brought by Czechoslovakia in June 1949 that the United States was discriminating between contracting parties in its administration of export controls. A later waiver has relieved both the United States and Czechoslovakia of all their obligations to each other under GATT.

[14] Except, of course, by those whose membership is drawn from one camp only, e.g. the Consultative Group Co-ordinating Committee (COCOM) in Paris, on which see UN, Dept. of Econ. and Social Affairs, *The Quest for Freer Trade*, 1955.

when the latter are of only marginal importance. But in many other instances it has acted as a check on the introduction of 'beggar-my-neighbour' policies, not only because most contracting parties fear a possible loss of reciprocal benefit but also because they are jealous of their reputation as good members of the 'club'. Indeed, perhaps the most powerful argument in favour of GATT is that it has provided the only available means for bringing collective pressure to bear on member countries, and especially on the United States, in order to counter the strong domestic lobbying in favour of protectionism.

THE REVIEW CONFERENCE[15]

Measured against the early post-war hopes for the establishment of a far-ranging international trade organization, the past achievements of GATT have not been very impressive. GATT is not a liberalizing force in its own right; its success is dependent upon the extent of the liberal intentions of its members. And, until recently, not only have the great majority of them considered that the strict application of the GATT code has been neither possible nor desirable, but the main effort towards the liberalization of trade within the non-dollar world has been made through OEEC.

However, the growing feeling in 1954 that convertibility was just around the corner refocused interest on the GATT code. In a 'convertible' world the stricter observance of the code would be of fundamental importance to Britain, since the bulk of her imports are essential to her economic life, while the exports with which she pays for these imports often do not constitute essentials for other importing countries and are, therefore, peculiarly vulnerable to the arbitrary imposition of restrictions. Clearly, it would be too grave a risk to make the pound convertible without some

---

15 For the background to the review conference see Michael Hoffman, 'The Future of GATT', *Lloyds Bank Review*, Oct. 1954.

assurance that other countries would not use restrictive or discriminatory measures as a means of accumulating sterling for conversion into gold or dollars. The use of quantitative and discriminatory restrictions could not, of course, be ruled out altogether even in conditions of convertibility; they might be needed in a crisis to safeguard the balance of payments or the size of monetary reserves, or as a measure of collective defence against a chronic creditor. The point stressed by Britain at the review conference was that they should be used not at the mere whim of individual countries but only in accordance with defined and agreed conditions and for so long as absolutely necessary, and that their use should be subject to collective review to encourage compliance with these conditions. In short, Britain's concern, expressed vividly if a trifle inelegantly by one spokesman, was with 're-gutting' GATT.

The outcome of the complicated and prolonged negotiations, which opened in Geneva on 28 October 1954 and lasted until 7 March 1955 can only be very briefly summarized here. The most significant result was the reaffirmation of the cardinal principles of the GATT code, implicit in the decision to amend the General Agreement rather than to scrap it and start again.[16] Several parts of the code were also strengthened. Not only has the basic principle that quantitative restrictions shall only be used for balance-of-payments reasons been reaffirmed, but the circumstances in which quantitative restrictions and discriminatory measures are allowed have been more clearly defined,[17] while provision has been made for the collective review of such measures by an Organization for Trade Co-operation, the task of which will be to administer the agreement and to provide a forum where differences can be thrashed out and grievances assuaged. 'The new plan is that countries imposing restrictions shall consult the organization about them

[16] For revised text see GATT, *Basic Instruments and Selected Documents*, vol. i (revised) (Geneva, Apr. 1955); or Cmd. 9413.

[17] The right of the contracting parties to apply quantitative restrictions 'having equivalent effect to exchange restrictions authorized' under the scarce currency clause of the Fund (Art. VII 3(*b*)) remains unaffected (Art. XIV (5)).

annually; the organization will notify them when their restrictions are inconsistent with their undertakings, and if they are inconsistent and cause harm and are continued, other member countries will be free to withdraw concessions.'[18] The collective review is to come after, rather than before, the restrictions are imposed. Sovereign states cannot be persuaded to defer action in times of economic crisis until the permission of an international body has been obtained. But the knowledge that policies will be subject to international review, and that they may evoke retaliatory action by other members, may set some check on 'beggar-my-neighbour' policies. To guard against withdrawal of tariff concessions if and when quantitative restrictions are further reduced, it was decided to prolong the life of existing tariff concessions until 1 January 1958; thereafter they will be extended automatically (subject to the re-negotiation of selected items) for further periods of three years. Thus a fair degree of stability in tariff levels should be assured for some time to come.

Of special significance was the proposal for a full-fledged Organization for Trade Co-operation (OTC). So far GATT has been operated by the Contracting Parties acting corporately. There have been annual sessions, rather makeshift arrangements for inter-sessional working groups and *ad hoc* committees, and a small but efficient secretariat headed by an Executive Secretary (Mr Eric Wyndham White); but there has been no 'organization' in the formal *de jure* sense. The structure of the organization now proposed is orthodox enough. It is to have an Assembly (Art. 5), consisting of all member states and meeting annually, an Executive Committee (Art. 6) of seventeen members, and a Secretariat (Art. 7). Unlike the International Bank and the IMF, there is to be no 'weighted' voting.[19] But there will no doubt continue to be a good deal of 'mental' weighting, while on the important question whether a member is suffering from such a serious decline in its monetary

---

[18] *The Times*, 27 Mar. 1955.
[19] As Britain at one time proposed during negotiations for the Havana Charter for an International Trade Organization.

reserves as to justify its use of quantitative restrictions, the OTC must accept the findings of the Fund; and these findings will, of course, be reached on the basis of 'weighted voting'.

In many respects the fact that GATT was not expected to play more than a stop-gap role was fortunate. The lack of elaborate rules and organizational structure encouraged flexibility and experiment and freed it from the follies of empire-building which have beset so many international institutions. If it is true to its small beginnings, the OTC should make for greater continuity and more effective administration without becoming top-heavy. However, OTC will not come into being until it has been accepted 'by governments . . . the territories of which account for 85 per centum of the total external trade of the territories of such governments' (Art. 17(*c*)). This means that acceptance by both Britain and the United States is necessary. Britain has already notified her acceptance,[20] but the United States decision, which is, of course, crucial, still remains in doubt.

The fear that Congress might not ratify the OTC, or, indeed, that the Administration might not adhere to its promise to try to persuade it to do so, was instrumental in overcoming the strong reluctance of most delegates, and especially of the Canadian delegates, to renew the waiver which allows the United States to impose quotas or other import restrictions on agricultural products (which are the subject of domestic price-support programmes), as required by Section 22 of the United States Agricultural Adjustment Act. The risk that the vast surplus stocks, which have been accumulated in the United States as the result of domestic price-support policies, will be dumped haphazardly on world markets at prices appreciably lower than prevailing prices is naturally a source of the utmost anxiety to other agricultural exporting countries. Furthermore, taken in conjunction with the distinction between primary products and other products, which, largely at American behest, has crept

[20] Oral answer by the President of the Board of Trade (Rt Hon. P. Thorneycroft), 19 Apr. 1955, H. C. Deb., vol. 540, col. 4.

into the additional provisions on export subsidies, the waiver suggests that one set of rules will apply to primary products and another set to manufactured products. For all practical purposes the effort to enforce the rule against quantitative restrictions in the agricultural field seems to have been abandoned.

The United States is not, of course, the only country that has been given 'legal permission to live in a state of sin'. The waiver granted to Britain in 1953 in respect of imports traditionally admitted free of duty from Commonwealth countries has been extended, while a further waiver allows Britain greater latitude in assisting industrial and agricultural development in her dependent overseas territories, by, for instance, according preferential treatment to imports from those territories. For not dissimilar reasons far greater latitude has also been given to underdeveloped countries.[21] A lengthy new Article XVIII enables them (*a*) to maintain sufficient flexibility in their tariff structure to allow of tariff protection for 'infant' industries, and (*b*) to apply quantitative restrictions on imports so that their balance of payments can be protected in face of the continued high level of demand for imports likely to be generated by their programmes of economic development. These concessions also tend to turn the revised code into a 'two-decker' code; but they are not inherently objectionable. Indeed, it has always been recognized that the GATT code needs to be stretched to meet the special needs of the underdeveloped countries. At least the reaffirmation of the principle of non-discrimination and the provisions for consultation and supervision by the OTC may help to curb the strong disposition towards economic nationalism in many underdeveloped countries. In addition, to cushion the shock to many domestic industries which might result from a sudden removal of quantitative restrictions that could no longer be justified on balance-of-payments grounds, a temporary waiver has been granted which allows the progressive elimination of such restrictions

---

[21] Defined in the agreement as 'contracting parties the economies of which can only support low standards of living and are in the early stages of development'.

over a period not exceeding five years. This should give a much needed period of grace in which to make the necessary adjustment, while, as a safeguard against abuse of the waiver, provision is made for an annual review of the progress made towards the elimination of these 'hard core' restrictions.

Three other points can only be touched upon. Neither the earlier nor the revised text of the General Agreement deals with commodity-stabilization schemes which Lord Keynes originally regarded as the main instrument for countering world slumps.[22] One reason, of course, is that the danger of a world slump has receded, while for the present the orderly disposal of surpluses (and the liquidation of strategic stocks) is a far more pressing problem. Nevertheless, underdeveloped countries, most of which obtain the greater part of their foreign-exchange earnings from the export of primary commodities, are still interested in ensuring greater stability in commodity prices so as to remove a dangerous element of uncertainty in their development plans. Britain's attitude on this issue is apt to be ambivalent, partly because different things suit her for different commodities, partly because, although her primary interest is in avoiding anything that might prevent an improvement in her terms of trade, she is also the banker of a sterling area, many members of which are primary producers. She has made no secret, however, of the fact that she would prefer commodity questions in general to be brought under the aegis of GATT rather than of the Commission on International Commodity Trade set up by the Economic and Social Council in August 1954.

Another rather complicated organizational problem arises from the fact that both the IMF and the contracting parties to GATT exercise jurisdiction over restrictions applied by governments to safeguard their balance of payments; the former is concerned with controls bearing upon the means of payment, the latter with restrictions upon the quantities of goods that may be imported.

[22] The Havana Charter had a chapter on commodity problems; its demise left a gap that has not so far been satisfactorily filled.

These are so much two sides of the same coin that the division of function between the two institutions is rather illogical and apt to be both confusing and wasteful. The ties between the Fund and the OTC (or GATT) need to be drawn as close as possible.

Finally, there is the vexed question of Japan's status in GATT. On 10 September 1955 Japan became a party to GATT. But Britain, together with 13 out of the then 34 contracting parties to GATT, have since notified their intention to invoke Article XXXV, which allows them to withhold from Japan all benefits of membership, including the right of most-favoured-nation treatment. The persistence of some Japanese trading practices of the 1930's—the disregard of patents, trade marks, and copyright, and the use of false marks of origin—as well as the alleged 'unfairness' of competition from 'cheap' Japanese labour, have been cited in justification of this rebuff to Japan. Thus Britain has intimated that 'before they can accept the obligations of the General Agreement towards Japan, and thus limit their full freedom of action to deal should the necessity arise with disruptive or unfair competition, they must see how the pattern of trade will develop'.[23] These charges have some substance,[24] but so far as Britain is concerned the rebuff looks more like a sop to those consumer-goods industries, especially the Lancashire textile industry, whose products compete with those of Japan. Japan's present considerable holdings of sterling reduce the urgency of the problem and perhaps in the not-too-distant future wiser counsels will prevail. The growing pressure of population in Japan on limited resources of food and raw materials makes a healthy volume of trade as vital a necessity to her as it is to Britain. It would not be surprising if, in face of widespread discrimination against her exports, Japan were to look less kindly on her ties with the West.

---

[23] Cmd. 9449, Apr. 1955.

[24] Although in October 1955 Japan offered to give effective guarantees against a revival of 'unfair' trading practices.

THE FUTURE OF GATT

The revised General Agreement on Tariffs and Trade is in many respects a judicious blend of principle and realism. In principle the goal is still a multilateral, non-discriminatory, 'free world' economy, in which the major currencies are freely convertible, quantitative restrictions are reduced to a minimum, and the national parts are kept in balance with each other by income and price or exchange-rate variations. But the goal is now more closely circumscribed by the realization that so long as the low level of monetary reserves in the non-dollar world persists, most governments are likely to be chary of taking the plunge into convertibility and of dismantling their import controls, even if the payments position were to become more favourable. The aim now is not so much to preclude the use of quantitative and discriminatory controls altogether (on other than development or balance-of-payments grounds) as to limit their abuse.

Consequently, the revised agreement, though strengthened in some respects, is less generally doctrinaire than its predecessors. Yet doubts about its viability must remain. There are still many doctrinal difficulties which cannot be manipulated away merely by 'interpreting' a clause or by extending further waivers. As always national policies are of crucial importance; and it is by no means clear how many of the contracting parties are willing to pay very much more than lip-service to GATT's 'rules of the game'. Certainly, many of them seem to have powerful mental reservations. In spite of the preference shown by Britain and others in recent months for the monetary weapon as a means of correcting an adverse balance, the suspicion that there is a 'hard core' to the dollar problem—that there is a dollar 'chasm' rather than a dollar 'gap'—which will force most non-dollar countries to retain exchange or import controls for several years to come, is not entirely stilled. Indeed, some still contend that the dominance and instability of the American economy is such that all plans for the future should be based on a preferential trading club made up mainly of sterling area and OEEC members (and, perhaps, Japan) rather than on GATT and a revitalized[25] Monetary Fund, while on the Continent those who pin their hopes to the more effective unity of Europe are often inclined to regard GATT as a potential threat to their efforts.

Outside the industrialized West, neither the underdeveloped countries, nor, for that matter, developing countries like Australia, seem to think that there is anything particularly deplorable about relying on quantitative controls to choke off the flow of imports and to protect the weaker elements in their newly 'diversified' economies. Quite understandably, agricultural exporters, whether in Australia, Canada, Denmark, or New Zealand, are apt to be struck more by the extent to which GATT condones agricultural protectionism than by the rules it sets out for industrial products. There is also some anxiety lest the commercial baits which the Soviet world now seems prepared to offer to the 'uncommitted' countries may cause them either to turn their back on GATT or to blackmail other contracting parties into making further concessions for fear of the political penalties of refusing them. Above all, there is the uncertainty that continues to surround American economic policy generally and the doubt whether Congress will agree to the United States' accession to the OTC.

Even such uncertainties are preferable, however, to the virtual certainty that without GATT the United States would be under far less pressure to go on paying careful heed to the interests and well-being of other contracting parties. Britain's fundamental and enduring interest in an expanding world economy and in stable trade conditions, together with the absolute necessity of securing the adherence of the United States and other major trading countries to a 'code of commercial conduct' which will work against domestic protectionism, makes the success of the revised GATT and of the OTC of very considerable significance for the well-being of the

---

[25] Revitalized by increasing its resources.

British people. Were there no common code and forum drawing together the dollar and non-dollar worlds, the commercial anarchy that would almost certainly ensue could not but have a most harmful effect on the unity of the Western world and on its relations with the free world.

CONCLUSION

This brief sketch of the interlocking Bretton Woods system does scant justice either to its ingenuity or to its complexity or to the extraordinary growth of international economic co-operation in the past ten years. Nor does it adequately convey the continuing doubts in Britain about the validity of several of the basic premises of the system and the growing inclination to give first place to the development of closer ties between Britain, the other members of the Commonwealth, and Western Europe. Certainly, our ideas of the world economy are much less simple than they were at Bretton Woods. The greater stability of the world economy in the last decade and the emergence of a fairly stable pattern of commercial relationships[26] are important factors in any reconsideration of the Bretton Woods system, but so are the growth of regionalism, the possibility that the dollar problem may have a hard core and that convertibility may have to be indefinitely postponed, the limited efficacy of exchange-rate variations as a mechanism of adjustment, and the insistence of underdeveloped countries and others on special trade rules. What has appeared in recent years in, for instance, the annual reports of the IMF about its own attitude to monetary policies is not so much a logical deduction from the speeches of 1944 as a response to circumstances not foreseen in 1944.[27] Moreover the persistent intrusion of political considerations

---

[26] Michael Hoffman, 'The Present System of World Trade', *Lloyds Bank Review*, Jan. 1956.

[27] Fortunately, the Articles of Agreement of the Fund and especially those of the Bank issue admonitions rather than prohibitions, so allowing for a considerable degree of flexibility in their application.

into the work of economic institutions, and the stubborn facts of national sovereignty, are taken more for granted than ten years ago. Institutions that many at Bretton Woods expected to operate untinged by political bias and to provide the framework for an economically indivisible world are seen today to be shot through with politics and to have become, in a sense, instruments of the 'free world' rather than of 'one world'. And even within the free world their authority is strictly limited by the refusal of governments to fetter their freedom of action too strictly or to give their international obligations precedence over their national responsibilities.

The experience of the past decade has been distinctly sobering, therefore, and many cherished illusions have had to be discarded. Few now think of the problem as principally one of hitting on the right formula; clearly what is of crucial importance is whether governments are prepared to play to the 'rules of the game' both in spirit and efficiently. Yet for a country like Britain, whose delicately poised economy can only flourish in a relatively prosperous and peaceful world, the basic philosophy of the Bretton Woods system still retains a great deal of its appeal. The system has already been appreciably modified to meet present-day conditions. It will have further to be strengthened if convertibility is to come about in the not too distant future; and even thereafter a long period of experiment and adaptation will almost certainly be necessary in which it would be extremely rash wholly to discard the present armoury of protective devices.[28] But the system still provides the only set of international economic and financial principles which are acceptable to Western Europe, the Commonwealth, and the United States, a group which accounts for about two-thirds of world trade. It is not a system to be lightly discarded.

---

[28] Which might, in any case, be needed to protect the economy against the worst consequences of failure.

OTHER
UNITED NATIONS
ACTIVITIES

PART FIVE

chapter fourteen

The United Nations
and Dependent Territories[1]

In the last decade the British Colonial Empire has undergone
a transformation nearly as striking as that of the Commonwealth.
For many territories[2] independence is no longer an idea to be
argued about but an actuality just around the corner; and nearly
all but the smallest or the most backward have attained or will
soon attain a wide measure of control over their domestic affairs.
This transformation can fairly be described as the consummation
of British colonial policy which, despite not a few mental reservations, has traditionally been based upon the premise that the natural

---

1 Some of the material in this chapter is based on a memorandum submitted
to the Group by Mr Kenneth Robinson, which has appeared in a slightly different form under the title 'World Opinion and Colonial Status', *International
Organization*, Nov. 1954.

2 e.g. Central African Federation, Gold Coast, Malayan Federation, Nigeria,
West Indies.

destiny of a dependent territory is responsible self-government.[3]
The change lies not so much in the spirit of British colonial
administration as in the tempo of advance towards self-government.
In the inter-war period many critics deemed it to be too slow and
alleged that the official concern with good administration—with
good government rather than self-government—too often served
as a brake on the gradual handing over of political power. Although
today there is a broad measure of agreement in Britain on the
general aims of colonial policy, there are still some who hold
this view and who regard the criticisms voiced at the United Nations
as a useful irritant in combating inertia and delay. In addition,
even many of those who consider much of the criticism to be
misdirected point out that anti-colonialism would still be rife were
there no United Nations; and they argue that the debates afford
a useful safety-valve for the more vociferous members of the anti-
colonial crusade and a valuable opportunity for demolishing the
more fanciful delusions about British colonial policy. The rather
more common fear amongst those well versed in colonial affairs
has been that the United Nations might unduly accelerate the
tempo of advance. They would be the first to concede that risks—
even grave ones—must be run if the orderly progress towards
self-government on democratic lines and within the Commonwealth
is to be maintained. But the economic and social foundations and
the political institutions and habits required for successful self-
government cannot be built in a day. Time and care are needed;
and any policy that threatened prematurely to abandon the colonial
peoples to anarchy or despotism would be generally regarded as
highly irresponsible. Probably many of the colonial peoples themselves would not strongly dissent from this view—at least in private.
But anti-colonial pressure at the United Nations shows few signs,
it is said, of this very proper caution. Indeed, to many in Britain

---

[3] See, for instance, Hansard Society, *Problems of Parliamentary Government
in Colonies* (London, 1953), app. C: 'British Colonial Policy: a selection of
representative statements'.

the useful part that the United Nations could play in colonial affairs appears to have been almost completely vitiated by the encouragement it has given to carping, and often malicious, criticism of Powers bearing colonial responsibilities by those whose policies towards their own backward peoples frequently leave very much to be desired.

THE CHARTER PROVISIONS

The Charter, in effect, establishes three categories of 'non-self-governing territories', namely:
  (i) trust territories (Arts. 75-85 of Chapter XII);[4]
 (ii) strategic areas under trusteeship (Art. 83);
(iii) territories whose peoples have not yet attained a full measure of self-government, other than those in (i) and (ii) above (Arts. 73-4 of Chapter XI).

The Charter provisions are far from precise but, from a practical point of view, the difference between the three types of non-self-governing territories mentioned above is to be found, so far as their relationship to the United Nations is concerned, in the extent to which, and the methods by which, their administration is held to be subject to the latter's supervision. And it is on this question of 'accountability' that most of the discussions at the United Nations are focused.

In ordinary trust territories the precise functions and responsibilities of the Administering Authorities on the one hand, and of the General Assembly and the Trusteeship Council on the other, are set out in trusteeship agreements which have to be approved by a two-thirds majority of the General Assembly (Arts. 79 and 85). But Article 88 also stipulates that the Administering Authority shall make an annual report to the General Assembly upon the basis of a questionnaire, formulated by the Trusteeship Council,

---

4 Arts. 86-91 of Chapter XIII set out the composition and powers of the Trusteeship Council.

on the political, economic, social, and educational advancement
of the inhabitants of the territory. Under Article 87 such reports
may be 'considered' by the Assembly, and, under its authority,
by the Trusteeship Council, which may also accept petitions,
examine them in consultation with the Administering Authority,
and provide for periodic visits to trust territories 'at times agreed
upon with the Administering Authority'.

Under Article 83 all functions of the United Nations in regard
to strategic areas under trusteeship, including the approval of the
terms of the trusteeship agreements, are exercised not by the General
Assembly, but by the Security Council,[5] which shall, however,

> subject to the provisions of the trusteeship agreements and
> without prejudice to security considerations, avail itself
> of the assistance of the Trusteeship Council to perform those
> functions of the United Nations under the trusteeship system
> relating to political, economic, social, and educational mat-
> ters in the strategic areas.

As regards the third group of territories, non-self-governing
territories, those Members of the United Nations who have or
assume responsibility for their administration, have made in
Chapter XI (Arts. 73 and 74) a 'Declaration' of the principles of
good colonial policy, principles which they recognize and accept.[6]
The obligations thereby accepted by the Administering Powers do
not depend—as do the obligations of authorities administering
trust territories—upon special agreements setting out in detail the
precise nature of the obligations concerned. On the other hand,
there is no provision in Chapter XI as regards the 'functions'
of the Organization, except in so far as by Article 73(*e*) the Secretary-

---

[5] Art. 83 has been held to conflict with, and to be limited by, Art. 10. The more
natural interpretation is that Art. 83 limits Art. 10 in the same way as does
Art. 12.

[6] Compare Art. 23(*b*) of the Covenant in which Members of the League undertook 'to secure just treatment of the native inhabitants of territories under
their control'.

General is authorized to receive, 'for information purposes'[7] and 'subject to such limitation as security and constitutional considerations may require, statistical and other information of a technical nature relating to economic, social, and educational conditions' in these territories. Moreover, it will be noticed that information about political conditions is not required under Article 73(*e*), despite the inclusion of the development of self-government and the ensuring of the political advancement of the inhabitants of such territories in the statement of the obligations 'accepted' by the Administering Powers.

It is not easy to disentangle, from the heated and often sophistical arguments to which these provisions have given rise since they came into operation, the initial British impression of what had been achieved—or successfully avoided—at San Francisco. Yet an account of this initial assessment is important to an understanding of Britain's position in the subsequent debates; and, since Britain's view of Chapters XI-XIII reflected fairly closely the ideas about British colonial policy current at the time, a word must first be said about the latter.

Throughout the inter-war years British colonial policy tacitly assumed that, the Indian sub-continent apart, British rule would be maintained for an indefinite period in the Colonial Empire. The colonial peoples might enjoy an increasing degree of participation in the management of their affairs, but, for as long a future as it was profitable to contemplate, ultimate British control was taken for granted. Accordingly, the main criteria of an enlightened colonial policy were held to be the prevention of certain malpractices —slavery and forced labour, the traffic in arms, the liquor traffic, and so forth—and a preoccupation with the welfare of the colonial people, rather than with the extent to which colonial policies might be expected to result in the early disappearance of colonial rule. This combination of assumptions was the essence of what

7 Not 'for consideration', as in the case of reports by the Administering Authorities of trust territories.

was then called 'trusteeship': a positive, though seldom avowed, conviction that the colonial relationship would endure for a long time, and an often rather negative conception of the duties of a good colonial Power. Furthermore, though in the League Britain recognized the obligation to afford independence to Class A Mandates,[8] this assumption of the virtual permanence of colonial rule was implicit in the rest of the mandates system and in most arguments for its possible extension to other colonial territories. The mandates system may have reflected a desire to safeguard the interests of the indigenous peoples and a feeling that outright annexation by the victors was incompatible with the allied proclamation of the principle of self-determination. But its main objective was to improve colonial rule, not to end it.[9]

However, there also existed in Britain (as elsewhere) a school of thought the origins of which can be traced back at least as far as the Congress of Berlin in 1885. There were two wings to this school. Both were based on the concept that overseas dependencies were not a matter of sole concern to the metropolitan Powers but were objects of legitimate interest to the international community. But whilst the one wing sought merely to extend an improved mandates system to all colonial territories, the other was opposed to the whole idea of colonial rule and was intent on outright international management. The inception of the campaign by Germany in the 1930's for the restoration of her colonies aroused wider interest in these proposals. Internationalization—in whatever form— came to be seen[10] as a means of removing one of the irritants making for international tension (and of placating the Axis Powers), whilst avoiding the treachery of handing over colonial peoples to the mercy of régimes in which racial intolerance was strong. In the

---

[8] Iraq, a former British Mandate, became an independent sovereign state in 1932; the other British Class A Mandates were Transjordan and Palestine.

[9] Moreover, the system applied only to the ex-enemy territories, a small proportion of the world's dependent territories.

[10] This was a predominantly, but not solely, Labour and Liberal view.

event this possibility was short-lived, and with the coming of the Second World War international management lost favour in Britain. Though some support for it was apparent at the Mont Tremblant Conference in 1942,[11] its main support towards the end of the war was to be found in the United States.

Some of the assumptions of the older British ideas of good colonial policy had, however, been considerably shaken before the outbreak of the Second World War. The series of riots in the British West Indies which began in 1937 suggested that good colonial policy implied the provision of external aid to make possible a positive policy of social and economic development as the basis without which any political development would be illusory. This idea was embodied in the Colonial Development and Welfare Act of 1940. The war accelerated this change in the climate of opinion. The eventual ending of colonial rule, and the achievement of some kind of self-government at a foreseeable date, came to occupy a larger place in definitions of good colonial policy; at the same time there was greater realization of the need for positive assistance towards the social and economic development of the colonial territories, as the necessary prerequisite of any genuine political advance. Though the size of the problem and the magnitude of the changes involved in such social and economic development were not fully appreciated, this more positive approach to colonial development was sympathetic to the inclusion in the objectives of the trusteeship system, and in Article 73, of positive, if vague, requirements to promote social and economic development. The references to self-government and independence were also in keeping with this new approach, even though they were still regarded by much of British official opinion as agreed but somewhat remote objectives rather than as criteria by which to assess good colonial policy.

But any hopes that the new arrangements for international supervision would reflect British policy as closely as had the

---

11 Eighth Conference of the Institute of Pacific Relations, Dec. 1942, vol. 9.

mandates system failed to allow for the changes in the international scene brought about by the war. Both the United States and the Soviet Union, which had now emerged as the two Great Powers, were traditionally hostile to colonial rule as such.

Most Americans considered 'colonialism' as essentially a political issue. It was the political relationship of subordination which was the root of all evil in colonial territories. In their view there was only one colonial problem: the absence of political independence. True to this traditional attitude, the American proposals presented by Mr Hull at the Moscow Conference contemplated the establishment of an international administrative organ with jurisdiction over all colonies to prepare them for independence.[12] However, by the time of Dumbarton Oaks, international supervision was to be limited to any 'territories for which assistance is requested by member states having control over such territories' and *a priori* it was to apply, as Mr Stettinius explained to Mr Churchill at Yalta, only to former League of Nations Mandates and to territories detached from the enemy during the war.[13] By San Francisco, the United States Working Paper had replaced the simple trusteeship proposal of 1942, applicable equally to all colonies, by the three types of colonial status set out in the Charter. How far this change was due to the firm British stand against any scheme for compulsory and universal international supervision, how far to the insistence of the United States armed service Departments that they should retain unfettered control of the Marshall and Caroline Islands,[14] and how far to a slight easing in American distrust of colonialism, is uncertain. But Mr Hull's deep disappointment at the emasculation of his original trusteeship proposals was naturally not shared by British official opinion.[15]

---

[12] Hull, *Memoirs*, ii. 1304-5; see above, p. 13.

[13] *White House Papers*, ii. 854.

[14] Former Japanese mandated islands.

[15] See McNeill, *America, Britain and Russia*, p. 597 n.

The precise effects on the colonial issue of the emergence of the Soviet Union as one of the two Great Powers were not clear at the time of San Francisco, but her insistence on a seat on the Trusteeship Council, on provision for United Nations inspection of Trust Territories, and on full national independence as the objective of trusteeship was an earnest of the future. Hence, though the motives behind, and the full effects of, Soviet anti-colonialism were to some extent concealed at San Francisco, and though the Soviet Union was already practising her own brand of colonial rule in much of Eastern Europe, it was already evident that it would be difficult to reconcile Soviet views with any arrangements that allowed for the maintenance of a colonial system on the Western model. It was also to be expected that many former colonial countries, such as the Philippines, would share the earlier American view and would press strongly for a general declaration that the ultimate goal for all dependent territories should be independence, and for the imposition of an international supervisory system on *all* dependent territories to ensure their rapid achievement of independence. But it was embarrassing to find that Australia, with some support from New Zealand, identified herself fairly closely with this group.

The Charter provisions agreed at San Francisco reflect these divergent attitudes.[16] Superficially, a verbal compromise was reached. But no real reconciliation was achieved[17] and the subsequent history of United Nations activity under these chapters largely represents the continuation of the debate at San Francisco. The official British view of the San Francisco discussions might have been expressed somewhat along the following lines. The more

---

[16] On the San Francisco discussions see Goodrich and Hambro, pp. 407-10 and 419, together with references cited therein. The United Kingdom draft proposals are to be found in UNCIO, iii, 609-14 (doc. 2, G/26(d)).

[17] The ambiguities of these parts of the Charter resulting from these political differences are reinforced by obscurities in drafting; for instance, on the question of which states are 'directly concerned' in the negotiation of trusteeship agreements (Art. 79), see *Repertory of United Nations Practice*, iv. 181-91.

positive obligations[18] to 'promote the political, economic, social, and educational advancement of the inhabitants of the trust territories, and their progressive development towards self-government or independence'[19] were generally welcomed, but there was relief that international management had not been an issue and that proposals for the international supervision of all colonial territories had proved abortive. World opinion had prevented the abolition of the rather anomalous arrangement by which special conditions had been applied to the administration of a few arbitrarily selected 'colonial' territories, but the new trusteeship system established by Chapters XII and XIII was essentially a revised mandates system, and, as such, was the best that could be hoped for. Although provision had been made for any territory to be voluntarily placed 'under trusteeship', Article 77 had been drawn up in the form of an 'enabling' bill,[20] and it was to such mandated territories as had not achieved 'independence' and to any similar 'colonial' territories which might, at the conclusion of the peace treaties of the Second World War, be detached from Italy or Japan, that the trusteeship system was intended to apply.[21] Moreover, some improvements had been secured in the conditions under which trust territories were required to be administered. These improvements included:

    (*a*) the elimination of the requirement that trust territories should be 'neutralized' and no fortifications erected or troops raised therein except for local defence;

    (*b*) the recognition that 'self-government' was a proper political objective for such territories, and not only 'independence',[22] in

---

[18] As compared with the negative prohibitions of the mandates system.

[19] Art. 76(*b*).

[20] In the sense that there was no legal obligation to place any territory in the three categories mentioned under trusteeship.

[21] On the question of what would happen if a country were unwilling to put a mandated territory under trusteeship—as in the case of South-West Africa—the Charter was deliberately silent; see below, pp. 363-64.

[22] Art. 76(*b*).

the sense of the eventual emergence of a separate sovereign state corresponding to each mandated territory;

(c) in place of the specific obligation to maintain the 'open door' to the nationals of all States Members of the League,[23] a requirement imposed in the interests of Powers other than the Mandatory rather than in the interests of the inhabitants of the territory, a less precise obligation to 'ensure equal treatment in social, economic, and commercial matters'[24] had been substituted and, even so, made subordinate to the more general social and educational advancement of the inhabitants.

On the other hand, in an effort to make international supervision more effective, the Trusteeship Council was empowered by Article 87 not only to consider the reports submitted by the Administering Authorities and to accept petitions, as had the League of Nations Permanent Mandates Commission, but also to provide for periodic visits to trust territories 'at times agreed upon with the Administering Authority'.[25] This attempt to back up the trusteeship system with a kind of international inspectorate was not at all welcome to Britain. Equally disturbing was the fact that, although Article 77 had been drawn up in the form of an 'enabling' bill, mainly to avoid what was considered to be the mistake made at Versailles of linking the Covenant with the peace settlement, paragraph (b) of that article clearly held out the possibility that the former Italian and Japanese colonies might be placed under some form of trusteeship.[26] This possibility, and the keen interest displayed by the Great Powers over the disposal of the territories, made it virtually certain that the Trusteeship Council would be composed of

---

[23] The Covenant, Art. 22, para. 5.

[24] Art. 76(d).

[25] For these and other contrasts between the League mandates system and the United Nations trusteeship system see H. Duncan Hall, *Mandates, Dependencies and Trusteeship* (London, Stevens for Carnegie Endowment for International Peace, 1948), pp. 277-81; also Goodrich and Hambro, pp. 421 ff.

[26] Art. 81 was drafted in such a form as to allow the United Nations to act as the Administering Authority.

representatives of governments instead of individuals acting in their
personal capacity, as was the Permanent Mandates Commission.
Moreover, the Soviet Union insisted that the Great Powers should
be permanent members and not merely eligible for re-election
(Art. 86(*b*)). In these circumstances, and despite the misgivings of
some members of the British delegation, Britain did not question
an American proposal for governmental representation, and she
went on to support the idea of having an exact balance on the
Council between Administering and non-Administering Powers
(Art. 86(*c*)), so as to ensure that the colonial Powers should not
find themselves in a permanent minority.[27] The inability of the
Trusteeship Council to meet until the trusteeship agreements were
signed was due to a drafting oversight.

No more satisfactory was the outcome of the discussions on
Chapter XI (Declaration Regarding Non-Self-Governing Territories).
Originally the draft proposals tabled by Britain,[28] which later
formed the substance of the opening paragraphs of Chapter XI,
had been intended to cover all dependent territories so as to make
quite clear that even when a territory was not under trusteeship,
the spirit of trusteeship should nevertheless prevail. Though partly
a sop to the demands of those who held that all colonial territories
should be brought under some form of international control, it
had also been thought useful to set out an international charter
of colonial rights as a signpost of the correct route for all and
sundry. On the other hand, it had been the intention that Chapter XI
should form an annex to the main Charter; as such its character
as a 'voluntary declaration' could have been preserved. Its incorpora-
tion as an integral part of the Charter appreciably modified its
legal status. Furthermore, in the subsequent process of elaboration,
the provisions of Article 73(*e*) for the transmission of information
to the Secretary-General proved a real problem. Britain saw no

---

[27] The majority of members of the Permanent Mandates Commission were
nationals of non-Mandatory Powers.
[28] In collaboration with Australia.

great harm in the Secretariat acting as a kind of information bureau on the analogy of Article 24(2) of the Covenant; but it was hoped that by excluding political questions and any provision for the discussion of information transmitted, the risk of United Nations intervention might be reduced to a minimum. It had been correctly foreseen, however, that whatever the wording of the article, the United Nations would probably insist on discussing the information. Accordingly this provision was only accepted with great reluctance. The Foreign Office commentary remarked optimistically that 'it does not empower the United Nations Organization to intervene in the application of these principles by the Powers concerned';[29] but most other United Nations Members were to take a very different view.

ACTION UNDER CHAPTER XI (DECLARATION REGARDING NON-SELF-GOVERNING TERRITORIES)[30]

United Nations activity under Chapter XI has, indeed, closely reflected the fundamental conflict between the minority of Members responsible for the administration of territories to which the Chapter applies, and the majority of Members who have no colonies. For the former, the chapter is a statement of principles designed to do no more than establish a clearing-house for information, of a technical kind, on the territories; it in no way implies that the United Nations has a right to supervise their administration.[31] For the latter, Article 73(*e*) represents the basis on which to establish

---

[29] Cmd. 6666, para. 53.

[30] For a fuller summary of United Nations proceedings under this Chapter see *Repertory of United Nations Practice*, iv. 5-87.

[31] In the early years of United Nations discussion of the significance of Chapter XI, United Kingdom spokesmen implied that the Chapter was no more than a 'voluntary declaration' of principles by which they would be guided in administering their dependent territories, and that to this extent it could not be said to import international obligations. This argument has since been abandoned.

a universal system of United Nations supervision of all dependent territories intended to result in their rapid advance towards 'independence'. Accordingly, they have attempted to set up under Chapter XI as close a replica of the trusteeship system as possible, and to treat the 'information' supplied from non-self-governing territories in a manner similar to the 'reports' of the Administering Authorities of trust territories.

The majority view first found expression in the establishment by the General Assembly in 1946 of an *ad hoc* Committee, composed of an equal number of Members transmitting information and Members elected by the General Assembly, to examine the 'summaries and analyses' of the information submitted under Article 73(*e*) (which are prepared by the Secretariat), 'with a view to aiding the General Assembly in its consideration of this information, and with a view to making recommendations to the General Assembly relating to the procedure to be followed in the future'.[32] In 1947 this body was reconstituted for a further year, under the title 'Special Committee on Information from Non-Self-Governing Territories', and was given the function of examining the information supplied under Article 73(*e*) and making recommendations 'relating to functional fields generally but not with respect to individual territories'.[33] In 1949 the Special Committee was reconstituted for three years, and enjoined to make, in 1950, a special study of education.[34] In 1952, when the question of its future again arose (the adjective 'special' in its title had been omitted in 1951), it was the subject of prolonged debate, and a proposal that the Committee should be continued 'for as long as there exist territories whose people have not yet attained a full measure of self-government' was rejected by the Assembly only after Britain, France, and Belgium had stated that they would not participate in the

---

[32] *GAOR*, 1st sess., Resolution 66(I).
[33] ibid. 2nd sess., Resolution 146(II).
[34] ibid. 4th sess., Resolution 332(IV).

work of the Committee if the proposal were adopted in that form.[35]
Similarly, at the tenth session (1955) of the General Assembly
Britain made it clear that she would not take part in the work of
the Committee if its terms of reference were extended; accordingly
the Committee's powers remain virtually the same as set out in
1947 for the further three years for which its life has been renewed.[36]

Britain's doubts about the legality of the Assembly's action in
setting up this Committee are based on the argument that nothing
in the Charter allows the Organization to exercise any 'supervision
or control' of the administration of non-self-governing territories
(other than trust territories), that the Administering Authorities
are, therefore, in no way accountable to the United Nations for
such administration, and that to make recommendations thereon
constitutes 'intervention' in a matter which is essentially within
their domestic jurisdiction.[37] In Britain's view the only precise and
definite legal obligation contained in Chapter XI is that in Article
73(*e*), namely, the obligation to transmit information of a technical
nature for 'information purposes'; since Article 73(*e*) must be regarded as qualifying Article 10, there are no grounds for the claim
that the Assembly has a right to examine this information. Similarly,
none of the 'undertakings' in Article 73(*a*) to (*d*) can be considered,
having regard to the conventions of international law, to justify
the anti-colonial contention that Chapter XI removes the 'political'
affairs of non-self-governing territories from the field of 'domestic
jurisdiction' and therefore of Article 2(7). The non-Administering
Powers have naturally taken the opposite view that, since the General
Assembly is authorized under Article 10 to discuss any matter within
the scope of the Charter, and since Chapter XI brings the administration of all non-self-governing territories within the scope of the

---

35 ibid. 7th sess., 4th Committee, 264-67th mtgs., 5-8 Nov. 1952; for the text
of the final resolution see ibid. suppl. no. 20, Resolution 646(VII).

36 *GAOR*, 10th sess., suppl. no. 19, Resolution 933(X).

37 Unless a situation existed which might lead to international friction likely
to endanger the maintenance of international peace and security; see also above,
pp. 262-63.

Charter, the Assembly has the right to discuss the matters to which the Chapter refers and to make recommendations thereon.[38]

The consequent efforts by these Powers to have political information included in that supplied, mainly so that the United Nations should be able to determine whether a territory remains or has ceased to be 'non-self-governing', have been particularly disturbing. In Britain's view the Assembly has no right to decide whether or not a territory has attained self-government (on which the transmission of information would cease); this is for the Administering Authority to decide in the light of the facts of each particular case. Accordingly Britain, with other Administering Powers, opposed a General Assembly resolution[39] at the eighth session setting out a complex list of 'factors' to be used as a guide in deciding whether or not a territory is self-governing, mainly because paragraph 3 of the resolution assumed a right on the part of the General Assembly to exercise a determining voice in deciding whether a territory had or had not attained full self-government and, to a lesser extent, because the circumstances of each particular territory would probably be so different as to make a list of general application of doubtful utility.

Although Britain from the start opposed the tendency to build up a counterpart of the Trusteeship Council which would subject *all* colonies to the same scrutiny and criticism as the trust territories, and has on these grounds more than once voted against resolutions

---

[38] At the eighth session of the General Assembly it was successfully proposed that resolutions recommended by the Fourth Committee on matters connected with Chapter XI should require only a simple majority for their approval by the Assembly. In the British view, these resolutions should be subject to the same two-thirds majority as the Charter requires for the adoption of resolutions on 'important questions', including resolutions on Chapter XII (Trusteeship) matters (Art. 18, para. 2). Thus in favouring the simple majority rule, the anti-colonial bloc implied that matters under Chapter XI were not 'important questions', despite their habitual insistence to the contrary; the fact is, of course, that they were finding it increasingly difficult to obtain two-thirds majorities for their resolutions. See *Repertory of United Nations Practice*, i. 582-86.

[39] *GAOR*, 8th sess., suppl. no. 17, Resolution 742(VIII). See also Cmd. 8035, pp. 28-29.

with the substance of which she did not disagree, at the same time she appreciated the importance of working with other Members of the United Nations in as co-operative a spirit as possible. She was also disturbed by the fact that the reluctance of the colonial Powers to co-operate in the Committee's work was taken by some delegates to indicate that they had something to hide and that their colonial policies must be as disreputable as the critics alleged. Here was fertile soil for those who were eager for an opportunity to discredit the colonial Powers and to increase the strains in Anglo-American and intra-Commonwealth relations.[40] Indeed, there were signs, in the first few sessions of the Assembly, that the case for British colonial policy since 1945 was in danger of being lost by default, and that current misapprehensions and delusions about that policy were being strengthened by Britain's attitude. Though some delegations had a strong vested interest in discrediting British colonial policy, a more co-operative attitude might induce others to examine that policy more on its merits; and there were few in Britain who doubted it would stand up well to such scrutiny. In 1950, therefore, at the first meeting of the Special Committee after its establishment for three years, the United Kingdom representative stated[41] that the British Government appreciated the importance of working with the United Nations and would henceforth play as constructive and co-operative a part as possible in the work of the Special Committee, while maintaining its determination not to accept any implication of United Nations supervision.[42]

One matter frequently debated in the Committee (and in the Fourth Committee) is worth citing because it gives a good insight into the prevailing climate of opinion about 'colonies'. The

---

[40] India and Pakistan now being amongst the foremost spokesmen of anti-colonialism.

[41] A/AC.35/SR.1, 21 Aug. 1950, pp. 6-7.

[42] This change of front was not welcomed or shared by all the remaining colonial Powers.

Administering Powers, and particularly Britain, have always urged that the Secretariat should be entitled, in preparing its 'summaries and analyses' of the information submitted under Article 73(*e*), to make use, for purposes of comparison, of information from sovereign states in which similar problems exist, since many of the problems of the territories arise from their natural environment and have little to do with their lack of political independence. This was permitted for a time, but it is now only possible with the consent of the Member concerned; this consent is not easy to obtain. Britain has also constantly sought to channel the information to the functional bodies of the United Nations, or to the specialized agencies, where the flaws in the accusing countries' own practices can more easily be pointed out and the information discussed more on its real merits. In general, the non-Administering Powers have hotly contested all attempts to draw comparisons between conditions in the colonial territories and those in similarly situated independent states; some, indeed, have argued that the only comparisons which are valid are those between the non-self-governing territory and the metropolitan country responsible for its administration. The fact is that for most of the anti-colonial Powers the only truly *colonial* question is that of political status; accordingly, the information transmitted under Article 73(*e*) is discussed by them not so much in terms of the material welfare of the colonial peoples as of the ills they are alleged to suffer from their lack of independence, a blind eye being turned to the existence of similar conditions in independent territories.[43] Nevertheless, those members of the Committee who are less doctrinaire in their attitude seem to have been impressed by Britain's policy, since 1950, of smooth persuasion rather than angry protest, and of taking more trouble generally to appear co-operative. In the Committee's recent sessions a rather better atmosphere has prevailed,

---

[43] In 1954 the ILO published a study on aboriginal groups (entitled *Indigenous Peoples*), the vast majority of which live in distressing conditions in the very countries where anti-colonialism is most rife; see below, p. 369.

and a number of delegates now seem inclined to take a more kindly view of Britain's efforts to improve conditions in her colonial territories.

ACTION UNDER CHAPTER XII
(INTERNATIONAL TRUSTEESHIP SYSTEM)
AND CHAPTER XIII (TRUSTEESHIP COUNCIL)[44]

As in the case of action under Chapter XI, the activities of the United Nations in respect of non-strategic trust territories[45] can be divided generally into, on the one hand, procedural questions in the consideration of which attempts have been made to enlarge the scope of United Nations supervision, and, on the other hand, questions of substance, the debates on which have often reflected deep suspicion of the activities of the Administering Authorities.

In what might be termed procedural matters, the tendencies at work in the Trusteeship Council can be illustrated by the initial attempt to compel the Administering Authorities to include in the trusteeship agreements provisions either for their revision at periodic intervals or of time-limits for the attainment of independence or self-government;[46] subsequently the Council has more than once been moved to recommend the fixing of target dates for successive stages of constitutional development. Time-limits of this kind have their uses (as, for instance, in the case of the Philippines and India),

---

[44] For a fuller summary of United Nations activities under this Chapter see *Repertory of United Nations Practice*, iv. 91 ff.

[45] The United Kingdom has no strategic trust territories. The three trust territories for which she is responsible are Tanganyika, and the western parts of Togoland and the Cameroons (all former Mandate territories). The trusteeship agreements in respect of these three territories were approved by the General Assembly on 13 Dec. 1946; the final texts are given in T/8, 25 Mar. 1947. For an analysis of the texts as compared with earlier United Kingdom drafts see Hall, *Mandates*, Annex XIII.

[46] The Administering Authorities made it clear that they would not accept trusteeship agreements including such provisions and that, accordingly, if their inclusion were insisted upon, the Trusteeship Council would never come into existence.

especially when a territory is already approaching self-government, but an empirical-minded colonial administration like that of Britain is naturally averse to setting rigid timetables for such a delicate and complicated process as the attainment of self-government in which the contingent and the unforeseen invariably enter in at every stage.

Among the substantive general questions[47] discussed in connexion with trust territories the following may be instanced as exemplifying the general trend:

1. the development of organs of self-government and of universal adult suffrage;

2. the protection of rights to land;

3. the pressure—of fluctuating intensity—for the immediate and absolute prohibition of corporal punishment, and of such 'uncivilized practices' as child marriage;[48]

4. proposals for the wider dissemination of information about the United Nations and for the establishment of a university for the inhabitants of trust territories in Africa, even though university colleges already existed in the Gold Coast, Nigeria, and East Africa;[49]

5. a recommendation (by the General Assembly)[50] that the United Nations flag should be flown side by side with that of the Administering Authority on public and other buildings in trust territories, a recommendation which the United Kingdom opposed on the grounds that it implied that the Administering Authorities were mere agents of the United Nations;

---

[47] See *Repertory of United Nations Practice*, iv. 107-42.

[48] In Britain's view the effective abolition of corporal punishment can best be sought by the progressive removal of the sanction, not of its immediate prohibition; similarly, the eradication of 'uncivilized practices' would be more likely to follow African recognition (through education &c.) of their undesirability. (This view seems to be borne out by the limited success of legislative efforts in India to abolish the caste system and is also shared by UNESCO).

[49] A University College has also since been set up in Central Africa.

[50] *GAOR*, 4th sess., Resolution 325(IV).

6. the problem of 'Administrative Unions' between trust territories (for example, Tanganyika and the British Cameroons and British Togoland) and neighbouring territories not under trusteeship; some members of the Trusteeship Council and many more in the General Assembly have seemed more intent on preserving the distinct political status of the trust territories (so that the United Nations can continue to exercise its supervisory functions over them) than on considering the needs and wishes of the peoples concerned.[51]

One omission from this list, namely, 'racial discrimination', may cause some surprise. Yet the issue of 'racial discrimination' has rarely been a burning topic in the Trusteeship Council, except for widely separated and sporadic attacks on land policy in Tanganyika. In fact there are no trust territories, with the possible exception of Tanganyika, where race relations constitute a serious problem.

An important and complex problem to which both the Trusteeship Council and the General Assembly have in recent years given much attention is the future status of British Togoland. Most of the non-administering members of the Trusteeship Council have been not insensitive to the advantages of its integration with a fully self-governing and independent Gold Coast; and, in the British view, if the people of British Togoland so decide, the objectives of the trusteeship system would be achieved and the trusteeship agreement could be terminated. In contrast, the Fourth Committee at the eighth Assembly (1953), largely on the instigation of unrepresentative petitioners, tried to preclude such integration; in this they were unsuccessful, but they were able to include in the eventual resolution the doubtful assertion that unification of British Togoland with its neighbouring trust territory under French administration was 'the manifest aspiration of the majority of their peoples'.[52] This view still found favour among many delegates at the ninth session when Britain proposed that arrangement should be made to ascertain the wishes of the people of British Togoland

[51] Since 1951 this problem has aroused little interest, however.
[52] *GAOR*, 8th sess., suppl. no. 17, Resolution 750 C(VIII).

about their future status.[53] In spite of attempts to prejudge the
issue in favour of unification of the two trust territories, a resolution
was adopted in accordance with which the Trusteeship Council sent
a special Visiting Mission to British and French Togoland. In its
report the Mission recommended that an early plebiscite should
be organized in British Togoland by the Administering Authority
under United Nations supervision. At the tenth session discussion
in the Fourth Committee centred on the main problems involved
in the plebiscite. The resolution finally adopted was based on a
draft tabled by India. It recommended that: (1) a plebiscite should
be held without delay, the territory to be treated as a single area
for the purpose; (2) the views of the inhabitants should be sought
not on the single question of the union of their territory with an
independent Gold Coast,[54] but also on the possible separation of
their territory from the Gold Coast and its continued administration
under trusteeship pending a final decision on its future; (3) the
United Nations, in its supervisory role, should be represented by
a Plebiscite Commissioner, assisted by observers and other staff
as necessary; and (4) the United Nations Plebiscite Commissioner
should report on the plebiscite, to enable the General Assembly,
in consultation with the Administering Authority, to decide at its
eleventh session what action should be taken in the light of the
outcome of the plebiscite.[55] Señor Espinosa Prieto of the Mexican
delegation was nominated United Nations Plebiscite Commissioner,
and he and a team of United Nations observers arrived in British
Togoland in January 1956. The plebiscite was held on 9 May;
it resulted in a substantial majority (93,365 to 67,422) in favour
of integration with the Gold Coast.[56] While the deliberations of

---

[53] See United Kingdom memorandum (A/2660) on the future of Togoland;
also full text of speech by the Minister of State (Rt Hon. Henry Hopkinson)
before the Fourth Committee on 30 Nov. 1954 (Cmd. 9394, pp. 62-64).

[54] As the United Kingdom desired.

[55] *GAOR*, 10th sess., suppl. no. 17, Resolution 944(X).

[56] *United Nations Review*, June 1956.

the Trusteeship Council and of the General Assembly have closely followed the course of action proposed by Britain they have helped to remove suspicions as to the latter's intentions and have, indeed, earned her considerable goodwill; in addition, United Nations supervision of the plebiscite may perhaps help to make its outcome more palatable to the very considerable minority in the south who voted to remain under some form of trusteeship.

An equally complicated question which does not directly concern Britain but which has provoked a good deal of comment in this country, is that of the status of the mandated territory of South-West Africa.[57] When, at its first three sessions, the General Assembly passed resolutions urging the Union of South Africa to place this territory under United Nations trusteeship, Britain abstained in the belief that the Union was under no legal obligation to do so. However, at the fourth session she supported a resolution referring the legal issues involved to the International Court for an Advisory Opinion. At the General Assembly's fifth session the United Kingdom delegate supported the Court's opinion[58] that South-West Africa continued to be under the international Mandate assumed by the Union Government on 17 December 1920; that the Union Government continued to have the obligations specified in the Mandate; that the supervisory functions formerly exercised by the League should now be exercised by the United Nations, but only to the degree, and through procedures similar to those, provided for under the mandates system; that there was no legal obligation on the Union Government to place the territory under trusteeship; and that the competence to modify the international status of the territory rested with the Union of South Africa acting with the consent of the United Nations. He also took the lead in urging the appointment of an *ad hoc* Committee to negotiate with the Union of South Africa on the procedure for implementing

[57] See *Repertory of United Nations Practice*, iv. 163-68 and 195-207.
[58] *International Status of South-West Africa, Advisory Opinion: ICJ Reports, 1950*, p. 128.

the Advisory Opinion. The efforts of this Committee, although not at first wholly fruitless, were rendered nugatory by the continued insistence of the majority of the Assembly that the territory should (despite the Court's Opinion) be placed under United Nations trusteeship. This did not deter the Assembly from setting up at its eighth session a Special Committee on South-West Africa with far broader terms of reference, intended to allow it to exercise supervisory functions over the territory.[59] Britain abstained on this resolution but at the tenth session she voted against a resolution[60] further extending the Committee's powers on the ground that, contrary to the International Court's Advisory Opinion of 1950, they were already in excess of those which applied under the mandates system. On the same grounds Britain has supported South Africa in denying the right of either the General Assembly or the South-West Africa Committee to hear oral statements from petitioners (for instance, the Rev. Michael Scott), and she was unable to share without qualification the International Court's Advisory Opinion of 7 June 1955[61] that the adoption by the General Assembly of the 'two-thirds majority' voting procedure on reports and petitions concerning South-West Africa would correctly interpret the Court's original Opinion.

Outside official circles there has been considerable sympathy with the criticisms voiced at the United Nations by the Rev. Michael Scott and others of conditions in South-West Africa, and of the Union Government's refusal to place the territory under trusteeship. Also it still appears to be the official British view (in contrast to the 'hands off' attitude of South Africa) that 'the United Nations has a direct and legitimate concern in the destiny of this former mandated territory';[62] but Britain also adheres to the Court's

---

[59] *GAOR*, 8th sess., suppl. no. 17, Resolution 749(VIII).

[60] ibid. 10th sess., suppl. no. 19, Resolution 941(X).

[61] *ICJ Reports, 1955*, p. 67.

[62] The Prime Minister (Sir Winston Churchill), 5 May 1953, H. C. Deb., vol. 515, col. 202.

opinion that South Africa is under no legal obligation to place the territory under trusteeship and that the General Assembly is only entitled to exercise supervisory functions to the degree provided for under the Mandate. The truth is, of course, that the General Assembly's resolutions may appear to many delegates to serve some high moral purpose, but without the co-operation of the Union Government the Assembly is powerless. Indeed, the attempt by the Assembly to exercise much the same degree of authority over South-West Africa as it does over trust territories generally would seem merely to have made for a more intransigent attitude on the part of the Union Government and to have effectively precluded the United Nations from exercising any practical supervision whatsoever.

One innovation (as compared with the mandates system), which has had a mixed reception in Britain, is the provision for periodic visits to trust territories by Visiting Missions appointed by the Trusteeship Council. The report on Tanganyika[63] of the first Visiting Mission to East Africa in 1948 occasioned some strongly worded observations by Britain.[64] Certainly, several of the Mission's recommendations reflected the brevity of the visit and the unfamiliarity of some of its members with the problems they had been asked to examine. But it is fair to say that many problems to which they drew attention, for instance, African pressure on the land and the problem of migrant labour, had not perhaps figured as prominently amongst the Administering Authority's preoccupations as might have been desirable, while the Mission's doubts about certain aspects of the groundnuts scheme were paralleled in Britain also. Subsequent events have suggested that not all the Administering Authority's strictures were well founded. The report on Tanganyika[65] of the 1954 Visiting Mission to East Africa was more open to criticism, for it was clearly based on a very doctrinaire study of the

---

[63] T/218.
[64] T/333.
[65] T/1142; for Britain's observations see T/1162 and Add. 1.

problems of that territory; Britain took particular exception to the Mission's belief that Tanganyika could become a self-governing community in less than twenty years. Happily, the Trusteeship Council did not endorse the major political recommendations of the Mission, and the reports of most other Visiting Missions have been constructive and helpful and have shown a commendable appreciation of the difficulties facing the colonial Powers. They have probably contributed a good deal to the more realistic note that is now sounded on the Council and have helped to educate their less experienced (in colonial affairs) Members into the facts of colonial life.

If the Visiting Missions are the eyes of the Trusteeship Council, its ears are the numerous petitions[66] submitted by those living in the trust territories. On the whole, the right to petition has proved another useful innovation; also the right to submit petitions direct and not through the Administering Authority (as, *mutatis mutandis*, was the case in the mandates system) has not been seriously abused. Occasionally the petitions submitted and the oral representations by petitioners have only served to confuse the picture, while the indiscriminate hearing of petitioners by the General Assembly and its Fourth Committee has more than once threatened to turn the United Nations into a forum for local political rivalries. But on the whole the system has worked reasonably well and is likely to continue to do so so long as the volume of petitions does not get out of hand.[67]

Although colonial affairs are discussed in Parliament and from time to time all-party delegations visit colonial territories, most Members seem today to be more concerned about the details of policy in particular territories than in the basic premises of colonial policy generally. This pragmatic approach is in the British tradi-

[66] The Council has set up a Standing Committee on Petitions to sift the petitions and to give preliminary examination to the more important ones; see *Repertory of United Nations Practice*, iv. 340-61.

[67] But see *The Economist*, 28 July 1956, p. 329, on the sudden influx of 33,000 petitions from the French Cameroons.

tion and reflects the wide measure of agreement on present colonial policy. Yet it is probably healthy for that policy to come under examination by an outside body in which rather different assumptions are held, so long as the consequent comments are well informed and made in good faith. The early debates in the Trusteeship Council were discouraging, being marked by much unrealism and irrelevant polemics, but recent discussions in the Council have become less embittered and more constructive. Indeed, Britain can take some comfort in the fact that in the past few years she has received nearly as many tributes as criticisms.

On the other hand, in the wider circle of the General Assembly and its Fourth Committee, many Members have persistently sought to discredit the work of the Trusteeship Council and of the Committee on Information from Non-Self-Governing Territories, to persuade the Assembly itself to initiate action in trusteeship matters, and to extend the competence of the Committee to cover political and constitutional matters. The colonial Powers have also been under pressure in other committees of the Assembly, notably in the Third (Social) Committee. One instance is worth citing. On a number of occasions the Committee has had before it a draft convention (for example, for the Suppression of Prostitution) dealing with matters which are within the competence of colonial governments. It is Britain's constitutional practice not to extend such conventions to colonial territories for whose international relations she is responsible without the agreement of the governments concerned.[68] Accordingly Britain has refused to adhere to conventions in which her signature would automatically bind all colonial governments and has sought to include in each case a Colonial Application Article which would enable the convention to be extended to individual colonial territories only after the necessary consultation. But many delegates have airily dismissed this real constitutional difficulty (which is a mark of the increasing autonomy of British colonial

[68] See J.E.S. Fawcett, 'Treaty Relations of British Overseas Territories', in *BYIL, 1949.*

territories in their domestic affairs) alleging, quite without justification, that it is a transparent device to exclude the territories
concerned from the benefits of such conventions.

Fortunately, matters are beginning to improve. For instance,
at the General Assembly's tenth (1955) session, despite the furore
over Algeria and race relations in South Africa,[69] the general debate on the work of the Committee on Information from Non-
Self-Governing Territories was noticeably milder in tone than the
debates of previous years, while the speeches on the report of the
Trusteeship Council showed a distinctly better understanding of
British policy. At first sight, therefore, Britain's policy of co-operation already appears to have produced useful results, and her good
intentions in the colonial field now seem to be accepted not only
by other members of the Commonwealth but also by the general
run of so-called anti-colonial delegates (excepting, of course, those
from the Soviet bloc and those who have ulterior motives for
discrediting Britain). On the other hand, although the virulent
and emotional attacks on the colonial Powers so common up till
about 1950 may have become less frequent, the anti-colonial members, usually under the skilful leadership of India, are pursuing
an intelligent, subtle, and much more coherent attack than was
mounted in the early years when frontal attacks were the order
of the day. There is still a risk that Britain's policy of trying to
educate delegates into the realities of colonial life may turn out
to be double-edged.

SOME GENERAL REFLEXIONS

Perhaps the first point that the foregoing experience suggests
is the rather arbitrary basis on which certain territories of a small
number of Western European Powers have been singled out as
'non-self-governing' territories. The fact is that the United Nations,
like the League of Nations before it, has fallen victim to the aptly

[69] See above, p. 265.

named 'salt-water fallacy'—the belief that any country that has expanded overseas must submit to a degree of international super-vision over its overseas territories from which nations whose ex-pansion has been overland are immune. Moreover, if the justifica-tion of such supervision is that the inhabitants of a territory do not have the same rights or the same voice in the selection of the government as the people of the metropolitan country, it is not easy to draw any clear distinction between the status of the peoples of the colonial dependencies of some Western European countries and, to take but one example, that of the 12 million or so Indians in North and South America, many of whom do not enjoy the same rights of citizenship as the other inhabitants of that continent, and who, according to a Director of the Inter-American Indian Institute, 'live in conditions of intellectual and material inferiority which are a disgrace to humanity'.[70] In short, the clear-cut line drawn between so-called colonial territories and the problems of 'minority' groups in any territory in which a dominant group exer-cises a monopoly of political power is a very arbitrary one.

It is also rather ironical to find that the vast majority of under-privileged and isolated aboriginal groups, whose unhappy lot is described in the ILO's report on *Indigenous Peoples*, live in the very countries whose spokesmen at the United Nations are often the most eloquent in denouncing the economic evils of imperialism and whose 'disinterested' supervision will, it is supposed, lead to the rapid eradication of these evils. 'A study of Indigenous Peo-ples, in fact, makes it perfectly clear that sovereign status is by no means a sovereign remedy for all ills.'[71] It is not surprising that the spectacle of Britain and other colonial Powers being harried at the United Nations by those self-styled champions of the rights of colonial peoples in whose own countries slavery or the secret

[70] M. Gamio, 'Some Considerations of Indianist Policy', in R. Linton, ed., *The Science of Man in the World Crisis* (New York, Columbia University Press, 1945), p. 399.

[71] Frances Boyd, 'Anti-Colonialism—The Biters Bit', in *United Nations News*, July-Sept. 1954.

police are still accepted institutions does not strike most people in Britain as being particularly edifying.

An examination of United Nations activities in respect of colonies also suggests that Britain has been obliged to form a close alliance with the other colonial Powers, which is not really in accordance with the general trends of British colonial policy. This alliance is no doubt reinforced by wider political considerations, but one consequence of it has been that Britain has not always been able to make the most of the extent to which her achievements and aims are in line with the ideas of her critics. Yet against this must be set the fact that the United Kingdom delegates have been forced by the attacks to present an attractive and coherent account of British colonial policies. This is not easy since they rest so largely on empiricism and a tendency to yield to the *fait accompli*, while the traditional solutions developed first in the older dominions and since extended to the Asian dominions, West Africa, the West Indies, and Malaya, cannot easily be applied to the remaining non-self-governing territories of the Commonwealth. Nevertheless, one of the possible consequences of these international discussions is that they may contribute, if only indirectly, to the working out of a much more precise and clear-cut objective in multi-racial or plural societies, and to the formulation of a more effective association in the British Commonwealth of those small territories for whom full membership may be impracticable. At the very least, recent speeches by United Kingdom delegates suggest that the attacks on British policy have nettled them into an eloquence which has impressed the more open-minded delegates.

Finally, a development which merits a brief word is that of associating colonial territories more closely with the technical and regional organs of the United Nations and of the specialized agencies. Not only is it explicit proof of their advance towards self-government, but it can help to introduce the indigenous representatives of these territories on to the international stage and to equip them for the exercise of their future international responsibilities. Thus it has long been the custom for British delegations to the ILO to include advisers from the indigenous peoples of colonial territories; it is now also possible for these territories to be represented at the General Conference by tripartite observer delegations, an arrangement of which Barbados, the Federation of Nigeria, the Gold Coast, Jamaica, Sierra Leone, Singapore, and Malta took advantage at the 38th (1955) session. Article 8 of the Constitution of WHO[72] has provided a model for a closer form of association which, on British initiative, has also recently been adopted by UNESCO;[73] also since 1949 a number of British territories in South East Asia have become, either separately or jointly, associate members of the United Nations Economic Commission for Asia and the Far East. In addition, a number of colonial governments take an active part in the technical meetings and in the regional activities of most of the specialized agencies. There is always the resulting risk of divided counsels, but such risks will have to be run if orderly progress is to be maintained.

CONCLUSION

It is perhaps inevitable that a colonial Power should be inclined to regard United Natoins action in the sphere of dependent territories as chiefly a source of criticism and advice not usually distinguished for its good sense or practicality. And, as far as actual colonial administration is concerned, probably the most material difference that the United Nations has made is to tie District Commissioners

[72] The first sentence of Art. 8 reads: 'Territories or groups of territories which are not responsible for the conduct of their international relations may be admitted as Associate Members by the Health Assembly upon application made on behalf of such territory or group of territories by the Member or other authority having responsibility for their international relations.' So far among British non-metropolitan territories, only the Federation of Rhodesia and Nyasaland has been so admitted.

[73] The following British colonial territories have become Associate Members of UNESCO: Gold Coast, Sierra Leone, British Caribbean Group (Barbados, Dominica, Grenada, Jamaica, Trinidad), and the Malaya/British Borneo Group (Federation of Malaya, Singapore, Brunei, North Borneo, and Sarawak).

z

to their offices under the irritating necessity of trying to answer often unanswerable questionnaires when their real job is 'up-country'. Indeed, of far greater practical importance has been the work of the Caribbean Commission, the South Pacific Commission, and the Commission for Technical Co-operation in Africa South of the Sahara. Members of these regional bodies can deal rather better with the problems and interests peculiar to their own region than can a quasi-universal organization like the United Nations.[74] Yet the United Nations system should not be judged too narrowly by its obvious defects or by the degree of irritation it arouses. It could, if it worked more smoothly and responsibly, provide a further incentive for the colonial Powers to ensure that their policies and administration offered as few targets for criticism as possible; even with the 'new look' in British colonial policy, a goad of this kind might have its uses. This was the hope when the Charter was drawn up. Unhappily, this initial hope has been sadly belied by the use to which the Charter provisions have been put by the less responsible elements in the anti-colonial school. Today few in Britain would quarrel with the position of the British Government as stated by Sir Anthony Eden in the seventh General Assembly:

> Either these lands can continue, with the help of countries like my own, their orderly progress towards self-government. Or they can be prematurely abandoned by us and exposed to anarchy or despotism, so that all liberal tendencies are smothered, perhaps for generations. There is no question in my mind as to which of these courses most closely fits the purpose of the Charter of the United Nations.[75]

The anti-colonial school of thought would, no doubt, indignantly deny that its advice, if slavishly followed, would frequently lead to the second alternative. But in Britain, rightly or wrongly, at present this is almost unquestioningly thought to be the case, and

---

[74] As anticipated at the Mont Tremblant Conference of the Institute of Pacific Relations (1942); see above, p. 347.

[75] *GAOR*, 7th sess., Plen., 393rd mtg., 11 Nov. 1952, p. 210.

the majorities the anti-colonial school habitually musters at the United Nations are deemed a poor substitute for the promptings of the British people's own conscience and the exercise of their own judgement. It is true that the increasing respect with which Britain's case is listened to by many members of the anti-colonial group suggests that the policy of co-operation is producing useful results and that the more ebullient manifestations of anti-colonial prejudice may indeed turn out to be no more than 'growing pains' to which any institution like the United Nations is inevitably subject. But if this hope should prove illusory, Britain would be forced seriously to reconsider her present policy of co-operation.

chapter fifteen

The United Nations
and the International Rule of Law

The role of international law in international society is complex and subtle; it must be stressed, therefore, that although for lack of space the treatment of the subject in this chapter is necessarily condensed, the issues involved are far from simple. Moreover, although few would deny that it is both generally desirable and in Britain's own interest to sustain the rule of law internationally, the precise methods to be adopted towards this end, and the part to be played therein by the United Nations (including the International Court of Justice), excite considerable controversy. It will be as well, therefore, to indicate very briefly, and rather dogmatically, two closely connected—but rather debatable—assumptions implicit in the argument in this chapter, namely, that international law is an adjunct to diplomacy rather than an arm of government and that law depends more upon order than order upon law (though the two are mutually sustaining).

Both assumptions derive from the fact that, unlike municipal law, which forms part of the process of government within a state and can, therefore, count upon both an executive—a police—to enforce the law and a legislature to change it, international law operates in a diplomatic milieu characterized by an overall absence of government; there is, therefore, no assurance that those who break it will suffer and almost no means of changing the law except by force or diplomatic negotiation.[1] If only for this reason the attitude of states to international law is fundamentally different from the attitude of citizens to the law of their land, and the degree of law-abidingness to be found in international society is far less than is usually the case in domestic society.

There are those who, with this distinction in mind, regard international law as little more than a sham, since, in their view, law that is not regularly enforced is not law in any real sense. It is, of course, the case that the deference most states show for the law is limited, although in varying degrees, by their disposition to look upon international law mainly as an instrument of state policy or a buttress to the interests of those who are suited by the *status quo*. Qualifying the operation of the pre-legal premise *pacta sunt servanda*[2] on which all treaty relationships rest—and on which the existence of international institutions is predicated—lies the legal loop-hole of *clausula rebus sic stantibus*,[3] together with the readiness of states to 'interpret' the law so that it does not work to their own hindrance and their capacity to set it aside altogether when their desire for change conflicts with their existing legal obligations. The fact is that legal considerations only rarely claim priority in the pattern of considerations which statesmen take into

[1] Hence, of course, the attempts in both the Covenant and the Charter to put a collective sanction behind the law and a premium upon peaceful rather than forceful change.

[2] That is, 'promises are made to be kept'; or, perhaps, more simply, 'good faith'.

[3] That is, that a treaty is binding only 'so long as things stand as they are' (see J. L. Brierly, *The Law of Nations*, 5th ed. (Oxford, Clarendon Press, 1955), p. 260).

account in their shaping of policy. To expect states, therefore, automatically to abide by legal obligations which are not closely attuned to shifting power relationships is to invite disillusion and even to court disaster.

Nevertheless, the tacit premise of all international negotiations, whether in the United Nations or elsewhere, is that states are not indifferent to international law. The great majority of the rules of international law, many of which deal with technical matters,[4] are in fact generally observed, while over the years most states most of the time behave *as if* international law were binding upon them. Indeed, if this were not the accepted diplomatic convention the contortions that states are wont to perform to persuade others that they are keeping within the law would make little sense. The point is not that international law is of no consequence, but that in modern times respect for the law is rooted for the most part not in fear of material penalties (except in the form of reprisals) or in any sense of moral (as compared with social) sanction behind the law (though that may occasionally be present),[5] but in diplomatic tradition and convention. Above all, it is rooted in the recognition by states of the convenience of preserving a system of legal relationships which can inject an element of predictability and stability into a closely-knit but politically fragmented society.

This may seem a very shaky foundation on which to foster respect for the law. It is indeed; but it is the only one available at present. Moreover, there is little reason to suppose that it will be strengthened merely by multiplying the number of legally binding obligations upon states. Such measures may occasionally be not unhelpful, but the essential need is to work for conditions in which

---

[4] The increased scale of state intervention in economic and social matters and the consequent proliferation of quasi-universal international institutions (for example, the specialized agencies) has, of course, led to a marked increase in the quantity of international law. See C. W. Jenks, 'The Impact of International Organizations on Public and Private International Law', *Transactions of the Grotius Society, 1951*.

[5] Especially in the West where the notion persists that international law embodies and expresses, albeit imperfectly, a morally binding 'natural law'.

respect for the law may more easily flourish. As Professor Brierly remarks, 'Our common phrase "law and order" inverts the true order of priority, both historically and logically. Law never creates order; the most it can do is to help to sustain order when that has once been firmly established . . . always there has to be order before law can even begin to take root and grow.'[6] In a world of sovereign states, therefore, international law has a valuable cementing role to perform, but its standing is primarily a function of the degree of order which has emerged in the course of history.[7] In other words, how to promote greater respect for the law is, first and foremost, a political not a legal problem. It is against this background that the Charter provisions and the activities of the United Nations need to be viewed.

THE CHARTER PROVISIONS

Despite the omission from the Dumbarton Oaks proposals of express reference to international law, the Charter is dotted with such references and the United Nations is well equipped with legal organs. The Preamble enjoins respect for legal obligations. Article 1 instances, as one of the 'Purposes' of the United Nations, the settlement of disputes in conformity with principles of justice and international law; under Article 13 the General Assembly is to encourage 'the progressive development of international law and its codification', while Chapter VI specifies arbitration and judicial settlement in general, and recourse to the International Court of Justice in particular, as approved methods of pacific settlement. The International Court, which is almost identical with the former

6 *The Outlook for International Law* (Oxford, Clarendon Press, 1944), p. 74.
7 Professor Oppenheim wrote, in the 2nd edition (1912) of his *International Law:* 'The first and principal moral that can be deduced from the history of the development of the Law of Nations is that a Law of Nations can exist only if there be an equilibrium, a balance of power, between the members of the family of Nations. If the Powers cannot keep one another in check, no rules of law will have any force, since an overpowerful state will naturally try to act according to discretion and disobey the law' (i. 193).

Permanent Court of International Justice, is cited as one of the 'principal organs' of the United Nations;[8] all Members of the United Nations are *ipso facto* parties to the Statute of the Court, while under Article 94 of the Charter each Member 'undertakes to comply with the decision of the International Court of Justice in any case to which it is a party', failing which the Security Council is empowered to 'make recommendations or decide upon measures to be taken to give effect to the judgment'.[9] Under Article 96 the International Court may be requested by the General Assembly or by the Security Council to give an Advisory Opinion on any legal question; other United Nations organs and the specialized agencies may also request Advisory Opinions on 'legal questions arising within the scope of their activities' if authorized to do so by the General Assembly. In addition, the General Assembly has a main committee (the Sixth) to deal with legal questions, it has set up an International Law Commission to assist it under Article 13, and there is a legal section in the Secretariat to advise the Assembly and other organs of the United Nations.

Taken at their face value, the provisions of the Charter would seem to testify to the importance Members of the United Nations attach to international law. Yet a characteristic feature of most United Nations meetings, as compared with the rather more than formal lip-service generally paid to international law in the League of Nations, is the atmosphere of general indifference to, and distrust of, legal methods and procedures and the disposition of many Members to brush aside legal considerations as technical quibbles—a form of 'legalism' or legal pedantry.[10] At one and the same time as a determined attempt is being made at the United Nations to extend the domain of international law (in international criminal

---

[8] Art. 7(1).

[9] On the model of Art. 13(4) of the Covenant.

[10] For some examples see G. G. Fitzmaurice, 'The United Nations and the Rule of Law', in *Transactions of the Grotius Society, 1952*, p. 138. This indifference to the law is not discouraged by the tangled wording of the Charter, which is full of ambiguities.

law and human rights), some governments behave as if international law were a mere instrument of national policy, while others denounce it either as an infringement of national sovereignty or as a derogation from some higher principle of international justice (for example, national self-determination).

This disrespect for international law is not, of course, peculiar to the United Nations, which is in any case a political institution in which political considerations will normally predominate. Nor is it to be assumed that the law should be deferred to if it is generally thought to be 'unjust' or if it conflicts with a state's 'vital interests'. The existing legal order is not sacrosanct and states acknowledge no duty to let their respect for the law threaten their very survival. But it is one thing to decide to evade legal objections out of sheer political necessity and quite another consistently to disregard the legal aspects of issues having a political character merely because they may be embarrassing or inconvenient. As a Power with a deeply ingrained respect for, and a strong vested interest[11] in, the rule of law, Britain has been deeply disturbed by the frequent failure of the organs of the United Nations to give legal considerations their due weight, by their habit of dealing with legal questions in a haphazard and light-hearted way, and by their seeming neglect of the International Court.

Britain has sought to contribute to the rule of law primarily by reducing the general level of international tension and suspicion and also by the example of her own deference to legal considerations. As has been seen,[12] within the United Nations Britain has repeatedly had to remind delegates that the Assembly's competence is strictly qualified by Article 2(7), the 'domestic jurisdiction' article, and that Article 73 in no way makes the 'colonial' Powers accountable to the United Nations for the policies they pursue in their overseas territories. She has not shrunk from incurring public odium in

---

[11] Mainly because of her interest in a more orderly world but also because her legal rights tend to outrun her capacity to defend them.

[12] See above, pp. 261-64 and 355.

doing so; although critics may dismiss the British arguments as mere technicalities, in the British view they are not merely sound in law but they need to be insisted upon if respect for the law is not further to deteriorate. Britain has also endeavoured to foster the rule of law in the United Nations not only by trying to moderate the bitterness which has marked so many exchanges at meetings but, more particularly, by her efforts to strengthen the Assembly's methods and procedures for dealing with legal and drafting matters, by her support of the work of the International Law Commission, and by encouraging more frequent recourse to the International Court.

THE GENERAL ASSEMBLY AND LEGAL QUESTIONS

At the sixth (1952) Assembly Britain introduced proposals[13] designed to prevent the legal aspects of issues under discussion at the United Nations from being entirely ignored or deliberately brushed aside. In introducing these proposals the Attorney-General (Sir Lionel Heald) said:

> An institution which handles legal problems . . . in a considered, objective, regular and orderly manner, will usually also be an institution in which the rule of law is respected . . . To pay proper regard to legal considerations, to give them due weight, to deal with them by means of an orderly and regular procedure, is always difficult, often tiresome, and sometimes exasperating. The institution that nevertheless does impose this discipline on itself will develop a mental attitude that will produce its effects over the whole field of that institution's work.[14]

The proposals fell under three main heads. It was proposed, firstly, that items of a political, economic, social or financial character, which presented legal aspects, should be considered at

---

[13] A/1897 and A/1929.
[14] 'General Assembly: Speech by the Attorney-General', *ICLQ*, Jan. 1952, p. 55.

some stage by the Sixth Committee so that these legal aspects could be given proper consideration. After the legal and non-legal aspects had been separately considered in the appropriate committees, the final resolution on the subject should be framed at joint meetings of the two committees. Secondly, that proposals to refer any matter to the International Law Commission, or requests to the International Court for Advisory Opinions,[15] or instruments for the amendment of rules of procedure, or the terms of reference, powers and functions of subsidiary organs, should be referred to the Sixth Committee for advice as to drafting.[16] Thirdly, that final drafts of all Assembly resolutions should be referred to a Central Drafting Committee in order to achieve greater uniformity of style and terminology.

These proposals met with a decidedly cool reception and were referred to a Special Committee for study. But the seventh Assembly passed a resolution[17] (based on the Special Committee's Report)[18] which followed the British proposals fairly closely (with the exception of omitting all reference to the drafting of Assembly resolutions). This resolution was permissive, not mandatory, but the discussion may have made delegates more conscious of the need for special care in handling legal and drafting questions. If the present more moderate tone in the Assembly continues and the political climate generally does not deteriorate, the recommendations may well gradually become accepted in practice. If so, they could contribute appreciably to the more orderly conduct of the Assembly's affairs.

On the other hand, Britain's approach to attempts by the Assembly to draw up an International Criminal Code of offences against the peace and security of mankind and to proposals to set up a so-called international criminal court or to adopt a conventional definition of aggression has been cautious and prag-

---

[15] This would at least relieve the International Court of the need to edit or interpret the questions referred to it before it could answer them.

[16] A number of other such items were also listed.

[17] *GAOR*, 7th sess., suppl. no. 20, Resolution 684(VII).

[18] A/2714.

matic. Nor has Britain yet ratified the Genocide Convention. All such schemes for codifying 'international criminal law' have apparently been regarded as either unsound in principle or at least as impracticable in present circumstances. Nor are expressions of regret at the Assembly's 'tendency to act as though deeply rooted social evils can be exorcised by issuing a manifesto against them'[19] uncommon. Similarly, initiatives to secure a conventional definition of aggression, however well intentioned in most cases, have usually seemed to Britain to be more likely to set what might be a 'trap for the innocent and a signpost for the guilty'. Might not the Soviet bloc's aim be to secure a definition which would lend authority to their claim that the Korean War (or similar wars in the future) did not amount to aggression but that the efforts of the Western Powers to organize resistance to such acts did amount to aggression?[20] Even apart from this danger, similar attempts in the League to arrive at an acceptable definition seem to most people to have been so much wasted effort or to have raised uncertainties which still remain unresolved.[21] There is little inclination to repeat this experience. Therefore, Britain has considered the readiness of the vast majority of nations to denounce a palpable act of aggression, and, of course, having denounced it, to combine together to resist it, more important than agreement upon formulae for the definition of aggression. Hence the prior significance of the Peace Observation Commission as a means of ascertaining the facts about any threat to the peace, and, within limits, of the 'Uniting for Peace' machinery as an instrument of collective resistance to aggression.

---

[19] Brierly, 'The Genocide Convention', *The Listener*, 10 Mar. 1949; see also the Attorney-General (Sir Hartley Shawcross): *GAOR*, 3rd Sess., pt. 1, 6th Committee, 64th mtg., *SR*, pp. 17-18; also G. Schwarzenberger, 'The Problem of an International Criminal Law', in *CLP*, 1950.

[20] See Fitzmaurice, 'The Definition of Aggression' (extracts from speech in the 6th Committee of the 6th Assembly, 9 Jan. 1952), *ICLQ*, Jan. 1952, pp. 137-44.

[21] See, for instance, International Studies Conference (7th and 8th), *Collective Security*, ed. M. Bourquin (Paris, 1936), p. 336, for an intervention by Professor C. A. W. Manning.

THE INTERNATIONAL LAW COMMISSION

The International Law Commission was set up by the General Assembly in 1947. Its fifteen members, elected by the General Assembly for a three-year term, serve in their personal capacity and not as representatives of governments.[22] The British members have been successively Professor J. L. Brierly, Professor H. Lauterpacht, and Sir Gerald Fitzmaurice. The Commission's discussions have ranged over a wide field; only a few salient features can be commented on very summarily here.

The Commission has devoted much of its time to advising the General Assembly on the proposals to draw up an International Criminal Code, to set up a so-called international criminal court, and to define aggression. It has also considered the general problem of reservations to multilateral conventions. The Commission's view,[23] which differed considerably from that adopted by the International Court in its Advisory Opinion on Reservations to the Genocide Convention,[24] had much to commend it, but it revealed an unfortunate conflict of opinion between the two leading legal organs of the United Nations.

The Commission's main task has been to prepare the way for the 'codification' of international law, especially in the fields of the régime of the high seas, the law of treaties, arbitral procedure, and nationality. The movement for 'codification' has a long history and much has been written on the subject. Widely differing views are to be found in Britain, as no doubt elsewhere, both on its merits and on its practicability.[25] Some contend that the imprecision and uncertainty of international law is one of the main reasons for its

---

[22] A point which many United Nations members are apt to overlook in the elections.

[23] See A/CN.4/48 (3rd Report), para. 28.

[24] *ICJ Reports*, 1951, p. 15.

[25] See, for instance, H. Lauterpacht, 'Codification and Development of International Law', *American Journal of International Law*, Jan. 1955, p. 19, and Lauterpacht, ed., *International Law* by L. Oppenheim, 7th ed., i. 60-65.

inadequacy and an invitation to states to interpret the law to their own advantage. It is argued that a code 'would provide a systematic arrangement of the law, would make its provisions clearer and more easily ascertainable, would remove uncertainties, and fill up existing lacunae'.[26] Thus the Attorney-General contended, at the Sixth Committee of the fourth General Assembly, that the Commission could 'do most valuable creative work in elucidating and clarifying topics of international law which are difficult or obscure, and in restating or codifying those parts of it which are suitable for that purpose'. His hope was that the rule of law would be promoted by the clearer enunciation of the existing rules of international law. 'When the rules themselves, as they exist today, are clearly and authoritatively set out, so that those who run to more aggressive or lawless courses may plainly read the rules they break, States are more likely to be guided by them in their conduct. . . .'[27]

Yet the Conference on the Progressive Codification of International Law, held under the auspices of the League of Nations at The Hague in 1930, revealed not only innumerable difficulties which still persist, but also the danger that efforts to codify international law may in fact weaken its authority by casting doubt upon principles hitherto generally accepted.[28] Moreover, it must be suspected that disrespect for the law stems more frequently from a readiness to brush legal considerations aside if they do not fit in with political predispositions than from ignorance or uncertainty as to what the law is. In any case codification, however successful, cannot remove all uncertainty

---

[26] Brierly, *Law of Nations*, 5th ed., p. 79.

[27] The Attorney-General (Sir Hartley Shawcross), 'The International Law Commission', *ILQ*, Jan. 1950, pp. 2 and 4.

[28] See Professor G. W. Keeton and Dr G. Schwarzenberger's comment: 'Foreign Offices added so many qualifications to what had been considered perfectly straightforward rules of international customary law that the attempt at codification merely compromised formerly unchallenged principles of international customary law.' *Making International Law Work*, 2nd ed. (London, Stevens for London Institute of World Affairs, 1946), p. 122.

for the main cause of uncertainty in any kind of law is the uncertainty of the facts to which it has to be applied. Law has necessarily to be stated in the form of general principles, but facts are never general; they are always particular, they are often obscure or disputed, and they were very likely not foreseen, and therefore not expressly provided for, at the time when the rule of law received its formulation.[29]

Nor does the experience of English common law lend much support to the case for codification. Indeed, Professor P. J. (now Rt Hon.) Noel-Baker's comment in 1924 that 'so far as the codification of English law is concerned, it is true to say that the best professional lawyers have nearly always been opposed to it' would probably still hold good today.[30] Arguments such as these are not, of course, decisive. But they do suggest that although there may be a case for codifying those parts of international law which have become 'well-settled' and thus ripe for codification, it would be imprudent to belittle the difficulties or to place much trust in codification as a means of building up greater respect for the law.

A connected difficulty, which The Hague Conference also met, is that the very term 'codification' is ambiguous.[31] In the Statute of the International Law Commission a distinction is drawn between codification proper, that is, the statement of the law as it exists—the clarificatory or declaratory task—and the development of international law by amending and supplementing existing law—the legislative task. Although it is a distinction which Britain has more than once emphasized, it soon became blurred in the Commission's discussions; nor have either Professor Brierly or Professor Lauterpacht been able to accept it without substantial

---

[29] Brierly, *Outlook for International Law*, p. 16.

[30] 'The Codification of International Law', in *BYIL, 1924*, p. 45. But see Sir Cecil Hurst, 'A Plea for the Codification of International Law on New Lines', in *Transactions of the Grotius Society, 1946*.

[31] Yuen-li Liang, 'Methods for the Encouragement of the Progressive Development of International Law and its Codification', in *YBWA, 1948*, pp. 258-61.

reservations.[32] It may well be that no hard and fast distinction is possible given the gaps and uncertainties (and inconsistencies) in existing international law. Yet there is a risk that by concentrating too exclusively on bringing about improvements in the existing law, by attempting, that is, to have it amended and supplemented rather than to formulate it more precisely, the Commission may merely give birth to a series of declarations *de lege ferenda* which not only have little immediate prospect of acceptance but may also undermine the authority of the accepted principles they seek to improve upon. The making of new law is primarily the function of the statesmen, not of the lawyers.

THE INTERNATIONAL COURT OF JUSTICE

The work of the International Court of Justice has already been discussed authoritatively elsewhere.[33] The following paragraphs will be confined to a brief reminder of those aspects of the work of the Court which have been of special interest to Britain. The limitations on the Court's powers hardly need to be recalled. The first is, of course, the voluntary basis of the Court's jurisdiction; the Court can only consider a dispute which the parties thereto have agreed to submit to it. That agreement may be given either *ad hoc*, or, in anticipation of such a dispute arising, by previous agreement between the parties, whether in a treaty or through

---

[32] For Professor Brierly's views when Rapporteur of the Commission see A/AC.10/30, p. 3; also quoted in B. Cheng, 'The International Law Commission', in *CLP, 1952*. Professor Lauterpacht has indeed argued that 'the task of codifying international law, if it is to mean anything, must be primarily one of bringing about an agreed body of rules rather than introducing systematic order and precision into legal rules already covered by customary or conventional agreement of states', in *American Journal of International Law*, Jan. 1955, p. 22.

[33] Fitzmaurice, 'The Law and Procedure of the International Court of Justice', in *BYIL, 1950* and subsequent years; also Schwarzenberger, 'Trends in the Practice of the World Court', in *CLP, 1951*.

signature of the 'Optional Clause'[34] contained in Article 36 of the Statute of the Court. The second limitation on the Court's powers is that its decisions (which are majority decisions) are binding in law but are not, in fact, enforceable. The record of compliance with the Court's decisions is in fact impressive, but recent experience —the example of Albania is well remembered—confirms that a sovereign state, however small, has the capacity to disregard them; in choosing whether to do so it is unlikely to be greatly deterred by fear of the Security Council's wrath under Article 94(2).

Since the Court was constituted in 1946, when the election of the first fifteen judges took place,[35] Britain has been the principal litigant before it, having been involved in the following cases:[36]

1. *Corfu Channel Case;*
2. *Case of the Monetary Gold removed from Rome in 1943;*
3. *Anglo-Norwegian Fisheries Case;*
4. *Anglo-Iranian Oil Company Case;*
5. *Minquiers and Ecrehos Case;*
6. *Ambatielos Case.*

Britain has also felt sufficiently interested to present statements to the Court in connexion with some of the matters referred to the Court for Advisory Opinions, such as:

---

[34] The 'Optional Clause' is a declaration whereby states recognize as compulsory *ipso facto* and without special agreement, in relation to any other state accepting the same obligation, the jurisdiction of the Court in certain kinds of legal disputes. The reservations appended to many declarations have, however, deprived them of much of their value. The United Kingdom first adhered to the Optional Clause in 1929. The United Kingdom declaration at present in force was made in 1955: it accepts the Court's jurisdiction subject to the exclusion, *inter alia*, of intra-Commonwealth disputes and 'of disputes with regard to questions which by international law fall exclusively within the jurisdiction of the United Kingdom'.

[35] Art. 2 of the Statute of the Court states that the Court shall be composed of a body of independent judges, elected regardless of their nationality and on the basis of their personal qualifications. In the complicated elections, in which both the Security Council and the General Assembly take part, this requirement tends to be overlooked by many delegates. However, considering present ideological differences, most judges show a remarkable degree of judicial independence.

[36] Not in chronological order.

a2

1. *Reparation for Injuries suffered in the Service of the United Nations;*
2. *Interpretation of the Peace Treaties with Bulgaria, Hungary, and Roumania;*
3. *Reservations to the Convention on the Prevention and Punishment of the Crime of Genocide;* and
4. *Effect of Awards of Compensation made by the United Nations Administrative Tribunal.*

Although Britain did not offer any argument in connexion with the Court's two Opinions on the problem of admission of new Members to the United Nations,[37] and on 'the International Status of South-West Africa',[38] these questions also involved matters of interest to Britain.

There is not space to deal here with the advisory jurisdiction of the Court except to note that in the *Injuries* case,[39] in the first phase of the *Peace Treaties* case, and in the case concerning the awards of the *United Nations Administrative Tribunal*, the Court's Opinions accorded closely with the views of Great Britain; but in the second phase of the *Peace Treaties* case, and in the case of the *Reservations to the Genocide Convention*, the Court's Opinions differed considerably from the views advanced by Britain.[40]

The results of the contentious cases in which Britain has been involved before the International Court of Justice will now be summarized very briefly.

---

[37] See above, pp. 223-24 and *ICS Reports, 1950*, p. 4.

[38] See above, p. 363.

[39] In which the Court was of the opinion, *inter alia*, that the United Nations was an international person, capable of possessing international rights and duties, and with the capacity to maintain its rights by bringing international claims (*ICJ Reports, 1949*, p. 179).

[40] Britain shares the view of many other countries that the Court's opinions, though not 'binding' in the strict sense, are nevertheless 'authoritative' statements upon the legal questions involved.

The Corfu Channel Case (1949):[41] This was brought by Britain against Albania after an explosion of mines in the Corfu Channel which caused the loss of many lives and severe damage to two British warships. Britain was successful in all three phases,[42] i.e. (*a*) Jurisdiction, (*b*) Merits, and (*c*) Assessment of Compensation; but the damages awarded (£ 843, 947) have not yet been paid by Albania.

The Case of the Monetary Gold removed from Rome in 1943 (1954):[43] This case, which was brought by Italy against France, Britain, and the United States, arose partly out of an attempt by Britain to enforce against Albania the hitherto unfulfilled judgment given by the Court in the *Corfu Channel Case*.[44] The Court rejected a British plea that the Italian application was invalid. It also found that it had no jurisdiction, although Britain contended that it had.

The Anglo-Norwegian Fisheries Case (1951):[45] Here the decision went against Britain in that the Court upheld by ten votes to two the validity of a Norwegian decree of 12 July 1935, delimiting Norway's zone of exclusive fisheries off her northern coasts and considerably extending the limit of the territorial sea to which Norway was entitled.

---

[41] The Court's jurisdiction was based essentially upon an expression of consent by Albania which Albania later tried unsuccessfully to withdraw. For details of the incident and its reference by the Security Council to the Court see J. Mervyn-Jones, 'The *Corfu Channel* Case: Merits', in *BYIL, 1949*, pp. 447-53; also RIIA, *Survey, 1947-8*, pp. 222-23.

[42] Although the Court declared that the action of British warships in entering Albanian territorial waters after the explosions for the purpose of sweeping the area clear of mines and of collecting evidence of the origins of the mines 'constituted a violation of Albanian sovereignty'.

[43] See D. H. N. Johnson, 'The Case of the Monetary Gold Removed from Rome in 1943', *ICLQ*, Jan. 1955, pp. 93-115.

[44] In the realization that Albania's compliance with the judgment in the *Corfu Channel Case* could not be secured by recourse to the Security Council under Art. 94(2).

[45] See C. H. M. Waldock, 'The Anglo-Norwegian Fisheries Case', in *BYIL, 1951*, pp. 114-71; also R. O. Wilberforce, 'Some Aspects of the Anglo-Norwegian Fisheries Case', in *Transactions of the Grotius Society, 1952*. This case was brought by Britain under the Optional Clause.

The Anglo-Iranian Oil Company Case (1951-2):[46] Britain was successful in obtaining from the Court an Order for the Indication of Interim Measures of Protection. The Iranian authorities denied the validity of the Order, however, and took no notice of it. Subsequently the Court found that it lacked jurisdiction in the matter of substance and therefore the Order of Interim Measures lapsed.

The Minquiers and Ecrehos Case (1953):[47] This concerned two groups of islets, mostly uninhabited, between Jersey and the French coast, sovereignty over which was in dispute. The case was referred to the Court by agreement between Britain and France. The Court found that both groups of islets belonged to Britain.

The Ambatielos Case (1952-3): In the first phase of this case, brought by Greece on behalf of a Greek shipowner alleged to have been 'denied justice' in the courts of Great Britain, the Court found that it lacked jurisdiction to determine the Greek claim itself, but that it possessed jurisdiction[48] to determine the question whether Britain was obliged to submit to arbitration in respect of the claim. In the second phase the Court found that Britain was indeed obliged to submit the claim to arbitration.[49]

In addition to the cases mentioned above, Britain has stated her willingness to refer certain other disputes to the International Court if the other party would agree, notably the dispute with Guatemala over British Honduras, the dispute with Argentina and Chile over the Falkland Islands Dependencies, and the dispute with Iceland over fishery limits. However, agreement has not been

---

[46] This case was brought by Britain under the Optional Clause. For further details see above, pp. 105-7.

[47] Johnson, 'The Minquiers and Ecrehos Case', *ICLQ*, Apr. 1954, pp. 186-216.

[48] In virtue of Art. 29 of an Anglo-Greek Treaty of Commerce and Navigation of 16 July 1926 (see *ICJ Reports, 1952*, p. 46).

[49] See ibid. *1953*, p. 10; also *Agreement regarding the Submission to Arbitration of the Ambatielos Claim*, Cmd. 9425, Apr. 1955.

forthcoming on the necessary terms of reference and so the disputes have not yet, in fact, come before the Court.[50]

The number of cases in which Britain has been involved before the present International Court is significant, though by no means spectacular. The main reasons for reference to the Court in each case are almost certainly to be found not in any doctrinal predilection for judicial procedures as such but rather in considerations of practical statesmanship. The *Corfu Channel* dispute was initially brought by Britain before the Security Council. It was only because the Security Council was unable to reach a conclusion (owing to a Soviet veto) that the dispute was then referred to the International Court upon the Security Council's recommendation. So far as the *Anglo-Norwegian Fisheries* and *Minquiers and Ecrehos* cases were concerned, not only were these disputes eminently suitable for judicial settlement in themselves, but also the friendly relations between the parties made reference to the Security Council almost unthinkable. In the *Ambatielos Case* Britain was the defendant and had no option but to appear before the Court. In the case of the *Monetary Gold removed from Rome in 1943*, Britain was nominally a defendant but herself took (along with the United States and France) the initial step which rendered possible reference of the question to the Court. It was, in fact, an adroit attempt to secure the damages awarded to Britain in the *Corfu Channel Case* out of some gold otherwise possibly due to Albania. In the dispute with Iran over the *Anglo-Iranian Oil Company*, although it was obvious from the start that the question of the Court's jurisdiction was doubtful, the chances that the Security Council would be both willing and able to uphold the Company's rights

---

[50] Although on 4 May 1955 Britain filed applications instituting proceedings against both Chile and Argentina on the grounds that their pretensions to sovereignty over parts of the Falkland Islands Dependencies were illegal and invalid, the two defendants refused to accept the jurisdiction of the Court, with the result that the Court was unable to take cognizance of the disputes.

must have seemed even more slender, while, for reasons already recounted,[51] direct intervention was ruled out.

Britain has clearly not been mistaken in treating the International Court of Justice as a useful piece of machinery for the settlement of international disputes, especially those in which the parties are in disagreement, either in part or in whole, as to their respective legal rights. Yet it is equally clear that in the present state of international society the potentialities of judicial settlement are strictly limited. There are at present only thirty-two[52] states which are parties to the 'optional clause'. It is to be hoped that this number will increase, but there is no evidence whatsoever to suggest that even the present signatories are willing further to extend the Court's compulsory jurisdiction. Their reluctance is not without good reason. The International Court must, of its nature, base its decisions on existing legal relationships. But the most serious international disputes arise out of conflicting political interests and ambitions, in which one of the parties is usually intent on having the existing legal order changed, not on preserving it. Nor can this particular difficulty be met by giving the International Court (or an arbitral or 'equity' tribunal) discretion to decide *ex aequo et bono*, that is, the power to abrogate or modify existing legal rights in favour of what is thought to be 'fair and just'. For this would in effect be to give it the power to legislate, to come to a political rather than to a judicial decision. The fact is that

> The dissatisfaction of a state with the *status quo* raises a question which is not a judicial one, and cannot be turned into a judicial question by adopting judicial methods of procedure; it raises a question which is essentially *political*, susceptible of amicable settlement no doubt, but only by appropriate *political* methods, by negotiation, by compromise, by mediation, or conciliation.[53]

In other words, in the absence of an international legislature,

---

51 See above, pp. 108-9.
52 Many with far-reaching reservations; see *ICJ Yearbook, 1954-5*, pp. 187-200.
53 Brierly, *Law of Nations*, 5th ed., p. 292.

that is, of a world government, the adjustment of shifting power relationships without bloodshed and in such a way as to remedy rather than to aggravate existing injustices is a task for the diplomats and statesmen, not for the lawyers.

Experience of the last twenty-five years has made it abundantly clear that the unruly forces of international life cannot be curbed merely by the enunciation of legal rules and restraints and that legal relationships are conditioned more by the facts of power than by the promptings of morality or of justice. Within the Atlantic Community, and especially within Western Europe, the domain of international law may steadily grow. Between the main Power blocs its role is bound to be limited so long as present mistrust and suspicion persist. Indeed, until at least a modicum of 'good faith' can be counted upon, the West cannot disregard the possibility that its signature of a treaty may be used primarily as a propaganda weapon against it. It is nevertheless the case that in much of the non-Communist world there is far too little recognition of the virtues of international law, of the benefits to be derived from the regular and systematic application of known legal rules and principles, or of the impropriety of brushing aside legal restraints not because they have become manifestly 'unjust' but merely because they have become something of an embarrassment. Nor is it sufficiently recognized that to weaken international law is to weaken an important check on 'self-help' by the more powerful members of international society. Misuse or disregard of international law by the smaller Powers may undermine a present source of protection. The remedies for this regrettable disrespect for international law lie, however, not in the extension of the compulsory jurisdiction of the International Court or in setting up 'equity' tribunals, but rather in the recognition by states of the need for 'good faith' and self-discipline in their dealings one with another. In short, the outlook for international law turns more on the attitudes of statesmen and the peoples they represent than on the activities of the judicial organs of the United Nations.

chapter sixteen

The United Nations Secretariat

In an institution like the United Nations the main difficulties arise not from any shortcomings on the part of the Secretariat but from the conflicting policies of Member States and from their inability to reconcile these policies. Nevertheless, a Secretariat which through its obvious impartiality, good political sense, and administrative competence, can win the confidence of Member States can often do a great deal to ease negotiations and to encourage latent possibilities of agreement, especially on those matters which do not impinge directly on problems of national security. This is recognized in the Charter, where the Secretariat is designated one of the 'principal organs' of the United Nations.[1] The Charter also recognizes that to enjoy the confidence of Member States the Secretariat must, like the League of Nations' Secretariat, be truly

---

[1] Art. 7, para. 1.

international in character. Article 100 states that 'the Secretary-General and the staff shall not seek or receive instructions from any government or from any other authority external to the Organization' and that they 'shall refrain from any action which might reflect on their position as international officials responsible only to the Organization'. The same article lays on each Member State the obligation to 'respect the exclusively international character of the responsibilities of the Secretary-General and the staff and not to seek to influence them in the discharge of their responsibilities'. Thus, instead of being national representatives responsible to their governments, members of the Secretariat are under an obligation to submerge their national loyalties in a wider international loyalty; and Member States are under an obligation to respect their efforts to do so.

This 'international loyalty' is not easy to define. The Preparatory Commission thought of it as a 'sense of loyalty to the United Nations and devotion to the ideal for which it stands'.[2] It has also been well described by Mr C.W. Jenks (now Assistant Director-General of the ILO) as a breadth of international outlook which is 'something quite different from the attitude ridiculed by Canning as that of "a friend of every country but his own"'.

> The international outlook required of the international civil servant is an awareness made instinctive by habit of the needs, emotions, and prejudices of the peoples of differently-circumstanced countries, as they are felt and expressed by the peoples concerned, accompanied by a capacity for weighing these . . . elements in a judicial manner before reaching any decision to which they are relevant.[3]

---

[2] *Report of the Preparatory Commission of the United Nations*, PC/20, 23 Dec. 1945, p. 85. The Commission went on to claim: 'Loyalty to the Organization is in no way incompatible with an official's attachment to his own country, whose higher interest he is serving in serving the United Nations.'

[3] C. W. Jenks, 'Some Problems of an International Civil Service', *Public Administration Review*, vol. 3, no. 2, 1943, p. 95; quoted in RIIA, *International Secretariat of the Future*, pp. 18-19.

That members of the Secretariat should not act as representatives of their countries or be a prey to narrow national interests and prejudices does not mean, however, that they should sever all links with their countries or rigidly avoid any contact with their national delegations. On the contrary, it can be a great help if a member of the Secretariat can

> bring some special knowledge, not possessed by his colleagues of other nationalities, of the main factors in the policy of his country, e. g. as to where that policy is likely to be elastic, and where rigid, in what directions concession is most possible or least possible.[4]

But it does debar them from advocating (or intriguing in favour of) a policy merely because it is the policy of the government of their country and it does require them to recognize the exclusive authority of the Secretary-General. And a necessary corollary of demanding this international loyalty from an international official is that he should not be subjected to pressure by his own country or 'penalized if his duties involve an attitude which is contrary to the policy of his own country on a particular issue'.[5]

In spite of subtle, and even open, sabotage by a number of totalitarian Member States, the League of Nations Secretariat and the International Labour Office have shown that the concept of international loyalty is a practicable one. There are bound to be individual backslidings, while even the most conscientious may at times find it difficult to resolve the tension between their national ties and their international loyalty[6] and to accustom themselves to ways of working and habits of mind that may be alien to them. But the

---

[4] Sir Arthur Salter, *The United States of Europe and Other Papers* (London, Allen & Unwin, 1933), p. 130.

[5] RIIA, *International Secretariat of the Future*, p. 20.

[6] Officials temporarily seconded from a national civil service or those on fixed-term appointments may find it particularly difficult to adopt an international loyalty for the limited period of their service with the United Nations.

inter-war experiment[7] showed that an international loyalty can be fairly rapidly developed amongst the general run of international officials and that an international administration based on international loyalty can be highly efficient.[8] Unfortunately so far, the United Nations Secretariat has, for the most part, not quite matched the high standards set by the League Secretariat. Indeed, in 1949 it was said that 'the homes of international organizations give the impression of centres of disillusion and frustration rather than of the hope and confidence which should be found there'.[9] Some of the specialized agencies could be exempted from this criticism, as could those departments of the United Nations Secretariat the work of which was not constantly stultified by political divisions, but for the earlier part of the first decade of its existence it was very true of much of the work of the United Nations Secretariat.

Obviously, one of the main reasons for this was the very difficult political climate in which the United Nations has had to operate. Another was the intrusion of 'witch-hunting'. Both of these originated outside the Secretariat; but some of the early shortcomings of the Secretariat were due to inadequate administrative leadership and to the fact that whereas Sir Eric Drummond's initial policy was *festina lente*, Mr Lie's was *carpe diem*. From the start there has, of course, been a hard core of persons of real ability and with the necessary tenacity of purpose; but far too many of those recruited in the stampede to join in 1946[10] were inexperienced and of indifferent quality. The general unwillingness to draw on the abundant experience of the League and the fact that the internal organization of

---

[7] Previous to the insistence of the first Secretary-General of the League (Sir Eric Drummond) on an international loyalty, the principle of national loyalty had been accepted almost without question.

[8] For a valuable study of the League Secretariat see Egon F. Ranshofen-Wertheimer, *The International Secretariat* (Washington, Carnegie Endowment for International Peace, 1945).

[9] 'U.N. and the Agencies: I. Staffing Problems', *Planning*, 23 May 1949, p. 304.

[10] About 350 officials moved from London to Hunter College, New York in April 1946. Six months later the total in New York was nearer 3,000.

the Secretariat was fashioned in the tradition of Washington rather than on truly international lines also added to the confusion and aggravated the tendency to over-expansion, over-grading, and over-staffing. The difficulties at this time were immense and much of the responsibility for the unhappy start rests on Member Governments, who were either busy thrusting often quite unwarranted responsibilities on to the Secretariat or, as in the case of Britain, were reluctant to release first-class people because of the dire need for them at home. Nevertheless, stronger leadership at the top (especially at the Assistant Secretary-General level) might have helped to avoid the worst pitfalls and to have curbed the rampant 'empire-building' in many parts of the Secretariat. These early failings were to take several years to remedy, but it is to be remarked that in 1952 the special Selection Committee, under the chairmanship of Mr. F. P. Walters, former Deputy Secretary-General of the League of Nations, was able to report favourably on the vast majority of staff members interviewed.[11]

THE ROLE OF THE SECRETARIAT

The Secretariat's main task is to serve the other organs of the United Nations, to prepare their meetings, to compile, translate, reproduce, and distribute documents, to interpret speeches, to write up and preserve records, to communicate to governments the decisions of the United Nations bodies, and, where required, to carry them out. The energies of the vast majority of members of the Secretariat are devoted to this task and to the running of the Secretariat's internal organization. On the whole the former job has been tackled efficiently and fairly economically[12] despite

---

[11] A/2364, Annex II.

[12] Apart from the excessive volume of documentation.

the very real difficulties;[13] the latter rather less so. But the senior officials are also expected to play a part in policy-making that would be thought highly improper in, say, the British civil service.

> An international administration has to exercise a special judgement and responsibility in circumstances in which a national administration would turn to its minister. The head of an international administration has . . . to take decisions which in a national administration would be called political.[14]

There are four main reasons why this should be so. In the first place, the Secretariat may often be required to interpret a resolution in order to give it greater precision; in doing so it may, in effect, be making policy. Or it may have to exercise the gentle art of persuasion in order to combat inertia or hesitancy in the execution of a recommendation. Neither of these roles would be looked upon kindly in the British civil service. In the second place, since the intergovernmental policy-making bodies meet infrequently, day-to-day ministerial guidance is lacking and the Secretariat provides the main element of continuity in the Organization. It may occasionally have to take decisions, therefore, which British officials would in the normal course of events refer to ministers. In the third place, 'in national governments the legislature and judiciary act as guardians of the constitution; internationally, this task may frequently fall to the Secretariat'.[15] In face of Member Governments' readiness to deflect the corporate purpose for the sake of national or domestic interests, the Secretary-General and his staff have a clear duty

---

13 Not the least of which was the frequent moves: from London to Hunter College, New York, in 1945; to Lake Success in 1946; to Paris for the third session of the Assembly in 1948; and to the present site on the East River in 1951. The atmosphere of New York is also apt to be unsettling and contrasts rather unfavourably with the calm and privacy (though tinged with provincialism) of Geneva.

14 E. J. Phelan, 'The New International Civil Service', *Foreign Affairs*, Jan. 1933, p. 12; quoted in RIIA, *International Secretariat of the Future*, p. 26.

15 'U.N. and the Agencies: II. The Secretariat's Role', *Planning*, 2 Jan. 1950, p. 167.

to remind Members of their obligations under the Charter and
to do their utmost to enhance the effectiveness and standing of the
Organization. In pursuit of this responsibility which is peculiar
to an international civil service, the Secretariat may from time to
time incur the wrath of Member Governments. So long as the
responsibility is exercised with impartiality and a sense of political
reality, this risk has to be run. In the fourth place, even at the conference table itself the Secretariat may play an influential role. Not
a few of the delegates may be inexperienced, may have had no
instructions, or may be unfamiliar with the subject under discussion.
They may turn to the Secretariat for advice, even for help in the
drafting of their speeches; perhaps a 'friendly' delegation may
be persuaded to put forward one of the Secretariat's own proposals.
A skilfully prepared Secretariat report or working paper may set
off delegates' thoughts in a direction from which it may be difficult
to recall them. And when, as at the United Nations, it is a question
of mobilizing the necessary majority rather than of securing the
unanimous consent of delegates, the Secretariat's influence can
be all the greater.

In the early months of the United Nations some members of
the Secretariat were inclined to take far too exalted a view of their
political responsibilities and to indulge in rather amateurish lobbying
which flattered some delegates but greatly irritated most. Ill-judged
lobbying of this kind soon became less common, however, while
the growth of tension between the Soviet Union and the West
tended strictly to limit the Secretariat's influence in most political
matters. This influence was further diminished by the appointment
by many Member States of permanent delegations to the United
Nations, which provided an element of continuity *in situ* at the
national level. Nevertheless, the Secretariat's political role has
remained by no means negligible, and in several of the so-called
non-political fields, such as technical assistance, the Secretariat
has been entrusted with unusually wide responsibilities which are
likely to expand rather than to contract. In part this is a tribute

to the technical competence and political impartiality that the Secretariat as a whole now possesses, but it is also indicative of the active political role played by both Mr Trygve Lie and his successor, Mr Dag Hammarskjöld.

THE SECRETARY-GENERAL

The role and standing of the Secretariat naturally depend very considerably not only upon the administrative leadership of the Secretary-General but also upon his interpretation of the duties of his office in the political field. The Charter places definite political responsibilities on the Secretary-General, for, in addition to designating him as the 'chief administrative officer of the Organization',[16] Article 99 accords him the right to 'bring to the attention of the Security Council any matter which in his opinion may threaten the maintenance of international peace and security'.[17] This still leaves a great deal to the Secretary-General's discretion; but it does not give him *carte blanche* to develop an independent political role. Nevertheless, it encouraged Mr Lie to model himself on the dynamic and overt leadership of M. Albert Thomas, first Director-General of the ILO, rather than on the more discreet approach of Sir Eric Drummond. Thus Mr Lie was an active adherent of the partition scheme for Palestine, sending a special emissary to London to point out to Mr Bevin that a change of British policy could do much to resolve the Palestine conflict.[18] He was influential in the selection of Count Bernadotte as Mediator, and marked his disapproval of the 1949 Assembly resolution on Jerusalem (against

[16] Art. 97. The functions and terms of appointment of the Secretary-General are conveniently set out in the *Preparatory Commission Report*, pp. 86-87.

[17] This right was not granted to the Secretary-General of the League of Nations, who had only the right (under Art. 11 of the Covenant) to call a meeting of the Council when asked to do so by a member. See S. M. Schwebel, 'The Origins and Development of Article 99 of the Charter', in *BYIL, 1951*, p. 371.

[18] Schwebel, *The Secretary-General of the United Nations* (Cambridge, Mass., Harvard University Press, 1952), p. 141.

which he had campaigned) by not including it in his final address among the achievements of the Assembly.[19] The action he took during the Berlin crisis and the criticism it incurred in Britain have already been described.[20] His reluctant acceptance of NATO did not help to stifle this criticism, and in January and June 1950 American opinion was alienated by his frequent reiteration of the view that the Chinese people had a right to be represented by whatever government has the power to 'employ the resources and direct the people of the State'.[21] He later incurred Soviet hostility when, at the beginning of the Security Council's meeting on 25 June 1950, he delivered the opinion that the Council was competent to act and had a 'clear duty' to do so.[22] His subsequent firm support of United Nations action in Korea earned him American and British gratitude, but made him *persona non grata* with the Soviet Union.[23] The most marked initiative he took to end the cold war was his 'Twenty-Year Programme for achieving Peace through the United Nations' and his round of visits to European capitals, including Moscow, in the spring of 1950.[24] His ten-point plan was well conceived and perhaps merited greater attention from the chancelleries than it received, but its timing and method of presentation were not altogether happy.[25]

---

[19] ibid. p. 71.

[20] See above, pp. 238-39.

[21] Schwebel, *The Secretary-General*, p. 145.

[22] ibid. p. 104.

[23] With resulting difficulties when, in 1951, the permanent members sought agreement on Mr Lie's successor (see Art. 97). The Soviet Union refused to agree to his reappointment or extension in office. The Western Powers refused to let Mr Lie appear to suffer for his firm stand over Korea, the United States publicly declaring its willingness to use the veto to block the appointment of any other candidate (*The New York Times*, 26 Oct. 1950). In the event, Mr Lie continued in office until 10 April 1953 when he was succeeded by Mr Dag Hammarskjöld.

[24] For details see *United Nations Bulletin*, 12 June 1950, pp. 509-13.

[25] Mr Acheson was in London to discuss rearmament at the time of Mr Lie's visit. For Mr Lie's own account of his political initiatives, see his *In the Cause of Peace* (New York, Macmillan, 1954).

On the whole the British attitude towards Mr Lie's conception of the post of Secretary-General was not enthusiastic. Britain has rightly been called the 'chief exponent of the primarily administrative interpretation of the Secretary-General's role'.[26] It has preferred 'the tradition which Sir Eric Drummond imported from the British into the international civil service, that civil servants, like children, should be seen but not heard'.[27] Certainly Mr Bevin personally was inclined to turn a deaf ear to most of Mr Lie's proposals and Whitehall was loth to accept his conception of the policy-making role of the Secretariat. It may be that the traditional British view of the latter's role is too narrow; yet there can be little doubt that it would often have been better if Mr Lie had stood up, as it were, in the background. Unlike M. Albert Thomas, who could usually rely on organized labour to back him up,[28] Mr Lie had no great body of organized public opinion within Member countries on which to lean. Yet it is only fair to add that in the state of tension that has existed since 1946 almost any initiative by the Secretary-General was bound to meet with criticism from some quarter. This risk had to be run. The fact that Mr Lie managed to irritate all the permanent members at one time or another may indicate a certain lack of political judgement, but it does not call into question his courage, impartiality, and sincerity. These qualities and his untiring exertions in steering the Organization through very troubled waters contrast very favourably with the dispirited quietism of the second Secretary-General of the League in not very dissimilar circumstances.

Mr Hammarskjöld takes a greater interest in administration than did Mr Lie and on the political side is more content to work behind the scenes. But he, too, has stressed the Secretariat's 'duty

---

26 Schwebel, *The Secretary-General*, p. 169.
27 Clive Parry, 'The Secretariat of the United Nations', *World Affairs*, July 1950, p. 363.
28 Each participating country sends a tripartite delegation to ILO conferences; government, employers, and organized labour are represented separately. Organized labour and the employers usually vote as solid blocs.

to anticipate situations that might lead to new conflicts or points of tension and to make appropriate suggestions to the governments before matters reach a stage of public controversy'.[29] Moreover, his initiative during the ninth Assembly's discussion on the retention by Communist China of American airmen serving with the United Nations forces, his subsequent visit to Peking, and his tour of the Middle East suggest that he expects to play an active role in political matters. That he should so rapidly have gained the confidence of the leading Member Governments—which Mr Lie only rarely enjoyed—is probably mainly due to his sound political judgement, to his belief in 'quiet diplomacy', and to his view of the Secretariat's relationship to governments as that of a 'trusted consultant' rather than, as Mr Lie sometimes seemed to suggest, of an actor trying to steal the lead.

PERSONNEL PROBLEMS

Some of the chief criticisms of the Secretariat have been lack of unity, over-staffing, inefficiency, and poor morale. As has been seen, many of these acknowledged shortcomings arose from the way in which the organization was initiated and have been or are being put right. In many cases they also arose from the lack of close co-ordination of programmes of work and of a strict assessment of priorities, especially in the economic and social field. Although delegates were mainly to blame for the fact that in the early years almost every meeting produced a crop of fatuous proposals, the Secretariat exercised little restraint and even initiated some of the proposals themselves. While the concealed (but usually discernible) guidance given by the Secretariat both before and during meetings can be, and often has been, most helpful, any tendency for it to become an exercise in sectional rivalries and competitive 'empire-building' is wholly deplorable; but this it frequently became. Happily matters were improving before Mr Lie

[29] U.N. Press Release, S9/336, 14 Sept. 1953.

relinquished office, and Mr Hammarskjöld has already shown himself well aware that the Secretariat has a major responsibility for helping to avoid dispersion of effort.[30] He has also achieved welcome economies in its internal administration while at the same time progressing towards the goal of a carefully recruited and more versatile and flexible career Secretariat.

One persistent difficulty that may militate against increased efficiency is the demand of many delegates for recruitment and promotion on a wider geographical basis. Under Article 101, para. 3 of the Charter, staff must be recruited not only so as to secure the 'highest standards of efficiency, competence and integrity', but also with due regard to recruitment on 'as wide a geographical basis as possible'. The problem of reconciling the two is a familiar one to most international bodies. In the United Nations the percentage contributions of Member States is taken as a rough guide to the proportion of staff to be drawn from each country, although a 25 per cent. deviation either way has usually been accepted in order to provide some choice between candidates on grounds of qualifications or specialized knowledge.[31] It is sometimes argued that geographical distribution should not be allowed to weigh against efficiency at all since it may result in a higher proportion of 'passengers' in the Secretariat, whose chief claim to their posts is their nationality. The creation of sinecures for the nationals of a particular country or the promotion of officials of inferior calibre mainly to obtain a more acceptable geographical distribution of the more senior appointments is certainly not unknown; and it is almost bound to affect adversely the Secretariat's efficiency and to have a chastening effect on its morale. Yet in the long run geographical distribution and efficiency are not necessarily incompatible.

Wide distribution enriches a Secretariat from the particular experience and culture which each member State can furnish.

---

[30] See especially his *Annual Report, 1 July 1953-30 June 1954* (*GAOR*, 9th sess., suppl. No. 1 (A/2663), p. xv, and E/2598, 13 May 1954).
[31] A large proportion of the junior staffs is excluded from the field to which the principle of geographical distribution applies.

Much of the more specialised work of a Secretariat may call
for a close and intimate knowledge of conditions of some part
of the world, which may only be possessed by nationals of
certain countries. Wide geographical distribution may also
help to strengthen the smaller Powers' sense of participation,
and may prevent dissatisfaction among delegations which
might otherwise find few familiar faces at the organisation's
headquarters.[32]

Some concession to national feeling among delegates may in the
long run result in more gain than loss, therefore. The need is to
strike a balance between technical efficiency in the strict sense and
the undoubted advantages which accrue from as wide a geographical representation as possible. In January 1953 Mr Lie claimed
that 'geographical distribution as envisaged by the Charter had
in the main been successfully accomplished';[33] but the recent admission of sixteen Members into the United Nations and the Fifth
Committee's request, in its report of 14 December 1955,[34] that the
Secretary-General submit a report to the General Assembly at its
eleventh session on the 'changes in geographical distribution'
suggest that the last has not been heard of this problem.

    Morale depends first and foremost, however, on the conviction
that a job is worth doing.[35] It is not surprising that the secondary
role forced on the United Nations in so many fields of activity
should have bred a sense of frustration, even amongst the many
competent and loyal members of the Secretariat. To this was added
in the early years of the Organization a feeling of resentment at
the inadequacy of administrative leadership and at the number
of 'passengers' receiving generous salaries. In addition, a fair
number of those who originally joined consisted of naïve idealists
who were soon disillusioned, or of the *déraciné* who often lacked

---

[32] *Planning*, 23 May 1949, p. 308.

[33] A/2364, p. 5.

[34] A/3103, p. 7.

[35] If only for this reason the level of morale is apt to vary a great deal from
one part of the Secretariat to another.

any real sense of purpose. Nevertheless, from about 1950, if not earlier, there was a very distinct improvement as the 'passengers' were weeded out; and morale greatly improved as a result of the vigorous action taken by the United Nations in the Korean War.

Unfortunately, morale then received a serious setback when earlier doubts in Washington about the loyalty of a few American nationals in the Secretariat culminated in the initiation, a day before the sixth Assembly opened (September 1952), by the United States Senate Sub-Committee on Internal Security under the chairmanship of Senator McCarran, of an inquiry to determine whether United States citizens who were United Nations employees had been 'engaged in subversive activities which are clearly beyond the scope of their employment'. With the same purpose a Federal Grand Jury sitting in New York almost simultaneously began to summon American members of the Secretariat for questioning.[36] These were not the first moves in the 'loyalty scare'. In 1950 the Secretary-General terminated the appointment of several members of the Secretariat, some apparently on 'security' grounds. Since they held temporary or fixed-term, and not permanent, contracts he maintained he could do so 'without showing cause'. The Administrative Tribunal[37] thought otherwise, but the fifth General Assembly (1951) amended the Staff Regulations to permit the Secretary-General to terminate the appointment of temporary staff at any time 'if, in his opinion, such action would be in the interest of the United Nations'. These events naturally aroused a feeling of insecurity and disquiet in the Secretariat, particularly since the grounds for dismissal were not divulged and the proportion of permanent contracts at that time was still low.

---

[36] For an authoritative and well-documented study of this aspect of personnel problems see Schwebel, 'The International Character of the Secretariat of the United Nations', in *BYIL, 1953*. See also L. C. Green, 'The Status of the International Civil Service', in *CLP, 1954*, and Lie, *In the Cause of Peace*, pp. 386-405.
[37] Established by the General Assembly in 1949 with competence to hear and pass judgement on applications alleging non-observance of contracts of employment or of the terms of appointment of United Nations staff.

The 1952 investigations were more serious and wider in scope. The refusal of a number of American nationals on the Secretariat to answer questions[38] before the investigating bodies about membership of the American Communist Party or, in some cases, about espionage and subversive activies, occasioned much unfavourable publicity for the Secretariat. Many Americans on the Secretariat who had not been in any way concerned with the questioning also felt that doubt had been cast on their loyalty when, in December, a federal grand jury reported that 'startling evidence has disclosed infiltration into the United Nations of an overwhelmingly large group of disloyal United States citizens', and declared that the situation constituted a 'menace' to the Government of the United States.[39] In fact, those called to testify before the two bodies were only a minute proportion of the American staff of the United Nations. And, as the Secretary-General stated in March 1953,

> not a single United States staff member of the United Nations Secretariat has ever, in the whole history of the Organization, been charged in any court of the United States—much less convicted—of espionage or any act of subversion or sabotage.[40]

The sense of uncertainty was aggravated by the Secretary-General's decision to discharge those on temporary contracts who had refused to testify, and to send those with permanent contracts on compulsory leave whilst he sought advice from a Commission of Jurists[41] as to what further action could properly be taken.

It may be that some of the American nationals who appeared before the investigating bodies were genuine 'security risks'. And

---

[38] They were able to do so by pleading privilege against self-incrimination under the Fifth Amendment to the United States Constitution.

[39] Council on Foreign Relations, *The United States in World Affairs, 1952*, p. 300.

[40] *GAOR*, 7th sess., Plen., 413th mtg., 10 Mar. 1953, p. 537.

[41] Sir Edwin S. Herbert (U.K.), William D. Mitchell (U.S.), and P. Veldekins (Netherlands).

it is understandable that the United States, like any other 'host' country, should wish to safeguard itself against subversion or espionage. But it is also essential that the international independence of the Secretariat (as provided for in Article 100 of the Charter) should be maintained and that no attempt should be made by Member Governments to deprive the Secretary-General either of his responsibility for appointments to, and dismissals from, his staff or of his responsibilities generally as the 'chief administrative officer of the Organization'.[42] The opinion[43] of the Commission of Jurists was severely criticized in Britain as elsewhere for not giving sufficient weight to these considerations.[44] So, to a lesser extent, was the decision of the Secretary-General (Mr Lie) to base his personnel policy on the Commission's recommendations[45] and to terminate the employment of those on compulsory leave.[46]

As a result of this criticism the Secretary-General submitted a report on personnel policy[47] to the second part of the Assembly's seventh session. The majority of delegates were disposed to postpone judgement until the new Secretary-General (Mr Hammarskjöld) had taken office[48] and the Administrative Tribunal had made known its findings. But the Jurists' statement that membership in the Secretariat 'in no way abrogates, limits or qualifies the loyalty a person owes to the State of which he is a citizen' came under heavy fire, since it was in flat contradiction to Article 100 and to the oath that members of the Secretariat take on assuming

---

[42] Art. 97.

[43] A/2364, Annex III, pp. 21-33.

[44] See, for instance, H. A. Rolin, *Advisory Opinion on the Rights and Obligations of International Civil Servants*, prepared for the Federation of International Civil Servants Associations, p. 19.

[45] Subject, however, to a number of important reservations.

[46] After they had refused to withdraw their plea of privilege. Those dismissed immediately appealed to the Administrative Tribunal.

[47] A/2364, 30 Jan. 1953.

[48] Mr Lie's resignation had been announced on 10 November 1952.

office.[49] There was also little support for the Jurists' view, accepted
in principle by the then Secretary-General (Mr Lie), that a plea
of privilege in an official inquiry on subversive activities[50] or
membership of the Communist Party should automatically constitute sufficient grounds for the dismissal of permanent staff.

It was, therefore, with considerable relief that the Secretariat
learnt in August 1953 that the Administrative Tribunal had found
in favour of those holding permanent appointments and had
awarded them compensation in lieu of reinstatement. Britain argued
at the eighth Assembly that the Tribunal had acted within its
competence and that the Assembly was under an obligation to
give immediate effect to the Tribunal's awards. However, in face
of strong opposition from the United States to such a course,
Britain then proposed, and after a long debate the Assembly agreed,
that an Advisory Opinion should be sought from the International
Court on whether the Assembly had the right to refuse to give
effect to the Tribunal's award.[51] The Court by a majority advised
that the Assembly had no such right.[52] At the ninth Assembly
(1954) the United States continued to disapprove of the Tribunal's
awards but reluctantly accepted the Court's opinion. A special
fund was constituted out of which the awards could immediately
be paid and it was agreed, in principle, that in future the Tribunal's

----

[49] 'I solemnly swear (undertake, affirm, promise) to exercise in all loyalty,
discretion and conscience the functions entrusted to me as an international
civil servant of the United Nations, to discharge these functions and regulate
my conduct with the interests of the United Nations only in view, and not to
seek or accept instructions in regard to the performance of my duties from any
government or other authority external to the organisation' (*U.N. Secretariat
Staff Rules*, 1955, Chapter I, Regulation 19, p. 6). For the United Kingdom's
comments see *GAOR*, 7th sess., Plen., 421st mtg., 1 Apr. 1953, p. 651.

[50] Unlike the Jurists, the Secretary-General took care to define subversive
activities and to pledge that he would only act upon the basis of 'tangible and
convincing evidence'. The Jurists had cited 'activities regarded as subversive
by the host country'.

[51] *GAOR*, 8th sess., suppl. no. 17, Resolution 194(VIII), 9 Dec. 1953.

[52] Advisory Opinion of 13 July 1954, *ICJ Reports, 1954*, p. 47; also 'Written
Statement of the Government of the United Kingdom', *ICJ Pleadings, United
Nations Administrative Tribunal*, pp. 122-30.

judgements should be subject to judicial review. A Special Committee on Review of Administrative Tribunal Judgements was set up to consider the proper method of review.[53] This Committee reported[54] to the tenth session of the General Assembly, which amended the statute of the United Nations Administrative Tribunal to the effect that objections to judgements by the Tribunal can now be submitted to a committee, which shall, if it decides there is a substantial basis for the objection, request an Advisory Opinion from the International Court of Justice. If no such request is made, the Tribunal's judgement shall be final. Otherwise the 'Secretary-General shall either give effect to the opinion of the Court, or request the Tribunal to convene specially in order that it shall confirm its original judgement, or give a new judgement, in conformity with the opinion of the Court'.[55] On the whole this would seem to be a fairly satisfactory solution to a very delicate question. Following the findings of the Administrative Tribunal, the Secretary-General also submitted to the eighth Assembly (1953) proposals[56] designed to clarify his power to dismiss permanent staff in cases of lack of integrity or improper political activities.[57] His proposals were accepted, subject to later review and to some minor amendments designed to define his powers as precisely as possible so as to safeguard the interests of staff members.[58]

It is difficult to avoid the conclusion that the United Nations Secretariat has had to bear the brunt of a good deal both of general American dissatisfaction with the way that the United Nations

---

[53] *GAOR*, 9th sess., suppl. no. 21, Resolution 888(IX), 17 Dec. 1954.

[54] ibid. 10th sess., Annexes, agenda item 49, A/2909, 10 June 1955.

[55] ibid. suppl. no. 19, Resolution 957(X), 8 Nov. 1955.

[56] A/2533, 2 Nov. 1953.

[57] 'Passive' party membership would be allowed and the Secretary-General was at pains to stress that a plea of privilege would not automatically lead to dismissal if, upon investigation, an explanation could be given which removed the unfavourable implications of the plea.

[58] See A/2615 for summary of Fifth Committee discussion and text of amended Regulations.

has been working and of American hysteria about Communist subversion. Perhaps in Britain people have been unduly reluctant to admit that some of those who pleaded privilege were probably not as disinterested in their loyalty to the United Nations as they should have been. Nor is the United States the only 'host' Government to reserve the right to safeguard its national security,[59] or to submit information to the Secretary-General on applicants for employment or on members of the staff, which in practice, if not in form, threatens to interfere with the discretion of the Secretary-General under Article 100.[60] Yet the activities of the investigating bodies before which American members of the Secretariat were summoned were not of such a nature as to inspire confidence, while the volume of support for the McCarran Bill (though it did not become law)[61] was alarming, since it would clearly have violated the United States' obligations under Article 100 of the Charter by making it a crime for an American to take a position on the Secretariat without a certificate of political 'loyalty' from the Attorney General.[62] It is, of course, generally desirable that the majority of such 'officials as are nationals of a particular state should be acceptable to that state';[63] but to claim that all officials should invariably be *persona grata* to the states of which they are the nationals is not only to give those states a virtual veto over their appointment but also gravely to jeopardize the position of those loyal and efficient members of the Secretariat who do not happen to enjoy the confidence of the present régimes in their countries.

[59] See Schwebel in *BYIL, 1953*, pp. 105 f.

[60] ibid. p. 83, n. 3. It should also be noted that the Soviet Union has virtually appointed the Assistant Secretary-Generals for Political and Security Affairs whilst most of the other eight Assistant Secretary-Generals were nominees of their respective governments.

[61] See *BYIL, 1953*, pp. 102-3.

[62] See F. R. Scott, 'The World's Civil Service'. *International Conciliation*, Jan. 1954, p. 288.

[63] Clive Parry, 'The International Civil Servant', *The Listener*, 18 Aug. 1955, p. 245.

The campaign carried on against the Secretariat was perhaps the inevitable price of locating the Headquarters of an organization which purports to transcend the ideological and power conflict in the territory of one of the two main contestants in that conflict. But it naturally tended to produce the unfortunate impression in Britain and elsewhere that the United Nations was regarded by much of American opinion as having some special obligation to conform to specifically American standards of 'loyalty' which completely disregarded the prior loyalty of the staff to the United Nations. With the weeding out of those who have pleaded the Fifth Amendment to the American Constitution, the eclipse of McCarthyism, and the growth of confidence between the Secretary-General and his staff on the one hand, and Member Governments on the other, this unhappy chapter in personnel problems at the United Nations may be nearing its end.[64] But the damage done will take some time to heal.

ORGANIZATION OF THE SECRETARIAT

The administrative structure of the Secretariat[65] was laid down by the first session of the General Assembly in 1946 on the basis of recommendations by the Preparatory Commission. These were to the effect that the Secretariat should be organized on a functional basis in eight departments, each under an Assistant Secretary-General. This structure[66] had the merit of organizing the Secretariat according to the work performed by each part, whilst to some extent linking the substantive departments with the appropriate inter-governmental organs of the United Nations. It also secured a wide geographical distribution and a place for the permanent

---

[64] Though some of the specialized agencies, for instance UNESCO, may continue to be troubled by them.

[65] And also its conditions of service.

[66] For details see *Preparatory Commission Report*, pp. 87-90 and A/41.

members' nominees at the most senior level. In practice, however, it proved excessively cumbersome and an encouragement to the centrifugal forces within the Secretariat. Each substantive department tended to become too specialized and self-contained and to insist on the final say in matters of recruitment and promotion, so aggravating the tendency to 'empire-building' and overgrading. Dispersion of effort and work of indifferent quality by highly-paid staff was particularly characteristic of the Economic and the Social Affairs Departments. Unfortunately, these departments served the Economic and Social Council, one of whose main tasks was to co-ordinate the activities of the specialized agencies; the inability of the Council to co-ordinate its own activities in these early years naturally reduced its influence with the specialized agencies. Nor did the signs of confusion in personnel matters encourage the specialized agencies to model their own practices on those of the United Nations.

As organizational weaknesses became apparent[67] a number of suggestions for reform were made which culminated in two reports by the second Secretary-General to the eighth and ninth Assemblies.[68] Mr Hammarskjöld's proposals were aimed at securing greater economy and flexibility in the use of staff. They were, firstly, to merge in a single unified department the two former Departments of Economic Affairs and Social Affairs; and, secondly, to bring more closely under his personal control budgetary, personnel, and legal affairs. At the ninth Assembly these proposals were welcomed by nearly all delegates, who were impressed by the very considerable saving they could effect, by the prospects of greater concentration in economic and social matters, and by the evident intention of the

---

[67] Especially the dissipation and duplication of effort in the economic and social field.

[68] A/2554 of 12 Nov. 1953 and A/2731 of 21 Sept. 1954. See also E/2598, *Review by the Secretary-General of the Organization and Work of the Secretariat in the Economic and Social Field*, 13 May 1954, and *Second Report of the Advisory Committee on Administrative and Budgetary Questions, GAOR*, 9th sess., suppl. no. 7. (A/2688), 27 July 1954, pp. 3-8.

Secretary-General to take a firmer grip on personnel policy and to make more use of the budget as a management device. The United Kingdom delegate voiced doubts, however, which were shared by many other delegations, about the decision to retain the Technical Assistance Administration (TAA) as a separate entity,[69] about the continued proliferation of top-level supervisory posts, and about the chain of command at the Under-Secretary level.[70] Some, but not all, of these misgivings were removed by the Secretary-General's assurance that modifications would be made in the light of experience. At the tenth session the Secretary-General submitted further proposals intended to devolve some of the social affairs work of the Secretariat on to the regional commissions and similarly to decentralize some of the responsibilities of the TAA. These proposals, which are to be initiated on an experimental basis, are to be considered at greater leisure at the eleventh session of the General Assembly.

There are good grounds for hoping that the new organization will secure much needed economies and also increased versatility and flexibility; and since the reduction in posts is to be brought about by the normal turnover of staff, members do not have to face the demoralizing prospect of dismissal through redundancy. Nevertheless

> The central and essential point is that . . . perfection of machinery can help substantially, but only if as much care is exercised in selecting the proper people to run the machine as is exercised in creating it.[71]

---

[69] Since it would have to co-operate closely with the Department of Economic and Social Affairs and might conveniently, therefore, form part of that Department.

[70] Several of the Under-Secretaries were to have Deputies who were, however, to be of equal status and not subordinate to them. For British criticisms see *GAOR*, 9th sess., 5th Committee, 437th mtg., 12 Oct. 1954. A summary of the discussion is given in the Report of the 5th Committee, ibid. Annexes, agenda item 53, A/2884.

[71] RIIA, *International Secretariat of the Future* (1944), p. 32.

Of paramount importance is 'a hand-picked recruitment[72] . . . [and] a leadership strong enough to create a common discipline and to animate the recruits with a common purpose'.[73] Not only is technical competence essential, but in the more senior posts it needs to be allied to sound political judgement and a genuine sense of vocation. That the Secretariat now has strong leadership and more members possessing these qualities augurs well for the future; what is still needed is closer co-ordination between the United Nations Secretariat and the secretariats of the specialized agencies. So far there has been only spasmodic progress towards the ideal of a single world civil service with easy transfer between agencies, comparable terms of service, similar administrative procedures, and joint staff organs. The difficulties are real, and the possibilities of interchange between agencies are more limited than is commonly realized;[74] but many of the difficulties would disappear were individual agencies less jealous about their autonomous status.

---

[72] The prospective candidate would be greatly assisted if the United Nations and the specialized agencies were to co-ordinate their recruitment procedures more closely, at least for the administrative grades.

[73] W. R. Crocker, 'Some Notes on the United Nations Secretariat', *International Organization*, Nov. 1950, p. 603.

[74] *Planning*, 23 May 1949, p. 319.

CONCLUSIONS

PART SIX

chapter seventeen

British Public Opinion
and the United Nations[1]

Although since 1945 the British public has probably been rather more interested in world affairs than in the past, for most of the period the United Nations has commanded neither the attention nor the fervour associated with the League of Nations, which for the best part of the inter-war period was the centre of an almost unparalleled controversy. Even the tempered optimism that accompanied the creation of the United Nations in 1945 quickly evaporated with the deterioration in Great Power relations. By the end of 1955 the United Nations had come to be little more than a dispassionately acknowledged fact, generally conceded to be a 'good thing', but little more. Consequently, charting the course of British attitudes towards the United Nations is mainly a matter of defining small gradations within a fairly limited range, a range varying from

---

[1] A good deal of the material in this chapter is based on a memorandum submitted to the group by Dr. F. S. Northedge.

sympathetic but often anxious interest at one end, to almost undisguised indifference at the other.

A further difficulty is that the views that the 'man in the street' occasionally voices about the United Nations are apt to be shaped mainly by his outlook on the international situation as a whole and by the part played therein by the two main protagonists in the cold war. In neither case is the United Nations itself the main object of his interest. In addition, in the comparatively small circle of informed and articulate public opinion[2] with which this chapter is chiefly concerned, the United Nations is usually thought of as essentially a form of 'diplomacy by conference', the effectiveness of which depends principally upon the performance of its Members; interest is, therefore, in the policies of those Members rather than in the machinery itself.

The generally rather tepid attitude towards the United Nations for most of the last ten years calls for fuller examination. But a further aim of this chapter is to search out those more fundamental beliefs and presuppositions which are implicit in much of British thinking about the Organization. This is a hazardous undertaking. It is difficult to write with any assurance, or other than in an impressionistic way, of something so elusive as the public mind. Yet even the most insensitive observer could hardly fail to note that those beliefs which were so prevalent in Great Britain in the days of the League have little currency today. The present public temper towards the United Nations can perhaps best be caught, therefore, by comparing it with that of a generation ago towards the League. Not that this will be easy. No inquiry into the deeper springs of human beliefs can be completely detached, particularly when, as in this case, it involves a certain amount of self-analysis. Interpretations as to why this or that belief is prevalent, or which experiences or ideas it may be supposed to reflect, are almost bound

---

[2] Consisting mainly of politicians, active members of political parties, journalists, university people, and members of such voluntary bodies as the United Nations Association.

to have a subjective ring about them. Nor can objectivity be attained or an accurate impression conveyed merely by the use of rigorous statistical methods. Such methods tend to produce rather questionable results where international matters are concerned. A great deal depends upon the way in which the questions in public opinion polls are worded; and if the use of a negative, or perhaps abstract, form of the question as opposed to a positive, or concrete, form is liable to make a substantial difference to the resulting percentages (and it often does), then for the moment at least the statistical or quantitative approach needs to be treated with caution, notwithstanding—or possibly because of—the scientific colour it gives its findings.

Nevertheless, the evidence of such polls as have been taken provides an interesting clue to the existence of an ambivalence in much popular thinking about the United Nations. On the one hand, despite the stresses and strains to which the United Nations has been subjected in the cold war, the majority of people still seem to wish it well and to feel that there is a strong 'social sanction' in favour of the internationalist case. According to a poll conducted by the British Institute of Public Opinion in March 1953, as many as 45 per cent. of those questioned felt that the United Nations had justified its existence as against only 25 per cent. who did not (30 per cent. were uncertain). And although the United Nations Association can no longer command the mass support that the League of Nations Union received, its membership still runs into nearly 60,000. On the other hand, for obvious reasons, dissatisfaction with the actual functioning of the Organization has tended to increase. In March 1946, 49 per cent. of those questioned by the British Institute of Public Opinion were satisfied with the progress of the United Nations as against 20 per cent. who were not; but by February 1953 the percentages were 32 and 39 per cent. respectively.

There is a marked difference between the little publicized findings of contemporary pollsters and the upsurge of enthusiasm which surrounded the 'Peace Ballot' of 1934-5. The polls can, of course, only record, not explain, this difference. Yet they lend some support to one possible explanation, namely, that the United Nations has not evoked the same partisan fervour because there has been little opposition to it and, therefore, fewer converts to be made. For much of the inter-war period the League of Nations was the focus of disagreement over foreign policy and so a major political issue which frequently benefited by a diversion of enthusiasm from other political causes. It was an object not of indifference but rather of either chilly disdain or ardent attachment. There was, indeed, a striking contrast between, on the one hand, the deep-seated scepticism of most ministers and officials towards what seemed to them to be a new-fangled excrescence on traditional forms of international intercourse, and, on the other hand, the crusading zeal of that appreciable and vocal section of the British people for whom the creation of the League marked the beginning of a new epoch in international affairs.[3] The intensity with which people were apt to be *pro* or *con* the League kept it in the limelight; but it had its drawbacks, for it contributed to a split in the British mind which was both novel and disturbing. It was novel because prior to the First World War public opinion usually had a negligible influence on British foreign policy, which remained the prerogative of a political élite. After the First World War no politician could afford to overlook the enthusiasms of the electorate, however ill-informed he might consider it to be. It was disturbing because the gulf between the short-sighted realism of the official mind and the often naïve idealism of the popular mind introduced an ambivalence into much of British thinking about foreign policy which was partly responsible for the fumbling and hesitancy to which it was so prone in the 1930's.

In contrast, up till December 1955 few people have found serious cause to quarrel with the broad lines of official foreign policy;

---

[3] See C. A. W. Manning, 'The "Failure" of the League of Nations', *Agenda*, Jan. 1942, p. 60.

criticism has for the most part been confined to points of detail or emphasis. Consequently, not only has policy tended to be more consistent, but the United Nations itself has rarely approached the area of party contention. It is true that the impotence of the Security Council and the protection the United Nations seems to give to the law-breaker has caused many people, not only on the Right, to view the Organization with a mixture of scepticism and irritation. Nevertheless, the leaders of all three political parties have continued to affirm their support for it; and it is difficult to get excited about something when one's government, whether Labour or Conservative, appears to be as active in its support as circumstances allow.[4] If, therefore, the typical attitude towards the United Nations has been tepid acceptance, it is probably very largely because there is little point in waxing enthusiastic about a proposition, whether the need for the United Nations or for women's suffrage, which has come to be accepted by almost everybody as self-evident. Why it has become self-evident is less easy to explain. Some of the credit should go to those zealous protagonists of international organization who led the League of Nations Union;[5] but the main reasons are doubtless very similar to those which have inspired official policy. There has certainly been a widespread realization that an institution that represents an attempt to curb the law of the jungle in international relations can be of greater benefit than ever to a United Kingdom whose power—relatively speaking—is on the wane. Above all, there has been the general belief that the United Kingdom's failure to fulfil her obligations under the Covenant in 1935 not only made the 'unnecessary war' more certain but denuded her of powerful allies when later her very survival was at stake. Thus when the Korean War came, 'the long drama centred around the League of

---

[4] One section of the right-wing press (especially the *Daily Express* group) has frequently attacked the United Nations, but this campaign has roused little interest.

[5] For example, Viscount (then Lord Robert) Cecil, Dame Kathleen Courtney, Dr Maxwell Garnett, and Dr Gilbert Murray.

Nations, the Peace Ballot and the Munich agreement had so conditioned Ministers and public alike, that a public revolt against supporting the United Nations in its first military test was unthinkable'.[6]

Most of those who have dispassionately accepted the United
Nations as an integral part of contemporary international life have
a very different picture of it, however, from that which dominated
the mind's eye of the typical League enthusiast. One reason for
this change in the public view of the nature of international organization is to be found in the contrasting impact of the two world
wars on the national consciousness. For the League enthusiast
the case *for* the League was basically the case *against* war. The
First World War had been preceded by a long period of peace
(interspersed so far as the United Kingdom was concerned only
by limited wars with little impact on the general public) accompanied
by a general air of optimism and by a belief in the inevitability of
progress (especially as regards the elimination of war). Out of this
sprang four long years of attrition warfare, the shock of which was
often accompanied by sheer incredulity that the traditional diplomatic
methods of the previous era could so easily be replaced almost
overnight by violence, force, and fraud. Yet the catastrophe was
ascribed not so much to the sins of national sovereignty or to the
rapacious nature of man as to a breakdown in the system of international relations. Thus, it was not only upon the hatred and fear
of a recurrence of such catastrophic folly but also upon the belief
that the cause of the breakdown could be removed that the League
was founded;[7] meaning by the League not so much the legal contract
between the Member States or the institutions at Geneva but the
public sentiment which made the League a popular myth, based,
as nearly all the great political mythologies are based, not on
rational calculation but on emotional experience. The repugnance

---

[6] Kenneth Younger, 'Public Opinion and Foreign Policy', *British Journal of
Sociology*, June 1955, p. 171.

[7] See, for instance, Viscount Cecil, *All The Way* (London, Hodder & Stoughton,
1949), pp. 124-27.

which so many people in Britain came to feel for everything which
had preceded the League,[8] and, conversely, the emotional attach-
ments they offered up to the League, were, in a sense, debts paid
to the 'doomed, conscripted, unvictorious ones' who had fallen
on the fields of Passchendaele and the Somme. Thus the fervour
with which the League was acclaimed in Britain in the 1920's
reflected the widespread belief that it represented not merely a
more expedient way of doing collectively what could not be done
so well unilaterally or bilaterally but a distinct revolution in world
affairs, a revolution which would substitute for these a kind of
uncontentious meeting of the minds of the democratic peoples of
the world, with diplomatic intrigue set aside. There was a millennial,
a messianic flavour about this vision.

It might also be said that the classical liberal doctrine of the
harmony of interests which was part of the general humane and
rationalist viewpoint of the nineteenth century came to full flower
in the outlook of the typical British supporter of the League. To
describe the League, as Mr R. S. Crossman once did, as an attempt
'to apply the principles of Lockeian liberalism to the building of
a machinery of international order'[9] is perhaps to read into the
minds of League supporters too close an identity of outlook.
Yet much of popular thinking about the League was in truth
impregnated with the belief that most nations, like most men,
were 'naturally' full of goodwill and of the desire to live in peace
with each other; that the rights and wrongs of almost any international issue could fairly readily be elicited by reference to
universally valid *a priori* moral principles; and that open discussion

---

[8] Sir J. W. Headlam Morley, official historian to the Foreign Office, wrote:
'The flood of light which recent publications have thrown upon every detail
of European diplomacy during the years preceding the war, cannot but have
a profound effect upon our action in the future, for on one thing every one
will be agreed, that this is not the way in which public affairs should be managed. The unvarnished record is the most complete condemnation of the system.'
Studies in Diplomatic History (London, Methuen, 1930), p. 6.

[9] Quoted in E. H. Carr, *The Twenty Years' Crisis* (London, Macmillan, 1942),
p. 38.

round the conference table by rational men would lead not only to better understanding but also to the discovery of an acceptable solution for almost every international problem. Nor did many question the premise that a threat to the peace could only come from a small minority, which would be restrained from resorting to force by the moral sanction of world public opinion, the mobilization and expression of which was to be one of the main functions of the League. If, unhappily, 'police action' (in the form of economic or military sanctions) did become necessary, in a lightly armed world,[10] it would, it was argued, be both effective and brief. It would be effective because the 'peace-loving' nations' strong sense of obligation to the Covenant would impel all (or virtually all) of them to act collectively against the wrongdoer—the 'hue and cry' of Article 11. It would be brief because the overwhelming preponderance of power on the side of the 'law-abiding' majority would bring rapid victory even if it failed in its primary purpose of acting as an effective deterrent to aggression.

Whatever might be thought of the validity of these assumptions, their emphasis on 'principle' rather than on 'interest', on 'morality' rather than 'power', was unhappily accompanied by a tendency to shy away from the concrete in favour of the abstract and to overlook the role of force in international society. High-mindedness easily became no more than a simple-mindedness which abhorred the uneasy compromises of politicians between the dictates of power and a deference to morality. Moreover, up till about 1935, the most vocal public support for the Covenant often came either from pacifists, who conveniently overlooked the sanctions provisions of Article 16, or from left-wing non-pacifists, who by ingenuously advocating both unilateral disarmament and collective security, helped to weaken the League's secular arm.[11] To all this must be

---

[10] To most League supporters in Britain the controlled reduction of armaments was the universal panacea and the *sine qua non* of an effective security system.
[11] For a discussion of these and other attitudes towards the Covenant, see R. B. McCallum, *Public Opinion and the Last Peace* (London, OUP, 1944).

added the debilitating belief that a 'League foreign policy' would place the least weight on the average citizen's shoulders and the assumption that the League was 'a self-propelling machine, a kind of miraculous automatic engine which, once set in motion, would perform its international functions *proprio motu*'.[12]

Of course, many level-headed League supporters looked upon many of these ideas as 'sublime mysticism and nonsense' and were acutely alive to the role of force in international society. Nor is this brand of 'idealism' entirely dead even today. Indeed, in 1945 many of the notions which had been current about the League a generation earlier were transferred to the United Nations. A Minister of the Crown[13] spoke of Britain's determination 'to use the institutes of the United Nations to kill power politics'. Others, including the Foreign Secretary himself (Mr Bevin), affirmed their belief that the United Nations should be the first step towards world government.[14] Nevertheless, on the whole, since 1945 it has been difficult to get much support for the view that the United Nations can ever purge international life of the cupidity and folly which have wreaked such havoc in modern times. Unlike its predecessor, the Second World War came not to a world that had known a long period of order, tranquillity, and progress, but to a generation whose minds had become accustomed to unrest and upheaval. By 1945 international politics of a peculiarly ruthless character had prevailed undisguised for over a decade. Most of those who fought in 1939 had grown up in the 'Great Depression'; they had reached manhood at a time when pictures of the war in China or of the bombings in Spain were almost a daily occurrence.

---

12 RIIA, *British Security* (1946), p. 11.

13 The Minister of State (Rt Hon. P. J. Noel-Baker), 20 Feb. 1946, H. C. Deb., vol. 419, col. 1262.

14 For the Foreign Secretary's statement see 23 Nov. 1945, vol. 416, coll. 785-86. See also Mr Eden's remarks in the same debate, ibid. coll. 612-13, and the Minister of State's affirmative answer on 28 January 1946 to the question 'Whether His Majesty's Government did mean to work the institutions of the United Nations in such a way that in due course we shall see produced the equivalent of world government' (ibid. vol. 418, coll. 630-31).

In addition, troubled in their consciences about an appeasement policy which seemed to sacrifice others in order that they themselves might escape, the vast majority of the British people by the summer of 1939 had come almost to welcome a 'show-down'. By that time, the practices of the Gestapo had persuaded many waverers to discard their pacifism and to take up arms in the belief that Western civilization was in real danger of a relapse into another Dark Age. Moreover, the subsequent course of the Second World War tended to confirm the belief that, although peace was still desperately wanted, war—even atomic war—could if necessary be endured if the alternative were totalitarian enslavement.

Thus in 1945 the United Nations did not have behind it either the hatred of the cruelty and waste of war or the belief that war was a mere accident to the same extent as did the League. Nor did victory bring the tranquillity of the 1920's. There was little time for the growth of comfortable illusions; the very depth and intractability of the cold war exposed only too clearly the harsh realities of 'power politics'—of the 'war of every man against every man'—which are now generally accepted as inescapable facts of international life, not to be easily wished away as many supporters of the League tried to do. Compared with a generation ago, there has been a notable change in the intellectual climate of thought about the nature and purpose of political action in the international field; and this has naturally affected attitudes towards the United Nations. For instance, there has been a discernible reorientation in favour of traditional diplomatic methods and the principles of the balance of power. And it is significant to note that, unlike the inter-war period, the Left now tends to join company with the Right in attempting to restore to diplomacy its traditional function of balancing and, if possible, reconciling necessarily conflicting interests, rather than in using it as a means of upholding a possibly rigid and subjective concept of international morality.[15] Although

15 For further discussion of this theme see *Times Literary Supplement*, 27 Apr. 1951, pp. 253-54.

to a surprising degree most people in Britain seem to have become mentally acclimatized to living in a civilization over which hangs a sentence of atomic death—to living in a state of 'Hobbesian fear'—for this and other reasons it is no longer a self-confident society. A note of fatalism about the political future sounds time and time again; instead of optimism, the predominant note is now apt to be one of pessimism, or at least of scepticism. After at least a century of optimism there has re-emerged the idea of original sin, of the 'Old Adam' in man. Most states, like most men, now appear to the majority of people to be predatory by instinct and to be at the mercy of impersonal forces they cannot control; belief in the inevitability of progress—at least on the international plane—is on the wane, and many in Britain tend to look back, rather than forward, to the Golden Age. Moreover, the fact that for nearly a quarter of a century one part of the world or another has been rent by armed conflict causes many to believe that war cannot be eliminated altogether[16] and that the most that can be hoped for is to postpone the occasion or to limit its incidence. With this more sober mood has also returned a certain cynicism about the respect shown by states for the 'pledged word', and so about legal rules and restraints; a distrust of political programmes and panaceas purporting to offer a once-and-for-all change in the quality of international life; and a predilection in an atomic age for those 'maxims which accept the fact of human conflict but seek to prevent conflict from overturning the whole civilized order of things'.[17]

In addition, the increased awareness of the infinite complexity of international issues and the present disinclination to expect of states the same standards of moral behaviour as are expected of

---

16 Even during the opening session of the General Assembly in 1946, *Mass Observation* found that 49 per cent. of its sample thought that another world war was likely within twenty-five years, as against 39 per cent. who thought it unlikely, and 12 per cent. who were undecided.

17 H. Butterfield, 'The Scientific versus the Moralistic Approach', *International Affairs*, Oct. 1951, p. 417.

individuals have made for a greater reluctance to judge international questions in clear-cut terms of right and wrong. Self-righteous moralizing is at more of a discount than in the past and the merits of patient realism and moderation are more generally extolled. Thus political conflict at the international level now tends to be visualized as a ceaseless impact of will upon will and aspiration upon aspiration such as can never be eliminated from human striving rather than as an all-out contest between good and evil, in which the former will inevitably triumph. Correspondingly, the United Nations has presented itself not as the complete answer to the world's ills but rather as an instrument the chief purpose of which is to curb and civilize the operations of 'power politics' by securing the more responsible exercise of power; and, however valuable this function may be, it is too subtle to excite mass enthusiasm.

Of course, these contrasts are overdrawn. Just as the Utopian, idealistic, view was never universally held as regards the League, so the realistic view has not entirely won the day as regards the United Nations. Elements of both views were present then and are present today. But their prevalence has noticeably changed. In proportion as fervour could be excited by the former revolutionary, or messianic, conception of the League, so it was dampened or smothered after 1945 by the widespread feeling that the United Nations was principally a glorified piece of diplomatic machinery and that power rather than morality was its very essence. Today it is as though the political temperature has fallen. 'Jerusalem' suggests more a hot and distant squabble than a call to mental fight; and the appeal to share in the battle against war is apt to fall on more sceptical ears and to be less able to draw on those formidable reserves of hopefulness which for so long buoyed up public support for the League.

The feeling of scepticism or even of pessimism about the United Nations has, of course, been deepened by the cold war, the depressing effects of which are too obvious to need setting out at length.

The impotence of the Security Council, the virulent slanging matches in the General Assembly, and the inordinate time spent on propaganda speeches in almost every one of its organs have been instrumental in evaporating the more optimistic hopes that were placed in the United Nations in 1945. A less obvious, but little less significant, source of indifference is the feeling—probably an exaggerated one—that Britain's voice does not command the attention it should in a United Nations that is fissured between two poles, neither of which is centred in Britain. National pride plays an important part in shaping the attitude which people adopt towards an institution like the United Nations. After the First World War people in Britain could feel that one of the main reasons why it was incumbent on them to support the League of Nations was that, as Professor Gilbert Murray wrote, 'if Britain is faithful to the Covenant, it will be hard for other nations to be obviously and grossly false'.[18] In the 1920's British supporters of the League knew that the world waited expectantly to hear what United Kingdom delegates would say in what was in many ways a European institution, small, intimate, modest. Indeed, it was because it was so widely believed that the League very largely stood or fell by virtue of what Great Britain did that the League controversy raged so vehemently in this country. But it is difficult for the British people to feel that Britain can effect as much in the United Nations as she did in the League. To some the United Nations seems more like a lavish transatlantic giant in which Britain is no longer the chief protagonist in a heroic struggle but merely a trusted and wise camp-follower—and then only one among several. The part Britain has played in tempering the acerbities of the debates and in keeping open possibilities of conciliation and mediation has been noted with pride. But it has failed to appeal to British self-esteem as much as did the belief that the success or failure of the League ultimately turned on British support.

---

18 *Problems of Foreign Policy* (London, Allen & Unwin, 1921), p. 119.

The not infrequent criticisms at the United Nations of some aspects of British colonial policy have also intensified the feeling that the United Nations is a place where British achievements and good intentions do not receive the recognition they deserve. The legitimacy of the United Nations' interest in colonial affairs has been generally accepted; it is the manner in which this interest has been exercised that has excited distrust. The advice of the Permanent Mandates Commission of the League was respected by most of those familiar with colonial problems, if only because its members were normally well versed in the problems of colonial rule and because, being appointed in their personal capacity, they were usually not mere mouthpieces of their governments. In contrast, neither the Trusteeship Council nor the Fourth Committee of the General Assembly (which is perhaps the most active in offering advice) excites much respect, not only because they are made up of government delegates, several of whom are abysmally ignorant about colonial problems, but also because much of the criticism comes either from governments which have shown no great capacity for improving the lot of their own people or from those that have the clearest political motives for showing up the colonial Powers in a poor light. This is not to say that there is no criticism in Britain either of official colonial policy or of the attitude taken by the United Kingdom delegates at the United Nations. For instance, considerable sympathy has been expressed for the Rev. Michael Scott's pleadings for the peoples of South-West Africa and some resentment has been evident at official opposition to his appearance before the United Nations. There have also been misgivings that the United Kingdom delegates, in siding with South Africa on the issue of domestic jurisdiction, might seem thereby to condone policies of racial discrimination which most people detest. But, on the whole, not only are the broad lines of British colonial policy accepted by both major political parties but there has been little inclination to question the position adopted by the United Kingdom at the United Nations. The situation might change if an issue should arise at the United Nations on which opinion at home was sharply divided; recommendations by the Organization might then be used by one or other of the parties as useful grist to their mill. But the reputation of the United Nations in these matters has not so far been such that its recommendations have been thought to be of great intrinsic merit; indeed, many have thought quite the opposite.

Three other aspects of the United Nations activities have had a disillusioning effect. The first has been the atmosphere of intrigue which has pervaded so many of its meetings. For instance, although the creation of Israel is now widely regarded as a United Nations success, at the time the United Nations handling of the Palestine problem produced some of the most severe criticism that the Organization has suffered in Britain, much of it from people and publications normally inclined to a friendly view of it. It is true that editorials in *The Times* and *Manchester Guardian*—as well as in the organs of Left opinion—implied that Britain was as much sinning as sinned against, and that the decisions themselves pleased the pro-Zionists. But the votecatching and lobbying manoeuvres by which they were reached disillusioned many as to the degree of objectivity and disinterestedness which could be expected in discussions at the United Nations. The defects of 'voting-power' politics have already been discussed; probably few in Britain have a clear picture of their precise nature, but from such accounts as filter through the conclusion is frequently drawn that an unhealthy air of intrigue and disregard for the real merits of any question marks far too many United Nations debates—in contrast to the church-like atmosphere of Geneva, the United Nations has been described as a 'den of thieves'. In addition, whereas in the inter-war period there were not a few Left writers very ready to belittle British achievements and the British way of life, there are very few today who, looking round the world, have not felt that parliamentary democracy in this country compares very favourably with political forms elsewhere and that there is little to be learnt from a United

Nations much of whose membership is drawn from countries of autocratic and despotic rule. Consequently, United Nations recommendations may have been treated with respect but they have not usually been regarded as the last word in wisdom, especially when, as on colonial questions, irrational prejudice has often appeared to be at the bottom of them.

The second has been the fairly widespread belief that the United Nations (and some of the specialized agencies) is extravagantly run; it has been said that the volume of documentation that issues forth is generally in inverse proportion to the importance of the topics discussed. The quality of some members of the United Nations Secretariat has occasionally been adversely commented upon, while the high salaries they command and the diplomatic privileges they are accorded have also aroused some resentment. These aspects are of no great consequence, but they have provided ammunition for the more peevish critics of the Organization. The third and more serious misgiving has been that the open debates, and the publicity that surrounds them, have tended to exacerbate relations. The third session (1948) of the General Assembly aroused particular criticism on this score, *The Economist* (11 December 1948) voicing a general opinion when it asked whether it was 'helpful to illuminate the chasm with so many flashes of vituperation'; since then the intrusion of television cameras into the debates has given rise to some acid comment. Coupled with this interminable wrangling, for which the Organization rather than its Members is often blamed, there is the inordinate time-wasting and the sad lack of brevity shown by most delegates[19]; indeed, it may well be precisely because Assembly meetings are so long and tedious that they receive so little attention. Thus, whereas to most League supporters 'secret diplomacy' was anathema, many loyal protagonists of the United Nations now share the preference of their ministers for open covenants, *privately* arrived at.

---

[19] For a typical comment see *The Economist*, 3 Dec. 1955, pp. 822-24.

From this brief sketch British opinion might appear to have been unduly lukewarm towards the United Nations. However, this conclusion needs to be treated with caution, and it should be remarked that the public has seemed no more inclined towards enthusiasm for either more far-reaching or more limited schemes. The various movements that have sprung up to advocate world government, federal or otherwise, have failed to take root and have withered away, except for a fairly small band of devoted supporters and a number of university societies. Indeed, the United Nations has generally been thought to have shown how impracticable are all schemes for world government. The number of those attracted by the United Europe movement or by the Friends of Atlantic Union has been statistically negligible despite influential support; and although amongst the élite the Atlantic Alliance may have come to take priority over the United Nations, this trend has not reached the mass of informed opinion. Nor is the public mood towards the United Nations solidly one of criticism or of merely sympathetic indifference. Not only has the prevalence of the mechanistic as against the organic conception of the United Nations meant that particular Member States rather than the Organization itself have frequently been the target of criticism, but there has been a real desire to keep faith with the purposes and principles of the Charter. A considerable body of informed opinion would almost certainly sharply reject any suggestion that Britain should abandon the United Nations or that the United Nations itself should be wound up. On the contrary, there has been fairly consistent support for preserving and enhancing its universal character—and so its ability to act as a bridge between East and West—by not driving the Soviet Union out and by letting Communist China in. In a vague way many people have come to associate the United Nations with 'getting along' with the Soviet Union; for them it has come to symbolize the possibility of 'peaceful coexistence'. Consequently, even its partial dissolution through the withdrawal of the Soviet Union and her satellites would probably be considered to mark a sharp deterioration in the international situation, even to presage a third world war. Furthermore, the moral sanction of the United Nations, as in the case of Korea, would almost certainly be of appreciable importance in mobilizing solid public support for armed intervention to check aggression, especially if the threat were far from home and the facts were obscure; without such a sanction many consciences might well be uneasy—and such qualms of conscience still matter.

The status of the United Nations in the public mind has turned principally on its political work, and press comment has tended to be linked with the Organization's success or failure in dealing with the more urgent political issues of the day. Its economic and social work has been less widely publicized, but it has generally been regarded as praiseworthy in principle although sometimes rather wasteful in practice. The plethora of schemes for economic and technical assistance are apt to bewilder but they have generally received a sympathetic press. Material on the technical assistance work of, say, WHO or the United Nations itself, especially when presented in the form of feature or television broadcasts or travelling exhibitions, has frequently reached an audience which would probably not have been greatly interested in the United Nations political work. Feature programmes put out by the British Broadcasting Corporation (for example, the broadcasts by Ritchie Calder or the films *World Without End* and *No Other Way*) have in most cases commanded a wide and appreciative audience; the small United Nations Information Office in London and the United Nations Association (and its Student Association) have done much to make both the general public and the more politically minded more aware of the achievements of the United Nations in the economic and social field; while U.N.A.'s Council for Education in World Citizenship has reached the younger generation by publicizing this aspect of the United Nations in over 700 schools throughout the country. Thus the publicity given to economic aid, or to the United Nations work for refugees or for children, has done much to counteract the widespread impression of the ineffectiveness of the United Nations political activities. It is, of course, the case that when the practical demands of 'mutual aid' are examined more closely, the material acquisitiveness of the ordinary individual is apt to conflict with his more generous impulses and that the more specious arguments in favour of increased aid are treated with reserve (for example, the contention that men when better clothed and fed will necessarily be more peaceably inclined). Nevertheless, there has undoubtedly been a considerable reservoir of goodwill and a sense of obligation towards the peoples of underdeveloped countries. Few charitable causes of an international character have so stirred the public imagination as the Lord Mayor of London's United Nations Appeal for Children in 1948 in support of UNICEF, which benefited comparatively little from large donations from the banks and great commercial enterprises but brought into being an army of collectors in almost every town and village and raised £680,000; in 1955 a similar appeal (though on a much smaller scale) realized over £160,000. The fact is that there is a substantial body of opinion which looks upon economic aid of this kind as essentially a moral problem in which it is incumbent upon the British people to play their full part.

The remarkable increase in the range of international activity in the economic and social field has also brought the work of the United Nations and its specialized agencies into the direct experience of professional people in a way that the League rarely did. Some ninety national organizations in Great Britain are affiliated to the international non-governmental organizations in consultative status with the Economic and Social Council. More directly, through their own Standing Conference on the Economic and Social Work of the United Nations and in other ways, they devote substantial time and effort to assisting in the United Nations work for refugees and displaced persons, child welfare, and human rights; for instance, the tens of thousands of displaced persons who have now built a permanent home in Britain have good cause to be grateful for

the more practical-minded supporters of the United Nations who
have sponsored them or helped to finance hostels for their aged
people. Still other bodies take a direct interest in the work of one
or other of the specialized agencies, whether it be WHO or UNESCO.
Familiarity with the inner workings of the United Nations and some
of these agencies occasionally provokes the comment that 'the
League did things better'; but for the most part familiarity breeds
respect.

Thus the present cooler and more sceptical attitude towards
international organization springs for the most part from a more
realistic appreciation of the international scene rather than from
any basic antipathy towards the United Nations system. There is,
of course, a fairly strong body of opinion, mainly but not only
on the Right, which is so struck by the system's obvious failings
and by the encouragement it seems to have given to forces hostile
to British interests that it has come to regard the Organization
chiefly as an irritating restraint on 'self-help' in the face of what is
considered to be acute provocation. But this view is by no means
universally held. On the contrary, any policy which appeared to
be clearly at variance with Britain's obligations under the Charter
would almost certainly deeply divide the country. The fact is that
public scepticism about the United Nations is on the whole
healthy, not hostile. In spite of its many vicissitudes the United
Nations still symbolizes, in however dim and inchoate a way,
those ideals of a just peace, the rule of law, and the mutual
welfare of the human race, to which the majority at least of informed
opinion in Great Britain feels itself committed.

chapter eighteen

The Role of the United Nations
and the 'De Jure' Revision of the Charter

In spite of its precarious authority and its somewhat chequered record, the United Nations is thus generally accepted in Britain as the essential framework for an international order and as a focus for the hopes and strivings of those seeking the material betterment of the human race. For obvious reasons it is no longer visualized, however, as an exercise in world government or as a decision-making authority with power to enforce its edicts. On the contrary, in most respects it seems the very antithesis of world government, and there is a strong suspicion that its operations may tend to encourage rather than to discourage national particularism and individualism.

THE UNITED NATIONS AND WORLD GOVERNMENT

Nor, with the exception of a small minority in such bodies as Federal Union and the Parliamentary Group for World Government, is there any real pressure to amend the Charter so as to give it a closer resemblance to a system of world government. In the foreseeable future such a system could hardly come about except through a third world war, and there is no certainty that it would be cast in a democratic rather than a totalitarian mould. Similarly, formulae intended gradually to transform the United Nations into some kind of supranational authority—world government by constitutional stealth, as it has been called—arouse little interest. However neat and elegant these formulae may appear on paper, most people are not so gullible as to believe that the world's ills can be remedied by drafting devices. On the whole it is only within Western Europe, or possibly NATO, that schemes for constitutional integration are thought to have any practical relevance.

THE SECURITY COUNCIL AND THE VETO

There are, of course, those who even today still picture the Security Council as a kind of supranational authority whose edicts would invariably be obeyed were it not for the constant Soviet use of the veto and who, therefore, argue that the first essential is to abolish the veto. As has been seen, this approach is based on two complete fallacies: the one that the Security Council has in fact been hamstrung by the veto, the other that if the veto were removed, collective security would become a reality.

It is, in fact, too little appreciated that the frequent Soviet vetoes are merely symptomatic of Great Power divisions[1] and that they have had surprisingly little effect on the actual course of world events. Over half have been used to prevent the admission to the United Nations of Western-sponsored candidates. This has been irritating to the states concerned, but otherwise it has been of no great moment.[2] Many of the remaining Soviet vetoes have been

---

[1] See above, p. 230.

[2] The question of the seating of the Chinese People's Republic, on which the veto has never been involved, has been of far greater importance.

cast merely to block resolutions which the Soviet Union did not consider strong enough,[3] to prevent condemnation of a Soviet satellite,[4] or to prevent investigation into events within the Soviet orbit.[5] One (in private) prevented the reappointment of Mr Trygve Lie as Secretary-General in October 1950, but it was countered by the General Assembly's extending his term of office. Although there is a risk that the Organization may temporarily have to do without an executive head, the use of the veto in connexion with the Secretary-General is in fact a valuable inducement to the permanent members to find a candidate acceptable to them all. The occasional Soviet vetoes on Western proposals concerning the Arab-Israel dispute have been more disturbing; but a number of the Security Council's edicts have been flagrantly disregarded with impunity in the past and it is doubtful whether the situation would be fundamentally transformed even if the Security Council found it easier to reach a decision. The vetoes over Indonesia came too late to make much difference, while the main effect of the six concerned with the Greek question was to hasten its transfer to the General Assembly. A Soviet veto in the earliest stages of the Korean War might have been more serious, but action could properly have been taken under Article 51 if desired. There remain the vetoes cast in regard to the regulation of armaments and atomic energy. Yet the present impasse is clearly the result of the underlying power conflict, not of the veto, the use of which simply records the failure to bridge the gap between the Western and the Soviet proposals. And there is, of course, little point in disarmament agreements

---

[3] For example, the draft resolution concerning the withdrawal of British and French troops from the Levant or the draft resolutions on Spain.

[4] For example, Albania in the Corfu Channel dispute.

[5] For example, two vetoes in May 1948 to prevent the establishment of a commission to investigate events in Czechoslovakia; or the two vetoes in July 1952 to prevent an investigation of germ warfare allegations. Even if the Soviet Union had not been able to exercise a veto, no investigation could have been made within its orbit without its consent; and the Soviet refusal to allow investigation of the germ warfare charges probably did as much to convince the world that the charges were baseless as any investigating body could have done.

among friends; the essential thing is that they should include those whose armaments are feared.

This is not to deny that the work of the Security Council has been hampered by the frequency with which the Soviet Union has used her veto. But the claim that this has of itself resulted in a deterioration in the international situation is quite unfounded. The veto mirrors political realities; its use is an outward sign of Great Power divisions, not a source of those divisions. Furthermore, even if the veto were amended so as to enable the Security Council to arrive at a decision more easily, it would still have no power to enforce its decisions so long as no military agreements had been concluded under Article 43. Till then sovereign states, whether great or small, may be voted down, but their capacity to ignore the Council's· decisions is little affected.

Attempts to amend or abolish the veto are all the more futile since amendments to the Charter have to be ratified by *all* the permanent members of the Security Council before they can come into force (Arts. 108 and 109(2)),[6] and it is almost certain that the Soviet Union is not the only permanent member which is firmly opposed to limiting its right of veto in respect even of the pacific settlement of disputes, let alone of enforcement action. Such attempts may indeed, be both wasteful and dangerous. They may be wasteful because they could better be devoted to persuading the permanent members to exercise their veto rights with greater forbearance by adhering, for example, to the 'code of conduct' set out in the General Assembly's resolution of 14 April 1949.[7] They may be dangerous because they might jeopardize conventions which have led to a useful *de facto* revision of the veto (for example, the convention that the abstention or absence of a permanent member does not constitute a veto),[8] and because if pressed too

---

[6] See above, p. 30.

[7] See above, pp. 233-34. ·

[8] They might also call into question the concession made by the Soviet Union at San Francisco that no one permanent member can prevent the discussion of a dispute; see Joint Statement on Voting Procedure and p. 28 above.

far they might well lead to the withdrawal not only of the Soviet Union and her satellites but also of many of the uncommitted Powers, who might be reluctant to remain in a Western-dominated institution. The value of the United Nations as a bridge both between present Power divisions and between the industrialized West and the less-developed East would then be lost. As a club of like-minded states it could do little more than duplicate NATO and its appendages.

THE UNITED NATIONS AND COLLECTIVE SECURITY

So much, then, for the first fallacy. The flaw in the second fallacy (that were it not for the veto collective security could be made to work) is that the main limiting factor in creating an effective collective security system is tnat the chief potential protagonists in any future world conflict—the United States and the Soviet Union—are not only Powers of much the same magnitude, who tower over their fellow Great Powers, but that the latter are also firmly committed to one camp or the other. With a multiple balance of five or six Great Powers of more or less equal weight, the majority of which were reasonably satisfied with the *status quo*, a collective security system could contribute appreciably to the security of all by holding out the prospect that an aggressive minority would be deterred or, if necessary, subdued by a majority coalition of overwhelming might.[9] In a nuclear world which has crystallized into two main Power blocs of about equal strength, with the uncommitted Powers nowhere near strong enough to give a clear preponderance of power to the side on which they might choose to throw their weight, each bloc has to rely for its defence solely on its own armed strength; nor can either bloc feel confident that the other may not attempt to achieve a quick victory by a surprise 'knock-out' blow. In other words, as the years leading up to the First World War showed, a two-sided balance is necessarily highly

---

[9] See above, pp. 40 ff.

competitive and precarious; it produces collective insecurity, not collective security. In addition, when each bloc is nearly self-sufficient economically, economic sanctions may perhaps serve as a useful form of diplomatic pressure but they are unlikely to be much more than an irritant—and possibly a dangerous irritant at that.

A further complicating factor is that the spread of the concept of the 'just' war (other than a war of individual or collective self-defence) has undermined an important prop of any collective security system. What in orthodox Western terms might seem to be a clear act of aggression and the occasion for a 'hue and cry' against the aggressor state may appear to others to be a righteous war of liberation.[10] In short, the contemporary international situation makes the creation of an effective collective security system quite impossible; the amendment of the veto, the conclusion of military agreements under Article 43, and the strengthening of the General Assembly's 'Uniting for Peace' machinery could in no way alter this basic fact.

THE UNITED NATIONS AS A DIPLOMATIC INSTRUMENT

Another illusion about the United Nations is that it was, and is, intended to supersede traditional diplomatic machinery. As has been seen, this is not the case; its prime function is to supplement and humanize that machinery by providing a diplomatic meeting place where the leading representatives of the nations of the world can attempt to reconcile conflicting national interests and to adjust

---

[10] As recently as the May 1955 issue of the *Young Communist*, Marshal of the Soviet Union S. S. Biryuzov reminded his readers of Stalin's saying: 'We are not against war. We are against imperialist war, since that is counter-revolutionary war. But we are in favour of liberation anti-imperialist revolutionary war, in spite of the fact that such war, as is well known, is not only not free from the "horrors of bloodshed" but is actually full of them'. But the Communists are not the only ones to believe in a 'just' war. A 'second round' against Israel, a preventive war by Israel, a war to 'liberate' Formosa, or a war to unite the Arab peoples, would probably be regarded by very many in the countries concerned as 'just' wars.

shifting Power relationships without resort to war. More precisely, the United Nations system, including, that is, the specialized agencies, can serve as an instrument for:

    (i) negotiation between the main Power blocs, especially on disarmament, and for mediation by the uncommitted Powers;

    (ii) rallying wider support for collective resistance to aggression;

    (iii) fostering the growth of world trade and alleviating economic distress and discontent in underdeveloped countries;

    (iv) diverting the currents of extreme nationalism and anti-colonialism into more constructive channels.

A brief re-examination of each of these functions will show how far their more effective performance calls for formal amendment, or *de jure* revision, of the Charter.

CONCILIATION AND MEDIATION

The United Nations' principal task is the reconciliation of conflicting interests. It is true, of course, that the Security Council is impotent in face of the intransigence of even one Great Power and that it is misleading to think of it as an impartial arbitrator between disputants; like other organs of the United Nations, it is primarily an instrument through which countries seek the national advantage. Nor does the extensive and heterogeneous membership of the General Assembly always provide a very propitious setting for negotiation, while there is always the danger that reliance on the United Nations may merely serve to conceal the lack of a coherent policy.

Yet the experience of the first ten years suggests that, when events are moving towards a détente, the United Nations can provide a readily available point of contact between the protagonists through which informal and private negotiations can be initiated without ceremony and on neutral ground. By encouraging personal diplomacy between foreign ministers (and their immediate aides) it may enable them to get to know each other's minds and fears and so act as a brake on mutual suspicion and mistrust; at least it can help to indicate how far a policy can be pursued without precipitating bloodshed. By universalizing what might otherwise remain limited conflicts of interest—admittedly with rather unpredictable results—the United Nations can open up new opportunities for mediation, especially (but not exclusively) by the uncommitted Powers. As an adjunct to traditional diplomacy the United Nations can enable a Power—even a Great Power—to climb down not only without loss of face but in such a way as to earn general goodwill, while it can serve as a convenient shelf—or 'cold storage'—for unresolved problems which might otherwise flare into armed conflict.

Apart from the Organization's potentialities for tackling this or that particular dispute, the Purposes and Principles of the Charter, which on the whole are sensibly conceived,[11] may also exert a beneficial effect on the general international atmosphere by inducing the free world to display a more scrupulous regard not perhaps for the general interest of the family of nations (which in the conventional sense does not exist), but at least for the interests and susceptibilities of their fellows. This deference may be faltering and at times rather hypocritical; but in marginal cases, and when bolstered by more material considerations, it may be of real moment. One possible source of embarrassment to the West is that it will almost certainly not be shared by the Communist states, which will no doubt continue to look upon this standard of international propriety as yet another expression of an outworn bourgeois morality, which need in no way inhibit their broad strategy. Yet on tactical grounds they may not infrequently pay it rather more than lip-service lest their reputation suffer in the eyes of the uncommitted Powers; and just as hypocrisy may be the 'tribute that vice pays to virtue', so may political conventions which later

---

[11] The obligation on states to refrain from the 'threat' of force in so sweeping a way (Art. 2, para. 4) is rather unreal; the threat of force is contingent in almost every diplomatic exchange between 'unfriendly' Powers.

acquire real binding force strike their first roots in political expediency.

Whether or not these potentialities for good are used depends primarily, of course, on the attitudes of Member Governments, on their moderation and good sense in debate, and, above all, on the policies pursued by the Great Powers. If the United Nations is used principally as a forum for 'diplomacy by insult', for pointing out the motes in other nations' eyes; if it serves mainly as an instrument for sowing dissension within the opposite camp and for wooing the uncommitted Powers; if it multiplies the number of international disputes by the exceeding facility it affords for raising them; or if it tends to poison relationships by publicizing disputes which could better be tackled through private diplomatic channels, then perhaps it would be better for it quietly to sink into oblivion. On the other hand, there seems a growing awareness of these dangers amongst more responsible delegates, while not only inertia but also the attachment to the United Nations ideal by many people in this country and elsewhere makes any proposal to wind up the Organization most unlikely in the foreseeable future.

The United Nations' potentialities as an instrument of conciliation and mediation would probably be strengthened if it were to become more fully representative of the whole diplomatic spectrum. A step in this direction was the admission in December 1955 of Albania, Austria, Bulgaria, Cambodia, Ceylon, Finland, Hungary, Ireland, Italy, Jordan, Laos, Libya, Nepal, Portugal, Roumania, and Spain. The continued exclusion of Japan and the absence of Western Germany is, nevertheless, regrettable, while it must be admitted that the increase in its membership will make the General Assembly more unwieldy than ever and will enhance the relative voting strength of the anti-colonial bloc. Yet there is little to be said for limiting membership to friendly states or to those which are avowedly anti-Communist. Indeed, although formal amendment of the Charter is evidently not essential to facilitate the admission of future candidates, it might be preferable if at some later date the qualifications on universality in Article 4 (para. 1) were watered down and if admissions could be effected simply by a two-thirds majority of the General Assembly (as in the League of Nations).

However, a more urgent step is that the Central People's Government of China should represent China in the United Nations and especially in the Security Council. Despite the denunciation of Communist China in 1951 as an aggressor, the issue is not primarily a moral one. It is whether disputes between the real protagonists in world affairs are to be handled in the United Nations or elsewhere. If Communist China continues for long to be excluded from the United Nations, they will be handled elsewhere. In that case the reputation of those who persist in excluding her may suffer appreciably in Asian eyes, as may the standing of the United Nations itself. Here no amendment of the Charter is involved; the question is one of the acceptance of one set of credentials rather than of another. On the Security Council such acceptance should be treated as a procedural matter, and so not subject to the veto, in accordance with the General Assembly Resolution of 14 April 1949,[12] or alternatively, whatever decision may be taken by the General Assembly (by a simple majority) could in due course be followed, as at present, by other organs of the United Nations.[13]

There are three further measures which could contribute to the more effective functioning of the Security Council. The first is to increase its membership so as to allow for the more equitable representation of Asia and, possibly, of Europe. The second is to create a sixth permanent seat on the Council for India. The third is to waive the present restrictions on re-election for such 'middle' Powers as Canada and Brazil. In these cases formal amendment of the Charter would be required, but a full revision conference would be quite unnecessary.

Too much should not be expected from measures of this kind; it is not merely the unrepresentative membership of the Security

---

[12] See above, p. 234.
[13] See *GAOR*, 5th sess., suppl. no. 20, Resolution 396(V).

Council that has caused recent Great Power talks to be held out-side the United Nations. Even if the international atmosphere were to improve and some of the main defects in the Security Council were to be overcome, a resuscitated Council of Foreign Ministers (or equivalent regular 'near-the-summit' meetings) might still have several advantages over the Security Council. It would not only bring those with authority face to face with a minimum of extrane-ous interference, but the privacy and limited membership of its meetings should allow more scope for hard bargaining on the basis of interest than does the Security Council, where negotiations would doubtless continue to be conducted more on the basis of principle. On the other hand, although the necessity of taking an attitude in public on the Security Council might militate against concessions, its public[14] debates now tend to be principally concerned with formally registering bargains struck in private. And if negotiations on the Security Council might occasionally suffer from the partici-pation of the not-so-great Powers, they might also greatly benefit from the mediation of the 'middle' Powers. The chief merit of the Security Council, however, would be that in a crisis its members would always be readily available, whereas the Council of Foreign Ministers would have to be specially convened. At the very least, therefore, by providing an everyday point of contact the Security Council[15] could serve as a useful complement to *ad hoc* meetings of the Council of Foreign Ministers.

COLLECTIVE RESISTANCE TO AGGRESSION

To dismiss collective security as wholly impracticable in a divided world and to give precedence to conciliation and mediation is not to rule out altogether the possibility that instances may arise in which the General Assembly's 'Uniting for Peace' machinery might help to muster slightly wider moral and material support for collec-

14 Though there is nothing to prevent the Council from meeting in private.
15 Or more accurately the permanent delegations of members of the Council.

tive resistance to aggression than could NATO and its appendages. In addition, in a world in which the deterrent effects of nuclear warfare may place a premium on 'local' wars and insurrections, the United Nations Peace Observation Missions may be of some help in checking infiltration and subversion. Thus, although regional organizations are now the main agencies for collective resistance to aggression, by encouraging states to stand up to both external and internal pressures the United Nations may be able to play some part in helping to avoid the 'one by one' technique of the aggressor. But its contribution cannot be more than individual member states are prepared to make, while there is some risk that the 'Uniting for Peace' machinery may not only entangle Britain in conflicts in which British interests are only remotely involved but that it may be used against Britain if she should ever be provoked into unilateral action to defend a vital overseas interest. Moreover, if in a nuclear age local wars are to be prevented from spreading, there must be a return to the concept of limited objectives, to the concept, indeed, of war as 'a duel in which contestants should be isolated and restrained by the rest of international society'.[16] In the event of local aggression, the United Nations' *main* task, therefore, should not be to mobilize states for punitive action but rather to prevent the conflicts from spreading and to terminate them as rapidly as possible.

ECONOMIC DEVELOPMENT AND WORLD TRADE

In the non-political field the United Nations and its specialized agencies have been overshadowed so far as Britain is concerned by regional and bilateral arrangements, but the specialized agencies have not been quite so subject to the frustrating effects of the power conflict as has the United Nations itself. The Soviet Union is still

---

[16] Kenneth W. Thompson, 'Collective Security Re-examined', *American Political Science Review*, Sept. 1953, p. 753. See also Herbert Butterfield, *Christianity, Diplomacy and War* (London, Epworth Press, 1953), pp. 91-93.

a member of the long-established Universal Postal Union and the International Telecommunication Union and she is a founder member of the more recent World Meteorological Organization. Despite political divisions, these specialized agencies, and others whose membership is limited to the non-Communist world (for example, ICAO), continue to foster much needed day-to-day co-operation in technical matters. In the economic and social field the specialized agencies such as the International Bank, the ILO, FAO, and WHO,[17] have already been of real assistance in setting in motion, or in speeding up, the process of development in economically backward territories and in helping to avoid the distress and dehumanization of personal relations that so often accompanied the industrial revolution in the West. Even if it be doubted whether economic betterment will necessarily lead to a reduction in political tension, the determination of the peoples of underdeveloped countries to be rid of the poverty, disease, and squalor which have been their accepted lot for centuries past is one of the major political facts of the contemporary international scene and one that rightly evokes strong sympathy amongst most of the peoples of the West. To ignore it would also be political folly, since the response of the industrial West, as compared with that of the Soviet Union, may play a major part in shaping the future political alignments of the uncommitted Powers. Economically also the West, and Britain especially, can expect to benefit from the increased trade which economic growth overseas portends. It is, therefore, incumbent upon the West to use its economic power and 'know-how' to assist the process of development overseas, and to do so on a scale, at a speed, and in a spirit which will match the gigantic nature of the task. The resources which Britain will be able to make available are likely to be limited, though by no

---

[17] The Soviet Union has recently rejoined the ILO, WHO, and UNESCO. Whether this is cause for congratulation remains to be seen. It is not, of course, unknown for countries to join an institution primarily in order to 'put a spanner in the works' or from fear that absence may damage their reputation in the sight of countries whose favours they wish to win.

means negligible, and it is right that her dependent territories and her fellow members of the Commonwealth should have first call on these; but she has a vast fund of experience of which more use could perhaps be made by some of the specialized agencies.

The basic problem is not, however, one of the adequacy or inadequacy of existing machinery, but rather of the ability and determination, on the one hand, of 'donor' countries to mobilize greater capital resources for overseas development and, on the other hand, of the recipient countries to put these resources to productive uses and to reduce the social and political barriers to economic change. Although bilateral and private channels will almost certainly continue to carry the major flow of capital going overseas in the near future, the International Bank and the United Nations Technical Assistance Programme (in which nearly all the specialized agencies participate) are often more acceptable channels to the recipients and are in a better position to ensure that overseas capital is put to productive uses; they need to be assured of more adequate resources than they at present command. Furthermore, if private investment, and especially private dollar investment, continues to be concentrated so heavily on the Western Hemisphere and on Middle East oil, the case for a Special United Nations Fund for Economic Development would be immeasurably strengthened.

In addition, the potentialities of the IMF and the projected OTC in drawing together the dollar and non-dollar parts of the Western world are of considerable economic and political significance. Despite the growing attractions of regionalism, they can still be of inestimable benefit to a country like the United Kingdom, whose economic livelihood depends so greatly upon a more orderly international economy and upon the freeing of trade channels throughout the whole world. Politically they can help both to draw the free world together and to disprove the Communist belief that the so-called capitalist system contains the seeds of its own decay and that, sooner or later, the stresses and strains inherent in the system will produce widespread unemployment and economic distress which will undermine the faith of the masses in their governments and pave the way for régimes which will first co-operate with Communism and then fall under Communist domination. The policies of the United States are, of course, of basic importance but it is also to be hoped that the resources of the IMF will be increased to the level necessary to ensure confidence in its ability to meet all reasonable demands upon them, that the Fund's Articles of Agreement which relate to exchange-rate variations will not be applied too strictly, and that the OTC will eventually come into being.

The record of the Economic and Social Council does not match up to that of the specialized agencies, whose work it was intended to co-ordinate. Although in the realm of economic stability, technical assistance, and land reform the discussions on the Council may have borne some fruit, it has hardly been commensurate with the energies which have gone into its twice-yearly meetings, at each of which agendas of well over fifty items—many of them of trivial importance—are considered. There is, therefore, a case for winding up the Council by devolving its responsibilities on to its Commissions, the Technical Assistance Committee, and the Secretariat, and on to the Second and Third Committees of the General Assembly. Such a proposal might, however, be misconstrued; it would certainly be greeted with genuine dismay by the majority of delegates. The more prudent course, therefore, might be to make a renewed effort to remedy some of the Council's worst defects by decreasing the frequency of its meetings, by burying the more incompetent of its Commissions, and by securing the more expeditious conduct generally of its business. None of these measures would be popular. Nor in themselves would they be sufficient to breathe new life into the Council; this depends first and foremost on the determination of delegates to eschew political demagogy and to grapple more closely with the often humdrum, but nevertheless important, economic and social matters, which should be the Council's normal fare.

But that there is also plenty of room for improvement in the Council's machinery can scarcely be doubted. None of the improvements suggested need wait upon formal revision of the Charter.

THE UNITED NATIONS AND ANTI-COLONIALISM

The rising resentment against any vestige of political servitude to the West has in many cases led to strong pressure for the 'nationalization' of indigenous resources which have been developed by Western initiative and capital and to persistent efforts at the United Nations to turn what the colonial Powers hold to be domestic issues into international issues. This would exist were there no United Nations; and it cannot be curbed merely by redrafting the 'domestic jurisdiction' clause in Article 2(7). But if the Charter is to be taken as excluding the Western Powers from protecting their property overseas, without providing any means of redress, it may tend to defeat its own ends and to become the bulwark for the irresponsible rather than for the law-abiding. Nor is the platform that the United Nations provides for the impassioned and often fraudulent denunciation of the alleged iniquities of 'colonialism' calculated to enhance its prestige in British eyes.

This is especially so since, as has been seen, the United Kingdom has for some time past been committed to the principle of granting self-government to her colonial peoples. She is, or should be, in sympathy, therefore, with the general aims of the more sincere and responsible members of the anti-colonial camp. Her differences with them centre mainly on timing and method. Britain must be expected firmly to oppose any attempt to usurp her responsibilities in colonial territories and to align herself with those who take a similar stand. But she does not claim that British colonial policy is wholly without blemish or deny the need for the colonial Powers to adjust themselves to the nationalist revolutions of the twentieth century. Indeed, if the United Nations were able to divert the currents of extreme anti-colonialism into more constructive channels and to educate delegates into the dangers of a disorderly handing over of power, then she might be more ready to concede the value of an occasional prod or word of advice from, for instance, the Trusteeship Council.

Unhappily, the policies of the colonial Powers are too often the butt of delegates who have no real concern for the welfare of colonial peoples, or, indeed, for the welfare of their own peoples, and are mainly intent on causing as much mischief as possible or on earning the plaudits of their countrymen and colleagues. United Nations meetings are also frequently used to publicize evils which exist—or are alleged to exist—in colonial territories, while the prevalence of these self-same evils—or worse—in many other parts of the world goes almost unremarked. No doubt some of these attacks are symptomatic of mere 'growing pains', which will disappear in due course. But they can be a serious embarrassment to those charged with the delicate task of helping colonial peoples to build the political and economic prerequisites of self-government. If they were to persist, or if the United Nations were to lose what remaining sense of responsibility it has in colonial matters, not only would the colonial Powers—and Britain amongst them—have good grounds for refusing to co-operate any further, but they might be forced to reconsider their attitude towards the United Nations as a whole.

Thus any attempt to blur the present distinction in the Charter between colonial territories and trust territories, perhaps by extending the scope of Article 73 so as to require the submission of information on political developments within colonial territories or the setting of target dates for granting them full self-government, could hardly fail to precipitate a grave crisis for the United Nations. So, almost certainly, would any proposal to place the present *ad hoc* Committee on Information from Non-Self-Governing Territories on a permanent footing. The fact that proposals of this kind would probably gain considerable support at any revision conference is, in the British view, one very good reason for not holding such a conference.

THE UNITED NATIONS AND THE COMMONWEALTH

Both because of the importance attached in Great Britain to the Commonwealth and because the latter is frequently held up as a model of what the United Nations might become, it is appropriate to say a word about the impact of the United Nations on Commonwealth ties. Perhaps the first and most obvious fact is that the airing at the United Nations of disputes between members of the Commonwealth marks a departure from a view generally prevalent in the inter-war period, namely, that intra-Commonwealth disputes do not fall into quite the same category as ordinary disputes between sovereign states. This discarding of the notion that the relationships among the members of the Commonwealth ought to be different from ordinary inter-state relationships might seem to reduce the already very light ties of the Commonwealth to invisible gossamer. Yet experience suggests that by helping to divert internal dissensions into less disruptive channels it may contribute to the tightening up of the consultative processes which constitute the main fabric of Commonwealth co-operation.

Nor is there any reason to suppose that loyalty to the United Nations is incompatible with loyalty to the Commonwealth. On the contrary, the strong attachment of most members of the Commonwealth to the United Nations is most noticeable.[18] Indeed, the concept of collective action often strikes a deeper chord than is perhaps the case in a Great Britain still wearing the mantle—albeit rather tattered—of a Great Power. Certainly in most countries of the Commonwealth the United Nations is still regarded as the chief hope for a more civilized and humane approach to international relationships; the first and often exaggerated hopes may have become dimmed, but they have by no means been extinguished. Partly for this reason, no United Kingdom policy which is too exclusively self-centred can hope to evoke a favourable response

---

[18] South Africa is the chief exception.

in the rest of the Commonwealth;[19] and the United Kingdom's reputation in the Commonwealth as a sympathetic and experienced partner turns to some extent at least on the deference she shows to the purposes and principles of the Charter and on the use she makes of the potentialities of the United Nations. Similarly, given the divergent interests, outlooks, and traditions of the members of the multi-racial Commonwealth, some highest common factor is needed to give meaning and purpose to the elaborate processes of consultation; as Professor Mansergh has observed, 'the policies which most firmly unite the Commonwealth are those that transcend exclusively Commonwealth interests'.[20] The United Nations can help to provide that common denominator. And even if from time to time it may increase some of the strains on the Commonwealth by requiring members to 'stand up and be counted' on one side or the other, it may also relieve the United Kingdom of the embarrassment of appearing to choose between different members of the Commonwealth or, indeed, between the United States and the Commonwealth. In addition, although intra-Commonwealth disputes which are projected into the United Nations may remain unsettled, at least they may be talked about and not fought about.

There is also no mistaking the sense of solidarity that has grown up among Commonwealth representatives at the United Nations, or the fact that in many ways the United Nations provides exceptional opportunities for Commonwealth consultation. It has, for instance, become the common practice for even the most controversial topics to be discussed at meetings of Commonwealth representatives before they are publicly debated. While the edge of the controversy may not be blunted as a result, there is usually a greater understanding of respective points of view and a more evident restraint in their expression than would otherwise be the case. Indeed,

---

19 As in the inter-war period; see Mansergh, *Survey of British Commonwealth Affairs*, p. 422.
20 Mansergh, *The Commonwealth and the Nations*, pp. 51-52.

precisely because it embraces peoples of nearly every race, creed, and tradition, as well as nations, both great and small, with very different views on such highly contentious issues as the cold war and colonialism, the Commonwealth can exert a most valuable moderating influence at the United Nations and can set an example of that mutual tolerance and respect which the Charter seeks to attain for all sorts and conditions of men. In addition it can, through the wisdom and ingenuity of its statesmen, open up hitherto undisclosed possibilities of reconciliation, while as the only political institution which effectively bridges the gulf between the industrialized West and the underdeveloped East, it can make a major contribution to the economic work of the United Nations and of its specialized agencies. Conversely, without the United Nations the example and influence of the Commonwealth in all these respects would be considerably diminished.

CONCLUSION

In almost every land there are those who have good cause to be thankful for the existence of the United Nations; refugees who after many years have set up new homes overseas; people of every race and colour who look to the 'shirt sleeve' diplomats of the United Nations and the specialized agencies to aid them in their struggle for economic betterment. Were it not for the efforts of the United Nations, they and their like might well be bereft of that small spark of hope which now illumines their lives. It is distressing that neither the United Kingdom Government nor the British people seem sufficiently to appreciate this aspect of the United Nations activities. Yet important as this work undoubtedly is, the primary function of the United Nations is the maintenance of peace and security, and, more specifically, the avoidance of another world war. And it is evident that for many years to come a long period of deadlock—of competitive coexistence—is the best that can be hoped for and that the prospects of world peace will turn not on the United Nations but on the effectiveness of global and regional balances of power and on the common fear of nuclear warfare.

For a long time to come, therefore, arrangements for the collective defence of the free world must claim pre-eminence over the United Nations in British foreign policy, as will the use of traditional diplomatic channels to resolve particular issues, and of meetings at the summit, or near the summit, to hammer out a general *modus vivendi*. But by securing time for tempers to cool the United Nations may act as a valuable additional check against the adoption of desperate courses, while the long-drawn-out disarmament negotiations may possibly help to counter what experience suggests is the inherently competitive nature of a two-sided balance-of-power (as each side seeks to achieve a slight margin of superiority in order to diminish its sense of insecurity and to strengthen its hand in negotiation). And is it too much to hope that the longer the world does without war, the more institutionalized may become the process of quarrelling without fighting? Above all, it should never be forgotten that the present Western defence effort is only a means to an end, namely, a world in which tension and suspicion will be reduced to more manageable proportions, a measure of disarmament become possible, and nations relieved of the present oppressive burden of fear and enabled to turn their energies to more fruitful pursuits. In such a world the United Nations might once again become the focal point of international politics and the foundation-stone of its Members' policies.

A word of warning may not be out of place, however. The special intractability of the East-West conflict is chiefly responsible for confounding even the sober hopes initially placed in the United Nations. This conflict may become less acute, but there is little reason to think that it will be resolved within the next decade or so. And even if it were, no doubt there would be other conflicts, little less irksome, to take its place. In other words, the Power conflict is part of the 'permanent baggage' of an international society in

which nearly all semblance of overall government is absent, and
the United Nations is bound to remain, in greater or lesser degree,
a cockpit of conflicting interests and ideologies. No world-wide
institutional framework, however skilfully devised, can eradicate
the clash of interests, the competing ambitions, and the deep-
seated incompatibility of temperament inherent in a society of
sovereign states each owning no superior and each, to a very large
extent, a law unto itself. Indeed, the self-centredness and egoism
of states and the follies and frailties of human nature are liable
so to corrupt and frustrate the work of such institutions that they
tend to become mere vehicles for competing national interests;
to guard against this is the supreme duty of the Secretary-General
and his staff—and it is up to Member Governments not to handicap
them in this duty. But one thing is as certain as can be. These harsh
realities cannot be removed by formal amendment of the Charter.
It is what states do at the United Nations and not the precise institutional pattern that matters most. There are no doubt any number
of inconsistencies and ambiguities[21] in a document which represents
a compromise between contrasting points of view, but any attempt
to remove them may merely resurrect old controversies and disclose differences which are certainly no less deep-seated than they
were in 1945; and the Charter's tangled wording may in fact allow
welcome scope for interpretation and so for adaptation to changing
circumstances. There are also any number of ways, some of which
have been instanced in Chapter 8, in which the practices and
procedures of organs of the United Nations could be further improved without amendment of the Charter. On the other hand,
apart from the changes in the composition of the Security Council
suggested earlier in this chapter, formal or *de jure* revision of the
Charter would be both inopportune and impossible until there is a

---

[21] For some examples see International Law Association, Committee on the
Review of the Charter of the U.N., *Report* by G. Schwarzenberger (London,
1954), app. 5: 'Memorandum on Technical and Minor Amendments', by
B. Cheng and L. C. Green.

marked relaxation of international tension. It would be inopportune not only because there are no major problems which wait upon Charter revision but because the amendments most widely canvassed would either be inimical to Britain's colonial responsibilities or would threaten the Soviet Union's withdrawal and so jeopardize the whole framework. It would be impossible unless the Soviet Union were to forego her present determined opposition to any amendment whatsoever, since, as is well known, amendments may be adopted by a two-thirds majority but they cannot come into force until they have been ratified by *all* the permanent members. Nor would there be much to be gained from a review conference. The work of the United Nations is in practice under constant review, both in the chancelleries and at the United Nations itself. Unless previous negotiations had elicited a widespread desire (including the Soviet Union) to hold such a conference and to accept substantial amendment to the Charter, it would most likely become mainly an occasion for mouthing rather empty platitudes (as did the Tenth Anniversary Conference at San Francisco) or be seized upon as an opportunity for apportioning blame for the Organization's defects and the world's maladies—in other words, a 'showdown' conference. In brief, the real need for some time to come will not be to revise or review the United Nations, but to use it.

These may seem sobering thoughts. Yet to dwell on the defects and inadequacies of the United Nations and the difficulties of overcoming them is to overlook not only the extent to which it is capable of growth without formal change but also its often unexpected resources. Even under present unpropitious conditions it can help to chasten the régime of power politics and to limit and control war, it can encourage states to be more alert to and to evaluate more correctly new forces at work in the world, and it can keep alive the notion of a family of nations in which co-operation rather than conflict is the norm and in which the welfare of each individual member is a matter of common concern. And even if the United Nations, like a lighthouse, can for the moment only help to prevent the ships of state from running on the rocks rather than piloting them into safe haven, is that not something to be thankful for? Moreover, despite the decay in international morality, the messianic urge to fashion the world in the image of the proletariat, and the primacy of national self-interest (checked, only intermittently and uncertainly, by a concern for the interests of others) the United Nations is still looked upon, by a majority of informed opinion in Britain as in many other countries of the free world, as a symbol of man's dream of a more peaceful and prosperous world. Belief in the possibilities of such a world must, of course, be a matter of faith rather than of fore-knowledge. But a dream may well be brought nearer realization by being resolutely pursued, while faith is the very life-blood of the United Nations without which efforts to sustain and develop such a modicum of co-operation as does exist would lose all momentum. As a Power with a strong vested interest in a more orderly international society, as the centre of a multi-racial Commonwealth, and as a leading member of the Western alliance system, Great Britain would almost certainly be very much the loser were her faith in the ultimate meaning and purpose of the United Nations to wither.

Index